Theorizing Art Cinemas

Theorizing Art Cinemas

Foreign, Cult, Avant-Garde, and Beyond

By David Andrews

University of Texas Press ◢◣ *Austin*

First edition, 2013
First paperback edition, 2014

Requests for permission to reproduce material from this work should be sent to:
Permissions
University of Texas Press
P.O. Box 7819
Austin, TX 78713-7819
http://utpress.utexas.edu/index.php/rp-form

⊚ The paper used in this book meets the minimum requirements of ANSI/NISO
z39.48-1992 (R1997) (Permanence of Paper).

An earlier version of chapter 1 was published as "Toward an Inclusive, Exclusive Approach
to Art Cinema," in *Global Art Cinema: New Theories and Histories*, ed. Rosalind Galt and
Karl Schoonover (Oxford: Oxford University Press, 2010), 62–74. Reprinted by permission
of Oxford University Press, Inc. An earlier version of chapter 6 was published as "Revisiting
the Two Avant-Gardes," in *Jump Cut: A Review of Contemporary Media*, 52 (Summer 2010).
An earlier version of chapter 9 was published as "Art Cinema as Institution, Redux: Art
Houses, Film Festivals, and Film Studies," in *Scope: An Online Journal of Film and TV
Studies*, 18 (October 2010).

Library of Congress Cataloging-in-Publication Data
Andrews, David, 1970–
    Theorizing art cinemas : foreign, cult, avant-garde, and beyond / by David Andrews. —
First edition.
        p.   cm
    Includes bibliographical references and index.
    ISBN 978-0-292-74774-6 (cloth : alk. paper)
    ISBN 978-1-4773-0205-7 (paperback)
    1. Experimental films—History and criticism.   2. Avant-garde (Aesthetics)   I. Title.
PN1995.9.E96A49   2013
791.43′611—dc23   2013000934

doi: 10.7560/747746

to Ruth, forever Darlin'

Contents

Preface

This theory goes back to at least 2003, when I was working on *Soft in the Middle* (2006), my study of American softcore cinema. During that research, I was struck by the connections between *Dr. Jekyll and Mistress Hyde* (2003), an ultra-low-budget softcore movie by Tony Marsiglia, and *Mulholland Drive* (2001), a mid-budget American indie by David Lynch. Not only did Marsiglia allude to Lynch and his oneiric devices, he also deployed Lynch's signature auteur rhetoric in refusing to explain his art, in waxing coy and ambiguous to avoid dispersing what was most ineffable, most fully mysterious about it. What is more, Marsiglia's studio, Seduction Cinema, stressed the Lynchian insistence on control that the director practiced in shooting films like *Mistress Hyde*, *Lust for Dracula* (2004), *Sinful* (2006), and *Chantal* (2007). Seduction promoted this arty obsessiveness as a sign of distinction in an otherwise flagging soft-porn industry. Unsurprisingly, Marsiglia's status as a softcore auteur was at that moment taken for granted in American cult subcultures.

Naturally, in writing about Marsiglia, I alluded to Lynch, just as I had alluded to Ingmar Bergman, another "serious" auteur with oneiric tendencies, when writing about Lynch. This was all natural and proper, for the allusions and historical connections were there, they were real—and given my background as both a Lynch scholar and a softcore scholar, they were obvious, so it would have been capricious had I failed to mention them simply because Marsiglia's oeuvre was produced, consumed, and acclaimed in a uniquely déclassé sector of moviedom. Still, it did not feel at all natural or proper to mix Lynch and Bergman into discussions of a softcore director. It felt criminal—or, worse, just incorrect. Those intractably mixed feelings, along with the attendant anxiety, prompted me to start the project that became this theory of art cinemas.

What I discovered in pursuing that project was that film scholars had never fully thought out the term "art cinema." Eleftheria Thanouli has acknowledged this dearth of theorization while also confirming that the term is nevertheless common, a combination that makes it seem both "fuzzy" and ordinary at the same time. Because of this oddity, I had trouble at first figuring out why it felt wrong to range across (sub)cultural stratifications when examining potential art cinemas. Was it that "art cinema" referred to a distinct movement or period within film history? If that were so, I might have made a mistake when looking for art movies outside those parameters. But in the end, I realized that the term did not refer to a closed historical period. Though some art cinemas, like the state-subsidized European art cinemas that helped make Bergman and Jean-Luc Godard household names, have left a deeper historical imprint than others, new art cinemas are today constantly emerging from the festival circuit and other institutional sectors. Was it instead that "art cinema" referred to a conventional genre, like the western or musical, which can have relatively regular forms and relatively stable expectations of effect (or *a*ffect)? If that were the case, I had simply erred when thinking of Marsiglia's softcore as art cinema. But this possibility did not merit much scrutiny, either. As film scholars have demonstrated time and again, not even the most traditional formats (e.g., the art film) can be reduced to specific forms, themes, or narrative tactics, for no art cinema has anything akin to the frontier backdrop of the western or the narrative-number structure of the musical. Nor for that matter does any art cinema deliver very consistent viewer effects, making audiences laugh, cry, or become sexually aroused, as is expected of "body genres" such as comedy, melodrama, and pornography, respectively.

Because these were the major ways that film scholars had approached art cinema, ruling them out from the get-go made me nervous. Still, as a student of cult film, I knew that there was another way to approach this foundational term. Such an approach would look at art cinema not as a set of films, stylistics, or viewer effects but as a more diffuse category like "cult cinema" or "mainstream cinema," concepts that allow people to define cinematic value in context-specific ways. As cult scholars and theorists of the mainstream realize, these terms refer not to genres, exactly, but to differential categories that classifiers use to carve out and sustain comparative forms of value, like political authenticity or social status. Thus a "cult classic" is often identified today as a midnight movie that is elevated through a culturally illegitimate mode of populist consumption that fetishizes illegitimate things, groups, and ideas. By contrast, a "mainstream movie" is a commercial feature that does not openly challenge dominant norms. The idea of a "mainstream cinema" may be used by cult fans and traditional cinephiles alike, who see in the category a debased background against which they may define their own values and tastes. Clearly, in this variety of usage, concepts like "art cinema," "cult cinema," and "mainstream cinema" do not mandate any particular forms or audience effects. Nor, from this point of view, must any of them be restricted to a specific context.

The benefit of the perspective that I propose in this book is that it allows theorists to think of art cinema as a subcultural aggregate, which was largely impossible under narrower ideas of genre. It does this by organizing art cinema according to its basic sociological utility, which I consider its aspirational, high-art function. This value-neutral idea of art cinema provides a rationale for folding into one flexible category the art cinemas that people used to call "art cinema" but don't much anymore (the film d'art movement, various interwar avant-gardes, etc.), the art cinemas that film critics continue to see as paradigm examples of the concept (e.g., postwar European and Asian new waves), the art cinemas whose relative place critics have long been on the fence about (American indie films, the New Hollywood, the postwar avant-gardes, etc.), as well as the art cinemas that few critics have ever called "art cinema" (e.g., the cult-art cinemas of Marsiglia and Anna Biller). These examples are not exhaustive, for the repertory model of art cinema that I employ here is *very* inclusive, despite the exclusivism that must remain art cinema's signature wherever it manifests. Indeed, this theory is hypothetically open even to aspirational cinemas that have not been, and may never be, recognized as art cinema in any subculture due to their peculiar aesthetics or to their lack of distribution.

In this book, I chart the most paradigmatic ways in which all these disparate art cinemas are bound together at the conceptual level as forms of cinematic high art. In pursuing this goal, I chose not to overcompensate in the direction of the untraditional. An expanded theory of art cinema cannot be *more* accurate if it ignores the category's most legitimate formats, rhetorics, institutions, canons, and social functions. Instead, this new theory weaves art cinema's most consecrated elements together with its unconsecrated elements as found in the conjoined spheres of mainstream cinema, experimental cinema, cult cinema, and so on. My aim is to look across the resulting diversity to analyze how this new conceptual inclusiveness affects our understanding of an ostensibly exclusive category. If I succeed in this project, future theorists may feel a bit less strange, a bit less illicit even, when moving among art cinemas that are, like Marsiglia's softcore, grounded in *very* particular kinds of legitimacy.

Just to be clear: this is not a theory that currently exists in the world. It has many historical precedents, but it is not already "out there." It is an invented

A production still from Tony Marsiglia's cult-art movie *Sinful* (2006). In the early 2000s, Marsiglia was the resident auteur at the New Jersey softcore studio Seduction Cinema. © 2006 Seduction Cinema, Shock-O-Rama Cinema, and El Independent Cinema. Used courtesy of Michael Raso and Pop Cinema.

theory designed to make sense of the way art cinema reverberates across national boundaries, time periods, and cultural stratifications. Though I hope it has an impact on academic film theory in general, I make no pretense of threatening the byzantine hierarchies that sustain art cinema in the practical world. In other words, individuals who subscribe to what Pierre Bourdieu calls the "illusio" of the aesthetic will continue to think it wrong or in bad taste to mention *Persona* (1966) or *Mulholland Drive* in the same breath as *Mistress Hyde*—for if they didn't, art cinema might well collapse. Fortunately, that is not the sort of impact humanities theories tend to have.

Several disclaimers are in order. First, I should probably say something about my construction of "film theory." In my view, film history, film theory, and film criticism have different ways and means. Film history subordinates conceptualization to archival detail, while film theory does the opposite; film criticism focuses on issues of convention, style, meaning, and narrative. This construction of film theory opens me to critiques. For one thing, it rejects the aims and politics of grand theory, an approach to theorization whose influence has waned in film studies but whose assumptions and practices are still often taken for granted in the field. More crucially, my approach to film theory implies that we can do it without performing new research in film history—which, given that historicism is by far the most substantive movement in film studies today, might seem controversial. Nonetheless, just because I haven't in *this* project involved myself in the nitty-gritty of empirical research doesn't mean I consider myself "above all that." It means instead that I consider it the film theorist's obligation to be reductive—to pursue generalities that unify in a logical, accurate way details gathered from across the cinema. Today, film history and criticism have supplied film studies with enough reliable data that scholars interested in crafting a synthetic theory of art cinema may do so. Another way to say this is that film theory is the unraveling of all the assumptions generated by our interactions with cinema.

A production still from Anna Biller's cult movie *Viva* (2007), which re-creates the period detail of classic sexploitation movies by auteurs like Radley Metzger. Besides directing, Biller also stars; in this orgy scene, she is wearing the headdress. Few critics have referred to cult auteur vehicles like *Viva* as "art cinema." Photo by Steve Dietl. Courtesy of Anna Biller.

Promotional art for Tony Marsiglia's cult-art movie *Dr. Jekyll and Mistress Hyde* (2003). This softcore vehicle alludes to David Lynch, remaking the themes, sounds, and images of *Mulholland Drive* (2001) in particular. © 2003 Seduction Cinema. Used courtesy of Michael Raso and Pop Cinema.

This unraveling can be useful, allowing us to re-stitch our understanding of undertheorized ideas like "art cinema," making them more coherent, comprehensive, and defensible.

I also want to qualify my use of concepts that may strike readers as elitist. I am aware of the intonations of terms like "legitimate" and "illegitimate," for I have a very clear memory of gnashing my teeth when first reading *Distinction* (1979), Bourdieu's classic sociology of art, taste, and status. By casually applying terms such as "legitimate" to high culture and "illegitimate" to low, Bourdieu risked reinforcing the essentialist belief that certain artifacts *deserved* their relative positions based on their intrinsic fineness. Of course, Bourdieu wanted to demystify our ideas of distinction; he was using these terms not to make an ahistorical graph of *real* intrinsic values but to make a historical chart of social positions based on received ideas of legitimacy. The problem was that there was no good way to avoid using such terms. They were convenient for plotting contingent forms of status, and any equally effective tools carried similar dangers. The same is true here. So let me say it plainly: things, ideas, and people don't deserve their status in any absolute way. This holds true even if *some* of the art preferences upheld by our received ideas of legitimacy have a natural or a hardwired basis, as I assume they must.

And finally, art cinema belongs to the world, but I am an American. I understand that the United States is not the core of cinema, much less art cinema, no matter how this book sounds at times. Indeed, this theory aims to dissect that easy sense of center that is one of art cinema's principal seductions. I apologize in advance, then, if my book, which aspires to a modest universality, betrays native biases. Such biases don't match my ideals, but I suspect they come with *all* our territories: for we are each somewhere, and we are, over long periods of our lives, only there. The best we can hope for is to approach universality. But we cannot hope for even that much if we don't first admit our constraints, integrating some sense of restriction, that feeling of containment by the world, into our theories. I have tried to do that here.

David Andrews
Chicago, 2013

Acknowledgments

I owe debts, intellectual and otherwise, to a great many people. One theme of this book is that none of us is ever autonomous or autochthonous—for whether we are film auteurs or academic authors, we rely on those who came before us and on all those who have offered us help and kindness along the way. This point has held true for me, so I wish I could thank everyone. Again.

Luckily, I have the opportunity to thank the people who have helped me on *this* project. Here my family deserves credit for tolerating my need for time, space, and silence. My gratitude and apologies, then, to my parents, Bill and Donna; to my wife, editor, and friend, Chris; and to my two smart, beautiful children, Samuel and Ruth. I should also recognize the artists who have contributed here, including Anna Biller, Jon Behrens, Robert Zverina, Tony Marsiglia, and Charissa King-O'Brien. Many of my colleagues have also supported this project. Chuck Kleinhans deserves special recognition for encouraging and assisting me on many occasions. Other scholars who deserve thanks include Michael Zryd, Michael Z. Newman, Karl Schoonover, Kathryn Ramey, Mary Adekoya, Giaime Alonge, Mark Kermode, Rosalind Galt, Linda Ruth Williams, Jean-Paul Kelly, Eric Schaefer, Mark Betz, Anthony Smith, Julia Lesage, Elena Gorfinkel, Mark Gallagher, Daniel Lindvall, and George Dickie.

I should also thank individuals affiliated with some particularly generous institutions. Many thanks, then, to Heather Middleton of *Screen*; Andrea Grover and Delicia Harvey of Aurora Picture Show; May Haduong of the Academy Film Archive; Michael Raso of Pop Cinema; David Levari, Andrea Nishi, and Michaeljit Sandhu of Doc Films; Anne Bustamante of Facets Multimedia; Laura Shaeffer of the Opportunity Shop; Shannon McLachlan and Mary Bergin-Cartwright of Oxford University Press; Jean de St. Aubin of the Gene Siskel Film Center; Brenda Fernandes of *Sight & Sound*; and, lastly, Julia Gibbs of the Film Studies Center at the University of Chicago. Academic conferences that have acted as sounding boards for single chapters in this book include the Society for Cinema and Media Studies Conference; the Popular Culture Association Conference; the Midwest Popular Culture Association Conference; and the Transforming Body in Popular Culture seminar series at the University of Southampton. Similarly, the editors and readers of *Jump Cut, Scope,* the *Journal of Popular Culture, Film International, Screen, New Cinemas, Cinema Journal,* and the *Journal of Film and Video* deserve credit for providing input that has helped shape individual chapters of this book in advance of publication. And thanks again, also, to the staff of the University of Chicago's Regenstein Library, as well as to the anonymous editor at Continuum who sent me a desk copy that I couldn't have afforded otherwise.

Finally, at the University of Texas Press, my deepest gratitude goes to Christopher Chung, who saw this project's potential; Jim Burr, who guided it to completion and lent me support in dark moments; my reviewers, whose critiques pushed me to refine my arguments; and Molly Frisinger, Victoria Davis, Nicholas Taylor, and all their colleagues at the press who helped copyedit, design, produce, and distribute the final product. I couldn't have done it without you—a fact so inescapable that I've only become more grateful over time. Thank you, *all* of you.

Theorizing Art Cinemas

Object to the Hollywood film and you're an intellectual snob, object to the avant-garde films and you're a Philistine. But, while in Hollywood, one must often be a snob; in avant-garde circles, one must often be a Philistine.
—PAULINE KAEL, "MOVIES, THE DESPERATE ART" (1956)

"What do you mean by 'good film'?"
—*LA MAMAN ET LA PUTAIN* (DIR. JEAN EUSTACHE, 1973)

Correcting Art Cinema's Partial Vision

Looking for the Elephant

Seven Blind Mice (1992) is a children's story by Ed Young based on the Indian fable of the six blind men. In it, seven mice investigate a new "Something" standing by their pond. They touch it each in turn before describing it and naming it for the group. Green Mouse, having felt its long trunk, deems it a snake, and Orange Mouse, having felt its floppy ear, thinks it a fan. The seventh rodent, White Mouse, takes a completely different approach, running all over the animal, and reports back that the first six were all wrong, for the Something was really an elephant. Hence, the Mouse Moral: "Knowing in part may make a fine tale, but wisdom comes from knowing the whole."

In a figurative sense, studying art cinema is similar: to see it whole, we should run all over it. Such inquiry may not lead to wisdom, but it might put us in position to see art cinema clearly. Why isn't this obvious? Because the ideologies and institutions that have given art cinema life and form have elicited partial views of the category—as if they were *directing* us to look only at the trunk or the ear, as if they were *telling* us to prioritize only a few parts. In such ways, this cultural area has prompted its participants to act as individual evaluators who are always ready to restrict art cinema to its "essence." And art-cinema insiders, forums, and promotional machineries have been specific about which kinds of phenomena are eligible for this status: auteurs, masterpieces, and new waves as defined by style, creativity, meaning, politics, and canon. Indeed, while making exceptions for themselves, even art cinema's most illegitimate participants have implied that we should focus our attention on the most legitimate institutions, such as the Cannes Film Festival, and the most legitimate formats, like the traditional art film.

This partial vision has of course been informed by many determinants, including academic compartmentalization, high-art ideology, and humanity's restless pursuit of status and value. But the most overlooked factor here may be our confusion over the kind of category that "art cinema" represents. Even scholars have at times assumed that this term refers either to a traditional genre—that is, an objective form produced in predictable milieus and manifest through style, narrative, or meaning—or to a closed historical period or movement, like the postwar European art film. But across film history, "art cinema" has frequently had more elastic usages, suggesting that it has more in common with a broad category like "mainstream cinema" or "cult cinema" than with a narrower genre term like "western" or "Italian neorealist film." Theorists of mainstream cinema and cult cinema today realize that the cultural phenomena these terms refer to are complex and always in flux.[1] The same holds true for art cinema—which over the past century has been a term that has designated many cinemas produced through a broad, institutional array of value-oriented, oppositional processes.

Strictly speaking, then, art cinema has *no* necessary-and-sufficient conventions at the formal level. *Indeed, I don't think of it as a form at all.* A practical way of imagining art cinema is as an idea of cinematic high art that has since the silent era inspired value-oriented events and value-oriented institutions as well as a multitude of aspirational forms in a multitude of contexts. This category's main consistencies are rhetorical in nature, for the cinephile discourses that govern art cinema regularly deploy high-art ideals such as anticommercial purity, authorship, and aesthetic disinterest in order to justify and defend the designation of certain movies as "art movies." Of course, when art cinema has been treated as a specific industrial area with specific formal and historical determinants, it has often been presented as a rival of an audience-driven Hollywood cinema, whose executives have favored everything that cinephiles claim to resist, including profits, standardization, distributors and distribution, technical innovation, celebrity culture, and entertainment. But when it comes to actual movies, art cinema is at most a value-oriented super-genre like "mainstream cinema" and "cult cinema," which have entailed different forms in different contexts. Its constituent works have thus been subject to much more debate than those unified by narrower terms like "western."

At its broadest, then, art cinema suggests an idea of cinematic quality. The corollary of this suggestion is that those films designated "art movies" often serve as the high art of whatever cinematic context frames them (which means that they wouldn't necessarily qualify as art movies or as high art in a different context). This high-art function implies a wholly *relative* antipathy toward commercialism—an antipathy in keeping with the "beliefs and values of Western societies," which, Shyon Baumann acknowledges, "deem commercial interests antithetical to the legitimacy of art."[2] It may strike us as odd to apply anticommercial ideals to the movies, for the relative costs and potential audience appeal of this particular medium can, as Baumann drily puts it, seem "incongruent with the aims of an art world and more in line with entertainment and amusement."[3] Nevertheless, the idea that high art opposes commerce is art cinema's most consistent myth.[4] It is part of art cinema no matter what. Of course, as we will see, this myth has been very flexible, meaning different things in different cinematic milieus. Consequently, high-art terms like "art cinema" and "art movie" have long been useful outside the global film-festival circuit where they currently seem most legitimate. Indeed, whether we are talking about the arrival of *Das cabinet des Dr. Caligari* (1919) in the United States or the earlier film d'art movement in France, aestheticist distinctions have been a staple of the many discourses on art cinema—and have never been confined to "official" art cinemas.[5] Instead, the proliferation of cinema as a medium has led to the proliferating application of high-art terms and distinctions. Hence, for the past fifty years these terms and distinctions have been available to insiders even within the most marginalized or abject cinemas, including the adult film. "Hollywood art cinema" is hardly, then, the oddest kind of art cinema to have emerged over the run of film history.

Today, the standard history of art cinema pays lip-service to the avant-gardes that coalesced in Europe in the 1920s and 1930s, but it mostly focuses on the achievements of the "new waves" that formed at postwar film festivals between 1946 and 1970 before flowing to art houses, grindhouses, and repertory theaters across the globe.[6] However, as I have implied, the standard history is too narrow. The potential inclusiveness of a category like "art cinema" suggests that it has more in common with the honorific sense of terms like "art" and "high art," which refer to broad, value-laden concepts whose flexible appeal has made them similarly plural, similarly resilient. In pursuing the origins of art cinema, we might, then, briefly consider the origins of those wider concepts.

Lately, the most intriguing glimpses into those origins have come from theorists in evolutionary biology, who view the ability to make, consume, and evaluate art *either* as adaptations that conferred reproductive and survival benefits on our ancestors *or* as by-products of adaptations like the big human brain, something that presumably evolved in the main to fill other functions. For two decades, Darwinian literary critics like Joseph Carroll and evolutionary aestheticians such as the late Denis Dutton have used new research in evolutionary psychology and cultural evolution as a bridge between C. P. Snow's "two cultures." This bridge has allowed them to generate "biocultural" insights in the humanities that are based on the premise that art is a product of "human nature," which is itself the product of selective pressures. But if these biocultural ideas have led to useful hypotheses pertaining to the material origin, persistence, and proliferation of art, they currently tell us little that is solid about art cinema's specific cultural formation. What we need, then, is a theory open to scientific evidence such that later scholars—who will know more than we do about how biology works through culture—will not be forced to dispense with our ideas of art cinema just to improve them.

The optimal framework for this purpose is one that starts by assuming the obvious: the human species has evolutionary origins and material constraints. Many of the best research programs in the humanities could be made more defensible if they simply stated these assumptions clearly at the outset. Indeed, according to Edward Slingerland in *What Science Offers the Humanities* (2008), even Pierre Bourdieu's work on taste and status would be made more sensible if we could imagine it against a "background of evolved human preferences and motivations." Had Bourdieu avoided the constructionist premises that are common in sociology and the humanities, he would from Slingerland's point of view have told a more "plausible story about how the sorts of novel, idiosyncratic, high-level cultural- or class-specific distinctions" that he "analyzed and catalogued with such nuance" were "grounded in basic and universal human capacities and dispositions."[7] The chapters that follow share this assumption. Hence, they refer on occasion to biocultural ideas, which open paths that would have been impassable under former regimes in film studies. At the same time, they are honest about the state of this research, which is early in its development and cannot be assigned too great a theoretical burden. It is up to later film scholars to pursue these paths further, which scholars like myself are leaving open for them.

Of course, I take it for granted that the scholars who follow these paths will have a grasp of art cinema's roots in post-Renaissance culture as well as its more immediate roots in film history. To ensure this, my next section offers a sketch of some of the most important developments in the history of art cinema as it exists today, with an emphasis on how those events have played out in American contexts. In the chapters that follow, we will often draw on this sketch, adding detail as we go.

Brief Historical Sketch

Art cinema, in all its multiplicity, is part of a vast cultural hierarchy that took root in Western society during and after the Renaissance. As historians like Lawrence Levine and Larry Shiner have documented,[8] economic pressures and philosophical innovations led post-Renaissance thinkers to divide the monolithic category of art, which had once referred to everything from chamber music and portraiture to popular narratives and embroidery, into fine art and useful craft. These high–low divisions became increasingly diverse and obligatory in bourgeois culture, reaching their apotheosis in the modernist era. The industrial revolution heightened these developments, enhancing the rarity and symbolic value of aesthetic objects made without obvious mercenary intent or "interest." Eventually, these cultural processes led to the romantic era and its "art for art's sake" movement, which claimed that high art was fully disinterested, antithetical to utility and to all didactic content. Hence, by the late nineteenth century, artists hoping for a rise in cultural status could not rely on their mastery of a craft. And practitioners of popular nineteenth-century media, like the novel and photography, were very insecure in their cultural rank, for the art classifier was no longer a straightforward identity based on craft-oriented effects like narration or realism. This classification had *also* become a status earned through cultural competitions wherein too much popularity bred suspicion. Thus, as the decades passed, high-art industries across the West increasingly promoted themselves through anticommercial rhetoric. And this tendency was especially clear among nineteenth-century producers of art novels and art photography, who were under some very heavy pressure to distinguish their work from "mere" genre fictions or from "mere" records of historical reality.

During the twentieth century, similar socioeconomic pressure led the distributors and audiences of cinema to recapitulate this process of cultural stratification. If anything, this process was only accelerated by the fact that the cinema was extraordinarily popular from the start with the working classes and the young, a fact that made the medium more worrisome to the cultural guardians who exerted the most influence over cultural status. In the United States, the cinema was under attack by progressives almost from the moment storefront theaters began exposing the working classes to the "nickel madness" around the year 1905.[9] Thus, in 1907, authorities in the United States and abroad began enacting prior censorship ordinances to control the distribution and exhibition of a potentially dangerous form. Given these factors, it is understandable that many film producers and distributors were anxious to protect the cinema by elevating its status through specialized forms.

An early example of this process outside the United States was the film d'art movement in France, which began prior to 1910. French producers like Charles Le Bargy, hoping to gain an educated audience and to raise the prestige of the cinema, began using literary adaptations and theatrical techniques in films like *L'assassinat du duc de Guise* (1908). As a self-conscious attempt to create artful films, these efforts were well publicized but could not ultimately survive financially—and film critics have retrospectively critiqued the movement for having failed to innovate in a cinematic (as opposed to a theatrical) vein. That said, the film d'art movement created a precedent for looking at cinema as an aspirational form that could potentially enjoy the same high-culture status enjoyed at the start of the century by elite forms of theater. Thus the film d'art movement paved the way for the European avant-gardes that made art films during the interwar period. These movements included French impressionism, German expressionism, Neue Sachlichkeit, and Soviet montage, which A. L. Rees and other scholars still call "Art Cinema."[10]

Just as vital to raising the profile of the art-film idea were several new distribution paradigms, including those of the film d'art movement, and new exhibition contexts, like little cinemas, *ciné-clubs*, museum theaters, and film festivals.[11] These new sites of exhibition emerged between 1908 and 1940, helping to circulate the art-film ideas of early film theorists like Ricciotto Canudo and Vachel Lindsay—and making it acceptable for people to discuss the cinema as art, especially in the European nations most amenable to the idea, like France and Italy.[12] In the interwar era, Hollywood focused on expanding its industrial hegemony by investing primarily in the most commercially dominant forms of narrative "entertainment." Nevertheless, Hollywood also contributed to the art-film idea through its ceaseless technological experimentation, through the artistry of individual Hollywood practitioners like Charlie Chaplin, and through its formation of the Academy system, which promoted the cultural status of certain varieties of Hollywood film.[13]

Clearly, there were many opportunities for discussing "art films" and "art cinema" prior to the Second World War that were encouraged by a significant, albeit nascent, art-cinema infrastructure that in select European capitals had succeeded in making art cinema a fairly mainstream concept. But not until after the war did aspirationalism become the key to reviving various European film industries—and, later, to reviving Hollywood cinema as well. One of the roots of this complex historical process was the disarray that the European film industries found themselves in after the Second World War. With their home markets flooded by Hollywood imports, the Europeans turned to subsidies and an "art" strategy to turn their industries around and reclaim former markets. The resulting state-subsidized art films had stable financing and were often mainstream critical favorites, for unlike many of the interwar avant-garde cinemas, their aspirations were couched in a fairly commercial narrative format accessible to large audiences. These art films were feted at major film festivals, like Venice and Cannes, and they were often exported to the United States, which was the most important movie market in the world due to its size, wealth, and influence on global film distribution. In this way, the postwar art cinemas began to solve practical problems that had marginalized earlier art cinemas like the film d'art movement.

In the United States, these European art cinemas were screened on an expanding art-house circuit that in the 1940s and 1950s was situated on the peripheries "between" exploitation exhibition and Hollywood exhibition. This circuit, which had developed in urban areas and university towns over the decades, had long exposed Americans to an eclectic mix of exploitation movies and foreign art films, which were in some respects equally obscene in the minds of domestic viewers used to the niceties of Hollywood sublimation as regulated by the Production Code.[14] But it was only after the war, during the advent of Italian neorealism, that distributors honed and expanded a more specialized model for exhibiting art films—and on a massive scale.[15] Often modeled on the "refined" exhibition practices of the Film Library of the Museum of Modern Art, the U.S. art house civilized what were potentially illicit visions through the trappings of gentility: the Francophilic promotion, the wine and cheese, the expert lectures, the air of obligatory disinterest. This exhibition circuit was engineered to sell European and Asian art films as eroticized but culturally inoffensive art.[16] For more than two decades, this business formula gave the art film a vogue in the United States, where its "opportunity space" was simultaneously enhanced by the return of American GIs from Europe, by increases in education, by status advantages imparted by the growth of television, and by a booming postwar economy.[17]

Beyond their cachet, these postwar foreign art films profited from two other advantages in the United States. First, in the postwar era, Hollywood's control over its home market was being corroded by Supreme Court rulings even as its popularity with its domestic audience was declining due to the introduction of television and other leisure pursuits. Hollywood's control over its home market had long been guaranteed by censorship. The authority of early American censorship ordinances had been codified through the Court's decision in *Mutual Film Corporation v. Industrial Commission of Ohio* (1915), which ruled that cinema was a business, not an art or an act of speech that deserved free-speech protection.[18] This ruling established the legality of film censorship in the United States, making Hollywood films subject to various regulatory bodies. In a defensive move, Hollywood moved to regulate itself through self-censorship in the 1920s and to this end enforced its own Production Code in 1934. Because they controlled exhibition through vertical integration, Hollywood executives did not at that point need to worry about the occasional success of a foreign art film, like *Ecstasy* (1933), or a domestic exploitation film, like *Mom and Dad* (1945). But this confidence was shaken once the Supreme Court began rattling Hollywood's foundations at the same moment that its audiences were being fragmented by new cinemas like Italian neorealism and new technologies like television. The main event in this long history was the Paramount decision of 1948, which disrupted a "classical" system built on vertical integration.

The slow collapse of the classical Hollywood system that followed the Paramount Decrees made many art cinemas more available to exhibitors. Suddenly, exhibitors could choose their own bookings, and art films and experimental underground films often proved lucrative, a development that Hollywood financiers quickly noted.[19] These trends were furthered when the Supreme Court overturned its *Mutual* ruling in *Burstyn v. Wilson* (1952), which suggested that European art films like Roberto Rossellini's neorealist film *The Miracle* (1948) were art and that similar films, however sexy, deserved constitutional protections. With the censors in retreat, more distributors and exhibitors felt comfortable taking on sexualized foreign art films in a postwar period during which most Hollywood producers were shackled by systematic self-censorship.

These industrial changes helped spur a rise in film's cultural status. Ironically, as Baumann has argued, the major determinant of this rise in cultural status was the rapid overall decline in the popularity of film following the Second World War, for that decline neutralized the factor—cinema's attractiveness to the working class[20]—that had made the middle class most anxious about cinema. When the working class began finding other entertainments, the middle class could then revalue cinema as a potential high art. This postwar process was further aided by a new idea, *la politique des auteurs*, which American critics imported from Europe. Though Andrew Sarris and other critics at first used the "auteur theory" to defend their judgment of the value of certain Hollywood films by certain Hollywood directors, it was also applied to the many foreign art films helmed by Italian, Swedish, and French auteurs, from Rossellini and Ingmar Bergman to Michelangelo Antonioni and Jean-Luc Godard. Especially in the United States, the idea of authorship central to the auteur theory was crucial to persuading an American audience schooled on Hollywood's anti-auteurist values and practices to re-see the cinema as an artist-directed medium. Moreover, auteurism gave academics the tools to claim an irreducible disciplinary specificity. By the 1970s, many major American universities had integrated film studies into their humanities curricula.[21] This process was most crucial to the stability of the American avant-garde cinemas, whose practitioners gained a secure place to produce, exhibit, celebrate, and teach experimental work as a result.[22]

But the auteurs and their theories may have made their most indelible impact through their direct influence on Hollywood. With its business model coming apart amid the ongoing reverberations of the Paramount decision, Hollywood became more open to innovation. In the late 1950s and early 1960s, the studios bought art-film distributors and began coproducing foreign art films. But Hollywood's most crucial experiment seems to have been the scrapping of the Code for a ratings system in 1968 and the reordering of the studio system such that Euro-style directors like Stanley Kubrick, Arthur Penn, Martin Scorsese, and Robert Altman had substantial new freedoms. These moves disrupted the market for foreign art films in the United States in that the emergence of the auteur-driven New Hollywood made it possible to exhibit adult-oriented Hollywood art movies, causing the "foreign film" to lose its cachet in the United States, as Sarris noted in 1999.[23] In time, this business model would fracture, too, with Hollywood retreating from its auteur excess after the flop of *Heaven's Gate* (1980). But by the late 1980s, a new "indie" movement had revived the auteur zeal so prominent in the 1970s. This American new wave gained traction through technological change: the coming of home video created opportunities for independent producers and distributors.[24] Later, this market showed such promise that Hollywood once again took notice. Since the 1990s, the indie-style studios—that is, the art-house divisions of major studios like Sony, Disney, and Fox—have once again dominated and disrupted the market for foreign or independent art cinema in the United States.[25]

From this sketch, we can see that there have been numerous potential art cinemas in global circulation since the silent era. In the United States, these categories have carried different labels—"avant-garde," "foreign," "mainstream," "indie," "video art," and so on—depending on their relative cultural positions and their usual distribution networks, with overlap always possible. The decline of the classical Hollywood system, along with the mainstreaming of auteurism and the relative wealth of American society, meant that the U.S. market, like developed markets in Europe and Asia, would become more segmented and stratified in the 1950s, inundated with relatively independent productions of all types by all types of directors—some of whom were self-styled "auteurs" long before they had directed anything. Often, these auteurs got their initial directing gigs in the 1980s amid the cult networks that exploded at the start of the video era, when legendary low-budget directors like Doris Wishman, Roger Corman, and Dario Argento were in the process of canonization. These populist networks developed their own film festivals, promotional mechanics, and modes of distribution, exhibition, and reception—and in time, they developed their own cult hierarchies, with domestic and foreign auteurs producing "cult classics," a category that could encompass movies peculiarly valued as "cult-art movies." Cult-art cinemas are different from other art cinemas in that their participants have exuded a conflicted attitude toward their own *subcultural* legitimacy (and their own *potential* cultural legitimacy). Though the high-art urge toward cultural status and artistic quality is relatively unproblematic even in *mainstream* art cinemas, this impulse is complicated in cult-art cinemas by the fact that cult networks and cult concepts purposely mystify illegitimate things, people, ideas, and status. Hence, as I detail in chapter 5, a confusing, unorthodox variety of art cinema was born in the late twentieth century, one whose cultural illegitimacy was often valued by insiders as a mark of its subcultural authenticity, in turn lending it subcultural legitimacy. Of the art cinemas, cult-art cinema is the least understood variety in academia.

Overcoming Art Cinema's Partial Vision in the Academy

Though brief, the U.S.-centered history sketched above offers hints at the truth of art cinema: that it is a concept that refers to the high-art social function of cinema, which has been manifest in different ways in different cultures, subcultures, and market niches. Why has this not been widely recognized? Or, to put it another way, why is art cinema in the United States still often boiled down to postwar foreign art films? There are many factors to consider. As scholars, we have not always been aware of the historical flexibility of high-art ideas in the cinema; we have not often focused on cult-art cinemas, an awareness of which would have sensitized us to art cinema's subcultural potential; and we have frequently deferred to the formalist schemas of movie critics and film scholars with cinephile dispositions. The last factor has been most problematic for film studies when highly distinguished scholars like David Bordwell or Dudley Andrew have written nuanced scholarship around the most traditional art cinemas.

Above, I noted that academic compartmentalization is one reason that partial visions of art cinema have been so prevalent in film studies. But if this compartmentalization is part of the problem, it may be part of the solution as well. Let me explain. The past two decades have witnessed the ascendancy of historicism in film studies. This trend has made it possible to write the history of art cinema I sketched above. Studies like Barbara Wilinsky's *Sure Seaters: The Emergence of Art House Cinema* (2001), Haidee Wasson's *Museum Movies: The Museum of Modern Art and the Birth of Art Cinema* (2005), and Thomas Elsaesser's *European Cinema: Face to Face with Hollywood* (2005) began to appear regularly. These studies charted art cinema's history while analyzing its industrial apparatus, global circulation, and distinctive appeal.

Today, these books seem to be appearing with even greater frequency. Thus recent years have seen the introduction of monographs like András Bálint Kovács's *Screening Modernism: European Art Cinema, 1950–1980* (2007), Geoffrey Nowell-Smith's *Making Waves: New Cinemas of the 1960s* (2008), Mark Betz's *Beyond the Subtitle: Remapping European Art Cinema* (2009), Tino Balio's *The Foreign Film Renaissance on American Screens, 1946–1973* (2010), Cindy H. Wong's *Film Festivals: Culture, People, and Power on the Global Screen* (2011), and Michael Z. Newman's *Indie: An American Film Culture* (2011). At the same time, several indispensable collections, like Barry Keith Grant's *Auteurs and Authorship* (2008), Rosalind Galt and Karl Schoonover's *Global Art Cinema: New Theories and Histories* (2010), and Dominique Russell's *Rape in Art Cinema* (2010), have come out; they have been supplemented by case-books on cinephilia that were released as crossover books or as portfolios in peer-reviewed journals.[26] Most intriguing of all has been the appearance of subculturally oriented studies that place art cinema in the context of exploitation and other lowbrow forms. The latter include two collections edited by Robert Weiner and John Cline, *From the Arthouse to the Grindhouse* (2010) and *Cinema Inferno* (2010), as well as a great many tightly focused historicist studies like Peter Stanfield's *Maximum Movies—Pulp Fictions* (2011).

The upshot of all this empirical activity is that scholars now have many tools with which to "re-see" art cinema, none of which existed during the auteur era or in the era of grand theory that followed it in film studies. Though the carefully defined historical parameters of much of this work can make it hard for academics to see *all* of art cinema—encouraging them to define certain art cinemas, like the postwar art film, as the "real" thing—scholars bent on creating a synthetic theory of art cinema can now get a holistic view by looking across *all* this work and *all* these historical parameters.

One theorist who has achieved an admirable balance of breadth, depth, and rigor is Baumann, a sociologist who fuses the new film-historical research with sociological methods and goals in *Hollywood Highbrow: From Entertainment to Art* (2007). Though hardly perfect,[27] Baumann's theory is valuable for three reasons. First, it offers a useful model for scholars. Baumann is unafraid to integrate different sorts of historical research into his sociological method, and the result is a scholarly analysis that is both meticulous and holistic. Baumann's theory is likewise helpful in that it offers a three-part "legitimation framework" that explains how cinema was legitimated as an art form in the United States during the postwar period.[28] Thus Baumann takes time to explain *how* this phenomenon occurred through shifts in the culture, industrial developments, and refinements in the ways that critics and scholars talked about movies at the technical level. Baumann's point is to show

how these transformations led to the consecration of the New Hollywood as a legitimate art form. In the process, he confirms that an American entertainment industry devoted to mass distribution could under the right conditions be deemed capable of producing high art. This aspect of Baumann's analysis will prove useful when we consider art cinema's hierarchies of value, including the differential cultural legitimacies of mainstream art cinema, cult-art cinema, and the like.

Despite the value of Baumann's book, *Hollywood Highbrow* still focuses most of its attention on just one untraditional, albeit briefly legitimate, variety of art cinema. Yet monographs like Wilinsky's and collections like Galt and Schoonover's hint at how films now valued primarily as cult vehicles have developed subculturally while also managing to circulate through legitimate networks. This is why today's film theorists should, if possible, familiarize themselves with the subcultural mechanics of the cult fields covered in books like Joan Hawkins's *Cutting Edge: Art-Horror and the Horrific Avant-Garde* (2000) — and why they should read the most essential collections in cult studies, like *Defining Cult Movies* (2003) and *The Cult Film Reader* (2008).[29]

One of the main engines driving the rise of the illegitimate cult-art cinemas since the 1960s has been auteurism. After the Second World War, auteurism was a boon to the legitimate art cinemas, helping to consolidate and publicize their central institutions. It is no wonder, then, that auteurism also proved inspirational in art cinema's less legitimate subcultures. After all, directors could emulate the auteur profile in low-budget areas, like the Italian *giallo* and hardcore porn, just as easily as they emulated it in more legitimate, state-subsidized areas. Unfortunately, auteurism and the high-art ideals that inform it have often blocked theorization of this unofficial auteurism. Critics have rarely dealt with the fact that auteurism justifies the aspirations of exploitation directors as much (or as little) as it justifies those of art-film directors or of avant-garde artists — and few books have tried to sort out the messy connections linking traditional art films, foreign art films, avant-garde movies, and video-art projects to mainstream art movies and cult-art movies, including both exploitation and hardcore pornography.

The goal of this study, then, is straightforward: to create a broad, synthetic theory of art cinema that resists high-art mythologies and throws off, where prudent, disciplinary blinders so as to see art cinema whole. This approach takes it for granted that we should not restrict our insights according to our appreciation for specific formats, new waves, auteurs, art-house styles, or cinephile tastes. Instead, we should look for the elephant, so to speak, by examining this category in three ways. First, we should connect the historicist dots and look *across* all the new historical accounts that have chronicled art cinema's industrial and cultural background. Second, we should learn from the history and theory of other super-genres like cult cinema and mainstream cinema, which might not seem relevant until we consider how contingent and intertwined the ideas of subcultural legitimacy that undergird super-generic concepts like "art cinema," "cult cinema," and "mainstream cinema" actually are. And third, we should be ready, as film scholars have historically been ready, to learn what we can from the other branches of the humanities, like art history and the philosophy of art, as well as from fields outside the humanities, like sociology, anthropology, and evolutionary psychology.

Preview of *Theorizing Art Cinemas*

This book consists of three main sections. The first chapter of the first section develops a definition of art cinema that construes it as a high-art phenomenon specific to cinema. In this definition, art cinema is an unfolding, super-generic event in which artists, promoters, and audiences typically reject a devalued, commercialized idea of the movie as a genre vehicle. Movies assigned to this category often secure their status through institutional means or through context-reliant canonical processes. The resulting complexity has plagued art-cinema scholars with problems of definition similar to those that once plagued philosophers of art bent on defining "art."

Chapter 2 moves on to auteurism, detailing the history of the auteur theory and distinguishing it from auteurism as such. Though the auteurist attitude has problems, auteurism has been a heuristic well suited to the human mind. It has been so useful in art cinema's development that it has generated tools that scholars may use to identify art cinema in traditional *and* untraditional areas. Clearly, we should continue to accent auteurism's shortcomings to avoid the human tendency to lapse into celebrations of the auteur. But because auteurism is unlikely to go away, we should also find legitimate uses for it. One such method is to use auteurism as a tool that can show us how and where untraditional art cinemas like "cult-art cinema" have arisen; this method expands our idea of art cinema even as its resists regressive uses of auteurism.

Chapter 3, the first section's final chapter, looks at the terms "foreign films" and "world cinema" in the United States. Until the late 1960s, "foreign films" denoted an "exotic" oppositional cinema identified with postwar art films; the success of these films led to industrial changes that encouraged Hollywood producers to begin distributing and then making art cinema. This had the effect of bringing foreign and domestic producers closer together, eroding the marketability of this class of films, and increasingly exposing the insensitivity of the term that lumped them together. Ergo, "foreign films" has gradually been replaced in college classes and retail outlets by "world cinema," a more neutral term that reverses the old perspective, aligning the "foreign," not the United States or Hollywood, with the "world." In academia, though, this classifying usage has remained controversial, for some see it as continuing to place Hollywood at the "core" of cinema, given that "world cinema" has not been used as a blanket term that includes Hollywood. Ironically, this practice implies that world cinema amounts to the "periphery."

The second section of the book focuses on four broad art-cinema formats. Chapter 4 looks at the "traditional art film," a format with such abundant cultural capital that it serves as a recovery-and-legitimation machine in mainstream film culture. In the United States, an art film of this category does not currently have to be praised or even liked to qualify as art cinema; instead, such a film merely has to fulfill its own institutional requirements. This is why today's indie art film, including its Hollywood variants, may be classified as a form of art cinema: this feature-length narrative plays in festivals and in art houses and is circulated by specialty labels, such that it functions as art cinema no less than do the art films of Europe, Asia, Africa, Australia, or Latin America. However, the most distinctive evidence that the traditional art film works as a recovery-and-legitimation machine is that this format has recovered debased content, like hardcore sex, for viewers in mainstream art houses. In this way, we may see art-cinema participants as exercising the "free pass" that has made art cinema so successful in global distribution.

Chapter 5 describes cult cinema as an oppositional cinema that has endorsed an active audience and that has embraced its own genre-based commercialism. Thus cult cinema diverges from high-art ideology, leading to an illegitimate form of mystification that is capable of fetishizing works from across the cultural spectrum but that focuses at the consumer level on inexpensive, lowbrow movies in sexploitation, horror, and so forth. Institutionally, this mystification has resulted in canonical processes and in the idea of the "cult classic." These canons and classics have on occasion made high-art claims that have been recognized in cult subcultures; on even rarer occasions, such claims have made cult films candidates for recovery by legitimate institutions. Ergo, these cult-art cinemas exemplify cult phenomena even as their aspiration to, or achievement of, high-art status threatens to erase their cult identity through legitimation.

Chapter 6 looks at American experimental cinema. The chapter traces this prestigious yet marginalized art-cinema sector through its roots in Europe, and distinguishes its distribution from that of other types of art cinema. The most concrete type of experimental cinema is the co-op avant-garde, which has since the 1960s been defined by its highly anticommercial form of "co-operative" distribution. This chapter focuses on the anti-institutional rhetoric of the co-op avant-garde to explore how this rhetoric has generated distinctive problems for avant-garde artists and avant-garde institutions as well as for the major external institutions, such as the academy, that have sustained this purist art cinema over the decades.

As the final chapter of the second section, chapter 7 rethinks the term "mainstream" so as to make sense of a seeming oxymoron, "mainstream art cinema." This chapter proposes that mainstream cinemas usually contain far more complexity than the derogatory connotations of the term "mainstream" imply. Indeed, cinemas of mainstream size and scope have frequently contained art-cinema canons, complete with mainstream art cinemas, within their own diffuse boundaries. To demonstrate this basic point, I take a brief look at various Hollywood art cinemas and consider the presence of mainstream art cinemas in a wide array of world and cult cinemas.

The third and final section of this book focuses on the contextual concerns so often downplayed by "cinephile discourse." Chapter 8 proposes that cinephiles have lavished attention on high-art issues like auteurism and style while often ignoring commercial concerns like stardom or technology. Such an approach belies the fact that the art film is no less involved with its stars and its technologies than are other areas of cinema. Though "cinephile discourse" feigns indifference to stars, the art film has actually relied on "niche stardom." What is more, the presence of a new kind of star in art cinema, the auteur, has resulted in significant subcultural synergies that have shielded actors, audiences, and distributors from censure, freeing female actors in particular to exploit their sexuality without fear of career-ending scandal.

Chapter 9 looks at art-cinema institutions, focusing its attention on the art-house circuit, the film-festival circuit, and the academic discipline of film studies. These global institutions have played major roles in promoting and anchoring auteurism in art cinema—and the combination of art cinema's auteurism and festival-based circulation has reinforced its tendency toward a heterogeneity of style and theme. This chapter argues that this heterogeneity is best understood not through a narrative- or form-based methodology but primarily through a culturalism that relates the genre's diversity to institutions like the art house, the film festival, and film studies.

Chapter 10 moves toward a distribution theory so as to develop an extended definition of movie distribution that covers many different cultural phenomena inside and outside the movie industry. By moving beyond the "bad old story" (which casts distribution agents in a uniformly negative light) as well as the "transit" metaphor (which sees distribution as little more than a pipeline), we can begin to see how movie distribution interacts with various forms of cultural capital and with crucial intellectual concepts. We can also begin to grasp some of the ways in which distribution shapes cinematic form. In the end, this theory of circulation gives us another means of looking at art cinema as an interactive whole.

My epilogue focuses very briefly on cinephilia. The affection for the cinema implicit to this term has long been identified with art cinema. Cinephilia is a crucial albeit "squishy" issue that combines our physiological responsiveness to art with our human capacity for love; indeed, it is an affection that has indirectly built art cinema's premier institutions, like the festival circuit. But as art cinema has fragmented and proliferated, so has cinephilia, to the point that aesthetes can no longer defend it in terms of an exclusive community of highbrow cinephiles (i.e., the "happy few").

And so the question remains: can the holistic art cinema charted in this book breed the kind of cinephilia that sent postwar film lovers to the barricades, or is this new aggregate cinema just another consumer category, without the old mystique to really move viewers? Only time, I think, will tell.

PART 1

Art, Auteurism, and the World

CHAPTER 1

Art as Genre as Canon
Defining "Art Cinema"

A Needy, Altogether Necessary Term

Way back in 1981, in his seminal article "Art Cinema as Institution," Steve Neale noted that "art cinema" had rarely been defined as a cinematic concept. Over time, the failure of scholars to confront this foundational notion has led to its becoming, in Eleftheria Thanouli's estimate, one of the "fuzziest and yet least controversial concepts in film studies."[1] Lately, however, theorists like Thanouli, Andrew Tudor, Karl Schoonover, Rosalind Galt, András Bálint Kovács, and Mark Betz have shown renewed interest in "art cinema" and its several offshoots. Thus, in a fairly recent analysis, Tudor points to the peculiarity of the term "art movie" by observing that in "everyday discourse we do not speak of 'art novel,' 'art picture' or 'art music.'"[2] Here Tudor is alluding to something that has long irritated the ex–composition teacher in me. "Art cinema" sounds redundant and almost needy. This is a category of cinema, the term almost shouts, that is also a form of art. Point taken—but what else could fictional movies be?

Non-art, naturally. I imagine that readers of this book will be dissatisfied with this answer; for me, it borders on the offensive. Still, it may just be a measure of art cinema's success that we feel this way. Though the cinema was, at the beginning of the twentieth century, a self-conscious medium that had to struggle hard in the United States (as in many other countries outside of France and Italy) to establish its high-art credentials, that battle has been so clearly won by the medium's status-heavy strains that *all* movies, not just the art movies and the cult movies that claim some special distinctiveness, stand revealed at the start of this century as art. Of course, it is more than just film history that tells us this.[3] The postmodernist "leveling" of so much contemporary discourse has modified centuries of hierarchical, post-Renaissance thought in the humanities. Throughout the academy, "art" no longer has the exclusionary resonance that it once had.

But this is not to say that art has lost its privileged place in our culture. This is why the honorific sense of "art cinema" can be illogical yet retain its distinction in mainstream criticism, at film festivals, and in the art houses that continue to operate. A similar value is also apparent in college courses as well as in the quasi-academic, crossover magazines where film studies has legitimated itself in the eyes of the world by showcasing aesthetically conservative attitudes. Ultimately, we might even speculate that this prestigious idea of art cinema is rooted in evolutionary capacities and preferences, which often favor talent and status regardless of their truth value. But despite all this utility, Tudor seems ready to say *yes*, the term is obsolete. He feels this way, it seems, due to the weight his Bourdieuian analysis places on art houses, an alternative exhibition circuit presumably beyond Hollywood's control that has long been challenged by the forces of consumer fragmentation.[4]

Indeed, according to Tudor, the past several decades have seen the decline of the art-house circuit and the fall of the art-house movie. This explains the elegiac note of his ending, where he interprets the "pluralisation of the field" as identical to the decline of art cinema.[5] But I disagree with Tudor here. A better interpretation is that "pluralisation" is tantamount to an oddly hierarchical democratization that has spread art cinema's aestheticist ideas in many directions at once, expanding its scope even as it has diffused the power of any one type of exhibition. So while art cinema's identification with the art house has weakened, the category is more robust than ever.

After all, as Tudor recognizes, it is not as if the rhetoric of the art house *ever* had logic on its side. Though this rhetoric aided art cinema's initial exhibitors by obscuring the economics of this ostensibly pure-art area, it never entirely obscured what Tudor calls art cinema's "ineradicably commercial character."[6] Indeed, film historians have shown that the art house itself was never a monolithic repository of "art-house taste."[7] It was instead a pluralist bazaar, interchanging sexploitation, horror, and mondo movies with an ad hoc muddle of traditionally highbrow foreign films and avant-garde movies. If the art-cinema impulse could persist even in these transparently commercial circumstances, it is not too hard to accept that it could thrive today, when its consecration is abetted by art-plexes, which often screen indie-style films on digital technology, and by fanzines, blogs, and DVD "extras," which tirelessly anoint auteurs for an age of home consumption.[8] Such conditions may seem profit-oriented by comparison to the circumstances of the art houses in the 1950s and 1960s, but this opinion may owe more to a sanitized memory of the classic cinephile era than it does to a clear and thorough view of today's cultural conditions.

Still, if we can go astray by identifying art cinema with a single site of exhibition, we can also wander off the mark by identifying it with cinematic forms derived from a historically specific set of new waves. Consider David Bordwell's "The Art Cinema as a Mode of Film Practice" (1979), which remains an influential expression of traditional thought in art-cinema scholarship. Here, Bordwell claims that "the art cinema as a distinct mode appears after the Second World War at a time when the dominance of Hollywood cinema was beginning to wane."[9] From there, he focuses on realism, authorship, and ambiguity as manifested in the narrative tactics of postwar European art cinema.[10] Bordwell admits that many scholars deem art cinema a heterogeneous category, but he is still confident that its "narrative and stylistic principles" remain "remarkably constant."[11] Unfortunately, as later scholars like Thanouli have shown, this aspect of his argument was bound to prove unpersuasive, no matter how sophisticated it was, for it has been refuted by the growing diversity of a status-oriented category that producers of every background have found desirable.[12] That is why Galt and Schoonover call art cinema a "mongrel" genre defined by "impurity."[13]

If we can agree that art cinema has historically been a diverse category whose one crucial function has, since the days of the film d'art movement, been to consecrate film, then Bordwell's project, which reinforces an opposition between art cinema and Hollywood, will seem suspect.[14] With few exceptions, scholars are now abandoning such positions, insisting instead on art cinema's basic diversity.[15] There is an awareness that, regarding form, the "art cinema" designation has a "nebulous" reality[16]—with the corollary that the term is "capacious enough and flexible enough" to tolerate different styles and audiences.[17]

But this awareness has also resulted in a new problem: the tendency to assert that a term that is "notoriously difficult to define" has little value.[18] Thus Thanouli argues that when "a category like 'art cinema' becomes so diluted over the years . . . it can contain practically everything, it is inevitably dried of any theoretical edge that it might have possessed in the past."[19] This tendency to give up on the term once its diversity is manifest has been noted by Angela Ndalianis, who writes in *The Cinema Book* that a "clear-cut definition of art cinema has always been elusive, increasingly so in recent years. As the boundaries that separate mainstream and art cinema practices become more porous, the question 'Is there such a thing as art cinema?' comes to the fore."[20]

Though I respect these questions and opinions, in the end they sound like excuses for burying our heads in the sand. Art cinema exists as a real human perception and as a shifting set of events and things unified and impelled by that perception. "Art cinema" in this sense has recently existed on Netflix, in Blockbuster, and at Facets Multimedia. And it has existed at Cannes, Sundance, Toronto, and Pusan. It has also existed in the pages of *Film Comment*, *Cineaste*, *Positif*, and *Cahiers du cinéma*. Art cinema is useful and desirable, tapping into a very human preference for status and hierarchy, so it is widespread, multiform, and ever changing. Why should we, as film scholars, question whether it "really" exists at this point when, if anything, it is more prevalent than ever? My feeling is not that we dislike art cinema's diversity but that we are intimidated by it, for that diversity overwhelms the existing theories. But we can no longer afford to simplify this category's diversity just because that diversity makes a hash of so many old theories. Nor can we afford to acknowledge this diversity while questioning whether the category itself has any value. The *old* concepts might have little or no value—but a new formula that helps us reconceive this sprawling cinematic category by defining its ideas and processes would have great theoretical value, for it would begin to address and explain a complex and increasingly dynamic super-generic phenomenon.

This chapter aims for such a formula. It ultimately defines art cinema as an ongoing set of events impelled by an aspirational idea of cinema. These events have left behind legitimate, quasi-legitimate, and illegitimate movie products that serve high-art functions in many subcultures, forming a diffuse and fluctuating super-genre across human cultures. Today, movies are often deemed "art movies" for one of three reasons. If they are made and distributed in a legitimate sector such as those devoted to traditional art films or avant-garde movies, they are typically designated legitimate art movies regardless of any later acclaim or denigration. By contrast, movies made in less prestigious areas secure a qualified legitimacy as art movies only through secondary recognition by accredited audiences and institutions. And we should not forget that both mainstream movies and cult movies can become art movies through the evaluative contexts of their original areas of circulation, meaning that they can act as high art even if confined to a quasi-legitimate or illegitimate subculture. In a subcultural approach like this one, all three kinds of art movie offer equally real (albeit quite distinct) ways of perceiving art cinema.

Before we can understand all this, we must consider what a super-genre is and how genre terms are used in practice. We must also review what a canon is and how canonization works, for these historical processes occur not just in legitimate areas but in mainstream and cult areas as well. But the first thing we must do is review how philosophers of art struggled during the second half of the twentieth century to arrive at contextual concepts of "art" that were both neutral and appropriately inclusive.

What Film Theory Can Learn from the Philosophy of Art

One model for developing a contextual definition of art cinema that is both neutral and inclusive is available in what may seem an unlikely place: the philosophy of art. The philosophy of art, or aesthetics, is a comparatively conservative field with fairly rigorous methods that prize clarity and logic over post-structural concerns like the position of the subject. However we feel about the politics of this method, though, we can hardly fault its outcomes, which have often been radical. Consider that aesthetics was distancing itself from aestheticist ideas of art at the same time that a wide swath of filmgoers in Europe and the United States were embracing an aestheticist idea of cinema for the first time. Long before *Screen* theory dismantled auteurism, aesthetics had given philosophers the equipment to see through the rhetoric enmeshing ideology-heavy genres. The value-neutral approaches of the philosophy of art allowed aestheticians to create increasingly catholic theories that could accommodate even the most popular forms of art, like porn.

Anglo-American aesthetics has been moving in this direction since at least 1956. That was the year Morris Weitz published "The Role of Theory in Aesthetics," a neo-Wittgensteinian article that contended that the term "art" is too variable to be defined through an evaluative idea of form. "If we actually look and see what it is that we call 'art,'" Weitz insisted, we will "find no common properties—only strands of similarities." Theorists can arbitrarily "close the concept," but this "forecloses the very conditions of creativity in the arts."[21] Weitz's article made him a leader in the field, a mantle that George Dickie tested by questioning the central assumption of his "open concept" approach: that we cannot define art. Dickie's argument was in its own way as simple and as elegant as Weitz's. Though we cannot define art through its textual forms, Dickie said, we *can* define it through its contextual institutions. Though the interventions of Weitz and Dickie gave rise to spirited objections, their detached rigor and their overall insistence on history remain crucial to the field. Today, few aestheticians use "art" as an honorific and fewer still define it formally. As a result, in aesthetics, popular genres like westerns can be enshrined as "art proper." Indeed, Noël Carroll has systematically critiqued ahistorical ideas of art and has identified all low art, including pornographic art, as art proper, while managing to maintain a flexible set of distinctions between high and low forms of art.[22]

But the formalist impulse in the philosophy of art did not go gently. To combat the revolutionary tide of Weitz, Dickie, and those who followed them, Monroe Beardsley in the 1960s and 1970s created an elaborate account of art that defines "'art' in terms of what is taken to be art's essential function or functions."[23] Beardsley thought that the point of art was that it rewards disinterested contemplation, or "the aesthetic attitude," with aesthetic feeling. He defined an artwork "as an intentional arrangement of conditions for affording experiences with marked aesthetic character."[24] A theory such as Beardsley's is classificatory but not neutral. For philosophers like Beardsley, "the act of classification is itself evaluative," for only works that reward the aesthetic attitude will "qualify as art. There is a threshold of merit, where merit is measured in terms of the efficiency of a piece in promoting the point of art, which a work must meet before it qualifies as an artwork."[25] Such a theory discredits works that do not spawn true *aesthesis* and thus delegitimizes entire areas of practice linked to impure, interested forms of experience like sexual arousal. Indeed, pornography has often been excluded from the sphere of art in similar terms.[26] It is no wonder, then, that Dickie also made a name for himself through his sustained critique of Beardsley's neo-Kantian idea of disinterest.[27] By attacking this conservative idea, Dickie took a jackhammer to the foundation of Beardsley's philosophy.[28]

One reason that the old accounts of art were so very seductive, though, is that they gave theorists useful tools for identifying art. Neither Weitz's approach nor Dickie's approach offered similar tools. Later philosophers such as Carroll and Jerrold Levinson, neither of whom wanted to return to the mistakes of formalist thought but who *did* want to find a tool of art identification, sought to correct this deficiency.[29] Like Weitz, Carroll doubted that art operates according to necessary-and-sufficient conditions, so he decided that what was most useful was a method for distinguishing art from non-art. But unlike Weitz, he was dubious of open-concept methods, which seemed to reduce everything to art. Instead, Carroll offered a historical approach, or "narrativism," which counted any work as art so long as a true account of its descent from more established works of art could be arrived at. Though not as open as Dickie's, Carroll's approach was still neutral and inclusive enough that it accommodated some of the most illegitimate forms.[30]

Whether Carroll's account is compatible with Dickie's institutional theory is a matter of some debate.[31] But such debate is irrelevant here. What matters to us is that Weitz highlighted the impossibility of defining art through its forms; that Dickie noted the possibility of defining art in an inclusive way through its institutional contexts; and that Carroll invented a neutral, historical tool for identifying certain forms as artworks. Along the way, one of the last great evaluative theories of art was demolished and dismissed, along with the "aesthetic attitude" on which it hinged so precariously. All four ideas— and especially Carroll's method of identification—will be useful to us as we move forward.

Genre, Super-Genre, Anti-Genre

Clearly, the development of a contextual definition of "art" in the philosophy of art is pertinent here. Without the new sense of inclusiveness yielded by these theoretical contributions, we might worry that mainstream movies and cult movies are simply not art and thus lack one of the main requisites for a high-art category like art cinema. But there is no convincing way of excluding mainstream movies and cult movies en masse from the art designation. A harder question is whether such movies can be said to have earned, or qualified for, the high-art status implicit to "art cinema." The answer is that they have long done so through a flexible mix of traditional and untraditional indices. As a result, the best way of defining "art cinema" is as an unfolding, high-art event that has for more than a century reverberated through the cinema, leaving many sorts of aspirational movies in its wake. The movies themselves may be categorized as forming a diffuse, value-added super-genre comprising (all) traditional art films and (all) avant-garde movies *plus* (all) the movies that have gained a more qualified and fragile high-art status by untraditional means either at the cultural level or, more usually, at the subcultural level.

These statements open a number of questions, all of which I hope to answer over the course of this book. But at this point I should focus on one pressing issue: the nature of genre. What is a genre? When we use the term "genre," we are traditionally referring to a group of formally similar movies that may be recognized by the presence of certain conventions that lead audience expectations in a given direction. Hence, a western has its frontier backdrop, a musical has its song-and-dance numbers, and so on. But as scholars like Steve Neale, Rick Altman, and Mark Jancovich have shown over the past decades, this traditional sense of genre is untrue to the internal formal complexity of even the most commercialized movies. What is more, it is difficult to reconcile this traditional idea of genre with the harum-scarum realities of genre usage. For example, Jane Campion's *In the Cut* (2003), which was no one's idea of a straightforward genre vehicle, shows that a genre-branded art movie can combine elements from many genres. These combinations can broaden an art movie's appeal—and it can activate the kind of slippages in genre usage that are anything but unitary even as they remain valid and logical. To wit: whereas one film reviewer might want to call Campion's movie an erotic thriller and apply that term reasonably, another reviewer might prefer to see it as a woman's film or a feminist film—or a work of neo-noir or soft-core or "art horror"—and apply any of those labels with equal good reason.[32] It all depends.

Traditional genres are, as Andrew Tudor argues, "what we collectively believe [them] to be."[33] They offer what Stephen Owen calls a "discourse of total order," which simplifies textual complexity and allows people to make sense of the cinematic realities in front of them.[34] It is unsurprising, then, that individual movies shift in their "objective" designations all the time, as we understand movies in new ways and struggle to express new ideas through them. But something subtly different happens, I believe, when we call a movie an "art movie," a "mainstream movie," or a "cult movie." These value-oriented classifiers have formal correlatives only in particular subcultures where these terms carry context-specific expectations in tow. Whereas the term "western" suggests the frontier backdrop in almost every example of this genre in almost every context, the same cannot be said of any motif in any art movie, mainstream movie, or cult movie.[35] Further, while it is often clear what a comic technique or a melodramatic narrative is supposed to do to the viewer in terms of affect, it is not always clear what an "art" technique *is*, much less what such a technique is supposed to do to an audience.[36] Making matters more complex is the fact that this juxtaposition of terms suggests another oddity of art cinema's relationship to genre. Though cinephiles speak of art cinema as if this category could be recognized by its forms, thus suggesting that it *is* a traditional genre, they seem reluctant to call it that, for in cinephile discourse the term "genre" smacks of commercialism and hence seems more appropriate to other categories, like mainstream cinema or cult cinema.

Theorists can solve these problems by switching from form- or text-based ideas of art cinema to context-based ideas. If we define art cinema as a sprawling super-genre such as mainstream cinema or cult cinema, we can retain all the elasticity apparent in the historical usage of "art movie" while admitting that such movies are defined as such not by their form or intrinsic value but by value-oriented traditions that have individual and collective functions. Indeed, a context-based definition of art cinema allows us to see that the concept of art cinema as an "anti-genre" distanced from genre movies is a value-generating illusion traditional in art-cinema contexts. Because this illusion is apparent even in art cinema's quasi-legitimate and illegitimate areas, we may assume that it is more universal to the category than any style or motif.

Within this illusion, the auteur vehicle represents the idiosyncratic opposite of the more standardized genre vehicle. This viewpoint was molded in part by the efforts of early auteur critics to distinguish art cinema from genre cinema,[37] and it has remained an article of faith among cinephiles ever since. Consequently, Lars von Trier and Thomas Vinterberg integrated this belief into their 1995 Dogme manifesto through their eighth "vow of chastity" ("Genre movies are not acceptable").[38] This kind of cinephile discourse reinforces auteur prestige, for it presents the auteur as a kind of priest, transubstantiating the dross of commerce into high art. As Linda Ruth Williams demonstrates in *The Erotic Thriller in Contemporary Cinema* (2005), promoters of genre-branded art movies (e.g., *In the Cut*) often stress the art-cinema affiliations of their movies when speaking within art-cinema contexts, as if art cinema were a place of refuge from genre affiliations and their low status — even if those low affiliations can, in other more commercial contexts, help their films circulate. Williams is right, then, to overrule this rhetoric, as she does when she notes that in this semi-mystical exchange an art movie doesn't become "*only* an auteur work"; clearly, it may still function as "a genre work."[39]

The contempt for genre visible in this anti-genre attitude has ample precedent in other arts. As Altman has noted, the nineteenth-century romantics were anti-genre, for "romantic inspiration was based on the breaking down of all generic differences."[40] The romantics tied their argument to debates surrounding the canon, so it is no wonder that the nineteenth-century artists who most wanted in on those debates — novelists — deflected their cultural abjection onto "genre fictions." This process continued into the twentieth century, when novelists like Vladimir Nabokov and Gilbert Sorrentino described their art as an ethereal magic, a "negative discourse," rather than a hands-on narrative craft that they had mastered over decades.[41] As aesthetes, they found it natural to deny that they were working in a commercial genre or in any genre at all.

Nevertheless, the idea that art cinema is *truly* an anti-genre beyond all genre usage is impractical. Genre usage, like all categorization, is supple, plastic, inescapable. Even if we were to differentiate auteur cinemas from "genre cinemas" along high-art lines, we would arguably be left with a high-art genre (albeit a very untraditional one). Moreover, auteur critics have not been that deeply invested in escaping genre. For example, in their critical capacities, Jacques Rivette, Jean-Luc Godard, and Claude Chabrol may have spoken ill of genre, but they spoke well of it at many other times and were influential in their elevation of popular Hollywood genres. (And here I am overlooking the fact that in their directorial capacities auteurs like Chabrol in particular made movies that were clearly both auteur vehicles *and* genre vehicles.) And, again, another problem is the fact that the anti-genre concept has not been limited to insiders in legitimate art-cinema formats like the art film or the avant-garde movie. Indeed, this idea has also been pushed forward by some of the most debased exploitation genres and subgenres, like horror, action, porn, and rape–revenge.[42]

This antipathy for genre is a conventional way that high-art status has been propagated across art cinema's subcultures, in a sense binding legitimate art cinemas to illegitimate and quasi-legitimate ones. Indeed, one irony of thinking of art cinema as an "anti-genre" is that this idea is a source of contextual unity across art cinema—meaning it helps us discern a high-status *super-genre* in a dazzling array of forms, some of which are quite commercial. If we accent issues of status by looking at the canon from theoretical angles, we can form a concept of art cinema that remains inclusive and neutral even as it covers all of this category's many hierarchies.

Canon, High Art, and Cult Cinema

Is it any more outrageous in the early twenty-first century to throw the names of the Mitchell Brothers and Radley Metzger/Henry Paris around in the company of Federico Fellini and Ingmar Bergman than it was in the 1970s to throw the names of John Ford and Howard Hawks around in the company of Herman Melville and Nathaniel Hawthorne?

—PETER LEHMAN, *PORNOGRAPHY: FILM AND CULTURE* (2006)

In the arts, a canon is often defined as a group of distinguished artists or a group of masterpieces in a genre or medium.[43] In common usage, this canon is thought to be fixed in time as a list of great artists or works that the culture has in a sense collectively agreed on through its mediating institutions. But in practice such a canon reflects thinking that has taken place throughout a culture. It changes over time and is never identical from one person to the next. In a sense, the concept of high art functions as a canonical super-genre of the arts. In this canon, we place super-privileged formats like classical music, ballet, modernist poetry, and abstract painting. Though this type of canon also has an illusion of permanence, it changes over time—and I doubt many people, experts included, would agree on its exact constitution. For example, the fact that jazz is a form whose populist roots are recent and obvious argues against its inclusion in high art. Still, the art jazz of virtuosos like Ornette Coleman has much in common with modernist painting and poetry. Arguments have been made, then, for including jazz in the pantheon of high art. Though such arguments rarely catch on quickly, they become entrenched over time as long as the candidate form remains a living one.

My theory of art cinema borrows from all these notions of canon. Art cinema comprises certain institutional formats that have been so successful over time that they now bestow a certain status on their members, regardless of individual achievements. The traditional art film is this sort of legitimate format.[44] So is the avant-garde movie and, in a sense that falls outside this book, video art.[45] Beyond these legitimate areas are others that have never succeeded in legitimating themselves at the cultural level but that contain a shifting canon of masterworks loosely agreed on by their institutions and participants. These works, whether they represent "art porn" or "art horror," exemplify local ideas of high art as put forth by each cult subculture. Some of these subcultural exemplars later secure individual acceptance in legitimate spheres, but most never do; and in any case, their status remains qualified pending the acceptance of their original areas as legitimate by the wider culture. Speaking of the movies themselves, then, "art cinema" refers to a dynamic, high-art super-genre comprising all legitimate art movies as supplemented by the qualified high-art canons of quasi-legitimate and illegitimate cinemas.[46]

To my knowledge, no one has articulated this exact understanding of art cinema before. It is in accord with neither an honorific idea of art based on modernist norms nor a more populist insistence on canonical fixity—nor is it in keeping with those who would ignore sociological function in calling only the most historically influential art cinemas "art cinema." But I bet that the assumptions of this understanding are reflected to some degree in all our tastes in art cinema, given that a personal canon gathers movies from illegitimate and quasi-legitimate sources as it grows in depth or breadth. It stands to reason that neutral theorists uninterested in defining art cinema in ways that validate their own tastes would include in "art cinema" art movies acclaimed as such in both illegitimate and quasi-legitimate subcultures, regardless of how they felt about those movies, just as they would include every case of a new wave like Italian neorealism regardless of whether they personally enjoyed those particular movies.

Given that this approach potentially locates art cinema in every movie hierarchy, from Italy, Germany, and France to Hollywood, Bollywood, and Nollywood, it may seem upsetting. But before dismissing this approach, consider these points: the hierarchies that American cinephiles made of the films of Roberto Rossellini, Ingmar Bergman, François Truffaut, and Federico Fellini are not essentially different from those that the French critics, including Truffaut, once made of the films of Howard Hawks, John Ford, Nicholas Ray, and Alfred Hitchcock. The French popularized a craze for making lists of favorite movies without placing much emphasis on high–low distinctions.

This habit of making personal canons was imported to the United States through prestigious critics like Sarris, and it is now widespread in our culture. Two egalitarian assumptions were built into this practice: first, that everyone is a potential cinephile, meaning that we all have the right to make a list, or canon, of our favorite films; and second, that the films on these lists may be gathered from almost anywhere, including Hollywood. (Hence the mid-century scandal at the prospect of building a "cult" mystique around the films of a Hawks or a Ford.) This hierarchical list-making, the bedrock of canonization, was built into the practices of influential cultural institutions like the Anthology Film Archives and those of influential critics like Sarris, Jonathan Rosenbaum, and Fred Camper; but it was also mimicked at the grassroots level by lay audiences who, more or less, shared their tastes in auteurs and in auteur works. But as the decades passed, these practices were also mimicked by cult institutions, cult critics, and cult audiences, whose reverse elitism was embodied through low tastes that fetishized downscale exploitation movies.[47]

The term "reverse elitism" comes from Sconce's *Screen* article "'Trashing' the Academy" (1995), which showed that cult cinema is regulated by hierarchical practices that in a sense mimic those of high culture. Cult cinephiles form distinctive groups, gathering subcultural capital through their knowledge of particular kinds of cult cinema, with the subcultures devoted to those cinemas in turn arranged in hierarchies that bottom out in the world of adult film. If there is a canon of high art, then, there is also a canon of low art. Inside these subcultures, specialized promoters, critics, institutions, and audiences make lists of their favorite movies and directors, regardless of their negligible cultural status. Thus we find many of the same canonical assumptions at b-independent.com and at *Bloody Disgusting* that we may find at the Anthology Film Archives and the Criterion Collection. Some of the canons that form through these subcultural processes accent the high-art potential of each subculture, working to differentiate the distinctive "auteur works" in these subcultures from the mere "genre vehicles" that dominate them.

Clearly, these processes don't happen only in the United States. But they only happen in this byzantine fashion in highly developed countries such as the United States, which has long had a sophisticated system of movie distribution. Distribution is important because it is one of the central ways that movies, genres, and auteurs are legitimated and canonized. The main legitimate channels in art cinema are those that lead through culturally sanctioned institutions, including the global film-festival circuit as well as the system of art houses, university theaters, repertory theaters, and museums that often exhibit art movies.[48] New cult-art cinemas, by contrast, emerge through cult

festivals and cult conventions, midnight-movie exhibitions, repertory theaters, and the many non-theatrical distributions that offer low-prestige outlets for exploitation films. The generic specialties of a film's production and
distribution labels are also important here, as are the forms and the styles on
display within individual films. In general, if a world cinema film like that of
Mikio Naruse comes to the United States after having been exhibited on the
legitimate festival circuit, it will be considered art cinema, whereas if a world
cinema film like that of Jess Franco is circulated in the United States through
a cult distribution label or after having been reviewed in cult forums, it will
be considered foreign exploitation schlock and treated accordingly.

Strategic and nonstrategic mixing can occur in this scenario, of course,
leading to changes in tastes and in canons over time. Cult-art movies and
entire cult genres can gain status through the attention of elite critics and elite
institutions. An example of this may be found in the recent issue of *Sight &
Sound* whose blurb for the cover story, "The Mad, the Bad, and the Dangerous: 50 Visionary Film-Makers," cites two cult filmmakers (Dario Argento
and Alejandro Jodorowsky) and three establishment auteurs (Catherine
Breillat, Werner Herzog, and David Lynch).[49] *Sight & Sound* is a major art-
cinema forum with a decidedly genteel interest in transgression, so the fact
that Argento and Jodorowsky are on the cover beside three recognized auteurs
indicates that by 2009 their reputations had been nearly legitimated. But not
completely. For example, Argento's reputation will, I expect, remain qualified
by his background in the *giallo* and in horror until those genres come to be
seen as fully legitimate sites for auteur work. This legitimation is currently in
process through the success that horror movies like the Bergmanesque vampire film *Let the Right One In* (2008) have achieved with legitimate critics such
as *Sight & Sound*'s Mark Kermode.[50] Even more crucial is the success of the
films of South Korean director Park Chan-wook, a virtuoso of horror, gore,
and other genre effects, at festivals like Cannes. But some crucial obstacles remain in place. As Joan Hawkins has noted in a recent *Jump Cut* article, Park's
movies have been popular with audiences and critics in the United States,
but they have encountered significant blowback from influential mainstream
critics like Manohla Dargis of the *New York Times*, who regretted Cannes's
elevation of "an *arty* exploitation flick" like *Oldboy* (2003).[51] What Dargis's
comment suggests is that the anti-horror bias traditional to "art-house taste"
is still somewhat intact; legitimate art cinema is not yet as open to distinguished horror films as it is to distinguished dramas and romances and even
thrillers. But it almost is. The fact that many "auteur horror" films are now
distributed as art cinema in American theaters after having been feted by

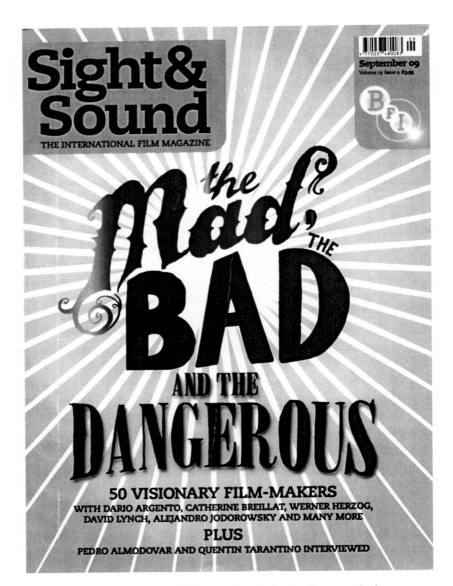

Sight & Sound's September 2009 cover story indicates the magazine's integration of cult auteurs and traditional auteurs. Used by permission of *Sight & Sound*, published by the British Film Institute.

prestigious European festivals indicates that our received ideas of legitimacy are continually being updated, just as they were after the arrival of Truffaut, Chabrol, and Godard.

I suppose that the main argument against the approach mapped out in this chapter is that it is a destabilizing, leveling value. After all, this sort of charge has long been brought against the postmodern theories that took root in film studies after auteurism experienced its temporary fall from grace. Hence, Geoffrey Nowell-Smith argues that the anti-elitist thrust of contemporary theory has raised impediments to

> a proper understanding of cinema. First, a canon continues to exist—but by default and determined more by the vagaries of fashion and the acci-dents of availability than by any form of reasoned argument. Secondly, in default of such argument the idea of the importance of cinema itself is undermined. If any film can be as important as any other, and if quasi-historical or idiosyncratically personal judgements take the place of aes-thetic reasoning, it is open to anyone to challenge the purpose of taking films seriously in the first place.[52]

But it is imprecise, I think, to say that *a* canon exists. Canon*s* exist—for dif-ferent ideas of the canon coexist and compete—and have always done so in accord with fashion and accident and never simply in accord with "reasoned argument." It is also not quite right to think that cinema has some ahistorical importance that obliges us to treat it "seriously." That seriousness is ascribed to cinema; it is not intrinsic. But it is not likely that cult fans with their own idea of the canon will pursue that postmodern truth, for they are cinephiles who love the cinema, too. They just love different movies.

Personal taste isn't the province of the film scholar. It is the province of the mainstream film critic. I prefer Naruse's melodrama *Yearning* (1964) to his more celebrated ensemble piece *When a Woman Ascends the Stairs* (1960), but it isn't my scholarly task to articulate or defend that very personal form of connoisseurship. Scholars are at their best when they are more detached, telling us what is going on and how that relates to what has gone on in the past—when they tell us what a canon has been *thought to be* by actual groups and institutions rather than when they tell us what it *ought* to be. When they get more personal, these commentators promote their own agendas, in effect playing a game they should be explaining.

My point in formulating a new definition of art cinema is to explain the game. To see art cinema clearly, I have neither embraced nor denounced any form, cinephilia, or site of exhibition. *But I do not want to level values*; rather, I want to observe the interplay of as many values as possible. I want to explain how all these values relate to one another and how the contexts that shaped them have developed over time. Theorists have often relied on formalist definitions of art cinema that focus on specific styles, motifs, and politics. And they have at times relied on contextual definitions that have focused on exhibition sites, new waves, or audience effects. But what has unified all these definitions is their effort to define art cinema in a way that credits its high-art potential. My definition prioritizes this shared purpose, making it the central part of the concept as a whole.

On the other hand, to settle on an extended definition of art cinema is not to endorse the evaluative, exclusivist meaning at the heart of "art cinema." It is instead to improve on the philosopher Ted Cohen by noting that in the arts the high–low distinction is not only indefensible *and* indispensable but *also* inescapable,[53] because this distinction is found in some form across the many subcultures devoted to art and art-making. If I were a betting man, I would speculate that this high–low distinction is a product of value-making habits that emerge in the growth of normal human behavior and is not something that we should attribute to specific cultural traditions. Rather, high art just *happens*—and it seems time to incorporate this idea of human nature into our art-cinema concepts. In any event, I can safely say that it makes no sense to endorse certain forms, outlets, or canons to sustain the seriousness of film, for this kind of activity only transforms film scholars from analysts of film culture into critics and evaluators, into makers of film culture. And that is to step away from any scholarly approach that is defensibly "serious."

CHAPTER 2

No Start, No End
Auteurism and the Auteur Theory

The attempt to move beyond auteurism *has to recognize the place which* auteurism *occupies, and the influence which it brings to bear.*
—JOHN CAUGHIE, *THEORIES OF AUTHORSHIP* (1981)

In a June 2009 letter to the editor, Michel Ciment argued that *Sight & Sound*'s celebration of the French New Wave in its May 2009 issue was deceptive, for it implied that the movement was "the origin of everything" and had even "established the auteur as the supreme creative force." To be clear, as the editor of *Positif*, Ciment did not have a problem with this idea of authorship. But he did have an issue with the idea that the New Wave inaugurated it. In his eyes, Ingmar Bergman, Luchino Visconti, Robert Bresson, Jacques Tati, and Andrzej Wajda had all become "cultural heroes" years before Jean-Luc Godard, Claude Chabrol, Éric Rohmer, François Truffaut, Jacques Rivette, and Agnès Varda had achieved a similar status. Indeed, as "early as the 1920s," Ciment wrote, the director stood out as the "auteur and the central creative role" across cinema. "Murnau, Lang, Sjöström, Lubitsch, Chaplin, Stroheim, Sternberg, Eisenstein, DeMille, Vidor, Gance et al were lauded and commented upon lengthily."[1]

Film scholars have made the same point many times. Thomas Schatz, writing in 1981, argued that anyone "who discussed 'the Lubitsch touch' in the '30s or anticipated the next 'Hitchcock thriller' in the '40s was, in fact, practicing this critical approach."[2] There is, then, a distinction to be made between auteurism, which is an attitude toward film authorship that has been with us since the silent period, and the auteur theory. The auteur theory was a specific articulation of the auteur idea that was first put forth by Alexandre Astruc in 1948 and over the following decade was refined as la politique des auteurs by the auteur critics of *Cahiers du cinéma*.[3] Then, during the 1960s,

Sight&
Sound

THE INTERNATIONAL FILM MAGAZINE

May 09
Volume 19 Issue 5 £3.95

BFI

THE
NEW WAVE
AT 50

DAVID THOMSON ON GODARD
MARK KERMODE ON 'LET THE RIGHT ONE IN'
KIM NEWMAN ON THE NEW HORROR
ARMANDO IANNUCCI ON SATIRE

EVERY NEW
FILM
REVIEWED

Does the May 2009 cover story of *Sight & Sound* establish the French New Wave as "the origin of everything"? Used by permission of *Sight & Sound*, published by the British Film Institute.

Andrew Sarris translated this auteur *policy* into the auteur *theory* as it is known to English-speaking audiences today.[4] As scholars like John Caughie, Edward Buscombe, David Gerstner, Janet Staiger, James Naremore, Pam Cook, and Barry Keith Grant (among others) have documented, this brand of auteurism was over the coming decades subjected to relentless attacks by critics, aestheticians, feminists, multiculturalists, historians, sociologists, structuralists, and post-structuralists.[5] Indeed, entire anthologies have been put together with the understanding that auteurism and its theory are deficient (e.g., Caughie's 1981 *Theories of Authorship*). But if, under the guise of its theory, auteurism was brutalized and left for dead, academically speaking, auteurism as a practical phenomenon never really left the scene. Instead, theorists have always "revised and revived" it, tailoring it to new circumstances.[6] And insofar as they did not exactly invent auteurism, the auteur critics followed a similar path: they retrofitted an existing auteurist attitude, one that was far too useful and far too *human* to ever be eliminated by rational argument.

In this chapter, I revisit auteurism, thinking about its influence, its shortcomings, and its persistence. In tandem with its signature theory, auteurism has made many things "go," but this functionality has come at a cost. Auteurism has turned attention away from the political, economic, collaborative, and biocultural contexts of the film industry, its romantic stress on the individual working to obscure many realities. Still, academics should not kid themselves into thinking this meme may be gotten rid of simply by highlighting its epistemological defects. Auteurism accesses something too basic in human nature for this to be possible. It simplifies in a way that is too convenient, too malleable. And it is now the foundation of too many institutions and investments. As scholars, we should face these facts head-on. We should be aware of auteurism's shortcomings as well as its utter stability. This dual awareness will help us recognize auteurism's best academic uses, which are in my view rarely evaluative and never celebratory. Hence, in my finale, I defend one modest use of auteurism that is modeled on the auteur critics' original application of the auteur theory to Hollywood directors of genre films. Because auteurism is one of art cinema's most basic building blocks, scholars may use its distinctive rhetorics as tools with which to identify art-cinema vehicles in cult areas, where auteurs are just as plentiful as they are in more traditional contexts. In other words, by refreshing our ideas of auteurism, we can refresh our ideas of art cinema, too.

Cultural Impact of the Auteur Theory

"I'm French. We respect directors in our country."

— *INGLOURIOUS BASTERDS* (DIR. QUENTIN TARANTINO, 2009)

According to Schatz, auteurism "would not be worth bothering with if it hadn't been so influential, effectively stalling film history and criticism in a prolonged stage of adolescent romanticism."[7] If anything, Schatz underestimates auteurism's mid-twentieth-century impact here. After all, auteurism didn't simply *stall* film history and film criticism; it remade those fields as well. What is more, the formalist tendencies linked to the auteur theory lent film studies some of its most productive methods. Thus Caughie has argued that the auteur theory encouraged scholars to attend to mise-en-scène with newfound rigor.[8] But auteurism has also had broader cultural effects. I agree with Caughie that scholars must come to terms with these effects, including auterism's most significant cultural, institutional, and even biocultural roles, if we hope to transcend its many defects.

Auteurism's effects have, it seems, been legion. For example, during the postwar period, auteurism helped push the sexual revolution forward through its auteur-inspired assaults on censorship. Its theory has also been given credit for helping to consecrate film as one "of the sanctified Arts,"[9] thus spreading cinephilia through cultures and initiating new-wave movements in a host of national cinemas across several continents. And auteurism temporarily settled a debate over film authorship. Thus, after 1970, even if a director's production role was qualified by collaboration, he or she was often credited as the film's "prime mover," the figure most responsible for the work's overall effect.[10] Adherents of the auteur theory believed with Sarris that a personal vision could be traced across the curve of an auteur's oeuvre; they also believed that the "best directors generally make the best films."[11] These ideas reinvigorated film studies, and they helped reorganize movie production—for even in Hollywood, they provided a rationale for subordinating all those involved in the production of a film, from the above-the-line talent to the studio head to the star auteur.

What occasioned these changes? If we examine the manifestos and interviews associated with the early auteur critics and their policies, we will begin, but *only* begin, to understand what it was about the auteur critics and their ideas that made them so influential. These documents include "A Certain Tendency of the French Cinema" (1954) by Truffaut; "Six Characters in Search of Auteurs: A Discussion About the French Cinema" (1957) by Rivette, Rohmer, André Bazin, Jacques Doniol-Valcroze, Pierre Kast, and Roger Leenhardt;

"The Face of the French Cinema Has Changed" (1959) by Godard; and "The Oberhausen Manifesto" (1962) by twenty-six German signers. To this list of documents we might add others, including "The First Statement of the New American Cinema Group" (1962) by Jonas Mekas and the New York Film-Makers' Cooperative, and various writings by Sarris, including "Notes on the Auteur Theory" (1962). These documents demonstrate the frustration of directors and critics irritated by literary traditions, economic constraints, and industrial hierarchies. Clearly, these burdens were felt more deeply as the success of the French New Wave became clearer. Thus Godard's insouciance in claiming that "film auteurs" have "thanks to us . . . entered the history of art" grows into the intemperance and outright sense of entitlement later expressed by the German and American directors. Their manifestoes demanded greater and greater freedom and ended up calling for open, artist-based experimentation, whereas the Godard of 1959 focused on *realistic* experimentation in the context of the film market with its commercial expectations.[12]

It should come as no surprise, then, that the early auteurs and auteur critics were responding in the main to their local conditions. The *Cahiers* critics in particular used their auteur policy to promote their favorite directors in a way that served their personal and professional necessities. For example, in "A Certain Tendency," Truffaut deploys his conservative brand of auteurism to praise certain French directors against the establishment directors associated with French cinema's "tradition of quality";[13] by contrast, in "Six Characters," Rivette uses la politique des auteurs in a similar way to promote certain Hollywood directors against the same French tradition.

These quintessentially French skirmishes had an impact on the studio organization of many different film industries all over the world as a result of the publicity machine that heralded the French New Wave, which was so tightly linked with la politique des auteurs. In other words, it is possible to see people like Rivette, who were shaped by local French conditions, as having an outsize impact on the local conditions of *many* different milieus through the intercession and amplification of crucial translators like Sarris. One reason this occurred was that film directors were in conflict with writers and executive producers all over the world, including Hollywood. This industrial correspondence gave la politique des auteurs resonance in many different labor contexts.

In the studio organization of classical Hollywood and the classical French cinema, the director was typically a supervisor, not a visionary, while the writer could have control over what a film said and even some control over its mise-en-scène. But the idea of authorship that impelled auteurism was a literary analogy that handed the director control over the dialogue, message, and style. Auteurists often thought it crucial that directors work with writers, since the latter could seldom be supplanted altogether for practical reasons. Thus Rivette makes it explicit that "the great American directors" are artists—not, as Bazin once put it, because of "the genius of the system," but because they "work on the scenario . . . from the beginning, in collaboration with a scriptwriter," while treating the writer as a technician akin to a gaffer.[14] On this basis, the *Cahiers* critics defended, as Rivette indicates with specificity, "Hitchcock rather than Wyler, and Mann rather than Zinnemann, because they are directors who actually work on their scenarios."[15]

Many wrinkles were added to this set of prescriptions. Some auteur critics, including Sarris, worked out intricate systems, frequently making the question of which Hollywood directors qualified as "true" auteurs a matter of complex and subjective formal criteria.[16] But the basic fact many Americans took from this new taste warfare was that the French had accepted Hollywood directors of genre vehicles—including westerns, comedies, and musicals—as serious artists. This was a staggering development, for Americans had not been trained to take their own cinemas seriously but *had* been trained to take the aesthetic declarations of the French seriously. Of course, the French context, bound as it was to specific conditions of labor, was lost in translation. And what has never been adequately considered is that it was the *job* of mainstream movie critics such as Truffaut and Sarris to evaluate movies, lauding some while denigrating others—which is one practical description of what the auteurists were up to, despite the breath and ferment. What enabled them to do all this so effectively was the accessibility of la politique des auteurs, which was adaptable to so many situations that it could be exported to markets where it could thrive not just on its own intellectual merits but also on the cultural credentials it gained in passage.

Problems with the Auteur Theory

Part of what made this new supercharged brand of auteurism effective was its generality, which made it uniquely portable. But this effectiveness—and this portability—also made it uniquely divisive.[17] Today, after five decades of industrial and academic debate, it is possible to differentiate narrowly epistemological critiques of auteurism (and its signature theory) from political critiques of the same. Epistemological critiques of auteurism condemn it for the false picture it gives of cinematic activity, which it simplifies at best and badly distorts at worst. By contrast, broadly political critiques condemn auteurism and its theory for the inequities that they have fostered in the cinema. These hierarchical divisions have distributed credit, control, and money unfairly among many different labor factions; have worsened the plight of women and minorities in the film industry; and have promoted the pursuit of the individual good at the expense of the collective good. Such critiques may be reduced to issues of honesty and accuracy on one hand and issues of social justice on the other. In practice, these issues overlap and provide the basic ingredients for the academic "complaints" about auteurism that have accumulated over the history of film studies. Such complaints may be divided into six very rough categories: the industrial complaint, the New Critical complaint, the structuralist or post-structuralist complaint, the feminist or multiculturalist complaint, the sociological complaint, and, lastly, the biocultural complaint.

The industrial complaint, as articulated in studies like John Caldwell's *Production Culture* (2008), considers auteurism and its theory untrue to the industrial practices of the cinema.[18] Thus one of auteurism's first critics, Pauline Kael, devoted *The "Citizen Kane" Book* (1971) to "the refutation of [Sarris's] theory that the director alone was the author of the film."[19] This falsehood was most apparent in commercial spheres, where the cinema's collaborative nature should have been obvious but was often overshadowed by the auteur aura that enshrouded the most prominent art-house directors. (Consider that directors like Alain Resnais, Luis Buñuel, and Peter Greenaway drew on Sacha Vierney's masterful camerawork in becoming auteurs, while Vierney himself remained a "mere" director of photography. Indeed, we might ask whether cinematographers like Greg Tolland, Sven Nykvist, and William Lubtchansky or editors like Dede Allen and Walter Murch have played similar roles in the construction of auteur celebrity.) In general, the industrial complaint considers the auteur's star status tantamount to a production credit that is negotiated, contracted, and constructed, and that is as much a result of movie promotion as it is of the director's role as "prime mover." Critics who take the theory too seriously, then, come off as naïve in this reading of the auteur tradition.

Then again, depending on one's scholarly perspective, anti-auteur scholars can be guilty of something equally problematic if they further the anti-collaborative thrust of auteur criticism by arguing for the ascendancy of different figures (or roles) within the industry, like the performer, the cinematographer, the writer, the editor, the producer, or the studio as a whole.[20] Through such arguments, scholars end up taking part in the industry's wranglings over credit rather than stepping back to theorize the collective processes that have shaped those conflicts.[21] On the other hand, this oddly auteurist brand of anti-auteurism can also have its benefits in that it can lead back to more modest claims of multiple authorship (as among the most crucial indus-

Hacks and Authors
Ben Hecht, the *politique des auteurs* and scriptwriting in classical Hollywood

Lunch discussion with
Giaime Alonge

Introduction by **Professor Rebecca West**,
Departments of Romance Languages and Literatures and Cinema and Media Studies

The *politique des auteurs*, in its worshipping of the director as a solitary genius, was intrinsically anti-screenwriter. So, it is no accident that when some film critics and scholars (Pauline Kael, *Raising Kane*, 1971; Richard Corliss, *Talking Pictures*, 1974), in the early 1970s, started to focus on the role of the screenwriter, they took a strong anti-auteurist stance. The paradox is that in many books and essays about screenwriters and screenwriting, the "myth of the author" comes back in a new form, that of the writer as the "real" author (or, at least, as the main co-author) of the film. To which extent can we consider the

screenwriter as an author, especially in a highly industrialized context such as that of classical Hollywood? Using Ben Hecht's career as a case study, Professor Alonge will lead a discussion on this question.

Giaime Alonge teaches Film History at the University of Turin (Italy) and at the Animation Department of the Scuola Nazionale di Cinema. His research areas are American cinema, film and history, and animation. In addition to his work on Ben Hecht, Alonge is also a screenwriter and novelist.

Co-sponsored by the Department of Romance Languages and Literatures

Tuesday, March 16, 12:30pm
Lunch provided for participants

5811 S. Ellis, Cobb 310
773.702.8596
filmstudiescenter.uchicago.edu
All events are free and open to the public

FILM STUDIES CENTER

This talk, led by Giaime Alonge, discussed the wranglings over credit that have shaped the "myth of the author" in both the film industry and film studies. Used by permission of the Film Studies Center at the University of Chicago.

trial figures, like directors *and* writers), or, similarly, of corporate authorship (as credited to a studio or a collective).[22] Such trends in the scholarship have seemed most reasonable when they have culminated—as they do in Bruce Kawin's essay "Authorship, Design, and Execution"—in the belief that the "shared vision" of the entire collaborative system is the ultimate author of a movie, and ought to be acknowledged.[23]

By contrast, the New Critical complaint contends that unitary film authors *do* exist, much as literary authors exist; however, these authors do not secure the value of the aesthetic object, as the auteur critics often suggest, but are instead irrelevant to that kind of value, which exists apart from extrinsic factors such as authorial and industrial activity.[24] The pioneering film scholars of the 1970s, like V. F. Perkins, had a great deal of disdain for the use of antiquated literary methods in film studies, and so they worked to differentiate their own auteur methods accordingly. They would, then, have been more than a little galled by the New Critical complaint, for it tends to lump auteurism with literary biography and other musty forms of evaluation.

But in the end, the New Critical complaint was less dismissive of auteurism than were the structuralist and post-structuralist complaints. These critiques are far too diverse to submit to efficient paraphrase. What we can say, however, is that many film theorists, especially those aligned with the post-1968 editions of *Cahiers* and the 1970s editions of *Screen*, were discomfited by the conservative drift of auteur theory.[25] To counter this trend, they drew on continental theorists like Jacques Lacan, Michel Foucault, and Christian Metz and the reigning contempt for authority in order to treat the auteur as "a kind of epiphenomenon," which was an ideological product of our shared history, our shared language, and the filmmaking apparatus.[26] Peter Wollen made compromises with this new way of theorizing cinema by inventing in *Signs and Meaning in the Cinema* (1969) the field of "auteur structuralism," which submitted films to semiotic critiques, and which treated the auteur as an "unconscious catalyst" for forces and meanings that the auteur neither fully created nor controlled.[27] If auteur structuralists continued to talk of auteurs, and often of the *same* auteurs, they no longer addressed those auteurs in the glorifying terms favored by earlier critics. Indeed, their demystifying approaches to the auteur drew on the death-of-the-author ideas popularized in this period by postmodern theorists like Foucault and Roland Barthes.[28]

The feminist and multiculturalist critiques about auteurism resembled the post-structuralist complaint in their attention to history, ideology, and the filmmaking "apparatus." This tendency is typified by Laura Mulvey's famous *Screen* essay "Visual Pleasure and Narrative Cinema" (1975).[29] Here, the visual pleasure normalized by the cinema, especially by Hollywood cinema and the commercial art cinema, was assumed to be informed by an array of prejudices that seemed to encourage mass audiences to overlook their own filmmaking traditions, including their own auteurs, in identifying with more hegemonic traditions. In its Great White Man approach to the cinematic tradition, the auteur theory was deemed complicit with this hegemonic power; it was also seen as encouraging lazy critical and theoretical habits, ones that quite often neglected auteur traditions outside the dominant Euro-American purview.[30]

The next demystification of auteurism, the sociological critique, has framed the auteur as an institutional status achieved through cultural and subcultural means. Drawing on theorists like Pierre Bourdieu and Howard Becker, sociologists have confirmed that cultural categories like "art," "auteur," and "art cinema" have been created in specific historical contexts, which were shaped by consumerist taste competitions, and have been governed by institutional standards of value.[31] Like the industrial critique, the sociological critique sees auteurs in terms of the credit they accrue through personal ambition, skill, and luck; but unlike that critique, the sociological critique does not necessarily see such status as an unrealistic response to collaborative production. Indeed, however unfair or unrealistic it seems in the heavily collaborative world of film, such status is the logical outcome of the social and economic forces that have shaped cinema in Western culture. Hence, Shyon Baumann, in his excellent book *Hollywood Highbrow* (2007), provides us with an exacting account of how Hollywood directors gradually grew to think of themselves as fine artists in the 1960s and 1970s, when Hollywood cinema's "opportunity space" became more conducive to such perceptions.[32] Of the critiques of the auteur theory mentioned so far, the two that remain most convincing today are the industrial critique and the sociological critique, which depart from grand theory long enough to sample realities on the ground, thus putting them squarely in line with historicism, the dominant trend in film studies today.

But there is one further critique of auteurism that has yet to penetrate film studies — the biocultural complaint. Unlike cognitive approaches to film, which often focus on the individual perception of individual works, the biocultural approach is more invested in evolutionary psychology and cultural evolution. In the humanities, its closest ties are to recent fields like evolutionary literary criticism, as promoted by literary scholars like Joseph Carroll, and evolutionary aesthetics, as promoted by philosophers of art like the late Denis Dutton.[33] These fields all take it for granted that the human species has evolved a common nature through prehistoric processes of natural and sexual selection. Though we have individual and cultural differences, these are limited by our fundamental human constraints — including our most essential functions, such as eating, sleeping, and reproducing, and our common traditions and practices, many of which have evolved culturally. Due to these constraints, which inescapably bind us as a species, we cannot meaningfully describe our differences through ideas of "free will," which have been crucial to the mystification of the director.[34] Overall, the biocultural complaint is that auteurism unduly elevates the individual at the expense of the group, hiding the fact that our individual natures and works are finite and contingent on processes of selection that operate through nature and culture. Indeed, like the wider idea of authorship, auteurism is itself a meme that has evolved culturally and that some evolutionists believe is a by-product of adaptive processes.

Over thirty years ago, Steve Neale noted in the pages of *Screen* that "authorship serves partly as a means by which to avoid coming to terms with the concept of film as social practice."[35] This criticism still holds true today, for it is the thread that runs through all the critiques noted above except for the New Critical complaint, which is even more vehement than auteurism in its rejection of the *human*. Indeed, in film studies, auteurism is one of the major ways that humanities scholars have avoided coming to terms with the idea of film as a *human* practice, one that is constrained not just by our shared social processes but by our common biological natures as well.

Why Auteurism Has Remained Dominant

Naremore has reported that the "ultimate answer" to the question posed recently by *Cahiers du cinema*—"What happened to the *politique des auteurs?*"—is, quite simply, "nothing." Auteurism hasn't gone anywhere, for as anyone can see, "the star director is more visible than ever" as an industrial role and as a complex institution.[36] Given that the attacks on the auteur theory enumerated above have proved so credible and so long-lived, we might wonder why auteurism has also remained so dominant both in the marketplace and in numerous sectors of film studies, from crossover journals like *Film Comment, Positif,* and *Sight & Sound* to the "little books" that Mark Betz sees as perpetuating the auteur tradition in the academy.[37] In my view, the most likely explanations for this persistence may be grouped under three overlapping headings: the irrational hypothesis, the pragmatic hypothesis, and the institutional argument.

The irrational hypothesis stresses that the belief in the auteur, like our idea of the author more generally, has never been subject to rational human control, whether inside or outside academia. For example, one way the auteurist argument has always gripped us is through the irrational strength of its literary analogy. As modern mass arts, the movie and the novel resemble each other in their narrative structures and in their modes of distribution and consumption. It has seemed commonsensical, then, to extend this analogy to production, using a modified argument-from-design to infer a discrete auteur for a movie. This wrongheaded analogy is reinforced by post-Renaissance art history, which has depended on ideas of individual creation and personal expression. But if this analysis provides insights into how auteurism initially gripped us, it does not explain why auteurism has continued to grip us long after its romantic analogy has been relentlessly exploded by film scholar after film scholar.

To gain a fuller explanation, we may need to look to new sources of knowledge, including evolutionary ones. For example, in *The Art Instinct* (2009), Dutton explains the persistence of authorship in the face of post-structuralist critiques by talking about the emotional tug exerted by the prehistoric functions of language.[38] Dutton hypothesizes that our languages, including our arts, evolved three functions in the Pleistocene, with the idea of authorship furthering each of them. Two of these evolved adaptations, the narrative function and the communicative function, are straightforward and can be clearly shown to develop spontaneously over the course of normal childhood development. Thus people find it easier to engage in the didactic and imaginary elements of a film if they can imagine that it was created by a single artist, not by a collaborative band. But Dutton's third linguistic function, the fitness evaluation, may be even more relevant to this discussion of auteurism. According to Dutton, "the idea of the fitness test" looms behind "every act of speaking, descriptive or artistic":

> Human beings are continuously judging their fellows in terms of the cleverness or the banality of their language use. Skillful employment of a large vocabulary, complicated grammatical constructions, wit, surprise, stylishness, coherence, and lucidity all have bearing on how we assess other human beings. Intentionally artistic uses of language are particularly liable to assessment in terms of what they reveal about the character of a speaker or writer.[39]

As a result, Dutton speculates that "it is from an evolutionary standpoint psychologically impossible to ignore the potential skill, craft, talent, or genius revealed in speech and writing," for our "intense interest in artistic skill, as well as the pleasure that it gives us, will not be denied: it is an extension of innate, spontaneous Pleistocene values, feelings, and attitudes."[40] For these linguistic functions to work efficiently in cinematic contexts, people will tend to see a single historical figure as the creator of a movie. What is more, people who have an inclination toward cinephilia will tend to believe that some directors are "better" than others and thus deserve the status of auteur.[41] Of course, these ingrained habits might not lead us to the truths of art, let alone the truths of a collaborative art like cinema. But even if we understood the truths of cinema, our human attachment to single authors would tend to "pull us back to assessing the capacities of a historical" figure.[42] As a result, the ideas of unconscious agency found in auteur structuralism and the theories of the postulated author found in post-structuralist film theory are in Dutton's view "bound to fail" in the long run.[43] They simply cannot compete with our preference for attributing the artistry of an artifact to a historical person, a preference that is an "adaptation derived from sexual selection off the back of natural selection."[44]

Here the irrational hypothesis fades into the pragmatic. In my vision of it, the pragmatic hypothesis has two major parts, the first of which emphasizes the overall convenience of using auteurism. This convenience is both cognitive and linguistic, since it is easier for our limited human brains to imagine and discuss a movie if we imagine it as "belonging" to an individual rather than a collective, which would include the crew as well as the above-the-line talent. This cognitive convenience, which is irrational as well as practical, has been built into our languages and our institutions, including the journals that require us to put the director's name after the title of a movie even in articles where we question the validity of auteur concepts. The other major component of the pragmatic hypothesis is the potential benefits of auteur status, which often accrue even to people who seem to reject it. A number of anti-auteurist new waves have made this dynamic clear, as when the Dogme directors refused directorial credit in their "vow of chastity" but continued to function as auteurs.[45] Such a dynamic is further complicated in feminist or multicultural contexts, where some theorists want to abolish the idea of the auteur as a white, male, heterosexual mistake while others want to build up certain identity categories by winning a more diverse range of auteur credits for black directors, female directors, gay-and-lesbian directors, and the like.[46] Though the latter commentators often agree with the former regarding auteurism's current biases, they part ways on status, which the latter believe has no color, sex, or identity. Indeed, the potential inclusiveness and overall practicality of auteur status is one reason theorists may want to adjust their ideas of art cinema, expanding it to make way for movies by auteurs from highly untraditional backgrounds, including the most déclassé cult contexts.

Closely related to the pragmatic hypothesis is the institutional argument, which is an explanation I detail in the third section of this book. Most generally, this argument posits that auteurism isn't going anywhere because it is integral to the many cultural and subcultural institutions that emerged during the postwar explosion of art cinema. Today, mainstream commercial cinemas—from Hollywood cinemas and cult cinemas to world cinemas—operate according to auteurist principles. Especially at festivals, auteur status is the fuel in the workings, the power source for the entire machinery. We see a similar phenomenon in art-cinema distribution, where individual distributors have traditionally relied on auteur prestige to expand the circulation of art movies—and have gone so far as to circulate anecdotes that make *themselves* look bad to buttress this effect. Auteur status also structures how art cinema's niche stars relate to their directors—and it may even give those stars the leeway to create explicit sexual performances. Mainstream film magazines, cult fanzines, and prestigious crossover journals all rely on auteurist principles, as do festival juries, granting agencies, and award bodies. Through these and other value-oriented institutions, auteur status provides directors and their communities with social prestige, which they in turn exchange for production funds, distribution deals, and cash in the form of opportunities for grants, stipends, or writing. This status is also useful in the academy, where avant-garde auteurs or "artisans" have made and taught experimental films, and where scholars have long used the auteur theory to their own ends. Thus, as Naremore and others have noted, even when innovative young scholars like Wollen were dismantling the auteur theory, they were often focusing on establishment directors like Hitchcock or Welles as they did so.[47] Like auteurism itself, these classic auteurs were so culturally entrenched that the attempt to demystify them in classic analyses only pushed them deeper into their classic status—and further reinforced the utility of auteurism as the proper lens for imagining the entire tradition.

All in all, film scholars have had reliable incentives to think in auteurist terms in their teaching and in their research. These incentives have served many roles. For one thing, these incentives have reinforced the sense that it is normal for film scholars to promote auteurism even when they are dismantling auteurist ideas. These incentives have also created the illusion that academic auteurism and the cinephile brand of auteurism, which is closely associated with mainstream film criticism, are one and the same. For this reason, auteurism in mainstream film criticism often seems authorized by academic authority even though its adherents regularly cast aspersions on other aspects of academic film studies, which can seem inaccessible or just plain flaky by comparison. On the other hand, if film-theory monographs have on occasion been pushed toward the imbecilic by the pressures and the mechanics of the academic market, mainstream film criticism has little to brag about here—for its "enduring truths" have been anchored by market necessities to auteur biases that are usually unexamined and always inadequate.

Reinforcing the importance of the auteur: a poster for a screening of Werner Herzog's *Bad Lieutenant: Port of Call—New Orleans* (2009). Used by permission of Doc Films Group.

Using Auteurism Modestly

"A 'personal' horror film? How does that happen?"
"When you put your heart and genitals into something, it always gets personal."
— *TIE ME UP! TIE ME DOWN!* (DIR. PEDRO ALMODÓVAR, 1990)

Given that auteurism is not going anywhere, we should look for uses of it that might coalesce with a clear analysis of cinema and especially of art cinema, which in the popular imagination is the auteur category. Ideally, these uses would be demystified—that is, they would be honest about the irrational, pragmatic, and institutional appeals of auteurism, meaning that they would be overflowing with disclaimers and qualifications warning readers against the irrational seductiveness of these appeals. Why is this so necessary? Because if scholars do not approach auteurism in an explicitly honest way, they are liable to slide back into naïve celebrations of the auteur and of the auteur vehicle—and even if they avoid such an outcome, they may encourage backsliding in others.

Consider *Authorship and Film* (2003), a volume edited by David Gerstner and Janet Staiger. This collection has been acknowledged as one of the most substantial on auteurism in the past decade.[48] And Gerstner and Staiger's introductory overviews are indeed splendid. Unfortunately, the chapters that follow seldom measure up because they often focus on individual auteurs and works—whether by looking at traditional auteurs (as in Wollen's "The Auteur Theory: Michael Curtiz and *Casablanca*") or by looking at less traditional ones (as in Sarah Projansky and Kent Ono's "Making Films Asian American: *Shopping for Fangs* and the Discursive Auteur").[49] Though this limited approach is in line with historicist precepts, its theoretical value is worth questioning. What can a single auteur tell us about the cinema? This sort of question recalls Schatz's point about the cinema's collaborative hierarchies: the more sense that we make of them, "the less sense it makes to assess filmmaking or film style in terms of the individual director—or *any* individual, for that matter."[50] My view is that our revised use of auteur methods should stress the fundamental contradiction of auteurism: that auteur status is hard and real even though the authorship to which that status refers is subjective, negotiable, and thoroughly marked by its multiple contexts.

Beyond that emphasis, our new auteur method could be molded to the specifics of whatever modest, mid-level questions we ask. For example, we could ask how to identify auteur works without devolving into naïve celebrations. One answer to this question is that it is usually safe to focus on cult auteurs. On its face, this answer may seem quite counterintuitive. After all, scholars have traditionally been compelled to pursue untraditional auteurs due to their interest in either the avant-garde or social justice. Ergo they have often focused on neglected directors in either experimental art cinemas or more traditional art cinemas whose sex, sexual identity, class, or ethnicity has not matched the white, heterosexual, male profile that has dominated the film industries of Europe and the United States. But because many scholars have wanted to redress such imbalances, they have also wanted to depict avant-garde, female, or minority directors as *deserving* their status—even though no filmmaker can be said to deserve any status absolutely. An understandable desire to level the playing field has thus discouraged film theorists from creating the scholarship that best describes how a director's auteur status flows out of a production context or how that status is formed through compromises with specific distribution constraints.

But when scholars look for auteurs among the creators of classic B movies—or among the creators of contemporary splatter movies or the past decade's torture-porn movies—they are much less likely to elevate those auteurs or to separate them from their contexts. After all, such movies are culturally illegitimate. Any form-based argument that ignores their social and industrial contexts will not be convincing in a legitimate sphere such as the academy. Though the dynamic at work here is unfair to cult auteurs, given that there is no absolute sense in which they deserve their status any less than traditional auteurs, the fact remains that the detailed contextualization that results from this biased dynamic benefits film scholarship, for it guarantees that the scholarship on cult auteurs will remain rooted in the collective, collaborative contexts that culminated in their being labeled "auteurs" and their movies being labeled "art movies."

We can see this contextualization emerging from the old and the new scholarship on cult auteurs. Consider, for example, the 1983 *Screen* article "My Name Is Joseph H. Lewis," in which Paul Kerr offers a detailed portrait of Joseph H. Lewis, the director of B films like *Gun Crazy* (1949) and *The Big Combo* (1955). Kerr's article accents the formal details that made Lewis's thrillers and noirs exciting to audiences even as it calls "into question the predictable—if problematic—promotion of Lewis to the auteur pantheon."[51] What I consider academically progressive about this essay is that it ends by insisting that the constraints imposed by the Hollywood B system on would-be-auteurs were not "merely negative in their operation," but were in a sense responsible for whatever excellence was later perceived in the movies they influenced. As Kerr puts it, working in "the B *film noir* meant simply that the opportunities for commercial and critical success lay in certain (industrial, generic) directions rather than in others."[52]

Sharon Hayashi's fine 2010 article "The Fantastic Trajectory of Pink Art Cinema from Stalin to Bush" makes a similar point about Koji Waka-matsu. Hayashi describes the process by which Wakamatsu—a director of Japanese eroductions or "pink" skin flicks like *Secrets Behind the Wall* (1965)—constructed himself as an auteur within the confines of the pink film industry. According to Hayashi, Wakamatsu was successful in this because of the "desires of an international art film circuit eager to read Japanese film in art cinematic terms."[53] As a result of the almost accidental global success of this "Pink Akira Kurosawa," subsequent "producers began the strategic mar-keting and distribution of some pink films as art cinema."[54] Once again, the achievement of the cult auteur is seen not as a product of towering genius or uncompromising personal vision, but as a product of accidents and con-straints over which the auteur had only partial control. If this way of seeing cult auteurs seems biased when compared to the romantic scholarship that ascribes "genius" to traditional auteurs from Orson Welles and Robert Bres-son to Claire Denis and Apichatpong Weerasethakul, this way of seeing has at least led to an honest view of these cult auteurs. It has helped situate them as one complex element in a more complex collective context that remains the true author of the "masterpieces" they have directed. All of which is, I think, as it should be.

Let me provide a different example of what I mean. When I was work-ing on *Soft in the Middle* (2006), I noticed that Seduction Cinema was bent on reinforcing the cinephile discourse around a director who went by the name Tony Marsiglia.[55] Marsiglia was often shown in the DVD extras for movies like *Dr. Jekyll and Mistress Hyde* (2003), *Lust for Dracula* (2004), *Sin-ful* (2006), and *Chantal* (2007) shooting scenes over and over, performing the same perfectionism that cinephiles have grown used to in promotions for Welles, Kubrick, or Hal Hartley. Later, I realized that Marsiglia's role at Seduction was to raise the studio's subcultural status by making low-cost soft-core art movies that benefited from his technique, creativity, and knowledge of film history. These factors made it possible for Seduction to bundle Mar-siglia's movies with DVD extras that testified to his control and his freedom as an experimentalist—and they also made it plausible for Marsiglia to claim that his interest in softcore was abstract and aesthetic, not commercial and certainly not prurient. These, it seemed, were very difficult claims to support in this particular distribution context, which, because it was dedicated to making softcore skin flicks, was shot through with the commercial. On the

The director Tony Marsiglia working with Julian Wells (*left*) and Misty Mundae (*center*) on the set of *Chantal* (2007). Marsiglia was promoted as an auteur by his cult labels, whose stock-in-trade were ultra-low-budget softcore and horror movies. Photo by Duane Polcou. Used courtesy of Michael Raso and Pop Cinema.

other hand, such difficulties have not usually been that difficult for *auteurs* to negotiate—for regardless of how or where an auteur has established him- or herself, the auteur aura has been capable of obscuring the commercialism evident in that auteur's distribution context.

Of course, there are reasons to pursue auteurism into cult contexts other than the fact that doing so helps us avoid decontextualizing the auteur. The auteur is a traditional emblem of art cinema, so finding high-art auteurs in cult cinemas contributes nuance and unity to a revised and expanded concept of art cinema. Given that anti-essentialist concepts of art cinema rely on inclusive, neutral methods to identify art movies, it seems only reasonable to deploy objective signs of auteur rhetoric as one of the main criteria (though not a necessary-and-sufficient one) for membership in expanded notions of the category. The point of identifying auteur vehicles in this way is not to prove that a cult-art movie is "authentic" art cinema or that the director in question is authentically aspirational. Instead, the point is to create a credible art-historical narrative that relates *potential* art movies to more established art movies through clear similarities in the auteur rhetorics that enmesh traditional and untraditional art movies. Adapted from Noël Carroll's idea of identifying artworks through historical narratives,[56] this tool could work in several different ways, but its point would generally be the same: to bridge the divide between traditional art movies and less traditional ones in the most reasonable manner available.

I take it for granted that the best evidence of auteurism is historical. That said, even if we do not have much contextual evidence to go on, we could arrive at a reasonable argument for labeling a cult director an "auteur" and a cult movie an "art movie" based on their use of motifs and techniques consecrated by gatekeepers like Bazin, Truffaut, Sarris, or Bordwell or influential auteurs like Godard, Andrei Tarkovsky, Miklós Jancsó, or Chantal Akerman. We should, of course, be judicious with this method, using it only if we have no better options.[57] But in the end, we cannot overlook that even in an Internet age background information is not always available—a problem that is especially acute in cult areas. In such cases, we might rely on formal evidence alone when such evidence is strong. For example, despite my inability to locate much background information on the late-night-cable movie *Anthony's Desire* (1993) or on its writer–director, Tom Boka, I could make a strong case for positioning this production as a cult-art movie and Boka as a cult auteur by devising an art-historical narrative that relates the movie's illegitimate narrative-number structure, a hallmark of porn, to its more accredited motifs. Such an argument is possible because Boka's movie uses many of the art film's most acclaimed techniques. Thus it focuses its plot on art, it foregrounds the act of filmmaking, and it often alludes to Godard and other auteurs. It also uses open, elliptical tactics in its development of characters; it contains a disinterested sexual vision and an orchestral score; and it relies on long takes, long shots, and relentlessly moving cameras. Still, when we use this sort of reasoning, we should avoid reducing cult auteurism to the mimicry of art-film traditions, as if to imply that the latter are somehow special or autonomous. Instead, we should stress that a cult-art movie such as *Anthony's Desire* integrates legitimate art-film motifs with an illegitimate pornographic structure, yielding the conflicted aspirationalism that is so characteristic of cult-art movies and cult auteurism generally. Clearly, to make this case we would need a grasp of the illegitimate subcultural traditions of the cult movie and knowledge of the legitimate cultural traditions of the art film. Such breadth is hard to attain, given the overall multiplicity, instability, and cultural debasement of cult conventions. But it is not impossible to attain.

The unexpected inclusiveness of auteurism suggests that this characteristic might be useful to theorists who want to formulate a more inclusive approach to art cinema, a category long deemed *only* exclusive. Critics might argue that looking for auteurism in cult contexts simply extends a flawed attitude to a new location. But the fact is that auteurism is already there, and it is functioning *very* well there. We need to know why.[58]

In the end, Michel Ciment was correct: neither the auteur critics nor the new-wave phenomena they spawned may be cited as the origin of auteurism. Auteurism does not have a single origin. It is, instead, rooted in ideas of authorship borrowed from other forms of art and other forms of communication, whose roots extend back beyond the historical record. But the fact that there is no real start for auteurism offers one explanation as to why it has not ended but is instead flourishing today despite the problems that we have observed in its signature articulation, the auteur theory. Auteurism is still flourishing because it is ingrained in our psyches and in our institutions, where it enables all kinds of activity. But as scholars have also realized, auteurism shuts down other kinds of activity—for in the academy, it often substitutes aestheticist myths for more rational truths. My view is that we can neither ignore nor dismiss auteurism, for it is an atavistic, revenant meme that will not stay dead. Instead, we should contrive rational methods for dealing with it. In this chapter, I have explained one such method that allows us to flesh out a more inclusive idea of art cinema; my final chapters, which often return to auteurism, suggest several other methods that we might develop as well.

CHAPTER 3

From "Foreign Films" to "World Cinema"

"Have you ever seen any of those, you know, those foreign films?"
"Yes, frequently."
"I don't like 'em."
— *LOLITA* (DIR. STANLEY KUBRICK, 1962)

Though terms like the "mainstream" or "mainstream cinema" are often used
with contempt in cinephile discourse, they are not always terms of derision in
actual art films. After all, these terms reflect common human desires ranging
from a straightforward, even hard-wired taste for accessible movies to an
equally natural desire to fit in. We often see such desires dramatized in art-
film narratives, depictions that are not always negative. For example, in my
epigraph, Dolores "Lolita" Haze signals her desire to return to the mainstream norms of American childhood by rejecting "those foreign films." It
does not bode well for Humbert Humbert that Lolita, who has been identified with Hollywood and pop culture, repudiates an oppositional film category that was in 1962 synonymous with outré depictions of sex. Through this
coded statement, Lolita returns to the mainstream, rejecting pedophilia and
Humbert's alternative lifestyle.

In 1998 I watched Stanley Kubrick's film with my undergraduate students
and was certain that these meanings did not come across. My supposition
at the time was that the term "foreign films" had long since lost its potency,
becoming a much more neutral consumer category that was even then being
interchanged with the term "world cinema" by retailers like Blockbuster.
Without a sense of that old exotic mystique, we might hear in this tragicomic
exchange no more than my students heard: namely, the obliviousness of an
American twelve-year-old who hasn't fully considered that her interlocutor,
as a European exile, would have seen many "foreign films"—and would prob-

ably have liked some of them, too. In itself, this lost meaning is not a big deal. But because the U.S. domestic market has had such an outsize impact on global cinema, this change in American idiom offers us some exceptionally intriguing insights, including a few new perspectives on our current academic debates over the term "world cinema."

Hence, in this chapter, I look first at the old American usage of "foreign films," a term that was in the postwar period identified with "art films" and "sex films." The sense of the forbidden implicit to this term softened over time until it became a fairly neutral classifier that in the United States now refers to non-American films across many genres.[1] The first purpose of this chapter is to abstract this transformation so that we might understand it clearly and perhaps relate it to similar phenomena elsewhere. The second purpose is to offer a concise perspective on "world cinema." After looking at the debates enmeshing this term, I argue that "world cinema" has been used in main-stream markets as a politically correct genre category that helps to maximize the distribution of the movies it classifies. It avoids obvious ethnocentrism and is useful the world over. However, because "world cinema" is still used as a classifier that distinguishes Hollywood from non-Hollywood cinemas, it has never escaped the hints of exoticism and neocolonialism that animated "foreign films." Thus it remains a focus of academic controversy. In the end, we can transcend these debates—and retain the classifying function of the term—by deploying "world cinema" with sensitivity and a sense of histori-cal context.

Brief Historical Survey

Whatever happened to that cachet? No one on either side of the Atlantic— or Pacific—wants to admit it today, but the fashion for foreign films depended a great deal on their frankness about sex.

—ANDREW SARRIS, "WHY THE FOREIGN FILM HAS LOST ITS CACHET" (1999)

What feelings did the phrase "foreign films" inspire in American audiences after the Second World War? Or, to put it a different way, what would an American audience have heard in 1962 when Lolita deployed the term? Fear and longing, most of all: fear of difference, fear of sex and art, and a simul-taneous longing for all the above. Specifically, "foreign films" referred to the postwar European imports that combined the allure of sex with an aspira-tion to high-art status borne out through hard-edged themes, gritty realism, and stylistic experimentation. These features—the cosmopolitan origin, the realistic, often erotic imagery, the aspirational aim—were the pillars of the exotic mystique assigned to foreign art films in the postwar milieu. Steeped in what Jack Stevenson calls "the myth of Europe," this mystique was made palpable by stylistic and thematic differences between foreign films and Hollywood movies.[2] The term "foreign films," then, denoted an oppositional cinema identified with art cinema.[3] When that sense of difference waned due to historical factors that brought the foreign and domestic producers closer together, this usage of "foreign films" quickly lost its idiomatic edge.

Where did this edge or cachet—which Andrew Sarris refers to as the "ooh-la-la factor"[4]—come from? The ultimate historical origin of this meaning was the commercial dominance of Hollywood in its golden era, which began in the late 1920s. Because major studios like Paramount had moved toward vertical integration by the 1920s, Hollywood was at the start of the sound era so comfortable in its industrial hegemony that it chose to regulate itself through the "Don'ts and Be Carefuls" of 1927 and the Production Code of 1930, rather than risk being regulated by outsiders such as censorship boards or federal agencies. Almost as soon as the industry began, censorship laws and paternalistic interest groups had depicted silent-era Hollywood as an immoral business that was a major threat to young people, women, and the urban poor. Indeed, before 1934, when the Code was first enforced, Hollywood was notorious for its permissive use of nudity and risqué themes. Clearly, the dichotomy implied by "foreign films"—that is, between healthy domestic entertainment and unsafe, yet oddly intriguing, foreign art—was inconsistent in the silent era.[5] But the adoption of new Code-era regulations opened up markets for alternative producers and alternative distributors, both foreign and domestic, which were happy to traffic in the licentious. Among other things, what these changes created was a new and very clear contrast between Hollywood product and foreign product.

This all happened quickly. Eric Schaefer has noted that foreign films had a prewar history on alternative distribution circuits, where they were "often wrapped in the lurid garments of exploitation."[6] According to Schaefer, the "most infamous foreign film to be released during the 1930s, and the motion picture that cemented the connections between imported films and salaciousness, was *Ecstasy*."[7] Gustav Machatý's film was imported in 1935 and had a troubled American reception, inspiring censorship concerns and intriguing debates about Hollywood entertainment as it related to foreign artistry. "Foreignness, art, and obscenity were conflated," writes Schaefer. "Because foreign films spilled over categories . . . they were not contained within traditional boundaries and thus were obscene."[8] Consequently, a precedent for presenting and receiving European imports as arty sexploitation had been set even

A frame capture of Hedy Lamarr as Eva in *Ecstasy* (1933), the Gustav Machatý film that helped shape American perceptions of the "foreign film" before the Second World War. © 1933 Elektafilm, © 2011 Televentures.

before the Second World War; after the war, this tool was standardized when those imports increased in number.

The promise of sex definitely helped circulate foreign art films just after the war. Borrowing "techniques from the exploitation market to 'sex up' film titles and advertising," as Tino Balio puts it, American distributors played up the sexual elements of foreign films even when their content was not that racy.[9] Armed with the "idea that it's European, therefore it's artistic and consequently it's risqué," in exploitation director Barry Mahon's words,[10] distributors of postwar neorealist art films like *Roma, città aperta* (1945) and *The Bicycle Thief* (1948) relied on their creativity to promote the limited sex content of these films. This sexploitation angle was crucial in acting as a "biological lure," drawing audiences to art-house films.[11] But it was especially crucial to circulating the idea of art in rural areas, where a film's cultural prestige might not have been enough to promote it. Schaefer suggests how "powerful the sex angle could be" when he cites *Variety*'s 1948 estimate that "the average foreign film made 60 percent of its revenues in New York, whereas 'sexacious

A production still of Brigitte Bardot as Juliette in *Et Dieu . . . créa la femme*
(1956), the movie that by itself raised the profile of the foreign art film in the
United States. © 1956 Cocinor, © 1957 Kingsley International Pictures.

pix' or those with a good exploitation angle garner 25% from Gotham and
the balance from the hinterlands."[12]

Once this selling point was identified, later foreign films—including *One
Summer of Happiness* (1951), *Sommaren med Monika* (1953), *The Game of Love*
(1954), *Et Dieu . . . créa la femme* (1956), *Les amants* (1958), *Hiroshima mon
amour* (1959), and *La dolce vita* (1960)—gave American distributors more of
what they wanted. Of these Swedish, French, and Italian films, the most influential of them all was Roger Vadim's *Et Dieu . . . créa la femme*, the Bardot vehicle that by itself raised the profile of foreign art films in the United
States.[13] Vadim's success spawned a dash to sexual explicitness that began at
the same general moment that the international festival circuit and its audiences were embracing auteurism in an increasingly organized fashion. The
synergies of this combination gave the new über-auteurs like Ingmar Bergman, Jean-Luc Godard, and Federico Fellini what amounted to a "free pass"
to shoot the "sexacious pix" that their producers wanted.[14] And by the early
1960s, commercially minded distributors from across the United States were

scouring Europe, looking for sexualized films like Mac Ahlberg's *Jeg—en kvinde* (1965)—which Radley Metzger rereleased as *I, a Woman* in 1966—to sell as auteur vehicles. Metzger later cut out the middleman, mimicking the stylization of these films while bolstering their sex content by shooting his own sex-art auteur films, including *Carmen, Baby* (1967), in Europe. The result of this trend was that "explicit sexuality became expected in foreign films, to such an extent that 'foreign film,' 'art film,' 'adult film,' and 'sex film' were for several years almost synonyms," as Peter Lev affirms.[15] Indeed, even foreign art films produced within relatively repressive filmmaking contexts could be influenced by this confluence of events, as a prerevolutionary Iranian film like Fereydun Gole's *Under the Skin of the Night* (1974) shows.

How did this all happen? First, we need to remember a point that Howard Becker emphasizes in *Art Worlds* (1982): people require a measure of political freedom before they can organize themselves into culturally significant art worlds.[16] Indeed, even liberal societies that grant their people many indi-

Highlighting the sexualization of the "foreign film": an ad mat for Mac Ahlberg's *Jeg—en kvinde* (1965), which Radley Metzger rereleased in the United States as *I, a Woman*. © 1965 Europa Films and Nordisk Films, © 1966 Audubon Films. From the collection of Eric Schaefer.

vidual freedoms are, due to differences in local conditions, at different stages in the development of their art worlds. As Shyon Baumann has noted, in the first half of the last century, "social conditions in Europe were more amenable to the development of an art world for film than they were in the United States."[17] It wasn't simply that the European industries that made relatively explicit foreign films faced no internal constraints, but that they had more incentives after a war that shattered their film industries to challenge those constraints—incentives that often included state subsidies and other monetary rewards. By contrast, classical Hollywood assumed its own vertically integrated dominance, so it had a smaller incentive to take on risk and thus accepted a measure of repression based on the judgments of censorship boards and Supreme Court decisions like the 1915 *Mutual* case. Given its strength in a field constrained by censorship, Hollywood could afford to give in to pressure groups that demanded it clean up its act. Indeed, even after Hollywood had in effect ceded certain materials to alternative foreign and domestic producers not governed by the Code, it didn't have to worry about losing domestic market share, which was ensured not only by community censorship but also by its own local control over exhibition and distribution.

All of this began to change, however, around the time that the first neorealist works arrived in the United States. Indeed, in 1948, the main support of the golden-era system—vertical integration—was knocked out by the Paramount Decrees, which opened new theaters to foreign and independent productions that lacked a Production Code Administration seal. After that, the Supreme Court, guided by American free-speech laws, overturned its *Mutual* decision in *Joseph Burstyn Inc. v. Wilson* (1952). Because of the latter case—which was related to the U.S. exhibition of a neorealist work directed by Roberto Rossellini, written by Fellini, and distributed by Joseph Burstyn, a significant American distributor of foreign art films—the censorship concerns that in a sense guaranteed the classical Hollywood system were wiped out. After that, exhibitors of films like Louis Malle's *Les amants* won more legal cases, opening even more mainstream theaters to risqué movies. It was perhaps inevitable, then, that Hollywood would copy the tactics of foreign producers, diminishing the sense of their difference—and contributing to the creation of a legitimate art world in a Hollywood industry that had traditionally been dominated by the entertainment ideal.

Lolita's release may be considered something of a high-water mark for this American usage of "foreign films." As Schaefer puts it, by "the early 1960s, the terms art theater and art film had become synonymous with nudity, completing the cycle begun with *Ecstasy*."[18] But the tide did begin to turn after 1962. With its old "entertainment" model looking obsolete, Hollywood devised responses to its new competitors, including foreign films and television, and new products for its newly educated and cosmopolitan American audience, which increasingly chose adult-oriented fare when choosing movies at all. Thomas Guback, Lev, and Balio have shown that Hollywood invested in European coproductions of the 1960s, including risqué films by foreign auteurs like Michelangelo Antonioni's *Blow-Up* (1966). At times, individual studios acquired entire subsidiaries just so they could distribute the racy foreign films in which those subsidiaries specialized without violating industry rules.[19] But domestic Hollywood producers continued to chafe at the self-imposed censorship at home. The early 1960s were characterized by challenges to the Code that occurred against the backdrop of declines in attendance for Hollywood movies and steady increases for foreign films.

After the success of adult-oriented, auteur-driven Hollywood films such as Mike Nichols's *Who's Afraid of Virginia Woolf?* in 1966 and then Arthur Penn's *Bonnie and Clyde* in 1967, Jack Valenti, the new head of the MPAA, installed a rating system in place of the Production Code. This system, which went into effect in November 1968 and remains in place today, allowed Hollywood movies to be distributed without a PCA seal. Under this system, R- and X-rated domestic films could match the explicitness of the imports without upsetting Hollywood's older entertainment model, which was retained through G and PG fare. This change ushered in the New Hollywood, an art cinema that challenged the assumptions of the traditional usage of "foreign films." (Indeed, by 1972, Lolita might have asked Humbert whether he had seen any of those *American* films.) These changes would prove "a mixed blessing," as Balio puts it, for they reinforced what Elena Gorfinkel calls the "falling fortunes of the foreign film."[20] Hollywood's decision to return to the thematic resources like sex and violence that it hadn't really exploited since the silent era stripped foreign art-film producers of a crucial advantage. Foreign art films could still push the envelope, as Vilgot Sjöman's *I Am Curious (Yellow)*, Just Jaeckin's *Emmanuelle*, and Pier Paolo Pasolini's *Salò* bore out upon their American releases in 1969, 1974, and 1975, respectively. But they could do so only by enhancing their sexual explicitness or their violence, calling into question their difference from more exploitative genres, including the emerging hardcore feature. This problem was only exacerbated by the fact that a large number of American films had, in the eyes of many, become full-fledged art movies. No longer would 80 percent of art-house offerings consist, as in 1958, of foreign films.[21] In this way, the terms "foreign films" and "foreign movies" lost their "cachet," as Andrew Sarris puts it, to the point that today in retail outlets like Netflix they are simple geographic classifiers.

A production still from Arthur Penn's *Bonnie and Clyde* (1967), an adult-oriented auteur vehicle whose success at the box office helped dispatch the old Hollywood Production Code. © 1967 Warner Bros.

Extensions and Ramifications

I began this chapter by noting the importance of the English-speaking American market, which in the postwar era was the most crucial world market due to the dominance of its domestic cinema as measured in box-office receipts and in global influence.[22] Not only could success in the United States lead producers to Hollywood riches, it could also lead to global recognition, as the Hollywood import–export machine has since the Second World War made a practice of absorbing the most successful foreign stars, auteurs, movies, and trends and recirculating them, often remade, to the world through its extensive distribution network. This process, which was given new life during the postwar period, has spurred auteur "waves" and elevated marginalized national cinemas across the world. Most crucial to this process at the formal level were signs of national difference, like language, that could be "exoticized," along with exploitable elements like sex.[23]

However, it is difficult to imagine that any future new wave could titillate the mature and segmented American market the way that the Italian, Swedish, and French cinemas did sixty years ago—not that individual auteurs, from Peter Greenaway and Lars von Trier to Catherine Breillat and Gaspar Noé, aren't still doing their best. The problem is that American audiences, including critics and journalists, are savvy to art-cinema codes, sex, and hype. Since the inception of the New Hollywood, American producers have used the same tactics, making these elements less exotic. And what has made contemporary Hollywood so stable is its ability to absorb and re-commodify stars and trends while sustaining its principal business in blockbuster entertainment. In a global environment like the United States, innovations, interventions, and provocations don't seem "foreign" for long, quickly reinforcing a blasé sense of "been there, done that." Though art cinema can still raise the profile of a national cinema, this process no longer seems capable of reforming the larger cinematic environment by forcing change on Hollywood.

This is not to suggest that new national cinemas cannot still extend art cinema's vast reach by spawning legitimate art cinemas in places like South Korea and Romania. The Korean New Wave has elevated itself through the global circulation of acclaimed and reliably eroticized auteur films, including Jang Sun-woo's *Lies* (1999); Kim Ki-duk's *The Isle* (2000) and *Spring, Summer, Fall, Winter . . . and Spring* (2003); Hong Sang-soo's *Virgin Stripped Bare by Her Bachelors* (2000) and *Night and Day* (2008); Lee Chang-dong's *Oasis* (2002); Park Chan-wook's *Sympathy for Mr. Vengeance* (2002) and *Thirst* (2009); and Bong Joon-ho's *Memories of Murder* (2003). However, in the absence of broader changes, these developments only add to the cinephile

resignation that art cinema is just a genre that goes through the same auteurist motions everywhere, from Japan, India, and the former Czechoslovakia
to Denmark, Israel, and the Philippines. But cinephiles should not get too
jaded. The formation of new art cinemas through emergent new waves and
global processes of consecration has in fact remained crucial to the consolidation of national and regional identities, as shown by the national cinemas
of Romania, Iran, Taiwan, Scotland, Mexico, Argentina, and Nigeria as well
as the regional cinemas of areas such as the Catalan and Basque regions of
Spain. For example, the Romanian Cultural Institute in New York has lately
been promoting the influence of Lucian Pintilie on much younger Romanian auteurs like Corneliu Porumboiu and Cristi Puiu, which in its opinion
makes Pintilie "the most important Romanian filmmaker" and thus a proper
representative of Romanian cultural identity in the United States.[24] The case
of Nollywood, the giant Nigerian video-making industry, is intriguing in an
opposite sense, for it fuses the populist, grassroots elements of a cult cinema
with the commercial elements of a mainstream cinema even as it is beginning
to develop the rudiments of an art cinema through a festival culture that is
just now taking shape. It might be possible, then, to discover a market environment somewhere in the world like that of the postwar United States,
where art cinema exploded with such great cultural and industrial power.

Still, as the case of Iran indicates, scholars should be careful in looking for
such a place. Iran corresponds to the U.S. model in several respects. It has
a distinguished film tradition despite the fact that its film industry has long
been subject to intense censorship as well as other repressions. In such a nation, even art films produced in Hollywood's fairly tame indie-style divisions
might carry some of the threat that "foreign films" once carried in the United
States. However, this analogy is limited by the extent of governmental control over production and distribution. Becker has noted the potential conflict
between state control and the formation of art worlds.[25] Indeed, in countries
such as Iran, China, and the former Soviet Union, there has been no guarantee that periods of openness would lead to expansions of artistic freedom
among directors—for such nations have not been governed by the liberal laws
that have over time expanded individual freedom and consumer choice in the
West. This observation is most evident concerning Iran. Azadeh Farahmand
has shown how the second Iranian New Wave that developed in 1983 and 1984
was pushed forward by a period of moderation in Iran's postrevolutionary climate, during which the reformist Mohammad Khatami served first as minister of arts and culture and later as president. In that period, Iranian directors
like Abbas Kiarostami were able to develop a recognizable style in movies like

Taste of Cherry (1997) that compromised between the necessities of a moderate Iranian government and the tastes of a global festival circuit.[26] But this period in Iranian politics, which led to the creation of a domestic art cinema acclaimed as such at home and abroad,[27] did not spearhead any permanent changes—for in the absence of a liberal constitution that could consolidate and defend all the new freedoms, there was nothing to stop hard-liners like Mahmoud Ahmadinejad from later tamping out creative expression.[28] Moreover, there has been no persistent ambition among global distributors to penetrate this market, for the Iranian film-going audience has had at most a negligible impact on cinema's global economics. Movie distributors, then, have had neither the opportunity nor the incentive to trigger the changes in the Iranian market that distributors of European art cinemas triggered in the American market.

On the other hand, the potential of global art cinema to foment change can be seen through the work of a Chinese filmmaker such as Jia Zhangke.[29] Over the last decade, Jia became a state-sanctioned director in China. He first gained his auteur prestige from films like *Platform* (2000), which were popular on the global festival circuit but hardly seen in mainland China except as underground films. His international success eventually led Chinese authorities to officially accept him. This arrangement allowed Jia more money for making films like *The World* (2004) and likewise allowed him to screen his work in more accessible venues. But the content of his films has not really changed: his focus remains the changes wrought by globalism and accelerating market dynamics in today's China, and his technique continues to show a mastery of the art-film conventions that also animate the work of Hong Kong auteur Wong Kar-wai, including the fusion of a gritty realism with long, luxurious takes; slow, sweeping camera movements; considerable visual flash; and ambiguous narrative arcs. Jia's work still contains extensive cultural commentary, but the elliptical nature of that critique, along with the prestige his films have generated through global festivals, has raised its status. If this kind of development becomes a trend among Chinese filmmakers, it would mark a shift from the tactics of Fifth Generation filmmakers like Zhang Yimou, who tended to avoid direct commentary on current events. In the long run, this trend could be a recipe for industrial and cultural change—provided the Chinese authorities do not follow the Iranian model. To me, a similar rollback seems unlikely, since China has shown consistent signs of becoming a consumer-based economy that depends on imports as well as exports.[30] (Indeed, this is the irony of Jia's work: his cinema critiques the same consumerism that has carried it to more diverse Chinese audiences.) It seems more likely that the authorities will control the flow of change. But even if this change were to occur very slowly, its cumulative effect on China could be huge, given the scale of its market.

The elements that informed the changing usage of "foreign films" in the postwar United States are, then, liable to be rare. But as the case of China shows, this rarity does not mean we should stop looking for parallels in world cinemas. Such scrutiny could help us distinguish between the business-as-usual manifestation of auteur cinemas in Asia, Europe, Africa, and the Americas and the more dramatic restructurings possible in places where the influence of the festival system on a crucial domestic cinema might signify an impending global wave, as occurred in the 1960s. This global wave seems likely to be triggered by reforms in a huge developing power like mainland China—whose potential audience and production capacity are so immense that they seem capable of not only transforming Hollywood but also marginalizing it.

Enter "World Cinema"

According to Dudley Andrew, the "term 'world cinema' is now permanently with us."[31] Though hyperbolic, this statement is correct in that "world cinema" has become an increasingly prominent classifier in academic classes and texts as well as in retail outlets, online and off. The term is also of interest to scholars of art cinema, for these cinematic categories are often conflated, especially on the festival circuit. As Andrew notes in his oft-cited article "An Atlas of World Cinema" (2004), "world cinema" has replaced the term "foreign art film," "which first slipped the heavily guarded university doors in the 1960s."[32] One source of this convergence is the hint of the unfamiliar and exotic implicit in the term "world cinema," which has made it yet another tool that teachers and retailers may use to distinguish Hollywood films from non-Hollywood films. Consequently, as Andrew notes, "world cinema" has even named "the resistance to Hollywood evident in the GATT debates over a decade ago."[33] It is predictable, then, that this classifier has also become a focus of academic debates, much as we might expect of an ethnocentric term like "foreign films" were it still a popular usage in the academy.

As it happens, the introduction of "world cinema" was part of the same dynamic that led to the obsolescence of "foreign films." The utility of that term was that it divided the world into an "us" and a "them," with the "us" often identified with English-speaking audiences, U.S. audiences in particular, and the "them" referring to an exotic, unfamiliar world that might be interesting for the "us" to see. But if this dynamic was unpalatable, it makes sense that people have needed some variation on it when making distinctions. Ergo, the utility of "world cinema." This recent term seems to be a consumerist update of "foreign films," one that reverses the old dynamic: it aligns the "us" with the "world," making the marketing and study of world cinema more respectful and less exploitative in tone.[34] But as Stephanie Dennison and Song Hwee Lim have noted in *Remapping World Cinema* (2006), this is just one of several ways that "world cinema" has been used. One of the other ways is to use it to refer to "the sum total of all the national cinemas of the world," making "world cinema" equivalent to "cinema."[35]

To get a sense of what is at stake in the competition between these two usages, we should consider the criticism that Andrew has taken from academic advocates of the latter usage. On first glance, Andrew is an unlikely target of criticism, given that he seems to consider even contemporary Hollywood a world cinema. This puts him in a decidedly progressive minority. If Andrew sees any cinema as the antithesis of world cinema, it is classical Hollywood cinema, which is long dead but well chronicled. Andrew's purpose in "An Atlas of World Cinema" is to arrive at much better classroom uses of the term for teachers and students of global cinemas. Thus, for his syllabus, he promotes a "'world systems' approach" that is at once broad and specific.[36] The overarching strategy of his method is to understand cinematic change as interactive and endlessly reactive "waves" that travel not through clean lines of national descent but through very messy, always specific interminglings of influence, counterinfluence, and the like. Andrew's most particular tactic is to discern the world through its various localities, examining "every local cinema . . . with an eye to its complex ecology."[37]

Andrew's ideas for tweaking the use of "world cinema" sound good to me. So it is a bit surprising to find that this nuanced essay has met with criticism. For instance, Lúcia Nagib has made a case for rejecting any use of "world cinema" that relies on a distinction with Hollywood, even one that limits its scope to classical Hollywood—and she rightly notes that "the distinction between Hollywood and the rest of the world still reverberates" in Andrew's approach, despite its better attributes.[38] This leads Nagib to renew her call for a more inclusive usage with a truly "positive definition":

> Despite its all-encompassing, democratic vocation, [world cinema] is not usually employed to mean cinema worldwide. On the contrary, the usual way of defining it is restrictive and negative, as "non-Hollywood cinema." Needless to say, negation here translates a positive intention to turn difference from the dominant model into a virtue to be rescued from an unequal competition. However, it unwittingly sanctions the American

way of looking at the world, according to which Hollywood is the centre and all other cinemas are the periphery.[39]

The problem that some theorists have with "world cinema," then, is that insofar as the term is still used to make distinctions between Hollywood and the "other," it only *seems* to place non-Hollywood films at the core of cinema. This use of "world cinema" as a classifier continues to a foster a hierarchical, unequal conception of cinema and, by extension, implies that the cinemas it labels "the world" actually amount to the periphery.

In all of this, I agree with Nagib. "World cinema" sounds like a blanket term, and Hollywood is certainly part of that blanket. And I agree with Rosalind Galt and Karl Schoonover that the kind of usage that Nagib is rejecting is a "world of commodified and sanitized exoticism."[40] But the spirit of Andrew's essay is to agree with all this, too, for in it, the author moves away from what Nagib rightly considers a simplistic search for origins toward an idea of film history as a set of endlessly interactive waves.[41] Drawing on Andrew, Eleftheria Thanouli has made a significant contribution to these debates through her argument that the complexity of global flows, along with their incredible interdependence, asymmetrical or otherwise, make terms like "core," "semi-periphery," and "periphery" seem imprecise.[42] The difference between these two sets of observers is that Andrew, Thanouli, and others would like to use "world cinema" as a practical tool, for they think that the term is destined to be around for awhile. What makes this durability an inviting prospect is that "world cinema" can be used progressively, for as Shohini Chaudhuri argues, it quite bluntly asserts "the importance of placing the national within the regional or global perspective."[43] Nagib, on the other hand, has no interest in using "world cinema" as a term of convenience—and its potential progressivism is not, in her opinion, *enough*. Unfortunately, her blanket usage of "world cinema"—which makes the term analogous to cinema with a lowercase *c*—does not do enough real work. While her usage has interesting theoretical dimensions, it is not capable of making a deep cultural impact, perhaps because it is at root so idealistic.[44]

Nagib's reservations also apply to one other use of "world cinema." In this usage, world cinema refers to an emerging art cinema, one whose presence at festivals suggests the arrival of a new new wave or a new national cinema. In other words, this type of usage refers to an unconsecrated art cinema.[45] Like the other uses of world cinema that Nagib rejects, this one depends on distinctions between Hollywood and non-Hollywood cinemas and on equally thorny markers between traditional and untraditional production locales. Because this usage is fraught by intimations of neocolonialism and differences in cultural status, it must be handled with care—that is, precision, mutual respect, and sensitivity to the workings of global cinema. But like the other usages, this use of "world cinema" cannot just be put aside. After all, theorists of art cinema cannot simply ignore the value-oriented mechanics of art cinema—for regardless of whether we like it, art cinema relies on (sub)cultural hierarchy everywhere. It can't exist without aspiration, distinction, and all the value-added details that so often ruffle cultural feathers—and whether scholars use a term in a certain way or not is entirely irrelevant to the ongoing reality of these hierarchical dynamics. That said, those who do use "world cinema" in this way can avoid ethnocentrism by looking at global art cinema precisely and with respect for its great diversity. Deployed with care, this usage will not reinforce art-cinema ideology in an exploitative way.

"Foreign films" fell out of use for two reasons: it exhausted its market value; and once that value was gone, there was no reason to retain an ethnocentric term that was out of step with the multicultural, *multiculturalist* drift of the liberal globalism that had allowed foreign films to come ashore in the United States in the first place. But as a context-reliant classifier, the term had its uses, making it logical that "world cinema" arrived to replace it, updating the older term in accord with a more postcolonial climate. Still, because "world cinema" was a *classifying* tool, it could never be correct in the eyes of film scholars who find classification itself problematic. So it is predictable that the debate around that term has threatened to empty it of the functions it was adapted to fulfill—a process that would presumably lead to ever-more correct terms to fill the same functions as "world cinema" and "foreign films" before it. We can only wait and wonder whether this process will be subverted when, or if, other developing cinemas like that of mainland China grow large enough to dwarf Hollywood through sheer economics.

Concluding Précis

Three conditions were crucial to the postwar meaning of "foreign films" in the United States. The first was the existence of a broad, middle-class society dubious of art and sex. This society enforced its norms through censorship. The second was a liberal capitalist system that corroded distribution barriers, aspiring to the free flow of goods, ideas, and capital. One of this system's profit centers was the idea that art was sacred, a belief that was legally protected though it did not always match mainstream sentiment. The third condition—and the hardest to replicate abroad—was the existence of a domestic movie industry that was so dominant that it could afford to be conservative, regulating its films so that they matched the values of its domestic audience.

This situation could not last, for the society's liberal laws could be used to smash the constraints (the censorship boards, monopolies, etc.) that had created it. Once the constraints were removed, distributors brought in increasingly liberated imports. At first, the foreign films inspired dread and desire in the domestic audience. But the films' notorious combination of art and sex also proved adaptive, helping them to circulate; at that point, their status as sacred art was crucial to cultural defenses of their sex content. But soon, so many of these films were in circulation that this mystification was no longer necessary to their flow. As the years passed, the society that once seemed repressive came to seem permissive, leaving the domestic industry out of step. It had to adapt or die; it had to revise its internal rules to mimic the success of the imports. These changes were made easier by the success of the imports—for, to paraphrase Baumann, it was the idea that foreign films could be art that made it possible to think of domestic films as art, too.[46] This reformation of the global hegemon reduced the foreigners' advantage and altered the meaning of "foreign films" until the term no longer inspired the dread it once had.

The foreign films never went away. But the encounter with "the other" that they occasioned led many citizens to see that there was nothing to justify the exoticism linked to the term "foreign films." Thus, a classifying term that had lost its economic value was outmoded terminologically by the same liberal processes that had brought it into being in the first place. Still, academics and cinephiles needed a term to distinguish among various kinds of cinema. In time, this necessity led to the ascendancy of "world cinema," a term that reversed the orientation of "foreign films" by identifying "the foreign" with "the world." Eventually, the most progressive film scholars of the newly global academy found fault with this term as well. A number of them seemed hostile to the fact that the term was a *classifier* that could still be used to make distinctions between Hollywood and non-Hollywood cinemas or between emerging, unconsecrated, "peripheral" art cinemas and well-established, consecrated, "core" art cinemas. Thus film scholars faced a choice: they could continue abandoning useful terminological tools in the interest of progressive politics, or they could invent a flexible, respectful, contextualized way out of an impasse that was created and exacerbated by cultural liberalism.

This film scholar chose the second option.

PART 2

Formats and Fetishes

CHAPTER 4

Recovery and Legitimation in the Traditional Art Film

Which art-movie format is now truest to art cinema's most legendary function, the legitimation of cinema as a high art? This is a question I seem destined to return to, for the answers that once tempted me — including cult-art cinema and mainstream art cinema — currently look misleading. On the one hand, the films and auteurs of these illegitimate and quasi-legitimate formats are today more popular than ever with global audiences — and their full legitimation as high art could validate gigantic swaths of the film world, much as the legitimation of classic art films once did during the auteur era of 1945 to 1970. Unfortunately, these answers no longer satisfy me because it seems highly unlikely that *under current cultural conditions* these untraditional formats could ever truly exceed or supplant the authority of the traditional art film, which remains the engine of legitimation across art cinema. After all, whatever legitimacy has been secured in these untraditional formats has typically been won through more traditional formats, especially the art film. Of course, as we will see in later chapters, both cult cinema and mainstream cinema do have their own specialized art cinemas, which they have generated internally. But to achieve a wider legitimacy, individual directors and individual movies within these untraditional art cinemas have had to secure stamps of approval from more official cultural institutions. For this reason, the traditional art film remains art cinema's legitimation machine and seems likely to retain that status and function for the foreseeable future.

To understand the mechanics at work here, we should reflect on the way the art film has throughout its postwar history managed to elevate comparatively debased movies, auteurs, and materials. I begin this process by suggesting that traditional art films do not need to be praised or even widely *liked* to be deemed legitimate; this legitimacy is instead a function of their institutional provenance, and especially their initial distribution channels and modes of exhibition. I then take a different approach by looking at the persistent squabbling over "authenticity" that has been characteristic of American independent cinema, a sector that has made art films, including Hollywood art films. Finally, I examine the art film as a recovery-and-legitimation machine by looking at how it has consistently found ways to smuggle contents once deemed déclassé or obscene into "respectable" culture. By exercising its "free pass," the art film has used some fairly predictable contents to market itself as risqué—and lately, it has backed up these claims by sometimes using unsimulated sexual imagery in its mise-en-scène.

What Is a "Traditional Art Film"?

One problem we should address from the outset is that the art-movie format I call the "traditional art film" throughout this book is only *comparatively* traditional. In fact, what makes this type of film "traditional" is not its native context or its historical origin or its method of production or its position in film studies, but rather its eligibility for distribution through institutions allied with the global festival circuit as they were established in the postwar period and as they continue to flourish today. By defining the "traditional art film" as a feature-length narrative geared toward this global circuit—while leaving other details open—we can distinguish this art-movie format from less traditional ones, like avant-garde cinema, cult-art cinema, and mainstream art cinema, all without devolving into arguments over form or authenticity.

That said, this concept of the art film is clearly *untraditional* in one respect: it does not define the art film as a foreign film that came to the United States from Europe in the quarter century after the Second World War. Especially (and primarily) in the United States, this is the most conventional idea of the "art film," and as such, it continues to crop up even in remarkable studies like Tino Balio's *The Foreign Film Renaissance on American Screens, 1946–1973* (2010) and Michael Z. Newman's *Indie: An American Film Culture* (2011). There are, however, several problems with restricting the art film to this classic phase. First, it is ethnocentric in a self-limiting way: it not only looks at art films through American eyes, it also denies American projects any possibility of art-film status. But the core problem with this kind of definition is that it sees "artfilmness" as belonging to certain kinds of movies rather than to certain kinds of institutions and social dynamics. I believe that art-film status is a sociological function of particular kinds of movie distribution and reception. If we fail to insist on this, we might settle for the conclusion that Newman settles for, which is to say that American indie films fill the same functions and niches as foreign films in the United States while never qualifying exactly as "art films"—because that category is not open to indie films, especially not indie films with Hollywood links.[1] To me, this is an overly academic idea of the art film, one that overstresses categorical consistency and that projects a somewhat misguided idea of generic closure. The history of the art film is not something that "closes."

This is not to deny that the feature-length art film has obvious roots in Europe. According to Andrew Tudor, the film-as-art idea originated with the same people who shepherded "art" audiences.[2] These promoters included writers like Ricciotto Canudo, who encouraged the art-house movement in France in the early 1920s, and impresarios like Ivor Montagu, who helped found the Film Society in Britain in 1925. In the United States, an emerging art-house circuit emerged during the interwar period, contesting Hollywood's vertical monopolization of domestic exhibition. This alternative circuit included museum theaters like that of the Museum of Modern Art as well as little cinemas, university theaters, repertory theaters, exploitation theaters, and film clubs.[3] Here, American viewers could witness experimental art films from Germany, France, and Russia, including *Das cabinet des Dr. Caligari* (1919). What is more, right after the Second World War, this art-house audience could attend movies that had been feted at European festivals, like the prestigious international events at Venice and Cannes.

Shyon Baumann has argued that these developments broadened the perception of the movies as a legitimate art.[4] According to this view, before the Second World War and immediately after it, cinema was deemed a potential high art mainly in certain European countries, like France and Italy—where the cultural and industrial conditions were very different from those in the United States—and in the pages of certain avant-garde journals.[5] But after the war, this situation changed rapidly due to shifts in industrial circumstances. Hollywood wanted to reclaim the European market share it enjoyed in the 1930s—and the shattered European film industries could no longer compete with it on anything like equal footing. Aided by state subsidies, European producers were thus compelled to adopt a niche "art" strategy that provided prestige and global export but not the most profits.[6] This strategy was crucial because it encouraged increasing masses of people to identify the cinema as a potential high art. Eventually, by the late 1960s and early 1970s, this paradigm proved so successful that it was even applied to Hollywood. Baumann has argued that the New Hollywood was able to have its films accepted as art primarily because European art films had already created precedents for reading relatively mainstream forms of aspirational cinema as high art, precedents that U.S. audiences could then use on Hollywood.[7]

Of course, this process would not have unfolded so cleanly had other industrial circumstances not appeared earlier. During the postwar era, distributors of European art films secured new distribution advantages in the United States through an array of Supreme Court rulings that broke up Hollywood's vertical integration and gave the cinema a number of new free-speech protections. As a result, U.S. distributors of European art films could exploit the sexuality, real or imagined, of postwar art films beginning with the Italian neorealists. The success of this strategy was rooted in the fact that classical Hollywood had, through the Production Code, barred itself from producing or exhibiting explicit themes and images in the theaters it controlled. Hence, art films were often marketed and exhibited in the United States as sexploitation, with tame movies like Ingmar Bergman's Swedish production of *Sommaren med Monika* (1953), which one exploitation distributor retitled as *Monika, the Story of a Bad Girl* to accentuate its sexual imagery.[8] Though this doctoring, which included dubbing and visual inserts, has historically enraged cinephiles,[9] it clearly furthered the market penetration necessary to familiarize Americans with the art-film concept, hastening the cultural process noted by Baumann. Seen in this light, actresses like Hedy Lamarr (*Ecstasy*, 1933), Harriet Andersson (*Monika*), and especially Brigitte Bardot (*Et Dieu . . . créa la femme*, 1956; and *Le mépris*, 1963) did as much as any auteur to popularize the film-as-art idea in the United States.[10] Given all this tradition, it is no wonder that the traditional art film has remained a reliably sexualized format (about which, more anon).

But the most crucial factor in the long-term success of the art-film format has been the expansion of the festival circuit since the Second World War. Festivals have acted as value generators, testing grounds, marketing points, and sources of legal protection for art films. Once the Cannes International Film Festival began distributing qualitative awards in 1946, the film-festival circuit proliferated across the globe.[11] Art films have often had their first exposure on this global circuit, earning wider release to art houses and to multiplexes by winning a distribution deal, preferably at a major festival.

Festival mechanics offer a persuasive explanation as to why a traditional art film has not relied on critical acclaim or audience praise for its cultural legitimation. Getting past the festival gatekeepers at Cannes, Venice, Berlin, Sundance, Toronto, or Pusan can be competitive, arduous, and very costly, especially if a film's producers are of more-or-less independent means. But once a movie has achieved festival exposure through hierarchical art-film institutions—institutions that in effect secured their own legitimacy as a growing network in the postwar era, when the change in the cultural perception of cinema gained mainstream acceptance—it does not *require* more praise to confirm that it counts as an "actual" art film. For a majority of critics, the tag "art film" often just means high-quality movie, and the festival system is

Popularizing the film-as-art idea: Brigitte Bardot with costar Michel Piccoli in Jean-Luc Godard's *Le mépris* (1963), an international coproduction that also starred Jack Palance. © 1963 Rome Paris Films, © 1964 Embassy Pictures.

clearly the foremost arbiter of cinematic quality. This seal of quality allows the art film to arrive on screens with a value-added character that suggests that sophisticated audiences have already approved it—a dynamic that in effect gives its distributors a "free pass." That is, distributors are provided an alibi for picking up even the most notorious art film, which might have had little hope of getting broad distribution if it hadn't possessed festival credentials. Consequently, when distributors attend a festival, they are free to focus on the movies they believe will appeal to their target audience, since the cultural credibility of those films is typically already assured.

Status and Legitimation in the Traditional Art Film

Today, the traditional art film is at the top of the cinema hierarchy, such that it is the only type of art movie that qualifies as high art in most cultural contexts just by being itself. Not even the cultural capital of the experimental art movie is equally useful, for avant-garde prestige is subcultural, valued primarily in avant-garde communities and in elite institutions like the art world or the academy. By contrast, the prestige of the art film is so expansive that we might say that it is "always already" consecrated, for once a film has been identified as an art film, its status is culturally—and legally—understood. This has not always been the case. As noted, the art film is still young— especially within the United States, where Hollywood's traditional identification of the movies as "entertainment" has served as a counterweight to the film-as-art (read: film-as-*high*-art) idea. To get a sense of the stakes here, we should look at the U.S. reception of two historically distant art films, Louis Malle's *Les amants* (1958) and Vincent Gallo's *The Brown Bunny* (2003). The divergent reactions to these two art films show how effective the change in American perceptions of the movies has been at moderating cultural responses to sexualized art films.

Malle's art film arrived in the United States after the auteur era had commenced but while the institutions of the art film were still in the process of validating the artistic potential of the cinema. So even though this foreign film was decorated by these institutions—after all, Malle was a respected French auteur who won the Special Jury Prize for *Les amants* at Venice in 1958—it was too early for these institutional credentials to prevent the brouhaha that erupted after this foreign film was exhibited in Cleveland Heights in November 1959. The problem, of course, was the film's erotic trajectory, which ended with a protracted sex sequence featuring an undraped Jeanne Moreau. Given that the theater owner, Nico Jacobellis, was fined for obscenity just for showing this film, its status as art was clearly still subject to

THE LOVERS (Les Amants)
Starring　Written and Directed by
JEANNE MOREAU　LOUIS MALLE　A Zenith International Release

The controversies that infused the American reception of Louis Malle's *Les amants* (1958) in the late 1950s now seem almost inexplicable, demonstrating that the film-as-art idea had not at that point fully penetrated the American market. © 1958 Nouvelles Éditions de Films, © 1959 Zenith International.

legal dispute, despite the fact that the Supreme Court had in *Burstyn v. Wilson* (1952) designated *all* movies as forms of art that deserved free-speech protections. Thus the defenders of *Les amants* marshaled its cultural credentials in order to corroborate that it had been produced with the intention of making art, not obscenity. In *Jacobellis v. Ohio* (1964), the Court accepted these and other arguments, reversing the fine through a decision made famous by Justice Potter Stewart's "I know it when I see it" obscenity standard.[12] Though the sex in Malle's film may now seem timid, the film had a definite cultural impact on the format, protecting the status of other art films even as it added to their marketable notoriety.

After the 1960s, art films that caused a stir in the United States rarely had to do more than to show off their institutional credentials to ward off threats to their circulation. This was in part because in the 1960s and 1970s hardcore and softcore pornographic movies were gaining public traction in the United States, creating a sense of their difference from traditional art films. This difference was a salient institutional reality regardless of the quality of a given art film according to critics—and regardless of whether the film itself seemed to exploit its freedom. Here Gallo's indie art film *The Brown Bunny* offers a case in point. Having produced the respected indie film *Buffalo '66* (1998) with an auteurist slant, Gallo amplified this aspect of *The Brown Bunny*, crediting himself for all significant production roles (including directing, writing, producing, starring, editing, and filming), as well as for roles that weren't so significant (such as makeup design). In that sense, then, *The Brown Bunny* would prove even more auteurist than *Les amants*, approaching the artisan ideal characteristic of avant-garde cinema. And *The Brown Bunny* had the same sort of credentials as *Les amants*. It had been released to art houses after being nominated for awards at festivals like Cannes. Indeed, at the Vienna International Film Festival, *The Brown Bunny* won a FIPRESCI Prize. In particular, the festival cited this movie for its "bold exploration of yearning and grief and for its radical departure from dominant tendencies in current American filmmaking."[13]

Despite these impressive credentials, *The Brown Bunny* is today primarily recalled for two things: its concluding sex scene, wherein Chloë Sevigny fellates Gallo on camera, and its reputation for bad aesthetics. The latter was precipitated by the catcalls the film received at its Cannes premiere and was reinforced when Roger Ebert called it the worst film in the history of Cannes, kicking off a nasty row between critic and auteur. *The Brown Bunny*'s cult legacy as "badfilm" lives on in the message boards of IMDb, which includes categories like "bad movie" and "TOO BAD no taste."[14] But the controversies that have surrounded the movie, unlike those that once surrounded *Les amants*, have never caused cinema experts to question its status as an indie art film. No matter how gratuitous viewers judge its fellatio sequence or how tedious critics consider its ostentatious pacing, no one has ever denied that it is an indie art film, because *The Brown Bunny* conforms to too many traditions of the format: it was independently funded; it was shot on 16mm by an auteur who has made other art films and has starred in art films by auteurs like Claire Denis and Francis Ford Coppola; and it was blown up to 35mm for art houses and festivals. Today, even the debates about its sex only seem to reinforce its status as an art film, which was certainly not the case of *Les amants*.

On the other hand, art movies that have been made by less traditional auteurs or that have arrived on the American stage through less traditional channels have long had to win their art-film status by winning over audiences and critics. In effect, this process exemplifies what Howard Becker, a sociologist of art, once said about distribution: that it "has a crucial effect on [the] reputations" of artists and their works.[15] We can see this fact borne out through the example of movies such as Joe Sarno's *Inga* (1968) and Rad-

INGA

Starring MARIE LILJEDAHL • MONICA STRÖMMERSTED • CASTEN LASSEN
Presented by JERRY GROSS and NICHOLAS DEMETROULES
A CINEMATION INDUSTRIES Release

An INSKAFILM, Ltd. Picture Photographed at EUROPA STUDIOS (Stockholm). A CANNON Production.

A promotional still for Joe Sarno's awakening-sexuality classic *Inga* (1968). The producers of this cult-art movie, which had an exploitation lineage, attempted to broaden its appeal and elevate its cultural status. © 1968 Cinemation, © 2002 El Independent. Used courtesy of Michael Raso and Pop Cinema.

ley Metzger's *Therese and Isabelle* (1968), which in the late 1960s crossed over from sexploitation theaters to mainstream art theaters on the basis of their strong, female-oriented narratives, their deflective aesthetics, and their docile sex appeal. Nevertheless, the fact that these movies originated on the exploitation circuit and were made by auteurs who later distributed hard- and softcore pornography has served to relegate them to a quasi-legitimate cult-art status. Indeed, some gatekeepers have gotten very personal in arguing for the prohibition of any legitimate recognition for these art movies. Thus, in a long *Spectator* article, Bart Testa has argued against any rehabilitation of Metzger's reputation, contending that this auteur of classical sexploitation was a mercenary and a "charlatan," an "interloper" whose "critical recuperation should [not] be sought."[16] Still, we should not forget that Metzger's art movies *did* resemble the art films of the day even if they haven't been accepted as such. They have been consigned to less-than-legitimate status, then, not by their texts but by their contexts: who made them and how; where they played and competed; and what, if anything, they won. Today, if a movie fulfills the institutional criteria of the art film, as *The Brown Bunny* did, it seems absurd to deny its legitimacy, no matter how bad or exploitative it strikes us. But if a film is of "cult" origins, it can secure its legitimacy only by winning praise from juries, critics, distributors, and audiences. The problem of *Inga* and *Therese and Isabelle*, then, is not that they were terrible but that they didn't generate sufficient acclaim to overcome their origin.

Problems of the Term "Independent"

It has become something of a cliché to note that most independent art films—like those produced by the American independent cinema, which is to many observers a clear example of an art cinema[17]—are only *relatively* independent.[18] As has often been pointed out, a strict construction of the term "independent film" would require that it be produced and distributed without any "corporate" funds,[19] much as Jim Jarmusch financed his realist indie classic *Stranger Than Paradise* (1984). But the vagaries of cinematic production and exhibition are rarely that clear or strict. Indie producers have routinely turned out to be only *relatively* independent, accepting studio funding through a variety of means, from coproduction monies to unreported distribution deals. The contradictions implicit in these arrangements have only been exacerbated when Hollywood studios have bought formerly independent studios, as when Disney bought the legendary independent Miramax in 1993 and tried to maintain its cred inside Hollywood, or when they have started indie-style studios of their own, such as Fox Searchlight or Sony Pic-

tures Classics, which the majors still call "autonomous" divisions. This practice has led many cinephiles to denounce movies made in these spheres as
"inauthentic." Thus they have often complained in crossover magazines like
Sight & Sound that a term that "should refer to films produced without studio
support" has been applied instead to what are really "genre" vehicles:

> These subdivisions may offer more directorial control, but it appears they
> also supply a full crew and enough money to afford major acting talents,
> music licensing and inescapable mass marketing. With this studio back-
> ground and their trademark "quirkiness," one can't help but find these
> "indies" to be as shallow and money-hungry as their bigger-budget, high-
> concept counterparts.[20]

Given how common this viewpoint is in art-film circles, one would think
that the recent economic downturn, which led Hollywood to pull back from
this minimally profitable area by closing or reining in a number of indie-style
divisions, would have been welcomed by cinephiles. But that hasn't been the
case. Instead, many cinephiles have acted as if the sky is falling, with Hollywood, that all-purpose bogeyman, again being blamed for producing or acquiring too few art films.[21] Clearly, Hollywood can only rarely please cinephiles, many of whom despise it by reflex.

But the debates over the term "independent" miss a bigger point. Regardless of whether cinephiles approve of its films, Hollywood has been making
and distributing traditional art films since the 1950s, having gotten into the
business even before the New Hollywood era. Today, indie-style films may
be "independent" in name only; nonetheless, they still circulate at the film
festivals for which they were made and where they often win awards that
boost them in their later release to art houses and multiplexes. They are,
then, *Hollywood art films*, and they maintain a dual status as traditional art
films and as mainstream art movies. This is no dark conspiracy, however, for
the festival system and the decentralized critical bodies that are the guaran-
tor of the art film's authority do not ban Hollywood from their events and
competitions. Indeed, as the ongoing recessions have demonstrated, many
art-film insiders profoundly *want* Hollywood to participate in this format,
for they understand that Hollywood financing and distribution offer art-film
auteurs and art-film fans unparalleled opportunities for exposure and access.
Of course, Hollywood has gotten many things in return for its investments,
including status in a category that is prestigious all over the world. In this
regard, the indie-style directors offer a case in point: while their subcultural
prestige on the film-festival circuit may not always have been as high as that

of auteurs from other continents or from more experimental (and under-financed) industries, these directors have consistently managed to achieve an enviable balance of mainstream penetration and high-art status through their art-inflected Hollywood distribution. That said, the fact that Hollywood has had *any* status in the institutions of the traditional art film is nothing less than remarkable, for the art film first coalesced as a commercial format in apparent opposition to Hollywood. What the presence of the Hollywood art film in the institutions of the traditional art film proves is that those institutions are, as legitimation machines, powerful and supple, capable of extending their prestige even to the entities they nominally oppose.

Another way that the current emphasis on authenticity misses the point is through its American focus. Obviously, I am sensitive to this because I am American. But it does seem odd to me that critics feel so free to criticize American art films for lacking independence when European and Asian art films have historically gotten help from Hollywood as well as from behemoths like the French studios Pathé, Gaumont, and StudioCanal or from top-down funding schemes such as public subsidies, tax incentives, coproduction agreements, and festival grants like the Hubert Bals Fund. Pierre Bourdieu notes that this last type of funding tends to subject artists to "hidden censorship," demonstrating that the freedom of European art films has always been comparative and context-bound.[22] This point is further borne out by the proliferation of recent articles and books that demonstrate how funding and distribution influence film form.[23]

Similarly, Mark Betz, Peter Lev, and Tino Balio have drawn on Thomas Guback to show that classic art films that were nominally European in production, attitude, and style were funded through Hollywood.[24] Such funding was part of Hollywood's emerging global strategy, which in the 1960s had Hollywood providing all or part of the budgets for 60 percent of British features, according to Lev and Guback.[25] Where their joint funding has come to light, these Euro-American coproductions have been "relegated," as Betz puts it, "to the despised zone of European popular cinema, wherein *popular* signifies a commercial betrayal of national traditions."[26] Betz notes how this critical devaluation has affected the reputations of films like *Blow-Up* (1966), *Zabriskie Point* (1969), and *The Passenger* (1975), which were financed in part by Metro-Goldwyn-Mayer. But he also wonders why director Michelangelo Antonioni's three previous films didn't suffer similarly.[27] Betz is referring to that trilogy of seminal Antonioni classics, *L'avventura* (1960), *La notte* (1961), and *L'eclisse* (1962). He believes that there is no reason to think that these Italo–French coproductions were any less compromised by global finance than was *Zabriskie Point*. Still, if the French contribution to the earlier films should in theory "corrupt" their identity as independent Italian productions, that contribution has been mostly overlooked because French money doesn't disrupt the comfortable and *marketable* assumptions about art cinema the way that American money does. My feeling is that critics who treat a movie like *Blow-Up* only as popular cinema, excluded from issues of a "legitimate" art cinema, are relying on the flimsiest stereotypes, the most mythical oppositions. Indeed, the illogic of this sort of exclusion is similar to that which has been invoked to exclude indie-style art films from legitimate art cinema.

But if these exclusions accentuate the hybrid status of these forms, they cannot detract from the fact that most of these films were made to be traditional art films — that is, to circulate among other art films in the culture of film festivals and art houses where they might be discussed by cinephiles, art lovers, and academics. And again, as with *The Brown Bunny*, it doesn't always matter whether viewers or critics actually *like* these films. Their institutional identities exist apart from evaluation.

Art Cinema's "Free Pass"

> *"How many film directors make films to satisfy their sexual fantasies?"*
> *"I would imagine most of them."*
> — *8 1/2 WOMEN* (DIR. PETER GREENAWAY, 1999)

So far, we have looked at several examples of how the art-film format has in effect acted as a recovery-and-legitimation machine. It has been capable of legitimating films that few people like — and, depending on circumstances, it has been capable of recovering films from commercialized areas that cinephiles distrust. Thus it can recover movies from the dustbin of direct-to-video distribution — and it can even legitimate whole classes of Hollywood film, such as the indie-style art film. But one of the art film's most spectacular capacities has been its ability to recover and legitimate certain types of imagery that are seemingly unfit for "refined" audiences due to their copious violence or explicit sex. This capacity should not lead us to think of the art film as an especially "benevolent" or "tolerant" format. The special permission at work here is a matter of institutional machinery rather than altruism. We should think instead of the art film as an adaptable market format that has grown more tolerant of genre-coded motifs, especially violent ones, since Quentin Tarantino proved through the towering success of his Miramax film *Pulp Fiction* (1994) the appeal of festival films that qualify as cult-art movies, mainstream art movies, and traditional art films all at the same time.

Indeed, ever since *Pulp Fiction* won the Cannes Palme d'Or in 1994, and

A production still from Quentin Tarantino's Miramax film *Pulp Fiction* (1994), a movie whose success at Cannes opened the festival circuit to more films featuring generic contents associated with cult forms. © 1994 A Band Apart and Miramax.

particularly over the past decade, art films featuring attributes identified with cult genres have been appearing with regularity on the festival circuit. In this time, there have been many urban art-crime films in the tradition of *Pulp Fiction*, from the Hong Kong film *Fallen Angels* (1995) to the Brazilian–Chinese coproduction of *Plastic City* (2008). But there has also been the entire art-house phenomenon that Joan Hawkins has referred to as "art horror." Over the past decade, art horror has had many practitioners, from Denis to Lars von Trier, but its signal auteur now seems to be the South Korean director Park Chan-wook, who has won awards at Cannes for *Oldboy* (2003) and *Thirst* (2009). Both films are gore-filled romps that combine elements of many cult traditions, including martial-arts movies, crime thrillers, vampire flicks, and sci-fi movies.[28] In other words, some cult-art movies no longer need to be "recovered" in the sense that Dario Argento's *Suspiria* (1977) or John Dahl's *The Last Seduction* (1994) were recovered for art-house audiences. Cult-art movies like Wong Kar-wai's *Fallen Angels*, Kim Jee-woon's *The Good, the Bad, the Weird* (2008), Park's *Thirst*, and von Trier's *Antichrist* (2009) have instead been legitimate from the start, for they were produced to succeed at art cinema's most respected institutions.

What directors are using the institutions of the art film to reclaim, then, are not specific movies or specific forms of production and distribution; they are instead reclaiming materials that art cinema has historically abandoned to lower-status formats. Of course, in using these materials, they must often reclaim debased market areas, such as those associated in the United States with the NC-17 rating. Art films have embraced this controversial rating more often than any other type of film, going back to Philip Kaufman's *Henry and June* (1990) and Pedro Almodóvar's *Tie Me Up! Tie Me Down!* (1990). But I believe that this enthusiasm is just a corollary of the art film's traditional emphasis on controversial content.[29] After all, the art film has, since the format's inception in films like Gustav Machatý's *Ecstasy* (1933), had a tradition of reclaiming lowbrow content from cult genres that include exploitation and porn. Thus, in the 1970s, Liliana Cavani's *The Night Porter* (1974) and Pier Paolo Pasolini's *Salò* (1975) used elements of Nazi exploitation (or "Nazisploitation") movies, a low-budget tradition in Italy at the time. But as the example of *Ecstasy* demonstrates, the longest, most robust art-film tradition has always been the recovery and legitimation for upscale audiences of sexual motifs debased by pornographic overtones. This tradition remains intact today; indeed, recent festival favorites like Julia Leigh's Australian art film *Sleeping Beauty* (2011) and Steve McQueen's British art film *Shame* (2011) have automatically benefited from this tradition. Some notable trends have emerged within this tradition over the past two decades—but we should recognize that these trends, striking though they may be, are new only *within* this specific tradition.

Let me explain. The art film's association with porn goes back in the United States and Britain to the 1930s and to directors like Machat, but this linkage was most prevalent in the postwar era, when the foreign films of Bergman, Federico Fellini, Roger Vadim, and so on came to stand for it. Thus, by 1980, Steve Neale had recognized that, "from the mid-1960s onward," art cinema had "stabilised itself around a new genre: the soft-core art film," which he defined in terms of legitimate art films like *Belle de jour* (1967), *The Night Porter*, and *Private Vices, Public Virtues* (1976).[30] Neale's use of "softcore" implies that the art films of the time were understood to be pornographic or semipornographic. These films relied on a simulated brand of sexual imagery that maximized its depictions of the female face, as justified by art cinema's new stress on psychology and interiority, as well as its depictions of the unclothed female body. The controversy that greeted this imagery, even in its timid, neorealist forms, often raised the profile of its creators and added market-ability to the art films in which it appeared. After Hollywood's 1968 switch to a rating system, these "softcore" art films were even made by American directors linked to the newly uninhibited New Hollywood.

None of this was happening in a vacuum, of course. In the United States, exploitation and avant-garde producers had long dabbled in unsimulated, or hardcore, sexual imagery. In tandem with a growing cultural permissiveness, producers of "mainstream" sexploitation and producers of underground stag films moved at about the same general moment to introduce the hardcore fea-ture, the first example of which was *Mona* (1970). Thus, by 1972, when Gerard Damiano debuted *Deep Throat* in New York, the porno-chic era had arrived in the United States. Besides its consolidation of hardcore sexual motifs like "meat shots" and "money shots,"[31] the hardcore industry was notable for using both unsimulated sexual imagery and the X rating, which the MPAA did not legally own. This association of the X with hardcore made that rating all but unusable by legitimate productions. Indeed, not even the introduc-tion of the copyrighted NC-17 rating in 1990, which was meant to replace the disreputable X rating, eased these stigmas, leaving the NC-17 designation largely unused, even today.

Of course, the hardcore industry has not been uniformly disreputable. Beside its mainstream triumphs in the porno-chic period, the hardcore in-dustry quickly engendered a loose hierarchy partly based on the high-art values of other cinemas. Hardcore auteurs like the Mitchell brothers, Gerard Damiano, "Henry Paris" (Metzger), and Chuck Vincent consolidated their credentials by aspiring to art cinema, as certified by celebrated classics that include *Behind the Green Door* (1972), *The Devil in Miss Jones* (1973), *Resur-rection of Eve* (1973), *The Opening of Misty Beethoven* (1975), and *Roommates* (1981). In 1984, *Adult Video News* launched the AVN Awards, an Academy Awards–like night bestowing honors in many categories, gradually elevating auteurs such as Candida Royalle, Stephen Sayadian, Andrew Blake, Michael Ninn, John Leslie, and Gregory Dark. The notoriety of this illegitimate value generator has served to disseminate hardcore's mix of traditional and untra-ditional values through the culture. European hardcore cinemas have pro-duced comparable hierarchies, especially in prestigious continental markets like France, Italy, and Germany, where directors such as Tinto Brass and Marc Dorcel have been hailed as auteurs. Still, the porn industry's attempts at self-legitimation have not been successful, because one of its global values has been the social transgression it aligns with taboos or "dirtiness." Along with the industry's mob history and humanity's clear evolutionary bias against pornography,[32] this self-conscious elevation of taboo, transgression, and dirtiness has served to block hardcore's entry into legitimate culture.

Thus, since the end of porno chic, auteurs have had to establish and maintain clear lines between their art films and "real" hardcore. Auteurs that make highly sexualized art films cannot be seen as trafficking in the same kind of content as hardcore pornographers, for doing so carries a greater risk of branding their art films as worthless—thus barring them from the mainstream markets to which they ultimately aspire—than it did before and during porno chic, when even softcore sexploiteers aspired to mainstream-ness through the crossover potential of their quasi-legitimate softcore art films (e.g., Sarno's *Inga*; Metzger's *Therese and Isabelle*; Just Jaeckin's *Emmanuelle*, 1974). Nevertheless, these auteurs *do* want to approach hardcore. They want to play with it, redeeming its explicitness; they want to prove that its signature imagery has legitimate purposes. And they want to harness its commercial appeal in a way that, over their careers, enlarges their distribution potential. Auteurs can do all this by relying on the freedom and legitimacy of the traditional art film and its value generators, the festival in particular.

But these auteurs have not necessarily wanted to cash in right away. As Bourdieu has shown, high-art producers usually approach their careers as vocations. As a result, they take the long view, understanding the long-term distribution benefits of a brand of cultural distinction that may not translate into economic capital all at once. Art-film auteurs are no exception here, which is why they have used sex to accentuate their notoriety even if, as Jon Lewis has noted, their employment of the most risqué motifs has not led to the biggest box office in recent years.[33] And the fact that the reputations of these auteurs often outstrip their profits works well for them, since auteurs like Catherine Breillat have not wanted to be confused with pornographers. Some of the evidence of this is formal: their art films have over the past decades contrived extremely specialized mannerisms that flirt with pornography but that may always be differentiated from hard- *and* softcore motifs. Thus, in recovering and legitimating explicit material, these auteurs may *seem* brave, but they have often performed these functions in a way that protects and enlarges their distribution potential over the course of their careers.

When it comes to unsimulated sexual activity, art-film auteurs have been pushing the envelope for over fifteen years. For example, Philip Hass's *Angels and Insects* (1995) contains simulated sex and is distinguished only by glimpses of an erection. Von Trier's *Idioterne* (1998), hardly a very "sexy" film, contains an orgy with hardcore inserts. Jang Sun-woo's *Lies* (1999) overflows with nudity, simulated sex, and sadomasochism. But it was the French auteurs of the "New French Extremism" who burst the dam.[34] Leos Carax included unsimulated imagery in *Pola X* (1999), Breillat included it in *Romance* (1999), Virginie Despentes and Coralie Trinh Thi included it in *Baise-moi* (2000), Patrice Chéreau included it in *Intimacy* (2001), and Bertrand Bonello included it in *The Pornographer* (2001)—which starred none other than the acclaimed French New Wave actor Jean-Pierre Leaud. From there, the trend went global, encompassing Julio Medem's *Lucía y el sexo* (2001), Larry Clark's *Ken Park* (2002), Gallo's *The Brown Bunny*, Dumont's *Twenty-nine Palms* (2003), Michael Winterbottom's *9 Songs* (2004), Carlos Reygadas's *Batalla en el cielo* (2005), Tsai Ming-liang's *The Wayward Cloud* (2005), John Cameron Mitchell's *Shortbus* (2006), von Trier's *Antichrist*, and Gaspar Noé's *Enter the Void* (2009).

These films, many of which have been released unrated, may include unsimulated fellatio, cunnilingus, heterosexual intercourse, same-sex intercourse, anal penetration, and ejaculation. (Incidentally, a number of these films use CGI or prosthetic penises, but the trend in question is not defined by its treatment of erections alone.) This imagery is distinguished from "actual" hardcore through its realistic style, which mostly avoids close-ups or "meat shots";[35] through its integration with the drama, which places spectacle in the context of narrative; and through its mostly (apart from *Shortbus*) downbeat thrust, which strips these art films of the pro-sex messaging common in porn. These films are also distinguished from hardcore by the production values they share with other art films: they are medium-cost narratives shot on film (as well as high-def video) and released to theaters, while most hardcore movies are today ultra-low-budget, shot-on-video, all-sex affairs distributed nontheatrically. The fact that these art films include *any* unsimulated sexual imagery at all differentiates them from softcore movies.

Nevertheless, we should avoid looking at these market-oriented differences naïvely. That would support the false dichotomies that have reinforced the illusory borders that separate art from porn, distinctions that have obscured the fact that porn is usually art.[36] Indeed, subliminally, these films actually seem to narrow the distance between themselves and hardcore. For example, *9 Songs* had to defend itself on its first release as much because of its openly pornographic format—which all but dispenses with narrative, oscillating between sexual numbers and musical numbers—as because of its fellatio, its intercourse, and its explicit ejaculation.[37] And some of these films incorporate aspects of "actual" hardcore by using crossover actors or by having characters witness "actual" hardcore imagery within the frame of the narrative. Hence, Breillat was celebrated for using Italian hardcore star Rocco Siffredi in *Romance* and *Anatomie de l'enfer* (2004)[38]—a practice that has since then become a standard element of films like *Baise-moi*, *Lucía y el sexo*, and Steven Soderbergh's *The Girlfriend Experience* (2009), which gains much of its "exotic" authenticity from exploiting the background of Sasha Grey, its female lead, within the adult film industry.[39] What is more, in their narratives, films like *Lucía y el sexo* and *Baise-moi* often expose their characters to carefully framed imagery taken from hardcore. These tactics are part of a trend to frame seemingly hardcore images in art films. This technique, which is linked to the "porn-in-film" effects that Catherine Zuromskis has discussed vis-à-vis mainstream films,[40] is at work in many recent art films. They include Hal Hartley's *Amateur* (1994), David Lynch's *Lost Highway* (1996), Noé's *Seul contre tous* (1998) and *Irréversible* (2002), Gough Lewis's *Sex: The Annabel Chong Story* (1999), Despentes and Trinh Thi's *Baise-moi*, Michael Haneke's *La pianiste* (2001), Medem's *Lucía y el sexo*, Ash Baron-Cohen's *This Girl's Life* (2003), Clément Virgo's *Lie with Me* (2005), Tsai's *The Wayward Cloud*, Jacques Audiard's *Un prophète* (2009), Giorgos Lanthimos's *Dogtooth* (2009)—and the list goes on.

What we should probably resist, however, is the standard rhetoric used to promote these films. The presence of hardcore images in films like *Romance* does *not* make them the most controversial cinema ever, and these films are definitely *not* going anywhere the cinema hasn't been before. Indeed, these sexed-up art films are neither the most explicit nor the most controversial movies ever made. After all, cinema has been used to record human sexuality since early in its history; and if we are talking about mainstream movies, *Deep Throat*, a "real" hardcore film, went mainstream in the United States four decades ago. Indeed, as Linda Williams has shown, even legitimate art films have a tradition of using graphic and pervasive unsimulated sexuality, as Nagisa Oshima's *Ai no corrida* (1976) confirms[41]—and if we focus on art cinema as a super-generic whole, we will see that Metzger, Blake, and Ninn have been purveying hardcore sex in art movies for quite some time. If there's anything authentically new here, it is the persistence with which these particular art films have used this particular imagery to create a seemingly permanent new commercial market for unsimulated sex within highbrow art cinemas. By looking across this trend, we can see that the art film and its institutions have in a sense exercised its free pass to recover these debased motifs—but only for use in this very specific market niche.

Before closing, we should remind ourselves that this freedom is a variant of the art film's traditional permission to circulate provocative and disturbing materials in broad markets where such materials might be subject to exclusion were it not for this format's cultural capital. In other words, this freedom isn't simply a matter of the art film's ability to show sex. It also applies to the format's habitual use of realistic, often downbeat materials, as in its focus on mental cruelty and abuse; misogyny and rape; violence and torture; substance abuse and sex addiction; carnage and gore; racism or the "exotic"; homophobia; profanity; pedophilia, incest, and bestiality; drug use; and existential despair. These motifs, which are routine in the American, European, and Asian art films of today, might seem unfit for the mainstream outlets where art films tend to be sold. But in context, they act as signs of the seriousness that is high art's rationale. By pointing to these signs, which evoke "art and a higher purpose," cinephiles have, as Dominique Russell puts it, reliably been able to "douse" cultural disputes over rape motifs in the recent art films of Pedro Almodóvar, Mike Leigh, and Lars von Trier—which means that they have done the same thing that cinephiles once did apropos the more classic art films of Ingmar Bergman, Akira Kurosawa, Robert Bresson, and so on.[42] The defenders of all these films have exercised art cinema's free pass.[43]

What does all this tell us? That the art-film format has tremendous cultural status. And that its producers and distributors have been able to bestow some of that status on previously illegitimate films, filmmakers, distribution channels, and cinematic materials, just as art-world insiders have always been able to bestow some of high art's cultural status on themselves and their audiences as well as on their art works, art materials, and art channels.[44] As a result, the art film's institutions have been supple enough to legitimate even the most questionable movies as "art films"—and its value generators have been able to sanctify even the most déclassé forms of production and distribution. What is more, the art film has been able to recover and legitimate culturally debased motifs. At its extreme, this trend has given a free pass to unsimulated representations of sexuality, thus establishing an upmarket outlet for "actual" sex in the art films of the past two decades. Ergo, the art film remains the format truest to art cinema's most legendary function, the consecration of new movie forms as high art—and it seems unlikely that a less traditional format will replace it as art cinema's legitimation machine anytime soon.

CHAPTER 5

Losing the Asterisk
A Theory of Cult-Art Cinema

In a 1986 interview with Andrea Juno, the cult-horror director Frank Henen-lotter made it clear that, unlike Sam Raimi and his cult classic *The Evil Dead* (1981), he was an unimportant director and his own classic film, *Basket Case* (1982), was an unimportant work, one that deserved at most a "footnote with an asterisk" by comparison.[1] What made his judgment something other than a straightforward expression of humility was the fact that it came at the tail end of a conversation that took it for granted that there was value in cheap, unimportant things and in any project governed by "bad taste." As a result, this interview displays all the earmarks of the 1980s cult sensi-bility that was just then taking shape. Even today, cult cinema remains a super-genre whose participants fetishize the illegitimacy of their own cult activities and forms, often wearing their "shame" as a badge of honor in cult contexts. In a sense, this cultural illegitimacy lends these people a narrow ~~...~~ icted legitimacy. Because this legitimacy is ~~...~~ outside the cult nexus, I refer to it as "sub-~~...~~

These are elementary assertions, to be sure, but their implications stretch beyond cult cinema. If we can apply them with understanding, we may be able to understand cult cinema's complex overlaps with other fields. As always, my goal here is to grasp art cinema in all its diversity and nuance. In this chapter, I approach this category through a peculiar combination of attitudes, activities, and forms that I call "cult-art cinema." Cult-art cinema happens in the subcultural spaces where cult cinema and art cinema over-~~...~~-art cinema is that it exemplifies the cult phe-~~...~~ to high-art distinction threatens to erase its ~~...~~ Henenlotter is careful to embrace through his idea of the asterisk that qualifies his work. In this multivalence, cult-art cinema shows us how imperfect most tra... really are. Its qualified aspirationalism sends u... ing board.

But before we can approach cult-art cinema, we must understand cult cinema as a larger whole. We must, then, struggle with questions of definition and history as well as with issues relating to cult production and cult consumption. Only then will we be equipped to tackle the issues most directly related to art cinema, including cult auteurism, cult canonization, and the astonishing diversity of the cult-art movie.

Definitions of "Cult Cinema"

What is cult cinema, anyway? More specifically, is it more accurate to conceive of this phenomenon as a group of subcultural artifacts or, instead, as a group of subcultural processes? There are, after all, traditions for presenting cult cinema in both ways. For example, in their introduction to *The Cult Film Reader* (2008), Ernest Mathijs and Xavier Mendik seem to define cult cinema primarily as a group of movies:

> Cult films transgress common notions of good and bad taste, and they challenge genre conventions and coherent stor... textual references, gore, leaving loose ends or ... talgia. They have troublesome production hist... often-limited accessibility, they have a continuous market value and a long-lasting public presence.[2]

There are, however, problems with presenting cult cinema as a group of movies. Even if cult fans, or "paracinephiles," seem mainly interested in the movies, which is usually the case, there is nothing permanent about which movies are designated as "cult movies." Much like philosophers of art before the interventions of Morris Weitz and George Dickie, cult theorists at times present the reality of *some* cult art as the ahistorical essence of *all* cult art. But this can't work. Have *all* cult films had "troublesome production histories"? Have they *all* "challenge[d] genre convention... And even if they had, how would any of this r...

A more serviceable approach is charted in *Defining Cult Movies* (2003). In introducing this collection, Mark Jancovich and his colleagues pursue a strategy of defining cult cinema in terms of "subcultural ideology":

The "cult movie" is an essentially eclectic category. It is not defined according to some single, unifying feature shared by all cult movies but rather through a "subcultural" ideology in filmmakers, films or audiences [that] are seen as existing in opposition to the "mainstream." . . . "Cult" is largely a matter of the ways in which films are classified in consumption, although it is certainly the case that filmmakers often shared the same "subcultural ideology" as fans and have set out to make self-consciously "cult" materials. . . . The mainstream remains central, despite its incoherence, because it is necessary so that cult fans can produce a sense of distinction. . . . To put it another way, it is necessary because it ~~is only through the idea of the~~ oppositional that cult audiences are able ~~to produce a sense of~~ themselves and the films around which they ~~congregate~~

This definition is useful because it acknowledges the textual multiplicity and contingency of cult cinema but still manages to move beyond it, pursuing the sociological realities that unify cult phenomena. Through their ideas of cult adversarialism, Jancovich and his colleagues indicate how cult participants revalue abject positions, achieving subcultural legitimacy through their opposition to the "mainstream." But we should be careful here, too, for this idea of cult adversarialism is easily overdone. The cult nexus is not deeply militant in its opposition to dominant sectors like mainstream cinema or art cinema.[4] Instead, this oppositionalism is often nominal, limited to subcultures or employed as a marketing strategy only. What is more, cult cinema is not the only super-genre to have constructed itself as an adversary to a context-specific "mainstream." Art cinema has also presented itself as adversarial, ~~oppo~~sing the mainstream and cult cinemas that ~~it is most useful to look at the cult nexus~~ that it is most useful to look at the cult nexus as a set of nondominant cultural positions whose oppositionalism and legitimacy are mainly limited to cult subcultures.[5] This point of view can help us avoid confusion with the avant-garde, which is of course a deeply adversarial sector of art cinema whose legitimacy, like that of cult cinema, is subcultural in nature — but whose values, unlike those of cult cinema, are claimed by the more traditional art cinemas.

A Brief History of Cult Cinema

"Even a bad movie can have a good trailer. Our lives should be so exciting."
— FULLTIME KILLER (DIR. JOHNNIE TO AND WAI KA-FAI, 2001)

Assuming that our aim is to grasp cult cinema as a set of dominated and illegitimate cultural positions and not as a set of underground movies, we need to forget for now all the movies that currently typify cult cinema. Once we do this, we will understand why it was that through the 1960s art-house tastes were often called "cult" tastes in the United States by critics like Andrew Sarris, Susan Sontag, and Amos Vogel.[6] These tastemakers weren't just wrong. Rather, in their day, the postwar European art cinemas did not yet represent a fully traditional or "legitimate" adjunct of the American cinematic establishment, which explains in part why art-film sexuality could be sold for many years beside exploitation sexuality on an American circuit mainly devoted to exploitation films.[7] With time, the status of the postwar art cinemas was recognized by more American critics and mark cialized circuit of film festivals, art houses, and the traditional art film could no longer be uphe in American circles; it had become far too highbrow and official.

After the 60s, traditional film could no longer be upheld as an oppositional cult taste in American circles; it had become far too highbrow and official.

The cult sensibility, as now constructed, does share some things with high-art sensibilities. For example, both cult cinema and art cinema portray themselves as indie outsiders in an industry dominated by Hollywood—and both cinemas, broadly conceived, seem equally disingenuous in making these claims.[8] But it is the differences between these two cinemas that should guide our thinking about them. The cult sensibility c art values by endorsing an active audience and based commercialism. Cult cinema would be hard pressed to reject these aspects of itself, given how often it has in the United States been identified with the trash aesthetic that emerged from a youth-oriented taste for the exploitation flicks and "midnight movies" first produced in abundance in the 1950s and 1960s. The déclassé popularity of these films coalesced into a distinctive sensibility in the 1980s, when cult established a nostalgic identification with the declining exploitation circuit. At that point, "cult cinema became self-aware of its status as cult," accordi "the ritualistic reception of cult cinema beca sequent growth of cult institutions—trigge that traditional critics were too willfully ignorant to say anything useful about low-end genres like horror films, sex movies, action movies, thrillers, teen

Cult sensibility departs from art cinema. High art values by endorsing an active culture and by embracing its own genre-based commercialism.

Cult cinema became self-aware of its status as cult.

comedies, and so on—meant there were "more means to 'cultify' films."[10] As a result, cult cinema grew rapidly. Its institutions came to include festivals like the Chiller Theater Expo and the Brussels International Festival of Fantastic Film, with similar events sweeping Europe, Asia, and the Americas from the 1980s on. (Of course, cult movies have also had a place at traditional festivals, where they've often been cordoned into midnight slots.)[11] In the United States, these institutions have included high-profile "zines" such as Michael Weldon's *Psychotronic Video* and much lower-profile mags like Bill Landis's *Sleazoid Express*. Eventually, of course, these institutions would come to include Internet sites like Softcore Reviews, b-independent.com, Bloody Disgusting, and Alternative Cinema, whose proliferation over the past fifteen years has greatly expanded the scope of cult subcultures.

What is more, since the 1980s, the study of cult cinema has taken its place in the academy as most of the grand theories have broken down, prompting ~~litional~~ auteur study and from psychoanalytic ~~torical,~~ culturalist analysis, one of whose aims is ~~stes,~~ including the most déclassé. This academic process has correlated with the growth of cultural studies and the publication of landmark works on popular genres like horror (e.g., Carol Clover's *Men, Women, and Chain Saws*, 1992; and Joan Hawkins's *Cutting Edge*, 2000), pornography (e.g., Linda Williams's *Hard Core*, 1989; and Linda Ruth Williams's *The Erotic Thriller in Contemporary Cinema*, 2005), and exploitation (e.g., Eric Schaefer's *"Bold! Daring! Shocking! True!"* 1999). Today, the most cited piece on cult cinema remains Jeffrey Sconce's 1995 *Screen* article "'Trashing' the Academy," which explained how cult participants could be adversarial and dominated at the same time, while the most cited books include *Defining Cult Movies* and *The Cult Film Reader*. And it is no wonder that the most influential sociological theory in film studies, Pierre Bourdieu's *Distinction: A Social Critique of the Judgement of Taste* (1979), has a decidedly culturalist bent. Along with academic sites in the United Kingdom, including the Cult Film Archive at University College Northampton and the Centre for Research into Extreme and Alternative Media at the University of Wales, these resources have led to the consensus that cult cinema, in its frequent trashiness, has much to teach us about the contemporary.

Cult Production and Cult Consumption

When I talk about "cult production," I am not talking about movie production per se. Instead, I am talking about the creation of the illegitimate value ; cult forums and films. Here some distinctions help. The first distinguishes intentional cult production by cult directors and promoters from unintentional cult production by hapless low-budget directors *or* by directors whose movies, regardless of whether successful on their own, have been appropriated as cult objects against their makers' manifest wishes. In the United States, intentional cult production is a relatively recent phenomenon that has gained traction only since the 1980s. Clear-cut cult directors like Troma Entertainment's Lloyd Kaufman often operate in the low-budget industrial sectors promoted by grassroots cult institutions. But there are also higher-budget cult directors to consider in cult niches; for example, in the United States, these directors include icons like George Romero, Wes Craven, Tim Burton, Robert Rodriguez, and Quentin Tarantino. Since cult production is so reception-oriented, we must also identify executive producers like Roger Corman and Michael Raso, distributors like Something Weird, and magazines like *Fangoria* [handwritten annotation] Without the specialized audiences that these p[...] energized, cult directors would have less incen[...] films in the first place.

On the other hand, unintentional cult production doesn't qualify as cult production in the sense outlined above, for it does not involve directors or promoters who knowingly apply illegitimate values to their movies with the intention of creating cult effects. Many of the most famous cult auteurs, including Ed Wood, actually qualify as unintentional cult directors. In celebrated cult classics like *Glen or Glenda* (1953) or *Plan 9 from Outer Space* (1959), Wood was a hapless outsider trying in hilarious ways to make the best films he could with little experience or funding. Some of these unintentional producers changed into intentional cult producers over the course of their long careers—which was arguably true of Wood, and which was definitely true of Corman. This cult avant-garde, so to speak, spawned today's cult cinema. These creators did not always foresee the outcomes of their efforts, but they were savvy enough to take advantage of the results, especially when it became clear that campiness had commercial appeal. By contrast, the other type of unintentional production is much less friendly to cult cinema. This type covers films appropriated after production from many different contexts, including everything from Robert Wiene's movie *Das cabinet des Dr. Caligari* (1919) and Leni Riefenstahl's *Triumph of the Will* [...] *Eraserhead* (1976), James Cameron's *Titanic* (19[...] piece *Man Bites Dog* (1992). In all these cases, t[...] films may be viewed as unintentional cult pr[...], leaving the main responsibility for their later cult status to secondary distributors and consumers who over time promoted their cult value.

We should also make an important distinction between cult consumption and the traditional reception of high art, which is often tied to art cinema. The neo-Kantian ideal of aesthetic disinterest is the linchpin of most legitimate aesthetics, and this applies to the cinema as well as to more traditional art media. Practical understandings of "disinterest" usually equate it with "close attention," a viewing posture that aids immersion, allowing viewers to gather as much of an artwork's detail as possible. The ideal of disinterest is also useful to cultural authorities and institutions in that it justifies and maintains social control; it has been thought that training people to adopt this aesthetic posture cultivates everything from fair play to individual restraint in public places, such as crowded museums and art houses. Hence, this ideal has been tied to notions of refinement and spirituality.

Cult consumption has long been celebrated as a class-oriented rejection of this high-art ideal. Consider the carnivalesque excitement inspired by screenings of midnight movies like *Freaks* (1932), *Reefer Madness* (1936), *Mom and Dad* (1945), *Blood Feast* (1963), *El Topo* (1970), *The Rocky Horror Picture Show* (1975), and *The Toxic Avenger* (1984). This kind of hullabaloo is a clear sign of cult cinema's rejection of aesthetic disinterest. The cult audiences that I have observed here in Chicago seem unified by their need to express themselves physically; they seem most pleased if they can laugh without regard for appropriateness.[12] It is not surprising, then, that this style of cult consumption has alarmed traditional auteurs (e.g., Peter Greenaway), who have always argued _____ be the sole determinant of the cinematic ex- _____ ur in the classic sense wants to do is to encour- _____ of the cinematic experience, which is the sub- versive goal of cult _____ galitarian, interactive modes of consumption.

But we should bear in mind that the oppositionalism of cult cinema is more nostalgic than militant. Cult fans seem more interested in celebrating _____ hting to create a more utopian present. This _____ cult consumption became self-conscious only _____ e déclassé films now linked to the cult sensibility began shifting from public, theatrical exhibition to a less threatening mode of private home viewing. In other words, the cult sensibility coalesced around the idea of public consumption at the same time that the public side of movie consumption was becoming a thing of the past.[13] The sense of a lost cinematic community that resulted from this revaluation of public consumption is today manifest in cult cinema's Internet orientation. The Internet has _____ ays to form communities and to register their _____ ws. But this experience has most often been _____ f computers and iPads, so it has guaranteed little in the way of flesh-and-blood togetherness—and *very* little in the way of social protest or of (sub)cultural revolution. In my view, there is nothing particularly aggressive here, especially given how insular most aspects of cult cinema actually are. Paracinephiles might style themselves as militants, as subcultural "avengers" even, but cult cinema as a whole in no sense threatens consumer culture. Instead, it reinforces that [...] for hegemony, cult fans and the sensibility the [...] distinction, struggling to maintain the viabilit[...] within the mainstream.

Cult Canonization, Cult Auteurism, and Cult-Art Varieties

To understand the concept of cult-art cinema, we must consider where we might locate a cult-art movie and how we might identify it within the confusing diversity of cult cinema as a whole. By definition, a cult-art movie seems to have, or to aspire to, two kinds of distinction: cult value and high-art value. It is thus found in the overlap of cult cinema and art cinema. This strain of cult-art movie may be identified in much the same way we identify more legitimate art movies: by presenting evi[...] cult canonization. But here cult-art cinema cr[...] cult fans have long sought to devise, in the v[...] "an alternative canon of cinema, pitched against the 'official' canon,"[14] we cannot assume that this canon amounts to cult cinema's high art. A canonical cult movie is often considered a "cult classic," but these classics come in many varieties, most of which are *not* ascribed high-art value. This is true, for example, of Henenlotter's movies and of Troma's gross-out comedies; it is also true of individual cult classics, from Herschell Gordon Lewis's aforementioned *Blood Feast* to Raimi's *Evil Dead* movies (1981, 1987), John Carpenter's *They Live* (1988), Lloyd Kaufman's *Tromeo and Juliet* (1996), Jay Lee's *Zombie Strippers* (2008), and many, many others. As it turns out, the cult-cinema canon has relied on a flexible array of criteria, which are very loose and derive from many different quarters. This is one reason the cult nexus is so rich and so byzantine—and why its canons are in such a rapid and continual state of flux.

On the other hand, as noted above, cult institutions have grown more entrenched over the past thirty years. With this institutionalization has come a newfound stability. During this time, an array of books, magazines, festivals, and websites have been devoted to the cult sensibility, with a few having proved so enduring that they are now recognized as ad hoc institutions unto themselves. (To cite just a handful of examples, consider the institutionalizing effects of Jonathan Rosenbaum and J. Hoberman's critical study *Midnight Movies*, 1983; V. Vale and Andrea Juno's book *Incredibly Strange Films*, 1986; and Gary Morris's magazine-turned-website *Bright Lights Film Journal*.) The presence of this literature in particular has made it more possible to distinguish cult-art movies from other kinds of cult classic. Thus, to make these distinctions, we should first peruse academic collections like *The Cult Film Reader* and *Defining Cult Movies* as well as Mendik and Harper's *Unruly Pleasures* (2000), Mendik and Schneider's *Underground USA* (2002), Mathijs and Mendik's *Alternative Europe* (2004), Sconce's *Sleaze Artists* (2007), and the interconnected volumes of Cline and Weiner's *From the Arthouse to the Grindhouse* (2010) and *Cinema Inferno* (2010). By examining the movies most often cited here, cult theorists may get a sense of what the cult canon has been held to be over time by fans, critics, and institutions, with the significant advantage of academic reliability. After we have achieved these goals, we will be in better position to make distinctions among various kinds of cult classic. Then we must lean on the distinctions we drew earlier in this chapter between intentional and unintentional forms of cult auteurism.

Before emphasizing three intentional kinds of cult-art movies, I want to discount two unintentional kinds. The first type involves cult-art movies appropriated from other spheres. The cult canon has often included experimental cinemas, mainstream cinemas, and world cinemas that were initially made and celebrated far from cult cinema as we currently imagine it. Some of these films represent unintentional cult-art movies, like *Das cabinet des Dr. Caligari*, *Triumph of the Will*, and *Eraserhead* as well as Luis Buñuel's "Un chien andalou" (1929); Riefenstahl's *Olympia* (1938); Orson Welles's *Touch of Evil* (1958); Jean-Luc Godard's *Le week-end* (1967); Stanley Kubrick's *A Clockwork Orange* (1971); Stan Brakhage's *The Act of Seeing with One's Own Eyes* (1971); David Cronenberg's *Videodrome* (1983), *Dead Ringers* (1988), and even *Crash* (1996); John Dahl's *The Last Seduction* (1994); the Coen brothers' *Big Lebowski* (1998); and Richard Kelly's *Donnie Darko* (2001), to cite only a few. The overlaps with more legitimate cinemas in evidence in this list indicate that the cult sensibility has not been restricted to movies with low budgets and lower cultural status (though those have been two of cult cinema's primary identi-
d, cult tastes are *underground* tastes that may
s that process is directed by subcultural audi-
values and who practice illegitimate modes
of consumption. If we blend these ideas of cult with an awareness that cult auteurism is often unintentional, we can reconcile and accept two conflicting

An unintentional cult-art movie: a still from John Dahl's noir-inflected indie, *The Last Seduction* (1994), starring Linda Fiorentino (pictured) as femme fatale Bridget Gregory. The film's underground success allowed it to be rereleased in theatrical art houses. © 1994 Incorporated Television Company and October Films.

facts: directors like Welles, Brakhage, and Kubrick were traditional auteurs whose main allegiance was to a traditional aesthetic; they were also auteurs whose films have often been praised as cult classics.

This kind of cult appropriation and elevation amounts to a populist intervention that forcibly reappraises a film that may have failed in legitimate forums or that may have fallen out of favor with mainstream critics—a description that applies as readily to indie films such as *The Last Seduction* and *Donnie Darko* as to Hollywood classics like *Touch of Evil*. *The Last Seduction* and *Donnie Darko* were both mid-budget indie art films that initially failed in legitimate channels: *The Last Seduction* failed to find a theatrical distributor, while *Donnie Darko* failed to earn back its production financing in its first go-round in theaters.[15] But in both cases, these movies earned an underground cult following during their nontheatrical releases that gave them a chance for a successful rerelease in theatrical art houses, which in turn allowed them to earn even more money in their subsequent releases through ancillary windows. It is as if the people spoke—and though their voice has always been te sectors, it lent these films an unintentional ox-office success and to positive reappraisals that in effect salvaged their legitimacy.

The second type of cult-art movie that I want to put to the side is the kind that results from the fetishization of directorial incompetence: in other words, "badfilm."[16] I have no problem with paracinephiles who celebrate "bad" movies. But we should remember that auteurism implies control, purity, individuality, and intentional aspiration—and cult auteurism implies these things as surely as any other auteurism. External critics have often mocked the very idea of the cult auteur. This mockery may be undercut by noting that such critics are seldom familiar with the traditions of the cult genres and subcultures that they mock. As a result, such critics have a tendency to confuse adherence to cult convention with straight ineptitude—as when antiporn critics laugh at softcore's narrative-number format, which only constitutes the genre's most fundamental formal convention. That said, badfilm—which I define as a tour de force of authentic ineptitude—is always difficult to reconcile with auteurism. If anything, the celebration of the badfilm signals an unintentional cult auteurism that is largely an effect of movie promotion and consumption. Of course, some campy, so-bad-they're-good cult movies have been made that way on purpose. Here we might think of Russ Meyer's *Mudhoney* (1965), Jess Franco's *Vampyros Lesbos* (1971), John Waters's *Pink Flamingos* (1972), Nobuhiko Obayashi's *House* (1977), the transgressive *Hardcore* shorts that Richard Kern made between 1984 and 1993, Rodriguez's *Planet Terror* (2007), Anna Biller's *Viva* (2007), and so on. But the intentional camp

A production still from Anna Biller's cult-art movie *Viva* (2007), which employs intentional camp effects to create a distinctive narrative texture. *Viva* re-creates the classic sexploitation movies of legendary cult auteurs like Radley Metzger and Doris Wishman. Photo by C. Thomas Lewis. Courtesy of Anna Biller.

irony of such works means that we do not need to label them "bad" in any straightforward sense; rather, these movies are rich in complicated aesthetic effects that their creators intended.[17] Although such films may be aligned with the cult of pleasurable bad taste, they cannot be aligned with directorial ineptitude—for their directors found a way to do what they wanted to do within their particular cinematic constraints. But the more common kind of bad movie—where the laughter works against the directors, not with them, and where the irony is a function of the viewers' reception—does not exemplify cult auteurism in any sense properly assigned to the cult audience.

One of the problems here is that bad cult directors typically disown intentional badness. Certainly, the first generation of bad cult directors—individuals like Wood, Doris Wishman, Larry Buchanan, and Andy Milligan, who have all been celebrated in critical forums as intentional auteurs—did not fetishize their own incompetence. Indeed, there is often little evidence beyond their embrace of what others have defined as their "trashy" aesthetic to support the idea that they were trying to make pleasurably horrid movies.

For the most part, then, their auteurism is a product of cult consumption, not of cult production—which means they are better positioned as significant "failures" whose technical and stylistic incompetence influenced later directors, like Jim Wynorski and Henenlotter. But not even the later directors have consistently promoted themselves in terms of an ironic camp control that functions as a subculturally legitimate auteurism. The latter might cast themselves as "unimportant," and they might glorify bad taste and cheap things, but they rarely take any explicit pleasure in the bad cinematic qualities imparted by their own incompetence. Bad auteurs become bad auteurs, it seems, despite themselves, with their authoritative ineptitude a product of certain styles of consumption and evaluation. This dynamic reminds us of [...] ethic. But it is so far removed from traditional [...] king whether the idea of the bad cult auteur [...]ts.[18]

As I have already noted, there are at least three main types of intentional cult-art movie. What unifies these types is their ambivalence about their cult identity, an ambivalence that seems to be a function of their makers' high-art aspirationalism—which is forever qualified, it appears, by cult cinema's metaphorical asterisk. Perhaps the best example of this ambivalence involves the cult movies that have *too much* legitimacy as a result of their provenance. This phenomenon is most evident on the festival circuit, where Bong Joon-ho, Tomas Alfredson, Tarantino, Park Chan-wook, Lars von Trier, and others have released movies that we might as well classify as cult-art films. In their production values, distribution, and prestige, movies such as Bong's moody toxic-creature film *The Host* (2006), Alfredson's equally moody vampire movie *Let the Right One In* (2008), Tarantino's riotous Nazi-revenge picture *Inglourious Basterds* (2009), Park's vampire comedy *Thirst* (2009), and von Trier's torture-porn meditation *Antichrist* (2009) are all traditional art films. They have won awards, critical acclaim, and global distribution through their mastery of the devices of the traditional art film and through the reputations of their makers. Indeed, these directors are veterans of the festival circuit, where they have served on juries, and where they have appeared at Cannes. [...] heir new movies as *cult*-art movies, then, is the [...]ody parts, the chills and thrills and spasms of [...] a different sense, what has made their movies cult-art movies is that traditionalists still do not always accept their genre-coded materials. Though horror and sex have been a regular part of film festivals for quite some time, horror films and sex films continue to face resistance from conservative cinephiles and critics. (See, for example, Joan Hawkins's apt critique of how Park's award-winning gore fests have been received by traditional critics like Manohla Dargis of the *New York Times*.)[19] Thus an argument remains for labeling these art films "cult" movies on a formal basis alone, even if such movies are a highly distinguished form of cult production that is more legitimate than illegitimate. But this argument is fading, I think, for other equally authoritative critics have been depicting cult sex and cult violence as more of the same, seeing in it all the tedium of art-world tradition. (See, for example, David Ansen's *Newsweek* essay "Shock and Yawn.")

A more sustainable, albeit still ambivalent, cult-art identity is evident in the quasi-legitimate films of cult auteurs like Mario Bava and Dario Argento, much of whose work has been released through illegitimate cult-movie mechanisms and not through legitimate art-film mechanisms, but has since then gathered acclaim in both illegitimate *and* legitimate circles.[20] Given that the cult nexus has grown more institutionalized over the past thirty years, we might say that *all* movies produced for cult consumption may claim the "cult movie" label, just as all movies produced for festival distribution may claim the "art film" label. Of course, this sort of cult movie has not earned any *classic* status, let alone any high-art status—but it is free to begin earning such status at the subcultural level. Cult auteurs, like traditional auteurs, first seek praise for their films through cult critics, viewers, and institutions, albeit in channels often defined as illegitimate. Indeed, the most respected films of many auteurs currently deemed "quasi-legitimate" (including Bava, Corman, Meyer, Koji Wakamatsu, Romero, Radley Metzger/Henry Paris, Craven, the Mitchell brothers, Wakefield Poole, Gerard Damiano, Tobe Hooper, Just Jaeckin, Obayashi, Argento, Tinto Brass, John Woo, Andrew Blake, Takashi Miike, Johnnie To, Eli Roth, Nacho Cerdà, and others) were typically identified with an illegitimate form of cult auteurism and an illegitimate embrace of genre-branded materials and genre-branded distributions. But as these movies achieved classic status within cult, the trend over time has been for those movies to become detached from their original channels and their original subgenres, freeing them to develop affiliations with more culturally legitimate institutions, including distri[...] lection.[21] Legitimate forums like film festival[...] theaters, and even crossover magazines like *Sig[...]* Mad, the Bad, and the Dangerous" identified many of these movies as auteur movies) have often been among the first forums to promote the canonical value of these movies and their directors at the cultural level.[22]

If we made a list of admired movies by these and other quasi-legitimate auteurs, we would find many cult classics that have been admired culturally or subculturally for their aesthetics, that is, for their contributions to the art of cinema. Such films include *Black Sabbath* (1963), *The Evil Eye* (1963), and *Blood and Black Lace* (1964); *The Masque of the Red Death* (1964); *Faster, Pussycat! Kill! Kill!* (1965); *Secrets Behind the Wall* (1965); *Night of the Living Dead* (1968); *Camille 2000* (1969) and *The Opening of Misty Beethoven* (1975); *The Last House on the Left* (1972); *Behind the Green Door* (1972); *Bijou* (1972); *The Devil in Miss Jones* (1973); *The Texas Chainsaw Massacre* (1974); *Histoire d'O* (1975); *House* (1977); *Suspiria* (1977) and *Tenebre* (1982); *La chiave* (1983); *The Killer* (1989) and *Hard Boiled* (1992); *Paris Chic* (1997) and *Hard Edge* (2003); *Audition* (1999); *Fulltime Killer* (2001) and *Breaking News* (2004); *Hostel* (2005); and "Aftermath" (1994) and *The Abandoned* (2006). In addition to these quasi-legitimate classics, we could add the Hollywood classics of cult directors such as Samuel Fuller, including *Shock Corridor* (1963), *The Naked Kiss* (1964), and *White Dog* (1982), and the high-art canons of cult Hollywood genres, like film noir. Indeed, we could even add a number of slashers and torture-porn films that have recently arrived from France, including *Dans ma peau* (2002), *Haute tension* (2003), *Frontière(s)* (2007), *À l'intérieur* (2007), and *Martyrs* (2008), along with certain Japanese pinks, including *The Glamorous Life of Sachiko Hanai* (2004). Praised as auteur vehicles and lumped into movements (e.g., the "new wave of French horror" and the "pink nouvelle vague"), these films are quasi-legitimate examples of cult-art cinema. When we add them and other cases to our idea of art cinema, we re-orient tradi-[...] xpand it both quantitatively and qualitatively. [...] t legitimate critics and legitimate institutions [...] n of this kind of cult-art movie. For example, it was legitimate critics from legitimate forums such as the *Village Voice* that canonized "the film noir high end" by praising films like "Jacques Tourneur's quietist *Out of the Past* (1947)" over the more "pulpy inventions" of lowbrow noir classics like "Edgar G. Ulmer's low-end *Detour* (1945)."[23] But there is one final type of cult-art movie, and it doesn't rely on legitimate critics for [...] does not have to be validated by outsiders in [...] *within* a given cult subculture. After all, cult [...] ons are more than capable of making distinctions among cult movies on their own.

To get a sense of the true scope of the art cinema super-genre, then, we must acquaint ourselves with sectors that legitimate critics rarely, if ever, visit. Thus, if we looked at contemporary American softcore, we would find a cult auteur like Tony Marsiglia, whose value has been beyond dispute according to sites like b-independent.com, Softcore Reviews, and Alternative Cinema. As a result, we would have to integrate ultra-low-budget, cult-softcore movies like *Lust for Dracula* (2004), *Sinful* (2006), and *Chantal* (2007) into our notion of art cinema. We would also have to add a number of very differ-

A still from Russ Meyer's cult-art movie *Faster, Pussycat! Kill! Kill!* (1965), a lowbrow auteur vehicle with a kinetic visual style refined on the exploitation circuit. © 1965 Eve Productions.

Promotional material for Tony Marsiglia's cult-art movie *Chantal* (2007). The status of this type of art cinema is generally recognized within a cult subculture but not outside it. © 2007 Seduction Cinema. Used courtesy of Michael Raso and Pop Cinema.

ent auteur vehicles, such as Tom Lazarus's corporate-softcore films, *Word of Mouth* (1999) and *House of Love* (2000). From there, we could move to Spanish exploitation and look at the independent horror auteur Jess Franco, whose output is praised in cult circles but is rarely recognized outside them. Franco's low-budget movies, though often exceptionally confusing, have achieved a patina of the personal through the passage of time and through their oddly recognizable swirls of psychosexual incoherence. Or we might study American hardcore by looking at single videos, like Gregory Dark's *New Wave Hookers* (1985), or entire oeuvres, like that of Michael Ninn. As a subculture, the world of adult movies seems to value Ninn productions like *Latex* (1995) over the "prestige" hardcore of the higher-profile Blake.

These lists could go on and on. Though it is helpful to compile such lists in untraditional contexts where high-end movies count as high culture, we needn't enumerate every auteur and every "masterpiece." Nor do we need to perform formalist inquiries, surveying cult cinema for traditional art-film techniques — including disinterested stylization, deep focus, the long take, the tracking shot, and slow pacing — or relevant cult mutations of these highly venerated techniques.[24] Cult-art movies clearly exist, as certified by the fact that movies in so many low forms — including the Italo-Spanish spaghetti western, the Japanese pink, the Italian *giallo*, the British Hammer film, the American torture-porn movie, and the Hong Kong action film, to name just a few — have functioned as high art with grown up around them. When made, circulate cult-art movies have even generated a qualifie subcultures.[25]

What is fascinating is that even the least recognized cult-art auteurs seem at best ambivalent about their cult identities. Such auteurs often have little prestige outside their subcultures and are mostly confined to cult sectors — and often happily, since they have so little real capital or status that they often can only express their gratitude to their backers for having taken a chance on them. But there is a crucial sense in which tl with a more established status: they have legi whether they have legitimate accomplishmen dom help having mixed feelings about their cult identity, which in legitimate contexts functions as a kind of psychological asterisk that qualifies their artistic status. Auteurs like Marsiglia, Lazarus, Franco, Dark, and Ninn count themselves as artists first and as *cult* artists second.[26] It is likely that they would be happy to leave the cult world fully behind if the canonical processes that elevated them within that world began to push them away from it, leading them (like Argento) to greater recognition and to greater opportunity in more legitimate cultural locations. Not only would a broader canonization help these illegitimate filmmakers make a deeper impression on cinema history, it would help them remove the asterisks from their reputations.

Unfortunately, because cult cinema rarely hides or denies its own commercialism, it can be difficult for aspirational movies produced in cult subcultures to come across as "pure" (unless we look at such movies from *inside* those subcultures, where they may be positioned as the purest cinema available). Thus, no matter how ready cult auteurs are to transcend their cult status, even directors like Argento tend to be defined by the cult provenance of their most ~~highly acclaimed~~ films. That distribution context becomes a permanent part ~~of their~~ directors reach the pinnacle of their career in a ~~~~ probably never lose their cult status entirely—not even if their ~~~~ ctioned as a kind of high art. Indeed, in such cases, their cult status seems even more likely to stick to them, to hang over them like an asterisk.

CHAPTER 6

Revisiting "The Two Avant-Gardes"

In 1975, Peter Wollen published his article "The Two Avant-Gardes" in *Studio International*. There he proposed that two experimental cinemas were at work in Europe, with one centered around a cooperative movement of avant-garde filmmakers like Peter Gidal, Malcolm Le Grice, and Birgit Hein, and the other around experimental auteurs like Jean-Luc Godard and the team of Jean-Marie Straub and Danièle Huillet, who often worked in a more commercial, feature-length format that relied more consistently on narrative. Wollen argued that the New American Cinema was the model for the first European avant-garde but that the United States lacked the second type. Though this last observation seemed to neglect classic experimental American auteurs both major (John Cassavetes) and minor (Susan Sontag), Wollen's piece was a good one whose virtues have continued to make it useful today, judging from how often it is cited.

But so much has changed since 1975 that Wollen's essay is now clearly ripe for an update. In pursuing this goal, however, we should revise Wollen's methods along with his coverage. For it is not clear that his avant-gardes were ever comparable at the ontological level. This is no knock on Wollen, whose public-intellectual purposes were adapted to a set of politics that weren't academic in the same sense as mine. But since it is academics who cite "The Two Avant-Gardes," we should consider the epistemological implications of its method. Wollen compared a large, inclusive, and institutional avant-garde tradition that was defined by its alternative distribution to a more exclusive, political, art-historical tradition that was defined by its auteurs, critics, and intellectuals. This isn't to deny that the second tradition had a reality as a concept; indeed, there is evidence that this concept has expanded since 1975 such that it may now cover even more experimental auteurs in Europe, Asia, and the Americas than before. But this second tradition has remained primarily evaluative, political, and conceptual. By contrast, Wollen's first avant-garde has, by dint of its alternative distribution scheme, an inarguable institutional reality of its own, which has allowed this experimental world to develop its own internal traditions.

Indeed, in the United States, these traditions have made it possible to perceive this avant-garde as loosely divided into two interconnected co-op communities: the grassroots communities that have gathered around do-it-yourself spaces, microcinemas, Internet lounges, and hipster scenes, and the more institutionalized (or "university-made") avant-gardes that have operated through colleges, museums, and the major media arts centers, which have relied to some degree on government subsidies.[1] Of course, these two co-op communities cannot be fully differentiated. Often, the more established avant-garde institutions have DIY roots, and individual participants in the co-op world can play roles in both spheres. That said, in American experimental cinema, there is a clear perception that a schism separates these two co-op spheres; this perception has in turn played an outsize role in the signature discourses that have helped shape the co-op avant-gardes.

In the final sections of this chapter, I theorize these avant-gardes, paying heed to how they differ from the avant-gardes as framed by Wollen and speculating as to what these differences tell us about art cinema as a whole. To make this discussion more concrete, I analyze recent scholarship on the subject, including Kathryn Ramey's "Between Art, Industry and Academia" (2002) and Michael Zryd's "The Academy and the Avant-Garde" (2006). These nuanced articles, which rely on ethnographic and historical methods, have allowed me to generate a new understanding of the cooperative movement and its place within art cinema. This understanding is grounded in an understanding of the avant-garde's anti-institutional logic, which creates an "authenticity problematic" that dogs experimentalists (as well as their promoters, whose interests differ from those of the artists) as they circulate through institutions, eking out careers. As it happens, this authenticity problematic—which resembles a similar dynamic evident in more traditional areas of art cinema, American indie cinema in particular—has not been a challenge for avant-garde communities alone. It has also been a challenge for the many institutions that support experimental cinema.

Art Cinema's Own Art Cinema

At this point, we should remember that in this book we are using "art cinema" as an umbrella classifier that allows its users to group different cinemas together through their common aspirationalism while allowing for subcul-

The interior of the original premises of Aurora Picture Show, the Houston microcinema founded in 1998. Founder Andrea Grover converted a 1924 wooden church, which she and her family lived in, for this purpose. The site was retired in 2009 as Aurora began a "nomadic" existence during its transition to a permanent site. Courtesy of Aurora Picture Show.

tural variations. The fact that this definition of art cinema is supple enough to contain mainstream art movies and cult-art movies as well as traditional art films implies that it can contain experimental movies, too. Indeed, there is a sense in which this definition virtually *compels* us to include the avant-garde, which exaggerates many of the high-art and indie dynamics found elsewhere in art cinema. For that reason, I look on avant-garde cinema as art cinema's most aspirational area—that is, its very own art cinema.

Before I do anything, then, I should make note of the common academic account that positions avant-garde cinema as totally separate from art cinema. In this separatist view, the avant-garde is motivated by activist purposes to occupy a rigidly noncommercial space, one that is far less commercial in its form, marketing, and distribution than is art cinema as traditionally defined.[2] But I would question this account in a number of ways. First, as I detail below, there is the common historical lineage to consider. Before the Second World War, it was common to interchange "avant-garde," "art cinema," and "art films" when referring to an aspirational cinema. Only after the war did the differences among these fields coalesce and come to seem

natural and obvious—largely due to the success of the postwar European art film, which dominated mainstream ideas of what counted as an "art cinema" or an "art film" after 1945. Around the same time, the avant-garde made itself more distinctive in cinema as a whole because its practitioners identified it more fully with anticommercial values, which culminated in the institutionalization of cooperative distribution in the 1960s. Nonetheless, the historical link between the avant-garde and art cinema remained strong. As a consequence, there are academics who still refer to the interwar avant-gardes as "art cinema," and a number of popular crossover critics still use that term to refer both to the postwar avant-garde and to contemporary video art.[3]

The reason these academics and critics can do this is that there is more than just a historical link between the two areas. There are striking consistencies in rhetoric, value, and ideology as well. Both the avant-garde world and the festival world depend on auteurist values—and though they express it in different ways and with different intensities, both subscribe to very similar anticommercial ideals. Further, both fields are energized by tensions between aesthetics and politics, for both are left-leaning sectors whose participants are divided between their concern for aesthetics on the one hand and for political imperatives on the other. If there is a true division here, it is one that has been maintained over the past fifty years in the co-op avant-gardes by non-profit distribution, which has encouraged far greater diversity in the form of experimental films and in the politics of their makers even as it has discouraged bigger-budget productions. This tradeoff has allowed co-ops to maintain their grip on the avant-garde label by leaving them firmly fixed within the marginal cultural position that has long defined avant-garde authenticity. Given all these factors, it seems reasonable to consider avant-garde cinema as a variant of art cinema with a *comparatively* separate place from more commercial forms of art cinema like the traditional art film. This distance is maintained by the avant-garde's reliably noncommercial distribution.[4]

Before reviewing the history of avant-garde cinema in more depth, we should say something about the terms in use here, including "avant-garde" and "experimental" as well as "alternative," "underground," and "independent." To be in accord with the militant implications of "avant-garde," any cinema that it names should be at the forefront of an art tradition that is both politically and artistically transgressive; it should also imply an active or activ*ist* connection to social experience. These expectations form what Jeffrey Skoller has called "the recurring refrain of the twentieth-century historical avant-garde: the problem of integrating social engagement and innovative aesthetic practice."[5] That said, not all avant-garde filmmakers have had to live up to these standards—and not all have tried. After all, if we survey the history of the field, the idea that avant-gardists must be in the vanguard of real change, or that they must be going somewhere radically new in the sense of style or politics, makes little sense. American avant-garde cinema has been marked by a diversity of individual purposes and a diversity of artisanal methods. So while its resistance to commodity-based media has generally been obvious, its use of experiment as a way of spurring Situationist revolt or as a tool for stirring civil-rights consciousness has been less consistent. Even the idea that the field is always experimental does not necessarily square with the fact that experimentalists are often simply pushing forward well-worn, albeit noncommercial and fairly political, art traditions.

These difficulties are not that odd, though, for in art, category designations rarely make perfect sense. And figuring out what sense they *do* make is often a question of gaining a wide enough perspective. We know at this point that avant-garde practice in American art cinema has been at its most diverse since 1960. During that span, many terms have been applied to this sector, with "avant-garde" and "experimental" having for some time been used almost interchangeably.[6] This near equivalence is fine, I believe; in fact, that is how I use the terms myself. While it does help to remember that "avant-garde" has more historical specificity than does "experimental," it does not help to get too hung up on the authenticity of our terms. On the other hand, some terms cannot isolate this cinema; these labels include "independent," "alternative," and "underground." Though these terms can describe the avant-garde, each is too broad in its references to distinguish this art cinema,[7] for each may be applied to cinemas that benefit from more commercial distributions. Only the terms "avant-garde" and "experimental" serve as fairly reliable signposts in this context—with the caveat that a label can isolate a field of art even if that field has never really lived up to the expectations implicit to the label.

As noted, the link between avant-garde cinema and art cinema is historical, rooted in the traditional designation of high-profile avant-garde films from the 1920s and 1930s as "art films" or "art cinema." But neither the idea of the traditional art film as a feature-length narrative form nor the idea of it as a new-wave phenomenon coalesced until after the Second World War. It was at that point that today's increasingly specific distinctions emerged.[8] This suggests that the history of experimental cinema is split. The first phase was an interwar period in which European directors were the leaders, theorists, and innovators. According to the film historian A. L. Rees, this first phase may be subdivided between a "poetic avant-garde," comprising artists working in an art-world capacity on more-or-less abstract films, and a "narrative avant-garde," comprising auteurs more closely involved with commercial industries and more likely to rely on some narrative and some realism in their experimental works.[9] In films such as "Le retour à la raison" (Man Ray, 1923), "Symphonie diagonale" (Viking Eggeling, 1924), "Ballet mécanique" (Fernand Léger and Dudley Murphy, 1924), and "Anémic cinema" (Marcel Duchamp, 1926), the artists of the poetic avant-garde constructed a playful, noncommercial cinema that dissolved realistic illusion in montage, abstraction, and surrealistic whimsy. The narrative avant-garde included the German expressionists and "the Soviet school of Eisenstein, Pudovkin, Kuleshov and Shub, the French 'Impressionists' such as Louis Delluc, Jean Epstein and Germaine Dulac, the Japanese director Kinugasa, and independent directors such as Gance, Murnau and Dreyer."[10] This second phase of the avant-garde was more political and far more plot-oriented than the first, as shown by its equivocal relations with photographic realism and classical narrative. This period also witnessed the birth of crucial American cinemas in both experimental categories, like the one that emerged from the Stieglitz circle through "city symphonies" such as "Manhatta" (Paul Strand and Charles Sheeler, 1921). These interwar avant-gardes fell apart for two major reasons: the coming of sound cinema and broader political events leading up to the

Second World War. After 1927, the coming of sound—which avant-gardists at first resisted on aesthetic grounds, though their resistance often spoke to economic necessities as well—contributed to the belief that Hollywood was both technically *and* economically superior.[11] But the most obvious problem facing the avant-garde during the 1930s was the coming of the war, which sent European filmmakers into exile, relocating much of the movement and its influence to the United States.[12]

In recent years, David James, Paul Arthur, and Chuck Kleinhans have added flesh to this historical narrative, with James adding insights on the "minor cinemas" around Los Angeles as early as the 1920s.[13] But the second phase of avant-garde cinema—which was contemporary with the rise of auteurism and the consecration of the commercial art cinema—had a more consistent North American character. During this crucial phase, the most influential movement was labeled the "New American Cinema" by Jonas Mekas and his many collaborators.[14] This avant-garde was influenced by the European poetic avant-garde, taking from films like Jean Cocteau's *Le sang d'un poète* (1932) the belief that cinema was an artist's medium no less than painting.[15] Its most famous image derived from "Meshes of the Afternoon" (1943), a neo-surrealist work produced by the European-born, American-raised filmmaker Maya Deren and her Czech-exile husband, Alexander Hammid. Deren and colleagues like Stan Brakhage formed the "visionary" phase of this avant-garde, which fused the sexual "psychodrama" of Cocteau to the lyrical modernism of American painting and poetry. Along with Kenneth Anger, Jack Smith, Shirley Clarke, Marie Menken, Jordan Belson, Chick Strand, Bruce Baillie, and many others, Deren and Brakhage pioneered an American underground that was, until the emergence of hardcore, as notorious for its opposition to mainstream sexual culture as for its opposition to mainstream aesthetics. Experimentalists like Anger and Smith had cult followings, and both fought to keep their films out of the courts.[16] Later, through the intercession of innovators like Andy Warhol, the trance films of the visionary era gave way to structural films like *Wavelength* (1967), by the Canadian filmmaker Michael Snow, and *Zorns Lemma* (1970), by the American director Hollis Frampton. It was under the disinterested aegis of the structural film that the New American Cinema made its surest entry into the "pantheon" of high art.

Just as crucial, I think, was Mekas's collaborative formation in the early 1960s of cooperative distribution. In some ways, this new form of distribution resembled an older system established by the Museum of Modern Art's circulating film library in 1935; like the later system, the museum library also encouraged the growth of film societies and of art cinema as a whole.[17] Moreover, neither system was designed for profit, so they were, in that sense, in keeping with the anticommercial rhetoric of high art. That said, after its first burst of success, major changes occurred in the American avant-garde. Until the late 1960s and early 1970s, avant-garde movies had been exhibited almost entirely in theatrical spaces. Whether displayed in museums or classrooms, co-op cinema offered a theater-type experience that the viewer was meant to take in from start to finish. But by the late 1960s, avant-garde movies began to proliferate in art galleries as part of art installations. Throughout the 1970s, these installations increasingly embraced the video artwork of nontheatrical artists such as Nam June Paik, Bruce Nauman, William Wegman, Bill Viola, and many others, a transition away from film technology that was more gradual in the theatrical avant-garde. Though they share common roots, these cinematic high arts have diverged since then, with video artists often unaware of their historical links to the filmmakers of the New American Cinema.[18] Though high-profile crossover artists, like Snow, Lynch, Greenaway, Akerman, Matthew Barney, Chris Marker, Isaac Julien, Apichatpong Weerasethakul, and Miranda July, have over the past decades straddled these divides, many moving-image artists now focus on a single area. Another change noted by scholars is the institutionalization of the field after 1970, the year the Anthology Film Archives was founded.

The institutionalization of experimental cinema has affected every segment of the field. For example, video artists have found opportunities for funding and exhibition through art schools, museums, galleries, and private foundations.[19] What intrigues me most, however, is the institutionalization of important theatrical segments of American experimental cinema. Since the 1960s, artists in this area have found jobs in film schools, film-studies departments, media-arts centers, and museums, and they have distributed their works through co-ops like New York's Film-Makers' Cooperative and San Francisco's Canyon Cinema. They have also exhibited films at festivals like Ann Arbor and MadCat; in microcinemas, like Total Mobile Home Microcinema in San Francisco and Aurora Picture Show in Houston; and through museum theaters, repertory theaters, college classrooms, university theaters, and a multitude of makeshift, DIY spaces.[20] This kind of institutionalization, ad hoc though it often is, has led James to highlight divisions in experimental cinema between "the student film and the faculty film."[21] But more telling divisions exist, I believe, between student artists and faculty artists, or better yet, between both classes of academic and what Ramey has referred to as the "homegrown" experimentalist.[22] These divisions, along with the many institutional conflicts they have fomented, have developed through the historical avant-garde's anti-institutional traditions, which have been extensively detailed by theorists like Bourdieu and Peter Bürger.[23] Such divisions are prob-

The current logo of Aurora Picture Show, the microcinema that has over the past fifteen years screened and funded many experimental filmmakers and video artists. Aurora's increasing institutionalization over that time period has multiplied those artist opportunities. Courtesy of Aurora Picture Show.

lems not only for auteurs but for academics, too, which is to say that they have over the past few decades become issues in academic disciplines such as film studies.

By the time that Wollen published his article in 1975, many of these institutional factors were also influencing the European avant-garde cinemas, particularly those that were organized by co-ops. But though Wollen refers to some of these factors in passing, as when he mentions the "hornet's nest" of video,[24] his focus is on political and aesthetic questions. To understand the strengths and weaknesses of such an approach, we should turn now to his classic essay, "The Two Avant-Gardes."

Wollen's Mixed Fruit

One of the most obvious strengths of Wollen's article is its simplified schema, which splits the European scene into two understandable tribes. It is to his credit that Wollen never pretends that all experimentalists fit neatly into these groups. Indeed, if his methods have value, it comes from the comparative way he deploys them to follow these avant-gardes through time and space, charting their relative cultural positions. As a result, Wollen shows his readers not only what has divided these avant-gardes but also what has united them. For instance, in the avant-garde perspective that Wollen clearly shares, the commercial Hollywood film is equivalent to the commercial art film of the "Antonioni or Fellini or Truffaut" variety, which aspires to the "narrative fiction 35mm film-making" that is Hollywood's specialty.[25] Hence, Wollen traces the

developments of the cinematic avant-garde primarily through the developments of the painters, poets, and musicians who had previously pushed for
anticommercial innovations, both political and aesthetic, within the confines
of the art world. And Wollen notes the conflicts that always arose from the
political bearing of the avant-garde, whose art-world context also included
its spiritual opposite within modernism, art for art's sake.[26]

To me, the strongest aspect of Wollen's article is the way that it depicts
European avant-gardists as specific cultural agents who are inevitably stuck
between one position and another. For instance, the militant, Godard-type
avant-gardist—who, in Wollen's view, emerged through the example of Sergei
Eisenstein—tends to differentiate him- or herself from the co-op avant-
gardist by presenting the latter as a "mere" formalist—that is, as an artist
whose interest in stylistic experiment resembles that of the aesthete, who
would never deign to inspire the masses. But the Godard-type artist must
also guard against "vulgar" Marxists, who depict *all* innovation as "mere" formalism, by claiming the Maoist justification of "scientific experiment."[27] For
the Godardian, revolutionary form must not be merely political at the level
of theme and story; it must also represent a "break with bourgeois norms
of diegesis."[28] The problem with this Brechtian position is that "unless it is
thought through carefully or stopped arbitrarily at some safe point, [it] leads
inevitably straight into the positions of the other avant-garde." For co-op
avant-gardists *also* consider themselves political. The difference is that they
tend to stress formal experiment more than Godard-type auteurs do, so they
must reconcile themselves to "minority status"—and to the public alienation
it yields.

But Wollen's essay leaves its reader with questions and contradictions. The
author notes in closing that, if he went further, he would discuss "the institutional and economic framework in which filmmakers find themselves."[29]
Indeed, had he delved into these topics, Wollen might have discussed the
price that auteurs like Godard had to pay to take part "in the commercial
system," with its stars and budgets—and its isolation from art collectives and
their sense of community.[30] The co-op system's "artisanal production" could
yield formalism, but its egalitarian collaboration could yield solidarity, too;
if these filmmakers lost touch with the masses, they had grassroots communities to fall back on. Viewed from this perspective, it is difficult to believe
that a cinema made in the hierarchical auteur system of the commercial art
cinema could ever be revolutionary.[31] Wouldn't this cinema have to "dilute"
its themes and forms to make itself accessible to broader audiences, trading
revolutionary effects for populist appeal, in the manner of Steven Soderbergh's *Che* (2008) or Olivier Assayas's *Carlos* (2010)? Or is it the other way

around—would this sort of cinema have to do those things in order to have revolutionary populist effects, meaning that Godard was occupying the right cultural position but making the wrong bets in ratcheting up his experimentation in mid-career works like *Le gai savoir* (1968)? On the other hand, could a grassroots community that disavowed popular distribution ever hope to be truly revolutionary? Granted, such a community would have the freedom to take many risks or none at all. But could it reach, let alone inspire, the masses if distributed noncommercially? Quandaries like these cannot be permanently resolved. But if Wollen had posed them in this manner—rather than spending time on the formal and political minutiae—he might have been able to frame his avant-gardes more clearly as overlapping fields.

This thought leads to my major concern. Assuming they occupy the same systems of production and distribution, could the Godardian auteur be objectively distinguished from the ostensibly less experimental Antonioni type?[32] Wollen suggests that this sort of distinction is clear-cut, but I think it comes down to notions of value (whether political or aesthetic) and of authenticity. On the other hand, Wollen frames the co-op avant-garde by distribution alone. This means co-op avant-gardists did not have to qualify as avant-garde through evaluative, political, or art-historical means. Rather, they submitted a film to a co-op and followed its policies, which were egalitarian and inclusive. (They could also qualify as avant-garde in this sense, even if they did not use co-ops—so long as they used other networks of distribution and exhibition favored by co-op artists, like the grassroots spaces, media-arts centers, and universities of urban centers like New York, Chicago, San Francisco, Houston, Los Angeles, and Seattle.) The disparities between these approaches should be clear. For one thing, the institutional method legitimates more avant-gardists. Whereas Wollen can offer only a few examples of the Godard type, he notes that in 1975 the co-op field included many practitioners in Britain alone. Because the Godardian auteur occupies an avant-garde *extreme* of the art-film field, the critic must decide which art-film auteurs do not make the cut, basing that decision on form, politics, and so on—a practice that leads to a highly subjective method that is inevitably evaluative. Thus, from Wollen's perspective, not many art-film auteurs deserve the avant-garde label; he even excludes Antonioni, who arguably had the right credentials. Today, after the cinema has encountered so many auteurs with similar credentials— including Godard, Straub-Huillet, Marker, Sontag, Cassavetes, Greenaway, Lynch, Alain Resnais, Joyce Wieland, Andrei Tarkovsky, Chantal Akerman, Derek Jarman, Béla Tarr, Apichatpong Weerasethakul, and Wollen himself (along with his codirector, Laura Mulvey)—it is still difficult to know which experimentalists "deserve" the label. Must these avant-gardists have shared

A promotional poster for a screening of Chantal Akerman's experimental 16mm film *D'Est* (1993). Filmed without dialogue or commentary, this feature-length film is about the immediate post-Soviet period in the old Eastern Bloc. Does this sort of project qualify Akerman as an avant-garde filmmaker in Wollen's Godardian conception of the term? Used by permission of the Film Studies Center at the University of Chicago.

Godard's Brechtian methods and Mao-inflected consciousness? Must they, in other words, have made intellectual think pieces that scorned the social realisms of their day and the bourgeois values that those techniques appeared to uphold? Or must they simply have made very experimental art films in any number of art-historical categories—films such as Resnais's *L'année dernière à Marienbad* (1961), Tarkovsky's *The Mirror* (1975), Jarman's *Caravaggio* (1986), Tarr's *Sátántangó* (1994), Greenaway's *8½ Women* (1999), or even Lynch's *Inland Empire* (2006)?

Wollen complains in his article about the scant attention given this second avant-garde relative to all the notice paid the co-op avant-garde. But this disparity simply reflects that his second avant-garde was a subjective tradition, a political, art-historical tradition, not a full-blown institutional reality like the co-op avant-garde. Though his essay verifies that the avant-garde and art cinema are indeed conjoined, its titular avant-gardes in the end seem less comparable than apples and oranges. Wollen's comparison of those fields appears to have been a critical–artistic intervention that lent his chosen style greater traction as he prepared to pursue that variety of experimental filmmaking with Mulvey. But even though the Brechtian products of their collaboration, including *Riddles of the Sphinx* (1977), have left their mark on experimental communities,[33] their status in those fields does not mean that this school of experimental filmmaking can be held up as truly comparable to institutional realities like co-op cinema.

Reconceptualizing American Avant-Garde Cinema

Though we should probably dispense with Wollen's mixed approach to the avant-garde, we should not necessarily dispense with his idea of seeing this cinema through its divisions. Indeed, such divisions have existed in the American co-op cinemas since the 1960s. How might we go about theorizing these internal splits? First, it is a good idea to identify the best scholars available. We should also remember what we have learned from Wollen: that it helps to divide the avant-garde into comparable areas. And finally, it helps to draw on cultural theorists like Bourdieu, who combines an understanding of art history with an in-depth knowledge of sociology and ethnography.

When it comes to describing the field's institutional splits, the scholars I think of most readily are Ramey and Zryd. In "Between Art, Industry, and Academia: The Fragile Balancing Act of the Avant-Garde Film Community," Ramey approaches co-op cinema along an ethnographic path. Like Wollen, Ramey is an avant-garde filmmaker; however, this vocation makes her no less detached as a scholar. Instead, she manipulates her insider status to academic benefit, using other "avant-garde filmmakers" as her "informants," as supplemented by interviews with curators, technicians, and professors.[34] She begins by describing the intentions of individual participants in this field ("to critique, subvert and provide an alternative to dominant, mainstream media production"), by tracing its history as a field, and by analyzing how its idea of the "avant-garde artisan" has been produced and reproduced.[35] Ramey then outlines the institutional structure of this experimental cinema by positioning individual participants in, between, and across subcultures and industries. She neither analyzes any avant-garde films nor evaluates them; instead, she observes how avant-garde subgroups make value claims based on forms, politics, and subcultural positions. Through terms like these, Ramey differentiates the "homegrown" experimentalist from the "university-made" artisan.[36] Throughout her essay, she depicts avant-gardists as struggling "with institutionalization and legitimization by the dominant film, art and university industries."[37] She concludes her piece by arguing that avant-garde "communities are supported by the art, film and university industries but are also threatened by their efforts to standardize and legitimate them."[38]

Zryd's essay "The Academy and the Avant-Garde: A Relationship of Dependence and Resistance" focuses on one part of Ramey's institutional triad, the academy. But as its title indicates, the article's premise is similar to Ramey's conclusion: the American avant-garde has long been conflicted, often resisting its own supporting institutions. What distinguishes Zryd is his use of historical methods to trace and contextualize the avant-garde's flimsy anti-institutional rhetoric—all as a prelude to collapsing that rhetoric by presenting contrary evidence in sections like "There Have Always Been Avant-Garde Institutions" and "The Academy Was There in the 1960s Too."[39] Zryd is making an economic argument that updates Ramey's account of a con-flicted field.[40] He wants to argue that the avant-garde's conflicted state has, *at the level of the field*, been a virtual smoke screen that has never truly interfered with its growth, which has been steady, sustained by a university system with which it shares interests, like the commitment to freedom of expression. The avant-garde's dependency has, then, culminated in a field of production more stable than the poor-mouthing of its individual practitioners suggests.[41]

These arguments can be framed usefully if we look at the way Bourdieu talks about the avant-garde in *The Rules of Art* (1992). Though Bourdieu wrote this book mainly in reference to developments in nineteenth-century French literature, he intended it to have a somewhat larger application and in one passage even implies its relevance to "'experimental' cinema."[42] As in other books, Bourdieu construes the avant-garde as occupying the pure-art sector of the field of cultural production, meaning the avant-garde is defined by its small-scale production and low economic capital, the compensation for which is its relatively rich cultural and symbolic capital. Bourdieu also defines the avant-garde as a field stridently opposed to the "banalization" of art despite the fact that its own processes seem to accelerate that outcome.[43] As producers, avant-gardists judge one another through their ability to impart an authentic sense of "rupture" in the "best informed consumers," namely themselves, their competitors, and critics savvy to what has been accomplished through the history of their field. Ergo, in this milieu, artists struggle to resist "the social signs of consecration—decoration, prizes, academies and all kinds of honours"—because these signs of institutional status seem to indicate that their works of art have aged, socially speaking, "through diffusion . . . in the process of canonization among a more and more extended clientele," with the result that those works of art can at most create a sense of rupture only in "simple lay people."[44]

If we put Ramey and Zryd together with Bourdieu, we can create a conceptual model that makes sense of the American avant-garde as an anti-institutional institution. Historically, co-op cinema has had a marginal presence in cultural institutions like the art world and the academy. Though this marginalization has been an economic burden, it is in accord with the larger history of the avant-garde, which has been defined in terms of a purist rhetoric that has had anticommercial, anti-institutional, and egalitarian inflections. Marginalization has thus been crucial to the identity and symbolic capital of this field—in part because, as Bourdieu has indicated, broader recognition signifies banalization in the avant-garde, much as it might indicate a sell-out in indie culture. At first, the American avant-garde movement lived up to this sense of dispossession, for its early practitioners, including Brakhage, Deren, and Gregory Markopoulos, were impoverished, homegrown filmmakers without much training and without immediate success. But as this avant-garde gained adherents and visibility as an underground, it got more organized. Its crucial innovation was a co-op system that distributed works without violating its purist values—though, predictably, its "purest" adherents rebelled even against this self-consciously grassroots institution. In the end, the cooperatives helped circulate art movies and served as a kind of anchor that encouraged the formation of new communities that flaunted their own DIY sensibilities. Though their use has changed over the intervening years— according to Ramey, co-ops are now "agents of history" that serve mainly as archives for older filmmakers—co-ops still have a stabilizing centrality within avant-garde cinema, holding it together by preserving its history.[45] After all, the field's history must be knowable if new generations of avant-gardists are to "surpass" that history in Bourdieu's sense.[46]

But even before the first successes of this purist movement, major institutions like the academy and the art world had shown an interest in it, serving as intermediaries that lent it publicity and that helped legitimate some of its practitioners. These ties to cultural institutions were controversial within this cinema, for they seemed to betray its grassroots ethos—and again, institutional status might indicate the banalization of a filmmaker's art or politics. Still, because its practitioners had needs—and because it is more difficult to make films without institutional resources than it is to make poems or paintings without them—more and more of these practitioners began to secure funding through these institutions, with the academy the most reliable option in this regard (just as it was during the 1960s already the leading consumer of co-op rentals).[47] As time passed, increasing numbers of these artists secured not only their publicity, funding, equipment, and even employment through the university but also their training—for film schools and art schools increasingly offered courses in experimental film production and scholarship. Consequently, as the movement reached its maturity, it contained (1) noninstitutional, homegrown experimentalists largely unaffiliated with the legitimate cultural institutions like the academy or the art world; (2) partly institutional, homegrown experimentalists, some of whose funding or training came through these legitimate cultural institutions; and (3) "university-made" experimentalists, most of whose funding *and* training came from these institutions. These distinctions were, of course, loose and pointedly relative, with mobility visible across all these sectors. Further, it is worth wondering how closely the homegrown filmmakers of the later periods truly resembled the earlier avant-gardists, since unlike their antecedents, the later artists had the benefit of looking back on more established traditions and benefited in many indirect ways from resources circulated by the academy and the art world, even if they were never personally part of either sphere. That said, even if these divisions are, as constructions, too brittle to contain the full complexity and fluidity of this field, they have profoundly shaped the thinking and the activity of experimentalists in the field.

Indeed, the perception of these divisions has activated a dynamic similar to one that is prevalent in many indie art cinemas but that comes across in a particularly striking way through these avant-garde divisions. The avant-garde reserves much of its subcultural sanction for the least institutionalized artists and scenes. Drawing on Bourdieu, we might say that authenticity or integrity is in the avant-garde a symbolic form of subcultural capital that *increases* as a participant's economic and cultural capital *decreases*. Trading it for distribution or funding can leave avant-gardists open to authenticity-based critiques in their original art-making subcultures. By contrast, the least institutionalized, most homegrown experimentalists often seem to contrive their subcultural capital from thin air as a perverse form of compensation for their nonexistent economic capital and equally nonexistent cultural capital. Hence, in the avant-garde, to have one's subcultural status recognized is to jeopardize it, especially if that recognition is re-articulated in more mainstream fields. Usually, this is not much of a danger. Though avant-garde prestige is *legitimate* — in other words, it is supported by a range of equally legitimate cultural institutions — it rarely has broad *cultural* power, as traditional art cinemas do, for mainstream audiences seldom recognize it. This is why avant-garde fads, like cult fads, are so frequently labeled "undergrounds": though one of these cinemas is legitimate and the other illegitimate, this sort of distinction is seldom obvious to the most mainstream audiences. As a result, an avant-garde cinema often requires an outside expert from the academy, the art world, or the festival circuit to corroborate that that cinema has high-art legitimacy and value. These indie dynamics can make avant-garde cinema seem open and inclusive, lending force to the egalitarian rhetorics wielded by its practitioners. But they also seem to echo the purist snobbery that Bourdieu has discussed in *The Rules of Art,* wherein any experimental work consecrated at the cultural level is assumed to be passé, déclassé, and no longer capable of inspiring an authentic sense of rupture in the best-informed consumers.[48] Overall, these dynamics make it possible to see the avant-garde as open and closed, at once purely populist and purely elitist.

Thus we have two fluidly interconnected avant-gardes, one of which is fairly noninstitutional and one of which is relatively institutional, as supplemented by a fully hybrid third category whose members may identify with either of the two other poles, depending on their needs and circumstances. These two fully relative sectors have the same sort of reality, given that they are both defined by the heterogeneous movie forms that circulate through alternative distribution schemes. Clearly, avant-garde cinemas cannot be defined through given styles or given themes. The co-op ethos that has united them has been too inclusive to sustain any form-based notion of authenticity, and the wider ethos of novelty-for-novelty's sake has also made such notions patently unworkable. Formally speaking, *everything* is in theory permitted there, from narrative, animation, and politically motivated documentary to the widest range of abstraction. This is why, as Kleinhans notes, the art-historical model first circulated by P. Adams Sitney in *Visionary Film* (1974) was at once an intervention that helped establish American avant-garde cinema as a "serious" art *and* an intervention that could not offer the final word on co-op cinema.[49]

Making Virtues of Necessity

At this point, I aim to backtrack to supply historical details left out of the subcultural model offered above. Once we have established such details, we will be better situated to understand the problems associated with this model (problems I discuss in the second half of this section). The first major detail is the fact that the economic rhetoric of the avant-garde was codified in the New American Cinema's most crucial documents, which tended to corroborate its sense of dispossession. For example, in his letters, Brakhage often made aesthetic virtues of the economic necessities thrust on his filmmaking by his chronically impoverished state; thus he framed poverty as a path to pure cinema. Brakhage was so adept at this mythmaking that he even transformed the theft of his 16mm camera, which he could not afford to replace, into myth by depicting it as the necessary break to get back to "basics" (i.e., 8mm filmmaking).[50] Later, when Brakhage explained his use of hand-scratched title and credit sequences, he linked the inexpensiveness of this technique to the modernist goal of prodding the audience into an encounter with the sensuous surface of the medium.[51] Using similar cues, Sitney's book *Visionary Film* (which, as I have noted, helped consecrate the leading filmmakers of the New American Cinema at the cultural level) presented Brakhage as the American avant-garde's crucial innovator.[52] It turned the pathos of this maverick artist, whose avant-garde tactics were often clever responses to economic austerities, into myths that seem to verify the aesthetic value of Brakhage's improvisations.[53] Sitney then proceeded to assign these myths to other filmmakers.

This romanticization of economic constraint was also apparent in the founding documents of the most important avant-garde institutions. "The First Statement by the New American Cinema Group" (1962), the manifesto of the New York Film-Makers' Cooperative, asserts that "the low budget is not a purely commercial consideration. It goes with our ethical and esthetic beliefs, directly connected with the things we want to say, and the way we want to say them."[54] For experimentalists like Mekas, having a low budget was not simply the economic consequence of working in a milieu devoted to free experiment; it was also a virtue that conferred pure autonomy, which had moral–aesthetic value. This anticommercial rhetoric did not change much as avant-garde cinema became institutionalized. It had a regular presence in Mekas's journal *Film Culture*, which championed avant-garde films from 1954 on, as well as in the regular columns that Mekas began writing for the *Village Voice* in 1958. And this rhetoric was just as often recycled to justify other institutions, such as the Millennium Film Workshop (and its journal) or the Anthology Film Archives (and its essential cinema list). Today, second-generation avant-gardists have continued this strategic rhetoric, making more virtues of necessity. Consider how Craig Baldwin—of *Tribulation 99* (1991) and *Sonic Outlaws* (1995) fame—has endorsed Bruce Conner's "cinema povera" tradition.

But this anti-institutional embrace of avant-garde institutions created problems from the start. American experimentalists like Baldwin have elevated themselves through their political hostility to what James calls "the commodity culture of bourgeois society," and this avant-garde posture has "axiomatically" entailed hostility to the mainstream.[55] Yet, as James points out, "the relations between avant-garde film and its own institutions have hardly been more amicable or stable" than the relations between avant-garde film and mainstream institutions.[56] Thus, even grassroots institutions like the New York Film-Makers' Cooperative have been susceptible to anti-institutional attacks from artists who have disagreed with their centralization of policy and power. Mekas knew that the best way to outflank critics of the New York Film-Makers' Cooperative was to adopt an egalitarian policy as well as a professional style that seemed disorganized or "non-institutional."[57]

An image from "The Astrum Argentium" (2006), a short film by homegrown experimentalist and Seattle filmmaker Jon Behrens, much of whose work is distributed and archived by Canyon Cinema. Image used by permission of Jon Behrens.

But the Film-Makers' Cooperative had so much subcultural success that it could not avoid all criticism. Indeed, many figures, including luminaries like Brakhage and Jack Smith, railed against the cooperative system, regardless of its anti-institutional stylings. According to Arthur, Brakhage and Smith deemed the Film-Makers' Cooperative a "parody" of Hollywood industrial filmmaking, with Smith characterizing the co-op as too rigid, too commercialized, and insufficiently anarchic.[58]

As suggested above, part of what made the Film-Makers' Cooperative a success despite such criticism was its egalitarian policy. Perhaps the signal event in the development of this policy was the moment in 1962 when Mekas decided not to work with Cinema 16, the New York society that exhibited and distributed alternative films from 1947 to 1963.[59] Mekas disliked this nonprofit because its programming in effect made its founder, Amos Vogel, "the sole arbiter of which avant-garde films were available and the primary arbiter of how they were presented."[60] Not only did the Film-Makers' Cooperative model opt against selection criteria, distributing any film that followed its policies, it returned a higher percentage of fees to artists, thus ensuring its competitiveness. Within a few years, Vogel had moved in other directions, becoming affiliated with the New York Film Festival and selling his Cinema 16 catalog to Barney Rosset at Grove Press; and soon thereafter, other distributors such as San Francisco's Canyon Cinema and Toronto's Canadian Filmmakers Distribution Center adopted the cooperative paradigm, whose policy of inclusiveness remained standard across the board. This egalitarianism still makes it possible for the most anti-institutional experimentalists to accept the co-op model as "authentic." Thus even homegrown avant-gardists such as the Seattle filmmaker Jon Behrens, whose work is distributed by Canyon, make distinctions between co-op institutions and more centralized forums like museums, which receive "city or state money."[61]

Indeed, in a useful article, Todd Bayma has argued that the co-ops, in tandem with "the small size of audiences, lack of wider recognition, and low financial return," have served "to discourage individuals and organizations from setting themselves up as evaluative gatekeepers."[62] This has in turn en-

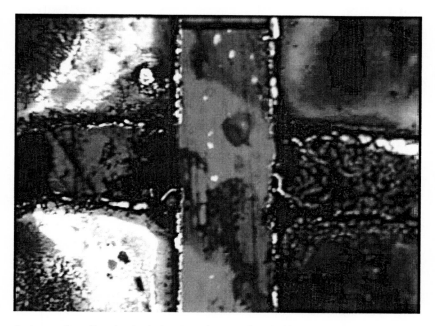

An image from the short, abstract, and very painterly film "The Production and Decay of Strange Particles" (2008) by Seattle filmmaker Jon Behrens. Much of Behrens's work is preserved and distributed by the legendary San Francisco film co-op Canyon Cinema. Image used by permission of Jon Behrens.

couraged the insider view that Bayma quotes, namely, that this avant-garde area is open and deserves its indie reputation, for it is "nothing like art, where you have a big, establishment art structure. . . . In film, anyone can blast their way into the area if they try hard enough, to some extent."[63] Fed over time by the easy availability of quality video equipment, this inclusivist, communitarian spirit has given hope to students and graduates of film schools as well as to homegrown artists, like Behrens, without much or any formal training.[64]

But in the end, this egalitarian spirit could not dispel the avant-garde's basic quandaries and shortcomings. Because the avant-garde's egalitarian logic, codified by its co-op policies, seems to endorse an antihierarchical position, it is in a continual state of revolt against institutions that would use any hierarchical canons — even the smallest, most rudimentary ones — as the basis for their programming choices.[65] Indeed, as Ramey has noted, the selection of first-generation avant-gardists like Shirley Clarke and Ernie Gehr as canonized faculty members "did not bring harmony to the avant-garde film community. Younger filmmakers became critical of their elders, accusing them of empire building, censorship and stagnation."[66] Thus Zryd has documented that in 1981 San Francisco Art Institute film students protested a screening of works by newly "official" artists like Gehr, Paul Sharits, and George Landow at the San Francisco Cinematheque, charging the theater with a "deliberate and systematic lack of responsibility in representing the current work of local filmmakers in [its] programming."[67] The problem for the avant-garde establishment was clear. The air of permanent, collective, indie revolt that animates the avant-garde — which is enshrined by its co-op policies, and which is a factor in its continuing appeal to student filmmakers and to homegrown artisans — was part of the co-op ethos sanctioned by that establishment. This ethos was in turn related to the broader avant-garde ethos that Bourdieu discusses, the one that considers banalization a natural outcome of canonization insofar as it entailed the distribution of a work, a style, or a thought along more mainstream pathways.[68] American avant-garde cinema was caught in a sticky albeit predictable authenticity problematic: as its members tried to benefit from their increasing consecration, its least institutionalized members could criticize them as sell-outs untrue to core values.[69]

What we cannot escape in all this is the fact that the avant-garde has championed the most abstract, difficult forms. Many of these forms fall outside normative capacities for human enjoyment,[70] meaning their appreciation can require a great deal of education or even "re-education." As a result, even the avant-garde's most secure institutions have faced scarce funds that have created limited opportunities for exhibition. (Co-op policies may be commendable in their egalitarianism, but they offer no guarantee that any-

The exterior of the original Aurora Picture Show, which was housed in a repurposed Houston church building. The increasing institutionalization of grassroots spaces like Aurora has led to new dilemmas of funding and programming. Courtesy of Aurora Picture Show.

one will screen the movies.) That the avant-garde has found it difficult to accept the realities of scarcity is indicated by the fact that small-press journals like *Spiral* have continued to ask naïve questions like the one cited by Zryd: "Is the anointing of certain films and filmmakers over others inevitable when the exhibition of film art becomes institutionalized?"[71] The answer to this question should go beyond just "yes." It should also include the fact that institutions cannot be blamed for practical realities. Programmers in these institutions *must* anoint one filmmaker over another; unlike the co-ops, they do not have the luxury of taking everyone. Indeed, programmers have had to choose among so many artists for such a limited number of screenings that they have quite naturally tied their programming choices to their own institutional priorities.

Consider the situation of the microcinemas. The microcinema movement began in 1993 through David Sherman and Rebecca Barten's Total Mobile Home Microcinema and grew over the next two decades through start-ups that were typically part of the founder's home, like Andrea Grover's Aurora Picture Show. By 2000, there were by some estimates more than one hundred of these exhibition sites.[72] Self-described descendants of the early-twentieth-century film clubs and the grassroots viewing spaces of the New American Cinema, microcinemas have hosted traditional avant-garde films as well as the more interactive, multimedia experiences associated with expanded cinema. (There is also room in the microcinema world for the eclecticism of the cult nexus; see, for instance, Baldwin's Other Cinema in San Francisco.)[73] Though the microcinemas have maintained their anti-institutional bearing over the years,[74] they have attracted institutional funding and have encouraged fierce competition for the few but fairly prestigious theatrical screenings (as opposed to less prestigious classroom screenings), stimulating grassroots hierarchies among local artists. But microcinemas have had no option but to balance conflicting interests when selecting which artists and which works they will program. Though they range from refined affairs to strategically ad hoc ones, they are all devoted to the artists, for whom some microcinemas have even arranged funding.[75] But today microcinemas are often dependent for this kind of funding on private granting agencies such as the Warhol Foundation or on government granting agencies like the National Endowment for the Arts. As Grover has indicated, these different kinds of sponsors have different requirements that must be met as a condition of sponsorship. By no means autonomous, the microcinemas walk a fine line in their programming.[76]

A very different set of dilemmas is created when avant-gardists bring their anti-institutional sensibility to the academy, hoping to benefit from academic largesse without sacrificing subcultural authenticity in the bargain. We shouldn't look on this issue as a one-sided moral affair, of course, for the academy has typically sought to exploit experimental artists, too. Especially when film studies was coalescing in the 1960s and 1970s, film departments hired experimental filmmakers because they brought the prestige and allure of a popular new sector of film culture. According to Zryd, hiring them "made fiscal sense as they commanded lower salaries and could usually bridge university cultures in the humanities and fine arts."[77] These trends have led to difficult professional lives. "Many avant-garde filmmakers are forced throughout their careers," Ramey has noted, "to piece together a living on adjunct teaching salaries."[78] Still, we should see that the exploitation is mutual and, on the avant-gardist's side, strategic. The adjunct life allows artists to access some of the legitimacy, money, equipment, and opportunity offered by the academy while still holding this institution at arm's length, allowing them to avoid the appearance of co-optation in their art-making subcultures—and allowing them to avoid the restrictions on creativity enacted by tenure pressures. Clearly, what is crucial in this field is maintaining direct independent control over one's art without threat of institutional compromise or banal-ization. Though the size of adjunct pay constrains the art of those who live on it, the fact that those adjuncts keep making avant-garde art seems to con-firm the authenticity of their vision. Indeed, filmmakers across experimental cinema who support themselves in similar ways—whether through construc-tion jobs, by waiting tables, or however else—in effect preserve their ability to "make virtues of necessity" when promoting their art.

But inside the academy itself, the downside of this strategic posture is that avant-gardists are in effect prevented from honing their skills as schol-ars. From an academic point of view, this is very disappointing, for it stands to reason that avant-gardists-cum-scholars would find themselves in perfect position to explain the avant-garde critically, historically, and theoretically. But the avant-garde's anti-institutional ethos is just one cause of this problem; another is the way the American academy rewards avant-gardists as artists first and scholars second (if at all). Thus, as Ramey has informed me, avant-gardists in fine-art tenure-track positions often chase the most conservative forms of artistic recognition in order to satisfy their promotion committees, which in effect hinders their credibility as artists within more authentic (i.e., less institutionalized) art-making subcultures even as it stunts them as schol-ars.[79] At times, avant-gardists-cum-scholars have made decisive contributions despite the many obstacles in their path. This has been true in the case of Ramey and that of Arthur, who was a critic and participant in the American avant-garde for over three decades. Regrettably, though, the achievements of these insider figures seem to be exceptions to the rule.

One of the areas in which "insider scholarship" can be most valuable is in figuring out which neglected figures warrant study. In avant-garde scholar-ship, the problem of the "neglected figure" is a daunting one, complicated as it is by the fact that even well-loved artists are neglected by mainstream standards. This problem is now improving under the influence of YouTube, streaming rentals, and various online archives,[80] but the fact remains that only the smallest portion of the American experimental tradition is available for mainstream consumption outside the co-ops. When this fact is combined with the multiculturalism of the humanities, which encourages the study of individuals from historically neglected traditions, the justification problem becomes much knottier. Not only are avant-gardists understudied as a group, due in part to their own anti-institutional intransigence and the realities of human scarcity, but a large number of them have also been subject to the same exclusionary dynamics that have suppressed the role of women and mi-norities throughout the history of American cinema.

Recent studies have begun to focus squarely on the experimental cinemas made by female and black artists as well as on those who identify themselves as queer artists. To cite two examples, Robin Blaetz has compiled a volume of essays called *Women's Experimental Cinema* (2007), which supplements an earlier volume called *Women and Experimental Filmmaking* (2005), which was edited by Jean Petrolle and Virginia Wright Wexman. Further, both Arthur's *A Line of Sight: American Avant-Garde Film Since 1965* (2005) and James's book *The Most Typical Avant-Garde: History and Geography of Minor Cinemas in Los Angeles* (2005), among other studies, contain sections on black experimental cinema.[81] These studies provide rationales for studying female experimentalists like Clarke, Wieland, and Barbara Hammer and black experimentalists such as Marlon Riggs, Cheryle Dunye, and Haile Gerima. But these studies do not always clearly elucidate the central problem of studying neglected minorities within avant-garde cinema: *to what extent is their neglect due to institutional factors that work against people in historically disempowered groups, and to what extent is it due to the anti-institutional ethos of their field?* It stands to reason that the scholars best equipped to tease apart these factors are those with insider knowledge. But because avant-gardists with dual roles in the academy have had incentives to avoid assimilating academic values and to avoid doing scholarship at all, they've rarely framed these questions in this way, let alone answered them credibly.

Nevertheless, some of the best analysts in this insider category, including Ramey and Arthur, have managed to isolate these questions to tackle them head-on. For example, after noting that the "avant-garde canon has frequently been chided by feminists and postmodernists as constituting a fringe bastion of conservative, idealist discourse," Arthur contends that, by respecting its own "identitarian impulses," the co-op avant-garde has evolved into a multicultural area with greater appeal to black experimentalists.[82] By approaching the topic rigorously, Arthur helps his readers discern why black cinema was considered separate from avant-garde cinema, how these cinemas have merged in the interim, and why black experimentalists like Riggs, Greaves, and Dunye deserve more recognition in the context of the avant-garde tradition.

All of which is to recognize that academic attention is finite. If it is unreasonable to expect exhibitors to dole out screenings to avant-gardists in egalitarian ways, it is also unreasonable to expect academics to study *all* of them, or *all* of their minority figures, just because their field has long been neglected. Nor is it reasonable to expect academics to pay attention to particular experimentalists based on their politics or aesthetics alone. Like the avant-garde, the academy is a competitive field with its own standards of truth and value. Generally, analytic claims that are authoritatively contextualized—laying out how specific experiments and specific experimentalists have embodied avant-garde notions of value in culturally significant ways at subculturally significant stages of the avant-garde tradition—have the greatest chance of acceptance. In my view, insiders who can internalize academic values and apply them to their insider knowledge of the co-op movement have the best chance of creating authoritative academic rationales for privileging certain avant-garde figures over others.

This book sees avant-garde cinema as a subset of art cinema. A perspective such as this takes account of the fact that the avant-garde is tied to art cinema ideologically as well as historically. Of many cinemas referred to as "avant-garde," the co-op avant-garde has had the least commercial distribution, allowing this postwar cinema to embody art cinema's opposition to commercialism in a striking way. Its nonprofit institutional structure has ensured that it has remained relatively free in its politics and in its forms—and this structure has likewise ensured that this experimental cinema has remained sturdily fixed in the marginal cultural position traditionally designated "avant-garde." Because of this stability, the co-op avant-garde has generated its own institutions as well as its own ties to cultural institutions, like the art world and the academy. These affiliations have fostered a peculiar set of internal rhetorics that call to mind the clashes over authenticity that have at times dominated the indie cinemas—with the caveat being that the payoff for selling out within the avant-garde has not been cash or mainstream fame, but rather a rise in institutional status, which in the avant-garde has often implied banalization and a corresponding loss of status within the avant-garde's own grassroots subcultures. In this kind of indie tradeoff, the social, political, and aesthetic dynamics of art cinema as a whole seem bracingly clear.

CHAPTER 7

Sucking the Mainstream
A Theory of Mainstream Art Cinema

"It's an art movie, it doesn't count. We're talking about movie *movies."*
— *THE PLAYER* (DIR. ROBERT ALTMAN, 1992)

So far, we have used the term "mainstream cinema" without establishing what it is. This may be par for the course, since one function of this seemingly straightforward idea is to relax us into thinking it is okay, even natural, to crowd gigantic groups of movies into a degraded background about which little is known but much is assumed. Using the phrase this way is a habit of convenience, for it helps us to think about the movies as a complex whole. Unfortunately, this habit also limits our understanding of how the "*movie* movies" lumped together as "mainstream cinema" relate to one another and how they relate to movies in other fields. The task of this chapter is to think against this habit in order to catch a glimpse of all that it obscures and how.

To do this, we must develop a context-dependent theory of "the mainstream," one that sees it as an idea of "the average" or "the normal" and helps those engaged in discourse on the cinema justify the value they ascribe to genres that seem outside the mainstream, like art cinema and cult cinema. Ironically, this tool gains its comparative power not by looking at the mainstream in depth but by ignoring the diversity and specialization that are inevitable aspects of any field large enough to be characterized as "mainstream." Because of this complexity, mainstream cinemas and art cinemas always share areas of overlap, much as cult cinemas and art cinemas do. These overlaps are evident when we look at the most dominant global mainstream, Hollywood. In this cinema, no stable distinction between "*movie* movies" and art movies is possible. Because this industry has long been specialized and hierarchical, it has given rise to many cinemas, art cinemas included. This chapter briefly surveys some of the varieties of Hollywood movie that people have referred to as "art movies." Because there are mainstreams outside Hollywood as well, we may also look for mainstream art cinemas in various world cinemas and cult cinemas. As it happens, these context-specific mainstreams have generated distinctive art cinemas of their own through their hierarchal subcultural processes.

Theory of Mainstream Cinema

In most critical discourses on film, the utility of "mainstream" derives from its function as a modifier, a comparative, and not as a noun. The term's nounal function imparts the idea that the mainstream is a stable thing. But in reality, the mainstream is not a thing but a complex idea of value that measures cultural and individual tastes. Thus, in cinema, "mainstream" measures value in terms of prominence, dominance, and pervasiveness. It is also an uncharitable term that suggests an ordinariness about which little must be said. Still, we should bear in mind that the mainstream sector of a cinematic field is not strictly real. Different cultures, different subcultures, different people: they all see different mainstreams, just as they all perceive different art cinemas and different cult cinemas. Ostensibly nonmainstream areas such as art cinema and cult cinema, whose identification is often inflected by affirmative valuations, could not lend their objects positive value without the more subtle negative fetishization of "mainstream cinema." After all, the phrase creates the illusion of a generalized background against which the virtues of an oppositional cinema may be foregrounded.[1]

What are the complaints against mainstream cinema? Usually, they consist of the following: that mainstream cinema is driven by greed or egotism, not aesthetics, and that as a result it is homogeneous and generic, lacking the authenticity, idiosyncrasy, and complexity we equate with oppositional cinemas. Such complaints are often found in art movies about filmmaking such as Jean-Luc Godard's *Le mépris* (1963) and Robert Altman's *The Player* (1992). Godard embeds a critique of the new global mainstream in *Le mépris*, implicitly separating the two, by demonizing Hollywood through the figure of Jeremy Prokosch (Jack Palance), a ruthless, unimaginative American producer who corrupts the creative process as smoothly as he seduces the protagonist's wife. In the sly American movie *The Player*, Altman lampoons Hollywood by depicting its producers as interested in the artistic status of their own projects only insofar as they are interested in marketing those projects through tag lines like "Movies *are* art—*now*, more than ever." But there is an insecurity in these intellectual metafictions that makes such criticism ring hollow. Godard was creating a fairly big-budget, star-driven, Euro-

American coproduction with Jack Palance and Brigitte Bardot. And Altman's movie contained over sixty cameos by Hollywood stars and power brokers; he even pitched *The Player* to Hollywood studios before raising the financing himself and distributing the movie through New Line, a label that was independent for only a few more years. These films had to distance themselves from Hollywood, it seems, because they were so close to it.

But neither movie really *looks* at Hollywood movies. Instead, they use the profit motive that drives many aspects of Hollywood as a reason for impugning the aesthetic quality of its products; and they take it for granted that art movies are not driven by commercialism, despite their development of stars and their use of entertaining, realistic stories meant to thrive in fairly commercial distribution channels. We find the same set of assumptions in academic articles. For example, in "Guess Who's Off the Hook: Inventing Interracial Coupling in Global Art Cinema" (2009), Jayson Baker belittles Hollywood as lacking the complexity and boldness to deal with racial mixing honestly. This essay—which looks at the shallowness of "American films" primarily through one film, Stanley Kramer's *Guess Who's Coming to Dinner* (1967)—spends its energy exploring foreign art films such as Godard's *Le petit soldat* (1960), Tomás Gutiérrez Alea's *Memories of Underdevelopment* (1968), and Rainer Werner Fassbinder's *Ali: Fear Eats the Soul* (1974). This kind of pejorative treatment need not benefit the traditional art cinemas alone. It can also benefit cult cinema or any oppositional cinema. To cite one example, consider Lloyd Kaufman's self-promoting essay "IA: I-Won't-Suck-the-Mainstream Art" (2002). Kaufman is the founder of Troma, the studio that has given us classics like *The Toxic Avenger* (1984) and *Teenage Catgirls in Heat* (1994). In his piece, Kaufman claims that "Troma has never sucked the mainstream." He means that his studio has never "gone Hollywood," which would amount to artistic prostitution, compromising his vision for cash. This view also entails his belief that a mainstream Hollywood hit such as *Pretty Woman* (1990) "should have been subtitled: *Girls who suck will be in luck*." [2]

I offer these examples not to embarrass anyone but to show how the mystifying usage of the term "mainstream cinema" generally works to the benefit of individuals and movies located in subcultures defined as outside the mainstream. Few people approach "mainstream" this way, preferring to see it as a noun, a thing, and not as a comparative process yielding subcultural distinction. As a result, the ideas of the mainstream that we find all around us are seldom constructed logically. But this situation is improving. Mark Jancovich has shown that, in areas like cult discourse, "the mainstream" is not a fixed, well-defined object, but "an undefined and vaguely imaged Other." [3] And Joanne Hollows and Jacinda Read have demonstrated that the cult nexus is heavy on masculinity talk and that "the mainstream" is, as a consequence, frequently depicted there as a passive, feminized other.[4] What is telling about this recent (albeit still uncommon) way of using "mainstream" is that it highlights the fact that mainstream cinema has long been a flexible punching bag. Paracinephiles are apt to lump art films and their promoters into this despised category—for in the eyes of cult fans, these works and individuals represent the dominant, the traditional, "the mainstream." Traditional cinephiles, by contrast, are more apt to lump cult movies and their fans into this sector— for in their eyes, these déclassé films and people are corrupted by financial motives and by their affinity for genre conventions.[5]

The fact is, though, that there is no reason to think that these genre terms must be distinct from one another. As I have noted, "mainstream cinema," "art cinema," "cult cinema," and "world cinema" make the most sense as groups of actual movies when they refer to overlapping super-genres. But these ideas are so plastic that they may be used in various ways, all of which are reasonable. Here it helps, I believe, to reduce these usages to their main variables: the classifier's institutional role and the specifics of the field under review. An American feminist critic looking at feminist art films might label Jane Campion's *The Piano* (1993) an example of "the postfeminist mainstream" while labeling Chantal Akerman's *Jeanne Dielman, 23 Quai du Commerce, 1080 Bruxelles* (1975) an "experimental feminist art film." This does not mean this critic has permanently devalued *The Piano*, which she might need to label an "art film" were she to widen her field to include all narrative features, not just feminist art movies, or if she were working in a more cinephilic capacity for the AFI, the BFI, or *Sight & Sound*. On the other hand, if cult critics were focused on a low-profile segment of cult cinema, they might identify Troma movies as a mainstream cult cinema based on their distribution through highly centralized outlets like Hollywood Video and their normalcy vis-à-vis more outré labels, such as After Hours or Factory 2000, with their fetish-oriented stress on strangulation videos. A mainstream field is more complex than the term "mainstream" implies, so a critic who looks closely at such a field may find another mainstream cinema—or another art cinema or another cult cinema—within it, just as we have found many such cinemas within art cinema as a whole. This variability is what makes it possible to consider the concept of "a mainstream art cinema," which may be defined as an area of cinema wherein a set of films somehow distinguished as "mainstream" seems to conflict in a value-oriented way with its own "mainstream-ness."

When introducing the idea of mainstream art cinema, it helps to begin by focusing on another maligned term: "Hollywood." Even a swift overview is sufficient to establish that Hollywood's historical reality is far more complex than the pejorative use of the word "Hollywood" often suggests. By acknowledging this complexity—which has given us specialized types of Hollywood art movie such as the prestige picture and the indie-style art film—we will position ourselves to understand how a mainstream art cinema manifests through sub-phenomena like "Hollywood art cinema." The perception of the conflicted nature of the Hollywood art movie results from a contradiction between a cultural commonplace (*Hollywood makes worthless movies*) and personal and institutional judgments (*these Hollywood movies seem comparatively valuable*). In the end, such perceptions would not be routine were Hollywood not more complex than its critics suggest.

What *Is* Hollywood, Anyway?

For over ninety years, the idea of a global mainstream cinema has been identified with Hollywood.[6] Those who by preference or necessity have found themselves outside this mainstream have seldom painted a happy picture of it. To them, Hollywood is a place of compromise, of prostitution and betrayal; it is a place where, as Kaufman has implied, people bend down or bend over but get stabbed in the back either way.[7] Given this rhetoric, which has so much in common with Frankfurt School notions of the culture industry, it is no wonder that Hollywood has so often been cast in paranoid terms as a "mechanical monster" or as a sinister "system," smug stereotypes that industry insider Joan Didion has lampooned as tantamount to the belief that Hollywood is "programmed to stifle and destroy all that is interesting and worthwhile and 'creative' in the human spirit," leaving empty products for empty people.[8]

But we don't need this rhetoric to understand that the association of "Hollywood" and "the mainstream" does have common sense on its side. Since the 1920s, Hollywood has dominated the global box office—and, as a result, its sales agents have dominated the global distribution of films. But I wonder how much statements like this tell us about the movies themselves. Rejecting Jeffrey Sconce's conflation of these terms, Jancovich contends that using "mainstream" as shorthand for Hollywood only deepens our confusion.[9] Of course, I am not suggesting that we abandon the conflation of these terms altogether, for such a maneuver would be unrealistic. But we do need a definition of each term that is so precise and so concise that even when we conflate these concepts in passing we do so with respect for the potential complexity available in each referent. Thus, as I work toward a definition of "mainstream" in this chapter, I am also hoping to construct a more accurate sense of "Hollywood" as part of the same project.

Even in the literature, Hollywood's basic reality remains a matter of debate.[10] It is not enough to say that Hollywood cinema has been the movie business conducted by the Big Five—and now the Big Six, counting Disney—major studios during the classical and postclassical eras. In more recent times, Hollywood studios have been conglomerate-owned and, apart from Disney, answerable to executives whose offices are located in New York, not California. Currently, there is no "stop" between the multimedia dealings of a parent company like Viacom or Time Warner and those of a studio like Paramount or Warner Bros. Partnerships like these have enabled studios to cross-promote their feature films and to profit handsomely from tie-ins. What we should recognize in such partnerships is an example of the drift toward specialization that has been a consistent part of the Hollywood studio system almost since its inception. Hollywood today may not be as solid in its vertical integration as it was during its classical heyday, but it is, as Tino Balio documents, more horizontally integrated across the globe,[11] and it has over time sought more specialized markets and ever-more specialized products as its domestic and global audiences have grown increasingly segmented.

Today, the major studios function mainly as distributors and financiers, and not as production companies that control studio lots, contract players, and places of exhibition. Thus most Hollywood insiders can now honestly claim some level of autonomy from the industry. Yet its executives can also, as John Thornton Caldwell shows, claim some level of control over vast distribution networks.[12] This flexible control extends not just to the majors' specialty divisions but also to the more-or-less independent companies that still do business with the majors and that still receive talent, equipment, financing, and even distribution through them. It also extends deep into foreign markets, where Hollywood executives have sold their own films through partial control of distribution channels and production labels.[13] As Balio, Richard Maltby, and Justin Wyatt have shown, Hollywood is today undergirded by the economics of the blockbuster or "tent-pole project," which is a spectacle-based, high-concept, ultra-high-budget feature. The global box-office of the blockbuster has in the post-Code era helped Hollywood weather losses sustained from projects that do not do well financially.[14] Many of these movies are fairly standardized, much as the films made in the classical Hollywood once were. But there is also a great deal of variety and idiosyncrasy built into contemporary Hollywood through the specialized, global reach of its postclassical business model—which has, to borrow Balio's phrase, sought a "major presence in all of the world's important markets."[15]

Given its macro- and micro-reaches, contemporary Hollywood cannot be reduced to a routinized assembly-line factory system. This stereotype—like much of the rhetoric attached to it—is either a conceptual relic rooted in an outdated conception of Hollywood or a gross simplification that reduces contemporary Hollywood to a maker of high-concept blockbusters. For the fact is that Hollywood has made contributions to almost *every* kind of narrative cinema, including those that are far from what most people label "the Hollywood mainstream."[16] The term "Hollywood" encompasses an astonishing degree of historical diversity, and this diversity has increasingly included very specialized sectors, like the indie-style art labels of the past decades. All we may say of Hollywood, then, is that it has produced narrative films, whose distribution potential it has sought to maximize. To lump all these movies together as "Hollywood" is to indicate that they share a common funding source, not a common form, theme, or level of quality.

The next section looks at two types of art movie that have been perceived within Hollywood: one that embraces its origins in genre vehicles and one that is ambivalent, even scornful, of such origins. In the first category, we may place genre vehicles by classical Hollywood directors who influenced the auteur critics, thus spurring postwar new waves. Here we may find everything from "prestige pictures" and the lean genre movies of a Sam Peckinpah or a Clint Eastwood to the grand art blockbusters of contemporary directors such as Tim Burton, David O. Russell, and David Fincher. At worst, these movies seem ambivalent about their use of Hollywood conventions. But in the second category—which includes the Hollywood-financed, Euro-American art films of the 1960s, the New Hollywood art movies of the 1970s, and the indie-style art films that came to the fore in the late 1980s and early 1990s and that still circulate today—there is open contempt for films and filmmakers who lean heavily on such conventions.

Mainstream Hollywood Art Cinemas

As areas of generic overlap, Hollywood art cinemas function as "real" mainstream cinemas and as "real" art cinemas. Thus it is perfectly reasonable to think of indie-style art films as mainstream art movies *and* as traditional art films. Still, these mainstream art cinemas represent different kinds of cultural and subcultural distinction depending on their type and context. Hollywood insiders consider many of them a distinguished kind of output. This is one reason indie-style movies have won so many Oscars over the past decades.[17] But viewed from art-world contexts that may include the avant-garde, the proximity of these art cinemas to Hollywood can call their own legitimacy into question. Thus these quasi-legitimate cinemas are marked by insecurity vis-à-vis more "authentic" art forms and display this insecurity through self-conscious attacks on Hollywood, which is at once their principal support and principal anxiety.

What is curious is just how important Hollywood movies were to the postwar new waves that cinephiles have accorded automatic respect. I am not talking about the general influence of an early Hollywood auteur like D. W. Griffith or that of a Hollywood classic like *Citizen Kane* (1941). Instead, I am talking about the elevation of John Ford, Alfred Hitchcock, Billy Wilder, Nicholas Ray, and other genre directors according to the auteur criteria circulated by *Cahiers du cinéma* before the French New Wave was even fully underway. To American eyes, these Hollywood directors produced "*movie* movies" that seemed mainstream in their codes and their distribution. But their films were, for the auteur critics, distinguished from other Hollywood projects in their stylistic control, which the critics often considered a result of a close collaboration between directors and screenwriters. This control distinguished such films not only from more mainstream Hollywood product but from more mainstream French product, too. By finding auteurism in the Hollywood mainstream, the auteur critics helped legitimate the belief that all cinema was art and that any cinema, even the most popular, could qualify as art cinema.

Interestingly, before the ideas of the auteur critics took root in the United States, American critics like Manny Farber were already praising the "soldier-cowboy-gangster directors," including Ford, Anthony Mann, Raoul Walsh, and Howard Hawks.[18] Farber betrayed his insecurity vis-à-vis the French critics and other intellectuals by resenting the incursion of "serious art" into the "masculine" sphere of the action film. For that reason, he invented an idiosyncratic auteur criticism that distinguished between an authentic Hollywood underground on the one hand, and an effete idea of "Cinemah" on the other. His attitude would sound like the sexist elitism that Hollows and Read identify with the cult critic except that Farber was a mainstream figure who focused on mainstream directors and published in mainstream forums. And he did not praise outsiders. Instead, he focused on the oppositional *insiders* that he deemed responsible for making covertly valuable movies. "Hawks and his group are perfect examples of the anonymous artist," Farber wrote. "To go at his most expedient gait, the Hawks type must take a withdrawn, almost hidden stance. . . . His films seem to come from the most neutral, humdrum, monotonous corner of the movie lot." These craftsmen taught viewers that "the obvious in art is a losing game." For Farber, the "sharpest work" was most likely to be created by "the most unlikely, self-destroying, uncompromising, roundabout artists."[19]

Had he been writing later, Farber might have applied this mainstream elitism to directors like Peckinpah and to unprepossessing movies like *Ride the High Country* (1962), *The Ballad of Cable Hogue* (1970), *Junior Bonner* (1972), and *Bring Me the Head of Alfredo Garcia* (1974). Celebrated as a "self-destroying, uncompromising" auteur who crafted a misogynist cinema in *The Wild Bunch* (1969) and *Straw Dogs* (1971), Peckinpah was a genre director whose projects resisted the "obvious in art." But like Hawks, he distinguished himself both from other Hollywood genre directors and from more high-brow directors skeptical of genre. A similar profile has been created by Eastwood, who has pressed the humble tradition of Hawks, Ford, and Peckinpah through the mainstream art movies he crafted in his late career for Warner Bros. Films like *Unforgiven* (1992), *Mystic River* (2003), *Gran Torino* (2008), and *Invictus* (2009) have the raw and "unpretentious" vigor that Farber admired. They create the illusion of coming straight from the popular Hollywood genres these directors loved.[20]

But there is today a different kind of art movie in Hollywood that embraces even more of the qualities that have caused mainstream cinephiles to feel insecure, like big budgets, big grosses, and special effects. This art cinema is found in the output of auteurs like Burton, Russell, Fincher, Terrence Malick, Michael Mann, Steven Soderbergh, and Christopher Nolan, who have all made "art blockbusters" in today's Hollywood system. This fairly big-budget format has meant that these directors have offered viewers accessible stories full of flash and vigor. Yet they have also pleased many critics, who've been impressed by their stylistic palettes and their auteur legends. Their films have certainly received no shortage of praise, for there are many critics, Baumann notes, that "argue that some blockbuster productions are true art."[21] This group of people includes Manohla Dargis of the *New York Times*, who has called vehicles like Michael Mann's *Public Enemies* (2009) "big-budget art movies," a category containing films with a "resolutely noncommercial" spirit.[22]

Some of these directors have, it seems, followed the standard (albeit inadequate) script of the starry-eyed filmmaker co-opted by Hollywood. After all, Malick made an impressive contribution to the new auteurism in American cinema with his early film *Badlands* (1973), starring the young Martin Sheen; Soderbergh added excitement to the burgeoning indie movement through the festival success of *sex, lies, and videotape* (1989); and Nolan generated tremendous buzz through the innovative narrative structure of *Memento* (2000). Why would such young, original directors begin making bigger-budget films for Hollywood executives if they were not "seduced" into doing so? Whatever their reasoning, these directors have all made movies that have defied the idea that it is impossible to make innovative auteur movies within Hollywood —

A flier for a screening of the Clint Eastwood film *Invictus* (2009), a mainstream art movie that was shown a week after a more traditional art film, Michael Haneke's *The White Ribbon* (2009), at a repertory art house in Chicago. Used by permission of Doc Films Group.

A *Sight & Sound* cover devoted to Michael Mann's mainstream art movie *Public Enemies* (2009). Can a movie that fits into this kind of coverage be said to have a "noncommercial" spirit? Used by permission of *Sight & Sound*, published by the British Film Institute.

including Burton's *Edward Scissorhands* (1990) and *The Legend of Sleepy Hollow* (1999); Russell's *Three Kings* (1999) and *I Heart Huckabees* (2004); Fincher's *Fight Club* (1999), *Zodiac* (2007), and *The Curious Case of Benjamin Button* (2008); Malick's *Days of Heaven* (1978), *The Thin Red Line* (1998), and *The New World* (2005); Mann's *Heat* (1995), *Miami Vice* (2006), and *Public Enemies* (2009); Soderbergh's *Traffic* (2000) and *Solaris* (2002); and Nolan's *The Prestige* (2006), *The Dark Knight* (2008), and *Inception* (2010). Several of these Hollywood art movies have been exceedingly profitable. Consider that *The Dark Knight*, which cost an estimated $185 million to make, had grossed $533 million in the United States alone by February 2009.[23] Given these numbers, it is perhaps surprising that critics have often positioned these directors as auteurs. But if we really look at their films—especially those of Malick, whose lush, whispery, antinarrative effects make genre designations seem beside the point—this auteur rhetoric will not seem that surprising at all.

These, then, are the Hollywood art cinemas that clearly produce *movie* movies. What I find interesting is that these cinemas have so often been accorded so little respect, even in Hollywood. This disrespect was highlighted at the 2009 Academy Awards, which failed to nominate *The Dark Knight* for Best Picture or Best Director, despite its acclaim and its formidable marketing campaign. There are many reasons for this disrespect. Savvy filmgoers recognize that cinephiles are at some level supposed to be anti-genre, so auteur projects that are also successful genre movies make them uneasy. But it is notable that, as Thomas Schatz notes, Hollywood, like other quasi-legitimate and illegitimate cinematic areas, has always asked its most acclaimed directors to work within genre constraints at least part of the time[24]—and European émigrés like Fritz Lang, Ernst Lubitsch, Douglas Sirk, Max Ophuls, and Otto Preminger adapted "effectively to Hollywood's genre-based system," often doing their best work in it, much as Hawks, Ford, Vincente Minnelli, and other thoroughly American directors did as well.[25] In other words, though Hollywood genre constraints have contributed to Hollywood's negative reputation among cinephiles, those constraints have helped shape an impressive artistic legacy.[26]

Mainstream art cinema has been highlighting its own aesthetic value or "quality" at least since the Academy of Motion Picture Arts and Sciences began the Oscars in 1929. Indeed, from the 1930s through the 1950s, a broad category of Hollywood production, the "prestige picture," gathered distinction in the mainstream, whether through the Academy Awards or through specialized kinds of exhibition. As *Time* magazine noted in 1937, the "cinema has a special category for what it calls 'prestige pictures.' Made with an eye to pleasing serious critics, these productions are intended primarily to stimulate the self-respect rather than fill the purses of their makers."[27] The film historian Chris Cagle has argued that these "middlebrow" art movies developed in two stages, paving the way for the more European aspirationalism of the New Hollywood.[28] Shyon Baumann concurs with this analysis, noting that even though prestige productions did not seek the same high-art mantle as the later auteur productions, they contributed "to the eventual redefinition of film as an artistic genre."[29] But, as *Time* also suggested, the danger of these aspirational movies was that they could lose money by striking viewers as "bores." The executives of the classical Hollywood wanted even prestige projects to be identified as "entertainment," not "art," for they were afraid that self-indulgent, arty films that strayed too far from classical realism or from popular genres might neglect the most common tastes of mass audiences, subtracting from their bottom lines. These executives wanted the distinction of art, but only if they could keep it in a box where it did not threaten the business of entertainment.

Such dynamics were drastically altered due to the postwar popularity of the new waves, which seemed to give Hollywood a way out of its postwar decline. Thus, since the 1960s, executives have been less averse to placing their movies in aspirational contexts, and Hollywood auteurs have become more contemptuous of Hollywood genre traditions. This pattern was most apparent during the New Hollywood era, when art cinema virtually overran Hollywood.[30] But contemporary Hollywood then righted itself through its careful development of specialty divisions—although the indie-style movies of Miramax, New Line, October, Fox Searchlight, and other art divisions have been as happy to condescend to Hollywood as Godard and Altman were in a more classic era. Two salient points may be drawn here. First, through the indie-style movie, Hollywood has put art cinema back in its box, creating a more sustainable system than was evident during the New Hollywood. Second, both the New Hollywood and the specialty divisions have had to dodge questions of authenticity, despite their anti-Hollywood postures and their European influences.[31]

Mainstream Art Cinemas Outside Hollywood

If these segments of Hollywood are reasonable constructions of mainstream art cinema, we should also acknowledge that similarly reasonable constructions can be found in complex mainstream fields far beyond Hollywood. Anywhere there is a metaphorical Hollywood, we are likely to find ideas of mainstream art cinema. These metaphorical Hollywoods exist not only in other nations but also within alternative cinematic traditions, such as those grouped under the rubric of cult cinema.

One excellent example of a mainstream cinema that parallels Hollywood was the classic French studio system and the "tradition of quality" against which French auteur critics like François Truffaut rebelled. Clearly, we should not take the opinions of the auteur critics as the final word here. Today, many French directors remain convinced that the French studio tradition was among the grandest in international filmmaking. As the cult auteur Pascal Laugier has put it, "Besides Hollywood, in the '40s French cinema was simply the best cinema in the world. It's impossible as a young French director not to be influenced by geniuses such as Julien Duvivier or Henri-Georges Clouzot."[32] What I would suggest is that "quality" directors like Duvivier, Clouzot, René Clément, and Claude Autant-Lara—none of whom Truffaut favors in "A Certain Tendency of the French Cinema"—form an art-cinema segment inside the mainstream French cinema of the period.[33] For example, Clouzot, director of *Les diaboliques* (1954), and Clement, who made *Jeux interdits* (1952), won festival awards and served on juries at the same time that their works, which often relied on genre conventions, were proving popular in a domestic studio system that was the French Hollywood.[34]

But we should not limit these investigations to the United States and France. Movies seen as fitting into the mainstream in their native contexts are often perceived as art films once they are exported through global distribution circuits. One example of such a movie is the recent Oscar winner for best foreign-language film, *In a Better World* (2010), directed by Susanne Bier, which *Newsweek* and the *New York Times* cited as an example of an art film that in its home context was interpreted as evidence of the "Hollywoodization" of Danish films (and of Dogme directors).[35] Here we should also mention the current trend toward quality productions in European cinema. For example, the film scholar Mary Wood has classified the contemporary European "quality" film as a fairly mainstream cinema that "has developed out of art cinema practice and represents an attempt by European filmmakers to compete with big-budget U.S. films."[36] Similar phenomena exist outside Europe, too. In Iran, directors like Nasser Taghvaee and Ali Hatami have made "popular art films," a category that is more commercial than the Iranian new waves but that often includes films by artists in those traditions, like Daryoush Mehrjui, director of *The Cow* (1969).[37] Yet another case is "middle cinema" in the Hindi tradition, where auteurs like Hrishikesh Mukherjee, Shyam Benegal, Mani Ratnam, and Guru Dutt have made movies whose niche is between the state-sponsored new wave (or "parallel cinema") and the more accessible and commercial movies of Bollywood.[38] The work of such directors may be classified in the United States as "world mainstream art cinemas."

If this concatenation of terms sounds strange, there may be even stranger ones to consider. In the cult nexus, we might refer to "mainstream cult-art cinemas," which we could conceptualize as *the art-cinema segments of the mainstream segments of cult subgenres.* Here we would have to adjust our ideas of the mainstream according to subcultural indices, not national or cultural ones. For example, the most mainstream element of the contemporary American softcore tradition is a strand that I have elsewhere classified as "corporate softcore" and distinguished according to theme, style, budget, and studio.[39] In softcore, the most crucial labels were once Playboy, MRG, and New City, which between 1997 and 2003 formed a low-budget softcore "Hollywood." Though this very mainstream softcore tended toward a weightless postfeminism, it included some adversarial elements. These were demonstrated when the Playboy auteur Tom Lazarus mocked his distributors and executive producers for their lack of imagination, railing against the corporate limits they put on his creativity.[40] Still, he remained at Playboy, where he had $300,000 budgets at his command for subculturally lauded films like *Word of Mouth* (1999), *House of Love* (2000), and *Voyeur Confessions* (2002).[41] Though Lazarus might have had more liberty at a more underground softcore label like Seduction Cinema, he would have had less money there, crimping his ability to craft the stylized realism that he favored. In a sense, Lazarus was a cult auteur who chose to "suck the mainstream."

If we follow this context-shifting path far enough, we will see that there are potentially as many mainstream art cinemas as there are mainstream cinematic fields. But we need not look at every mainstream cinema to understand this. All we need to remember is that a "mainstream art cinema" results, first and foremost, from the deceptive function of the idea of "the mainstream" — which, in intellectual discourse on the cinema, typically obscures the complexity of a comparatively large field to the benefit of fields defined as outside "the mainstream." But experts *within* that mainstream will have the ambition and knowledge to make field-specific distinctions. They will applaud certain styles and themes while seeing others as more mainstream, more humdrum, more worthy of neglect. But we may shift this context-dependent discourse in other directions, too. From certain angles, avant-garde ones in particular, even the postwar new waves may be considered "mainstream art cinemas." There is, then, no end to the mainstreams that may be discerned in the cinema — and no permanent inferiority marks any of them.[42]

PART THREE

Institutions and Distributions

CHAPTER 8

Re-integrating Stardom
(. . . or Technology or Reception or . . .)

One point I make across this theory is that art cinema's high-art status is dependent on consistent myths that are circulated through equally consistent intellectual discourses. By highlighting the anticommercialism or the auteurism of a given cinema, these discourses lend that cinema an air of disinterested seriousness crucial to it being perceived as high art. That said, *many* factors must coalesce before such perceptions can crystallize, for the status of an art world results from what Howard Becker has called the "collective activity" of that world.[1] Though many of these activities are just as crucial to the cultural elevation of an art cinema as the high-profile activities that cinephiles emphasize, most of them are forgotten as the art cinema in question is publicized and defended in the standard ways. If we want to promote a more holistic understanding of art cinema, we should, it seems, consider *more* of those activities while also theorizing the broader processes of distortion and omission.

The dual task of this section of the book, then, is to begin analyzing the contextual issues that have been either warped or neglected by what I call "cinephile discourse"—and to hypothesize why those negative processes have worked as they have. Thus this section ranges across institutional concerns like film festivals, film studies, and art-cinema distribution. But it also contains portions that focus on less obvious issues whose connections to art cinema have been marginalized. For example, in this chapter, I theorize stardom in art cinema by leaning on helpful ideas like "niche stardom" and "auteur stardom." Because cinephile discourse implicitly frames Hollywood as the natural site of celebrity, it characterizes the art film as antagonistic to celebrity. Ergo, it burnishes the anticommercial credentials of the art-film field, ironically creating conditions conducive to auteur stardom. Of course, auteur stardom *does* have real star power in art-film sectors, even if that power seldom matches in sheer dollar value that of an A-list actor in a mainstream production. But what is distinctive about this industrial role is that, unlike Hollywood stardom, it generates part of its commercial potential from the illusion that it has no such potential. The negative rhetoric of implicit Hollywood comparison enshrouds the art-film format in the impractical aestheticism that is the stuff of art cinema.

Cinephile Discourse, Technology, and Stardom

In using the term "cinephile discourse," I refer specifically to the quasi-academic, crossover discourse that has traditionally lionized global cinema in its auteur phases. At least in the United States, this taste formation is identified with a postwar sensibility that took root in the 1960s, when it was linked to cinephiles like Susan Sontag. Today, festivals as well as highbrow magazines like *Film Comment* have carried on this sensibility, perpetuating an identity that generates its positive energy from its negative outlook on contemporary Hollywood. Since I focus at length on cinephilia in my epilogue, I won't say more about "cinephile discourse" as such here. But I will offer an extended example that helps us recognize this discourse and understand its functionality. This example derives from the hullabaloo that surrounded the recent release of Werner Herzog's *Cave of Forgotten Dreams* (2010), an art documentary that premiered at the Toronto International Film Festival before running at other festivals like Berlin, San Francisco, and Hong Kong.

Cave of Forgotten Dreams is notable here in three of its details: its production by Herzog, a global auteur with a long and storied history in film-festival circles; its content, which required Herzog to secure permission from the French government to film in the Chauvet caves of southern France, something no other director had gotten; and its use of 3-D technology to accent the caves and the Paleolithic artwork that adorns them. When this film was advertised for the theatrical markets, critics and promoters focused on Herzog's auteur credentials. What was intriguing about this straightforward marketing plan was that it presented 3-D as a degraded technique that auteurism might redeem. To wit, in a *Facets Features* blog entry, Susan Doll declares that

> Werner Herzog has directed the perfect film for those who despise 3-D.
> In *Cave of Forgotten Dreams*, he uses 3-D as a true cinematic technique to
> enhance and support his content, unlike most Hollywood blockbusters
> in which 3-D is merely a gimmicky spectacle to distract the audience
> from sophomoric stories or dull animation.[2]

According to the *New York Times*, the anti-Hollywood prejudices that enmeshed 3-D were shared by the filmmaker, who, according to a colleague, deemed the technology a "carnival trick," something that might sell a Hollywood blockbuster like *Avatar* (2009) but not an auteur vehicle. To market the film to cinephiles, its promoters had to confront this predictable cinephile prejudice and recast it through auteur rhetoric. Thus Judith Thurman, a collaborator on the project, opined in the *New York Times* that "the 3-D is an essential element, a real stroke of brilliance and imagination, and the slow revelation of the paintings themselves is staggeringly beautiful."[3] In cinephile discourse, the auteur is someone who rediscovers the "essence" of techniques, technologies, and motifs that might otherwise be subject to exploitation.[4] These adventures of discovery allow the auteur to create high art and avoid commercialism—an artistic profile that Herzog's supporters were under pressure to preserve given the French government's idea of Chauvet as sacred ground. Herzog's use of 3-D was, then, a meaningful and potentially treacherous choice, due to its Hollywood associations.

Cinephile discourse treats the star in much the same way that it treats 3-D. Technology and celebrity are both colored by commercial associations, as if they are actually the property of an overly commercialized Hollywood. As a result, these concepts must be "redeemed" before they can be legitimated in cinephile circles—something that only artistic treatment, preferably by an anointed auteur like Herzog, can accomplish. Ergo, in cinephile discourse, the star, like the technology, either is subordinated to the auteur or *is* the auteur. These traditions may seem fussy, but they do have a significant upside. If directors act in accord with these cinephile prescriptions, they can circulate images and technologies with real commercial potential through the relatively mainstream channels open to the traditional art film—where that commercial potential might help their art movies flourish.

From Mainstream Stardom to Niche Stardom

Why is stardom identified with Hollywood? During the golden era of the movies, Hollywood stardom was tied to the economies of scale generated by vertical integration. In the first half of the twentieth century, Hollywood stars often remained under contract to the studios, which systematically recruited, developed, and exploited them. But this system began to fall apart after the Paramount Decrees of 1948. In the system that emerged after 1968, Hollywood stardom was usually tied to the economies of scale that were generated by the global or "horizontal" reach of the ultra-high-budget, high-concept movie. Amid the impressive turmoil of the New Hollywood, this stardom was driven by agents and by the skyrocketing salaries they negotiated for their clients. In the intervening years, the studios used these fees to their advantage. Since they were among the only sources of financing large enough to pay such steep costs, the studios were able to use these salaries to block competitors from accessing the most bankable stars. Consequently, movie stardom has been routinely identified with the mass audience that only Hollywood stars, with their mainstream recognition, seem able to deliver.[5]

Clearly, it is reasonable to identify stardom with Hollywood. This identification, along with the poverty of successful postwar European art cinemas, Italian neorealism in particular, reinforced the attitudes of significant postwar cinephiles like Sontag, André Bazin, and Amos Vogel, who saw the art film as occupying a "different economic and commercial space from the run-of-the-mill commercial production," which could presumably afford stars.[6] Unfortunately, the cinephile view was neither nuanced nor accurate—and it required an implicit comparison with Hollywood to make any sense at all. For the truth is that art movies of *every* kind have relied on their stars. Art-film promoters may insist that auteurs reject "Hollywood systems and values," but scholars have found star systems in art cinema that closely "parallel Hollywood's own."[7] Indeed, Jill Forbes and Sarah Street have noted that even the Soviet cinema of the 1920s, which was often exported as an art cinema, had its own stars, despite its institutional "rejection of Hollywood's norms and the capitalist associations of star systems."[8] These confusions have made it more difficult to discern that the art film has developed distinctive forms of stardom that are adapted to the values and expectations of cinephile discourse. The challenge, it seems, is to theorize these realities in a clear way that frames the art film as a rather coy star vehicle, one where some standard and not-so-standard forms of stardom have developed and flourished.

We should begin this analysis with a clear idea of what movie stardom actually is. Stardom is not some mysterious essence. It is instead a combination of audience recognition (of the star performer) and audience desire (for more star performances). The Hollywood star machine has been effective at building star personae, creating attractive figures like Marilyn Monroe and James Dean who have the coherent, multiply meaningful mystiques that Richard Dyer has famously referred to as *"structured polysem[ies]."*[9] In the classical era, the studios manufactured and maintained these personae by themselves; today, they often outsource much of the work to agents, publicists, and the media. When the work is done efficiently, producers and distributors can make lucrative matches between a known quantity—that is, the star—and the unknown quantity—that is, the new star vehicle with mainstream box-office potential. In a sense, the new Hollywood star vehicle promises its audience the same thing that the new Hollywood genre vehicle promises its audience: an intriguing experience of standardization within difference.[10]

There is no reason to think that the art film is at odds with these facts of stardom. The art film's salability has long hinged on an audience's desire to repeatedly experience the known qualities of art-film actors as manifest in new art films. Indeed, at times, art-film stars have been all but indistinguishable from mainstream stars—and in significant cases, these stars have made a major impact on the world. The best example of this sort of impact involves Brigitte Bardot. According to Peter Lev, the "leading personality in the breakthrough of foreign art films to larger audiences in the United States was not Fellini or Resnais . . . but rather the French actress and sex symbol Brigitte Bardot," whom Lev calls a "female James Dean."[11] Mark Betz argues that Bardot's attraction was a multivalent blend of modern spirit and primitive allure.[12] Her mystique was exploited by distributors looking to extend the reach of art films like *Et Dieu . . . créa la femme* (1956) and *Le mépris* (1963). Because Hollywood was at that time still limited by the Production Code, Bardot became an almost instant celebrity. In other words, Bardot's success was the result of an implicit comparison between her celebrity and the more demure stardom allowed in Code-era Hollywood. As Ginette Vincendeau puts it, "Bardot was launched as *the* female sexual myth of 1950s France, and a valuable export when international markets, especially Hollywood, craved the 'natural' sexuality of European actresses."[13] This art-to-mainstream strategy led to extensive imitation, with waves of European and Asian stars like Catherine Deneuve, Emmanuelle Béart, and Gong Li hoping to rekindle the Bardot magic for global markets. Lately, this global marketing of art-film stars has been most evident at international festivals—which, as Liz Czach notes, have increasingly played a double game, both emphasizing and downplaying the power of a global "star culture." Through this bivalence, festival directors hope to enhance their prestige while preserving "the status and visibility of the cinephiliac moment," through which festivals maintain their difference from Hollywood.[14]

For the most part, though, the art film has not succeeded in commodifying its star actors to the extent it did with Bardot. Its more typical reliance has instead been on "niche stars" like Marcello Mastroianni and Toshirō Mifune. Niche stardom reminds us that the idea of the "star" is not absolute. Stardom is instead a context-dependent idea that its user may adjust according to various indices. So while it makes sense that Hollywood, as the most economically dominant cinema of all time, has a historical identification with stardom, this logic in no way entails that Hollywood "owns" the star concept

Catherine Deneuve in a still from the highly sexualized Luis Buñuel film *Belle de Jour* (1967), which greatly enhanced her global star power. © 1967 Paris Film and Five Film Rome, © 2012 The Criterion Collection.

or that it is restricted to A-list examples—for stardom is more variable than this specific historical identification implies. Niche stardom—which relies on actors whose appeal is limited to specific markets but is nevertheless functional in that specific context—offers a fine example of this variability.

To better understand the concept of niche stardom, we should consider the career of Parker Posey, the indie queen whose metro-caffeinated star persona was in the 1990s and early 2000s identified with the American indie-film movement. Posey, who has worked repeatedly with indie directors like Hal Hartley, is the subject of a fine article by Diane Negra in which Negra speculates that niche stars, "while perhaps not fully meeting criteria of stardom in the conventional sense," do indeed "generate personae that operate as legible, functional trademarks."[15] The familiarity of these personae "functions to guarantee that the films in which they appear will support a certain aesthetic and status economy with which independent film-goers are likely to affiliate."[16] Similar things might be also said of actors like Steve Buscemi, Chloë Sevigny, and, more recently, Greta Gerwig, who took many roles in low-budget "mumblecore" projects before getting parts in bigger indie films and eventually in studio films. For Negra, even cameo appearances by such stars have given indie art films an economically significant stamp of authenticity. Their participation in a project can convince producers of its profitability and persuade viewers of its generic benefits.

The celebrity of the niche star often seems better at traveling through time than through space. This quirk is due to the cultish tactics that cinephiles and archivists have used to sustain art-film stardom. They have supported retrospectives devoted to prominent art-film stars like Mifune at festivals and at museum theaters, university theaters, repertory theaters, and so forth, just as they have devoted such retrospectives to prominent auteurs. Though the fame of such stars can be limited by the narrow scope of the niche they occupy, the temporal persistence of their fame has been ensured by the memory of the cinephile. Indeed, in this regard, the celebrity of an art-film star can rival or eclipse the celebrity of the more mainstream star in the more mainstream market.

Auteur Stardom in the Art Film

One way that niche stardom is adapted to its art-cinema context is that it sells an art film without overshadowing its auteur. This practice offers a contrast with Hollywood practice, where the A-list star is often *meant* to overshadow the director. In the art film, the niche star functions as an accessory to the auteur and is often part of an ensemble or troupe bound to that auteur. In-

Chloë Sevigny as Debbie in the Steve Buscemi indie art film *Trees Lounge* (1996). Sevigny was one of a handful of "niche stars" identified with the American indie-film movement during its 1990s heyday. © 1996 Addis Wechsler Productions and Live Entertainment.

A poster for a Toshirō Mifune retrospective held at the School of the Art Institute in 1983. Through institutional interventions such as this, art-cinema stardom travels through time and space. Used by permission of the Gene Siskel Film Center.

deed, some of the brightest stars in the art-film firmament gained their celebrity by working repeatedly with the most prestigious auteurs in the history of art cinema. Thus Max von Sydow, Setsuko Hara, Jean-Pierre Léaud, and Mastroianni often appeared in the films of Ingmar Bergman, Yasujirô Ozu, François Truffaut, and Federico Fellini, respectively. More recent niche stars have filled similar roles in the films of Hartley, David Lynch, Mike Leigh, Claire Denis, the Dardenne brothers, Michael Haneke, and so on. By participating in an ensemble bound to an auteur, the art-film star subordinates his or her celebrity in a way that accommodates cinephile values.

What this phenomenon highlights is that the auteur is a celebrity director, and as such, the most important star in the art-film environment. This stardom has been almost as useful to audiences, distributors, and actors as it has been to directors. As an organizing principle, the auteur replaces the familiar face of the star actor with the familiar style or philosophical approach of the star director. This method of classifying a movie confers prestige on the classifier, for it displays knowledge and taste. But in the end it is just as easy for a cinephile to say, "Have you seen the new Fassbinder film?" or "I loved the new Herzog movie," as it is for a fan of Hollywood to say, "Have you seen the new Monroe film?" or "I loved the new Stallone movie." Hence, as Steve Neale puts it, the name of the auteur often works "as a 'brand name,' a means of labeling and selling a film and of orienting expectation and channeling meaning and pleasure in the absence of generic boundaries and categories."[17]

But we get a different sense of the benefits of this form of celebrity by focusing on distributors and actors. For example, distributors and actors have benefited from a distinctive director–actor dynamic that could not manifest outside an aspirational movie. In the art film, the prestige of the auteur gives actors a clear alibi for participating in projects that use their bodies as specifically sexual resources. Such nudity is read as an extension of personal cinema and consequently represents vision, not exploitation. Because this reading is available, even standard (in this context), executives have often encouraged directors to take advantage of it. Without the prestige of the auteur, which the executives can hypothetically point to in a legal setting to defend the mainstream circulation of an explicit art film, this socio-aesthetic dynamic could not work.

The potential appeal of this art-film dynamic is only enhanced, it seems, when combined with accessible genre conventions. This is the formula that allowed the Italian auteur Michelangelo Antonioni to secure one of his biggest hits with the Euro-American coproduction *Blow-Up* (1966), an arty erotic thriller in which Vanessa Redgrave parades without a top in one long segment. Later, in 1974, Julie Andrews was reportedly to star in a studio-

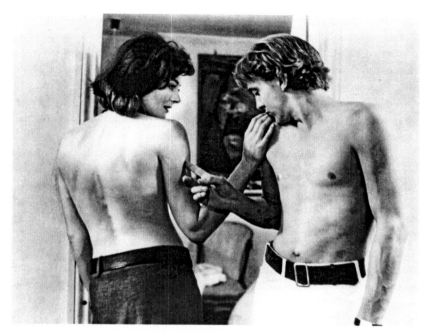

A still from Michelangelo Antonioni's Euro-American coproduction *Blow-Up* (1966), a traditional art film that features a long scene in which Vanessa Redgrave wears no top. The sequence is alternately racy and chaste, much like art cinema itself. © 1966 Bridge Films and Metro-Goldwyn-Mayer.

made hardcore movie conceived by Stanley Kubrick, written by Terry Southern, directed by Mike Nichols, and funded by Warner Bros.[18] Though this film was never made, that it was considered at all demonstrates the power of the auteur. This power has only grown more entrenched over the past few decades, when audiences have been able to claim they were viewing a David Lynch film, *not* a Patricia Arquette erotic thriller; or a Stanley Kubrick film, *not* a Nicole Kidman (or Tom Cruise) erotic thriller; or a Jane Campion film, *not* a Meg Ryan erotic thriller.

Thus, as I have often noted, the rise of auteurism led to less timid film-making in the art film. The alibis of art and individualism allowed for personal excess, letting the art film develop into an area in which the nonstandard was standard. Consider, for instance, the New German Cinema. In its ecstatic stress on the "Autorenfilm," the New German Cinema became what Neale has called "a series of star films by star names, the films themselves almost obliged to contain marks of personal eccentricity."[19] Like the world of visual art, where the art industry has promoted authorship while obscuring the economic underpinnings of the artist's industrial role, the art-film industry has promoted the auteur while obscuring its economic place—thus allowing a tremendous amount of commercial activity to be justified through a generalized auteurist fiat.

It is safe to say, then, that the art film has adapted its own relationship to stardom. Though art-film stars like Jean-Paul Belmondo have never had the mainstream appeal of a Humphrey Bogart, the American star that the French actor mimics in Godard's *À bout de souffle* (1960), Belmondo is today a "name" recognized by a niche audience scattered across the world—and this fame is no less durable than Bogart's.

Art-Movie Stardom in Hollywood and Beyond

The star dynamics discussed above rely on comparisons with the Hollywood star machine. What happened, then, in the New Hollywood period, when so many Hollywood movies openly mimicked European art films? And what can we say about the role of stardom in art cinemas located outside the art film?

The answer to the first question is that these industrial distinctions loosened up and became considerably less obvious. Once Hollywood absorbed art-film paradigms and rhetorics, it became more difficult to defend the idea of a simple contrast between Hollywood and the postwar art cinema. In that era, the status distinctions distinguishing different kinds of art movie grew more significant. Indeed, the New Hollywood period witnessed the emergence of the questions of authenticity that still dog various kinds of art movie, including some that arguably deserve art-film status. In cinephile circles, an art movie's authenticity then came to depend on its distance from Hollywood. Was the so-called art film "actually" an American coproduction? Was the so-called indie production a "true" indie, or was it merely indie-*style*? When the judgment was being made *within* Hollywood, however, this type of question seemed less pertinent than the commercial thrust of a movie as gauged by its relationship to auteurism. If the actors were more crucial than the director, the production probably wasn't an art movie. If the actors were accessories to a directorial aesthetic, it probably was.

To an extent, similarly direct judgments regulate the status of an art movie in cult cinema. After all, the idea that a movie's status as "art cinema" is an absolute is relatively weak both in Hollywood cinema and in cult cinema, for cinephiles typically classify both as commercial. (Of course, art films are commercial, too, but they are seldom seen as such outside the avant-garde—which is a good reason to include experimental cinema when recontextualizing art cinema.) To admit that there is such a thing as a Hollywood art movie or a cult-art movie is already to have admitted relativism into the matter. This admission makes the film's status hinge on the *extent* of its commercialism, not on the *possibility* of its commercialism. When such admissions are made, then, auteurism and the role of the star become major determinants of how a project is defined.

But, to answer the second question, we should note that stardom in a Hollywood art movie or cult-art movie does not work in exactly the same way that stardom works in a festival art film, and it probably does not "feel" the same to the stars themselves, either. For an art movie in a cult sphere, auteur arrangements in a production can help the movie circulate more efficiently relative to other films in the same context. But cult-art movies seldom arrive in art-plexes from the world of cult cinema using the rationale of art and auteur as their pass into our homes. Their internal hierarchy may give them a status-based distinction and sanction in cult contexts, but this sort of subcultural capital rarely leads to greater success in the mainstream channels open to the art film. Similarly, cult prestige rarely helps individual stars or individual auteurs move into more mainstream projects. This sort of prestige may even do the exact opposite.

The recognizability that defines the niche star can be a mixed blessing, for it can leave that star with little room to maneuver. This was certainly true of Posey, who was at first typecast as an indie queen. But since her niche was in a legitimate segment of art cinema, Posey had more leeway in the mainstream than do most cult stars. Illegitimate niche stardom can furnish both actors and directors with subcultural capital, but that capital can actually block a niche star like Misty Mundae or a niche director like Radley Metzger from crossing into more legitimate sectors. For this reason, Mundae once articulated careful aspirations to cross into low-budget horror films before setting her sights any higher.[20] Her incremental approach was a response to the scope of her success in an illegitimate field. Though she starred in the subculturally acclaimed ensembles that cult auteur Tony Marsiglia put together for Seduction Cinema, her broader recognizability as a softcore performer disqualified her as a mainstream actor. Thus the best she could hope for was to become a "scream queen" à la Debbie Rochon. It is to the point, I think, that Sasha Grey's smaller reputation in hardcore—and greater training as an actor—allowed her to cross into the lead in a mainstream indie film, Steven Soderbergh's *The Girlfriend Experience* (2009). Though Soderbergh openly

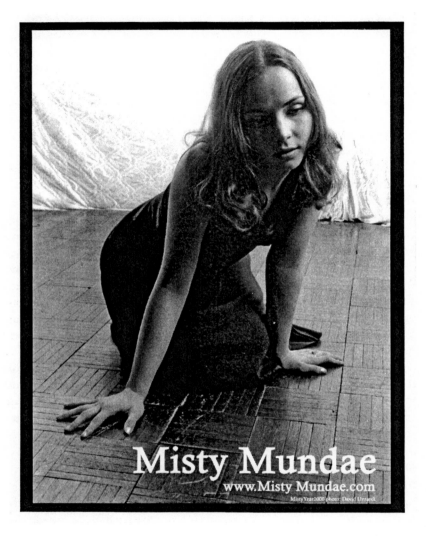

The recognizability of the niche star can prove a mixed blessing. A promotional still for Misty Mundae, a niche star featured in many of Tony Marsiglia's subculturally acclaimed cult-art movies. Photograph by David Uzzardi. Used courtesy Michael Raso and Pop Cinema.

exploited Grey's hardcore "authenticity," he did not want her reputation as a porn star to overwhelm his own status as a star auteur, and so he didn't reach out to the biggest porn names he could think of.[21]

Issues like stardom and technology have typically been marginalized in cinephile discourse because they fall outside the narrow circle of topics that cinephiles present as most essential and valid: artist, style, authenticity, masterpiece. It is predictable, then, that when we examine those marginalized issues in detail, we discover unexpected things about how the aura of art cinema has been created, sustained, and disseminated.

Stardom is as crucial to the art-film industry as it is to any other movie industry. Movies make stars, stars make movies. But it is also inescapable that the star, like 3-D technology, is associated with the kind of Hollywood commercialism against which art cinema has historically defined itself. For that reason, the art film's inescapable reliance on stars and stardom is specialized in an oddly negative way. What seems most crucial is that art films not be perceived as dependent on A-list stars (whom they cannot afford at A-list prices). Instead, art films have typically relied on niche stars and star directors. These distinctive forms of stardom are adapted to the auteurism prevalent across all art-movie formats. What I find fascinating is that the submersion of star actors within a hierarchy that elevates the auteur as the main celebrity has granted actors a distinctive functionality, including cultural permission to play explicit roles that might otherwise end their careers. That an anticommercial illusion has had a commercial role in the art film may not explain where that illusion came from, exactly, but it goes some ways toward explaining why that illusion has persisted through time and is still here today.

CHAPTER 9

Art Cinema as Institution, Redux
Art Houses, Film Festivals, and Film Studies

In a recent issue of *Scope*, Eleftheria Thanouli observes that, thirty years on, the two most influential articles on art cinema remain David Bordwell's "The Art Cinema as a Mode of Film Practice" (1979) and Steve Neale's "Art Cinema as Institution" (1981). Thanouli then critiques Bordwell's "canonical account" of art cinema—which, as she notes, he expanded in *Narration in the Fiction Film* (1985)—"to underline a number of weaknesses that undermine the applicability of art cinema as a cohesive paradigm of narration."[1] In the course of her essay, Thanouli argues that Bordwell's account of this category is incompatible with recent trends, including the appearance of American "smart films," Danish Dogme films, and second-wave Iranian art films—to the point that she wonders why we would want to use a concept that has been "so diluted over the years that it can contain practically everything."[2] Nevertheless, she continues to press for better terminology, even if our search for formal precision convinces us "to abandon the idea of 'art cinema' as a grand narrative paradigm once and for all."[3]

This is an effective essay, but we should reinforce its premises to embrace its conclusions in a more explicitly institutional way. First, it is imperative to perceive that Thanouli is questioning "art cinema" as a *narrative* category. This might be hard to discern if we are mostly familiar with Neale, for he and Bordwell treat art cinema quite differently. Neale looks at the category as a diffuse generic and industrial institution, while Bordwell treats it as a historically specific set of narrative forms arising from a circumscribed set of European attitudes, movies, and directors.[4] So when she dismantles Bordwell's account by showing how varied art cinema has been as a narrative form, she does not prove that we should dispense with this term as a generic concept. All that Thanouli verifies is that we should stop thinking that the concept still makes sense in the narrative terms that were put forth by Bordwell. On this, I fully agree with Thanouli. "Art cinema" makes little sense as a term that implies static or even *coherent* narrative forms.

Indeed, Thanouli comes close to saying that Bordwell's analysis — which places certain works by Robert Bresson and Jean-Luc Godard outside the art-cinema category while placing those of Ingmar Bergman and Michelangelo Antonioni squarely inside it — was never sensible.[5] I wish that she had said it. For it makes no sense to me to define art cinema, whose cultural and institutional status has been so universally sought, as a tightly restricted subset of an already rigid set of narrative films. This point is only magnified, I think, when we consider how Bordwell reduces the scope of "art cinema" from the outset of his account. Not only does he distinguish what he considers an authentic art cinema from the many art cinemas referred to as such before the Second World War, but he also distinguishes it from all the postclassical art cinemas that do not match the new-wave phenomena he prefers.[6] By contrast, in "Art Cinema as Institution," Neale refuses to make this sort of exclusionary distinction. He accepts all historical art cinemas as "art cinema," for he hopes to grasp the logic of art cinema's institutional eclecticism, which Rosalind Galt and Karl Schoonover refer to as its "mongrel identity."[7] So he immediately confronts the fact that art cinema has entailed a diversity of forms that already included everything from Jean Cocteau and the French avant-garde of the 1920s and 1930s to Francis Ford Coppola and the New Hollywood of the 1960s and 1970s. He does not pretend that art cinema could be equated with one narrative idea. Could a single idea cover the very different art vehicles of Marcel Duchamp, Werner Herzog, Marie Menken, Robert Altman, Chantal Akerman, Radley Metzger, Nagisa Oshima, and Dario Argento?

This implies that Thanouli's closing point — that the "crisis of 'art cinema' as a coherent mode of narration in contemporary cinema is at least partly due to the inherent deficiencies of this paradigm and partly to the transformations of the entire cinematic terrain over the past two decades" — is imprecise.[8] Though neither Thanouli nor anyone else has focused on one of the principal sources of art cinema's diversification over recent decades (i.e., the emergence of the cult-art cinemas), she is still mistaken to suggest that the problem is even *partly* the fault of contemporary cinema. Given that the potential for formal diversity has always been present within the art-cinema concept, the blame for this "crisis" rests entirely with theorists intent on squeezing diverse forms into exquisitely narrow categories. But abandoning this mistake would not mean that poeticians would have to abandon their analyses of art cinema, for Thanouli has herself advocated a method that maps narrative properties in a "bottom-up manner."[9] Nor would they have to dispense with art cinema as a generic (or a *super*-generic) institution. Attempting to dispense with this concept would be futile, for art cinema is an active cinematic category that is not going away just because scholars have had a hard time figuring out what each new manifestation of "art cinema" means at the stylistic or narrative level. As Thanouli knows, art cinema is a dynamic, global category that theorists must come to grips with somehow. But they can't do so through a unified theory of art-cinema narrative.

This critique of Bordwell's method should instead prompt scholars to embrace Neale's much more supple institutional approach, which Thanouli introduces but then looks at only in passing. Indeed, her essay leaves us with a question: why did she focus on Bordwell while all but neglecting Neale? Her choice might have made sense had she used her article in the manner that Morris Weitz once used "The Role of Theory in Aesthetics" (1956): as a way of showing that the diversity of forms referred to as "art" make a hash out of the evaluative, formalist logics that try to explain *all* art in terms of *some* art. Such an approach would have been an elegant way to lead back to Neale, since it was Weitz's innovations that led George Dickie to construct the institutional theory he finished in *The Art Circle* (1984). But Thanouli hasn't done this. She seems invested in solving Bordwell's problems within the terms of his project.

But if we are not restricted by this sort of disciplinary investment, we may take Thanouli's advice and subject Neale's essay to careful scrutiny. This effort reveals that the assumptions of "Art Cinema as Institution" are still relevant to contemporary art cinema, despite the "enormous changes" affecting the category since the 1980s.[10] After we have accomplished this inspection, we will be in a better position to update Neale by joining his early institutional account to later ones. The subsequent accounts, some of which are still just emerging, cover art-cinema institutions that Neale surveys only in brief, like the art-house circuit, the film-festival circuit, and the academic discipline of film studies. These art-cinema institutions have, it appears, anchored our notions of the category in flexible but stable evaluative paradigms like the "festival film" and auteurism.

Thinking Institutionally

Before turning to Neale, we should consider the term "institution." When theorists like Neale, Dickie, or Andrew Tudor refer to an "institution," what they mean is a social construct that is collectively created and maintained over time. Such a construct can be broad and diffuse, like film studies, or it can be compact and concrete, like *Cahiers du cinéma*, but it is in any case mediated by our group nature, not by our individual nature or biological nature. Thus "institution" is often contrasted with "form" such that fields that promote the idea of intrinsic properties and the study of single texts seem to oppose institutionally minded fields such as film history, cultural studies, and even sociology.

Both Neale and Bordwell begin their respective pieces with an assumption that qualifies as "institutional": that art cinema gained traction as a category through Europe's opposition to Hollywood's domination of its film markets.[11] But whereas Bordwell uses this idea as a reason to return to a conventional idea of form — and to the belief that art-cinema narrative *must* oppose that of Hollywood — Neale remains focused on institutional specifics, like the efforts of "European countries both to counter American domination of their indigenous markets in film and also to foster a film industry and a film culture of their own."[12] As a result, Neale manages to look at postwar European art cinema as an important instance of art cinema but *not* as the only one. And this makes it plausible for him to subsequently present the post-Code, New Hollywood tradition as embracing *some* European attitudes and forms without having to present it as embracing every practice associated with European art cinema simply to justify it *as* an art cinema. In this way, Neale remains open to art cinema's historical diversity.[13]

Though Neale often refers to the distribution and exhibition of postwar European art cinema, he is strongest in reference to its production. According to Neale, this strain of art cinema came to seem "European" through the contributions of major European powers to its production in the postwar era. Specifically, he looks at art cinema's postwar development in France, Germany, and Italy. In each case, his "point of historical and theoretical departure [is] the fact of Hollywood's increasing domination of the mass market in these countries after the First World War."[14] Neale predicates each case on the idea that the advent of sound technology contributed to the early industrial hegemony of Hollywood. Producers in these nations, aided by government subsidies, in effect ceded their mainstream "mass" markets to Hollywood, opting to compete through a niche "art" strategy that supplied cultural prestige, national identity, and global distribution but never the most profits. This class-based strategy became more unified in the decades following the Second World War, when foreign producers were handed distribution advantages in the U.S. market, beginning with the Paramount Decrees.

To make my next section more concrete, it helps to summarize what Neale says about the government policies that helped art cinema grow in these European nations. As András Bálint Kovács has noted, "It was already apparent — in the early 1930s — that the semicommercial narrative art-film institution could not survive without state support."[15] Consequently, as Neale indicates, the postwar art cinemas of France, Germany, and Italy each got their start through national strategies designed to protect domestic industries and reinforce a sense of native cultural identity, which seemed threatened by imports from Hollywood and elsewhere. In France, a centralized system of quotas, tax incentives, and prizes for artistic and cultural merit was established through the formation of the Centre National du Cinéma Française in 1946, the passage of the Loi de Développement de l'Industrie Cinématographique in 1953, and then the interventions of the Assemblée Nationale and Minister of Cultural Affairs in 1958 and 1959, respectively.[16] Having subsidized its own silent-era cinema, Germany returned to these policies at a later time, establishing production incentives in the 1950s, with a full system emerging after the 1962 Oberhausen Manifesto through "the setting up of the Kuratorium junger deutsche film in 1965, the Film Subsidy Bill of 1967, and the various interlocking systems of grants, subsidies, and prizes since then, each feeding into the establishment of the 'New German Cinema.'"[17] Other systems were established in Italy through the Andreotti Law of 1949 and the Aid Law of 1965, which taxed imports and gave awards for merit.[18] These systems also offered incentives to distributors and exhibitors. In France, a policy of "tax concessions" encouraged what Neale refers to as the "development of a numerically powerful Art house circuit" that grew out of the *ciné-clubs* and *cinemas d'art et d'essai*.[19]

Still, according to Neale, it was only through art cinema's international dimension that it became truly influential and prosperous. This dimension, which clashed with the nationalism that had underwritten postwar art cinema, reconciled the category's contradictions through the universals of art, status, and culture.[20] This new internationalism relied on the equally global dimensions of the art concept, which had traditionally submerged a tremendous amount of heterogeneity, both political and artistic, under the universals of "authorship" and "aesthetic value." The first signs of this increasing internationalism were evident in the coproduction agreements that emerged in this period, such as the one signed between France and Italy in 1949, as well as in "international film festivals, where international distribution [was] sought for these films, and where their status as 'Art' [was] confirmed and re-stated through the existence of prizes and awards, themselves neatly balancing the criteria of artistic merit and commercial potential."[21] By having their credentials certified nationally and internationally, highly sexualized European art films could later become viable in the crucial American market. It is no accident that *Roma, città aperta* (1945)—a film that significantly encouraged the growth of the American art-house circuit by causing a stir there upon its U.S. release—won a Grand Prix at Cannes in 1946.

Neale does not, then, neglect form. He looks at just a few narrative and stylistic features that run across art cinema, such as sexualization, psychological realism, and the difference between art cinema and the dominant forms of Hollywood narrative, but he does address directly the profound degree of heterogeneity that has traditionally been submerged under the term "art cinema," which critics like Thanouli and Cindy H. Wong continue to notice today. In so doing, he shows how this classifier managed to contain art cinema's expanding formal heterogeneity over its long history. These explanations clarify why this heterogeneity persists to this day. And they are even more helpful if we update Neale's account so that it touches directly on more recent decades. Hence, we may begin to see how institutions in the areas of distribution, exhibition, and evaluation have encouraged the production of diverse art-cinema forms while also encouraging the use of a single concept to cover them all.

As noted, one necessary limitation of Neale's account is his focus on the production end of European art cinema. Thus Neale leaves out major developments in European art-cinema exhibition and reception, including those in the festival network; he also leaves out most developments in North America and Asia. Still, Neale does cite the impact of Hollywood, which helps to explain how the Production Code came to influence Hollywood's postwar competitors: by way of the Hollywood Production Code, European producers and distributors learned all the things that Hollywood could *not* do, meaning that they learned many of the *same* things that they *should* do. This counter-Code approach helped art-cinema producers and distributors bind their films into what seemed to American eyes a real genre despite its diversity: the "foreign film." Such a result was in part the by-product of a process designed to enhance the appeal of these films in the United States, which, as I have noted, was the crucial world market due to its huge collective audience and its outsize impact on the films that Hollywood exported to the rest of the world. From 1948 to 1968, the U.S. market opened up to foreign films, giving power to a lucrative art-house circuit — and playing a role in Hollywood's flirtations with art cinema and its eventual scuttling of its Production Code.

Here a few words about American art houses are in order. Until the middle of the twentieth century, viewing art films in the United States meant attending one of the little cinemas, repertory theaters, museum theaters, university theaters, or film societies available to cinephiles, mainly in college towns and in select urban areas. But after the Supreme Court's 1948 Paramount decision and its 1952 Miracle decision, these outlets became more prolific, profitable, and organized.[22] Indeed, after those events, the art-house circuit rapidly developed into a regular network with complex relations to other "alternative"

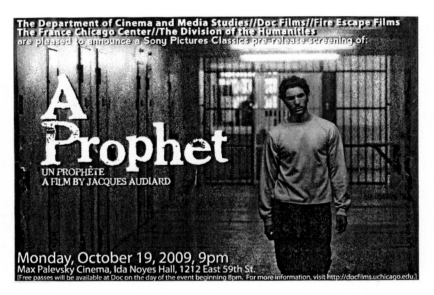

A poster for a special promotional screening of Jacques Audiard's *Un prophète* (2009), a traditional art film showing at Doc Films in Chicago. Doc is a university theater exhibiting films on a repertory art-house model. The oldest student-run theater in the United States, Doc's antecedents stretch back to 1932. Used by permission of Doc Films Group.

sites of exhibition, like the grindhouses and drive-ins of the exploitation circuit.[23] This circuit tolerated a great deal of formal diversity, exhibiting a range of foreign art films as well as exploitation movies by foreign and domestic producers. As in the United Kingdom,[24] the U.S. art-house circuit entered a period of decline during the late 1960s that lasted into the 1980s. It was adversely affected by competition with the New Hollywood art movies and high-concept blockbusters that played in Hollywood's standard outlets. This circuit was also affected by suburbanization and the proliferation of multiplexes; later, it suffered the coming of home video. Despite these setbacks, the American art house survived the 1980s to thrive in the 1990s after the resurgence of American independent film, which encouraged the establishment of new art houses, multiscreen art-plexes, and a range of microcinemas. If American critics still use terms like "art-house style" and "art-house film" in their reviews today, it is because this circuit has been a flexible and resilient host, not because the circuit has actually made movies.

But there is one component of art cinema's exhibition apparatus that *has* had a generative role in art cinema: the global festival network that began at

Venice, Cannes, and Berlin, and which is still anchored by those institutions as well as by relative newcomers like Sundance. Of course, the art-house circuit and the festival circuit have shared many roles. As Neale notes, both were devoted to the reverential exhibition of art films, so both reinforced the neo-Kantian sense that such films *deserved* or *mandated* their accolades. Through their evaluative functions, these two networks helped bind art cinema into a category that has been more unified by its institutional claims to high-art status than by its formal attributes, which are as diverse as those of any other form of high art. What gives the festival network an edge over the art-house circuit in cultural significance is that, as the "major clearinghouse for art cinema," it has been in a position to dictate which art movies have received distribution to art houses across the globe—and scholars such as Wong, Thomas Elsaesser, Azadeh Farahmand, and Mark Betz have shown that the festival system has had a direct generative role by way of the constraints and incentives it uses to enmesh directors, whom this system has traditionally if ironically referred to as "autonomous" auteurs.[25] Because the significance of this system in art cinema cannot be overstated, we should look at it as a major mechanism through which art cinema has sustained the ideas of value that bind it. These ideas include auteur mythology and the notion of the festival film.

But we may also choose to look at one other segment of postwar reception and evaluation, the academic discipline of film studies. Film studies is noteworthy because, "as with film festivals, academic study bestows artistic worth on its object," as Shyon Baumann puts it.[26] Film studies has for the most part been a postwar phenomenon (albeit one that has undergone dramatic changes since Neale wrote "Art Cinema as Institution"). Indeed, its institutionalization in the Anglo-American academy is loosely correlated with the mid-century consecration of the cinema as high art, which justified the medium's role in academia. This is noteworthy because, if my analysis is right, film studies has played a significant, albeit underreported, role in sustaining the art-cinema concept. Though film scholars have at times been hostile to auteurism and to art cinema itself,[27] their participation in the "crossover" forums, which reinforce art cinema's auteurist assumptions, has been crucial to the long-term maintenance of art cinema's high-art value in mainstream forums.

The Film Festival as Contemporary Institution

Before we examine the film-festival system as a contemporary institution of some significance, we should look at its long history. This system, which began in Venice in 1932, is rooted in Europe. As Elsaesser has noted, the film festival is

> a very European institution. It was invented in Europe just before the Second World War, but it came to cultural fruition, economic stature, and political maturity in the 1940s and 1950s. Since then, the names of Venice, Cannes, Berlin, Rotterdam, Locarno, Karlovy Vary, Oberhausen and San Sebastian have spelled the roll call of regular watering holes for the world's film lovers, critics and journalists, as well as being the market-places for producers, directors, distributors, television acquisition heads, and studio bosses.[28]

Still, as both Neale and Elsaesser have acknowledged, this institution was not confined to Europe for very long. As a distribution network, it has performed its commercial role by reproducing itself through export and imitation. Once the circuit gained glamour through its capitals, Venice and Cannes, it spread to North America, South America, Asia, Australia, and Africa. Today, there are over 700 festivals held across the globe.[29] The system has traveled every-where but Antarctica, carrying its cinephilic values along with it.

Consider the United States. Though the festival system is European in ori-gins and bearings, the first U.S. festival was held in 1953. The circuit spread to major American cities in 1957, when the San Francisco Film Festival was held. After that, the American festival system grew explosively, with seventy-three festivals already active in 1985, many of which were juried, and most of which judged their entries using auteur assumptions.[30] The juried festivals in-cluded the U.S. Film Festival, which was renamed the Sundance Film Festival in 1985. The expansion of the American festival circuit has been steady since then, with important festivals taking root in major cities as well as in smaller ones like Austin. Today, some cities have multiple festivals and even mul-tiple *major* festivals: New York, for example, features the New York and Tri-beca Film Festivals. Many festivals have a sprawling, catholic sensibility while others (such as Ann Arbor, which concentrates on experimental cinema) have specialized tastes. Specialized festivals may be devoted to a genre, theme, or style, or to an identity or subculture that cuts across the lines of gender, class, race, and sexual orientation; thus festivals for gay-and-lesbian directors form a dynamic segment of today's American scene. Another notable segment is the cult festival that focuses on the "paracinema" aesthetic—that is, on an alternative taste regime that often presents itself as a cult variation on the art-house sensibility.[31]

Like the art-house circuit, the festival circuit is a loose, decentralized system with a variety of extensions.[32] But it grows tighter and much more institutionalized as cinephiles and insiders move from its outer reaches to the inner sanctum of international "A" festivals at Venice, Cannes, and Moscow as well as Montreal, Tokyo, Cairo, and so forth. These festivals form a compact "network with nodes and nerve endings" that operate through imitation and competition.[33] Elsaesser observes that elite "host cities compete with each other regarding attractiveness of the location, convenience for international access and exclusivity of the films they are able to present. The festivals also compete over desirable dates on the annual calendar."[34] This competition has raised standards across the network, adding

> value to the films presented. Competition invites comparison, with the result that festivals resemble each other more and more in their internal organization, while seeking to differentiate themselves in their external self-presentation and the premium they place on their (themed) programming.[35]

A festival offers a stamp of prestige and raises tourist revenues. But what intrigues me most is how its cultural capital flows among producers, distributors, critics, films, and genres through a self-sustaining, circular logic of association. Everything is so colored by the festival hothouse that the sources of value and the objects of reverence mix and merge. This cultural capital has very practical uses. As Baumann has noted, postwar critics could refer to "the awards that a film had won as testimony to its artistic worth,"[36] and sales agents and distributors could follow suit. To justify this evaluative atmosphere, festivals have had to speak the language of the absolute, the unquestionable. Thus they have from the start adopted an air of bogus religiosity that makes their film judgments seem "impervious to rational criteria or secondary elaborations"—for as Farahmand notes, "Festival awards would not be useful for distributors if the public were aware of the capital-dependent and politics-driven dynamics of film festivals that . . . influence the selection of films and allocation of awards."[37] This protective religiosity is not new, for André Bazin had noticed this dynamic by 1955, when he made it a premise of his essay "The Festival Viewed as a Religious Order."

If a festival is especially durable or successful, it may even provide its prestige to entries that win nothing, for just getting into a festival can be competitive and costly—and potentially useful to movie distributors. Thus Marijke de Valck argues in *Film Festivals* (2008) that the value "added by festival selection and programming reaches beyond the level of personal preference and becomes more or less—according to the festival's prestige on the international film circuit—globally acknowledged as evidence of quality."[38] Much like a festival award, this participation-based prestige may be invoked by sales agents to market a film to distributors, exhibitors, and audiences, including viewers who watch on computers, cell phones, and iPads. Festivals are "turnstiles taking directors into the industry," making them useful as high-pressure sites for deal-making between sales agents and distributors.[39] They have been used by exhibitors as guides for programming art houses, art-plexes, microcinemas, and even museums, and they have been used in this way by executives at Blockbuster, Facets, and Netflix as well. The festival is art cinema's fundamental institution, then, the one that best captures the naked contradictions of a commercial area whose marketability is determined by aesthetic rituals that testify to its purity.

This sort of contradiction is also important to Elsaesser's comments about how, in its effects on production and distribution, the festival has come to resemble Hollywood.[40] Elsaesser's argument in this section of his fine essay "Film Festival Networks" (2005) is based on what he considers a crucial shift that took place in 1972 when Cannes supported the move away from national selection committees. Because any shift at Cannes tended to reverberate across the entire system, this change in effect gave festival directors across the globe the final say over the entry process. Thus it marked a significant moment in the development of what Elsaesser calls an increasingly "postnational" festival system. As Elsaesser has recounted, "The gold standard of the European festivals under the rule of Cannes [after 1972] became the auteur director," not the nation or the national cinema.[41] By stressing the "auteur" and other signs of universalism, festivals could better facilitate the international flow of cultural and economic capital on which they depended. But as Elsaesser has also pointed out, the increasing auteurism of this postnational system has also been in fairly open conflict with industrial realities.

For example, though festivals promote the autonomous auteur, film directors face a variety of constraints when they take their films to festivals. These constraints tend to reinforce formulas approved by festival directors. "Films are now to some extent 'commissioned' for festivals," Elsaesser notes, meaning that the "power/control has shifted from the film director to the festival director," who is put in the position of a "star curator" or a studio executive.[42] Consequently, many of the Iranian films that Thanouli mentions are festival films,[43] for directors like Mohsen Makhmalbaf and Abbas Kiarostami have tailored their films to festival criteria in order to win reliable acclaim.[44] On the other hand, the fact that these auteurs have faced specific subcultural constraints does not mean the "festival film" is all that restrictive as a category; indeed, it has as much leeway as the "art cinema" category. Festivals do not have to adhere to centralized criteria, so their dispersal through time and space, in tandem with the incentives that festival directors have to offer new choices and to discover new auteurs, new waves, and national cinemas, has encouraged a great deal of formal heterogeneity. (Here it is to the point that the other hard cases Thanouli cites, including American smart films and Danish Dogme films, have also been identified with film festivals.)[45] Wong has charted many of the commonalities of festival films, including the "seriousness" that binds those that prove most successful at festivals, but at the same time she repeatedly insists that there is no "single formula for festival films or festival success."[46] As Farahmand makes clear, the fact that art cinema's "generic boundaries remain loosely defined . . . ensures that festivals can continue to offer fresh products, or at least a new take on the products they showcase."[47]

One last point about the festival system: though it is a vehicle for conservative aesthetic values, it may also be an agent of political and artistic change. For Elsaesser, the existence of gay-and-lesbian festivals, which are as value-oriented as any other festivals, is a positive force for those who identify themselves as nonheterosexual; similarly, the fact that Cannes awarded *Fahrenheit 9/11* (2004) the Golden Palm said negative things about American foreign policy in the Bush years.[48] Another way that film festivals have provoked change is by acting as a register for the changing tastes of juries, audiences, and auteurs. I have noted the existence of cult-movie festivals, which have appeared in Europe (e.g., the Brussels International Fantastic Film Festival), North America (with significant events in San Francisco, Austin, and Montreal, among other cities), and several other continents. These festivals may seem to form a separate system with their own rituals and audiences. But this separateness is not unique to cult festivals, given that festivals devoted to experimental cinema and gay-and-lesbian cinema also display this separate-yet-connected nature.[49] There are, then, ways for movies to flow across these systems into the most culturally prestigious circuit anchored by Cannes, Venice, and Moscow as well as Toronto, Rotterdam, Berlin, and so on. Moreover, festivals like Tribeca have often included screenings dedicated to films classified as having a cult flavor.[50] These cult areas are crucial to the festival circuit's overall diversity and even more crucial to the flow of cult movies across the globe, a circulation that has been more difficult to ensure than that of more traditional art films.

Consequently, in an age in which a fanboy like Quentin Tarantino has become a true fixture at Cannes, it may be a harbinger of things to come that the last decade has increasingly seen cult motifs and cult ideas penetrate the most prestigious levels of the circuit. For instance, art-horror films like Park Chan-wook's *Oldboy* (2003) and Tomas Alfredson's *Let the Right One In* (2008) have won prizes at both traditional festivals and "fantastic" festivals, with *Oldboy* winning a Grand Prix Second Prize at Cannes. This should cause observers no particular surprise. If art cinema and its auteurist emphasis have proved useful to Hollywood directors and to studios in mainstream areas, there is no reason to think they couldn't prove similarly useful to directors with cult sensibilities specializing in cult forms and themes. Here Cannes in particular has been in the vanguard, as confirmed in the July 2009 issue of *Sight & Sound*. The points of crossover between cult and traditional forms have demonstrated that cultural tastes evolve over time.

Of course, it is traditional for mainstream critics and traditional cinephiles to see in this process of transformation the "erosion of a certain *idea* about art cinema," as Joan Hawkins puts it, for these observers often still believe that art cinema is "superior to and distinct from exploitation."[51] Thus they follow Bazin in lamenting the state of the festival, whose ever-present corruption they identify as a fall from the grace of cinephilia.[52] What they fail to perceive is that art cinema is perpetuated by the rituals of the circuit, *including* its tendency for lamentation, and not by any particular tastes favored by those rituals. Thus the fact that many status-laden festivals like Cannes and Venice still award prizes through these rituals is sufficient to certify that the art-cinema institution is alive and well—and the fact that cinephiles continue to lament the "sorry" state of contemporary cinema is sufficient to certify that a "certain *idea* of art cinema" has been successfully handed down through that institution.

The Institutional Function of "Crossover" Forums

Another institution that plays an important role in art cinema is film studies. This is a tricky case to make, since film studies is usually considered an academic institution, not a cinematic one. However, once we see that the mainstream world of movie reviews, trade presses, and blogs cannot be cleanly separated from the academic world of peer-reviewed journals, university presses, and professional conferences, we will be more open to the idea that film studies promotes art cinema in a variety of fashions. Still, if all these forums may claim to be "doing" film studies in some sense, they clearly do it in different ways, bringing varying levels of expertise and legitimacy to the conversation. The most expert forums are peer-reviewed academic publications, where film scholars have critiqued the ideological bases of art cinema, particularly its stress on auteurism. These expert forums have the most *sub-*

cultural legitimacy inside academia. However, scholars have also been free to participate in crossover forums where they may appear alongside more mainstream critics. The quasi-academic crossover publications can have large circulations and may constitute the most academic form of publication on cinema that nonacademics encounter—and for that reason, they have more *cultural* legitimacy than do peer-reviewed forums. Crossover forums are significant in that they channel their academic credibility to promote the cinephilic discourses that have been mandated by their specific market constraints. Consequently, mainstream readers who do not recognize the difference between a fully academic, peer-reviewed text and a more popular, quasi-academic, crossover text may presume that all academics are in full agreement with art-cinema assumptions—and with auteurism in particular. To understand what this means vis-à-vis the genre itself, it helps to review two interrelated histories: the development of auteurism and the emergence of academic film studies.

Because I dealt with auteurism and the "auteur theory" in chapter 2, I will only outline my conclusions as they relate to film studies. We should first recall that the idea of film authorship is as old as film itself, and that the belief in the director as the most logical creative "center" of a movie goes back to the silent era. Ergo, we should look at the success of *Cahiers du cinéma* and the French New Wave at promoting la politique des auteurs—which later became known as the "auteur theory" through critics like Andrew Sarris and journals like *Movie*—as a moment in the history of auteurism but not as the start of that history. However, the auteur theory did add momentum to the emerging discipline of film studies. Partly under the aegis of auteurism, academic film studies grew quickly in Western countries from the late 1950s through the 1970s. The Society of Cinematologists (currently named the Society for Cinema and Media Studies) was inaugurated in 1959 and followed by film-studies departments across the United States and the United Kingdom.[53] These departments blended the professionalism of the older film-production schools with the critical slant of the highbrow journalism that appeared in *Cahiers du cinéma, Movie, Film Quarterly*, and many other crossover periodicals. One crucial aspect of this broad historical process, however, was that the auteur theory offered this emergent discipline an accessible and respectable sense of rigor that film scholars could then invoke to justify their field to outside administrators. Moreover, an auteurist brand of art cinema offered film studies a very popular subject that students were motivated to study, adding even more momentum to this disciplinary shift.

Once the new field was established, however, it came to operate according to the mechanics that ruled across the humanities: to get ahead, its participants had to publish innovative research in peer-reviewed forums. What this meant was that the academic segments of film studies *had* to go beyond the auteur theory, while the field's mainstream segments could *not* go beyond it. The incentive behind the academic market is the pursuit of academic capital, which is principally useful within its own academic subculture. There, its institutionally subsidized presses and journals are designed to experiment with ideas that are often inaccessible to laypersons, meaning that film scholars have had incentives to critique more popular theories, such as the auteur theory, when necessary. And that kind of critique often seemed necessary after 1968, when a combination of academic and political pressures led scholars to demolish the auteur theory in the publications of cutting-edge university presses and theoretically radical journals like *Screen, Jump Cut*, and many others.

Thus, in "Art Cinema as Institution," Neale voiced what was by then recognized as the summary knock on auteurism: that it was "a means by which [film scholars] avoid coming to terms with the concept of film as social practice."[54] Film scholars pursued this idea in a variety of ways. They argued that auteurism was untrue to the communal nature of film production and the industrial necessities of film promotion. They also argued that it was untrue to the realities of language, discourse, and consciousness; that it was untrue to the racist and patriarchal "apparatus" of cinema; and that it was untrue to the nature of auteur status, which derived not from intrinsic talent or value but from the sociological processes of art, society, and the film industry.

Many of these attacks were convincing. But auteurism didn't go away. Instead, it turned out to be a very human attitude that grew more stable despite the criticism. Indeed, this stability seems impervious to all scholarly argument, in part because auteurism has enabled so much activity, helping people to talk, to think about film—and because it has grown ever-more institutionally entrenched, providing its users with both collective and individual benefits over time. Among its collective users is film studies itself, whose auteurist lineage has proved adaptable, open to diverse agendas, including many that are politically progressive. As a result, even in the most academic sectors of film studies, we may still find auteurist thinking, from the standard conference paper on feminist and queer auteurs to the psychoanalytic treatise that is actually a loosely veiled variant of auteur study. And university presses still regularly publish openly cinephilic (i.e., theoretically retrograde) explorations of a single auteur oeuvre or single "masterwork."

I make these points to explain why so many of us have taken part in the crossover forums. It is not that we are pursuing a mainstream form of success. Contrary to popular belief, scholars are humans, and auteurism appeals to us as such. Plus, auteurism has an ancestral legitimacy in academic film studies, where it is still accepted as a normative stance. Scholars who conform to the auteurism that dominates crossover publications are not, then, necessarily betraying academic traditions. What I want to stress, though, is that it is our participation in the crossover forums that gives them a quasi-academic bearing, reinforcing the legitimacy of such forums in the mainstream. And that dynamic has in effect protected the traditional understanding of art cinema as a special genre, one that "deserves" its privileged place as a movie institution.

This should not surprise us, given Baumann's idea that the cinema could not have been consecrated as a legitimate art medium without expert intellectual discourses working to justify it. These justifications emerged through the growing ties between the academy and the film industry and through the growing specialization of review-oriented publications, which evaluated movies in increasingly professional ways.[55] Haden Guest claims that by "the 1950s one can see productive debates . . . between popular film writing and the more rigorous academic writing beholden to standards of evidence and argumentation."[56] Indeed, the more rigorous journals, like *Films in Review*, *Cinemages*, and *Film Culture*, may have been even more important outside film departments, where they "played a foundational role in establishing film studies as a major intellectual force across the humanities."[57] Consequently, they spoke to the educated general reader and the budding scholar. Today, journals in this crossover category include the U.S. *Film Quarterly*, *Film Comment*, and *Cineaste*; the French *Cahiers du cinéma* and *Positif*; the British *Sight & Sound*; and the Canadian *CineAction*, among many others.[58] These crossover journals have juxtaposed mainstream critics with film scholars. Though they have regional tendencies, they are unified in their stress on auteurs as well as on art, with the corollary that the default subject of these magazines is the plastic notion of the "auteur work."

Much the same might be said of certain presses—including Wallflower, Berg, BFI, Continuum, and Twayne—which support the foundations of art cinema by subsidizing accessible academic tomes on auteurs, masterpieces, new waves, national cinemas, and even cult-art cinemas. Recently, Betz has published an essay focusing on the "little book" in film studies: the small, sophisticated book written by specialists for nonspecialists. To reach the widest audiences, imprints like the *Sight & Sound*-affiliated series Cinema One, which was active between 1967 and 1976, stressed in Betz's view a "circumscribed set of subjects," including "directors" and "nations/movements or the 'new' cinema."⁵⁹ This trend has persisted through today, Betz claims, noting the general prominence of British publications and the specific prominence of Wallflower:

> The sizes and formats of [the Wallflower] series cut a swath between some of the much smaller little books in current publication and that of the standard university press monograph, denoting Wallflower's crossover address among those studying film within the educational sector and a new generation of the cineliterate fueling their passion from without. On the production end, there is room in its stable for both the academic scholar and the belletristic critic.⁶⁰

Betz's insight is born out by *dekalog³: On Film Festivals* (2009), a Wallflower volume that I have cited in this chapter. This physically small volume is very useful despite the programmatic cinephilia that makes its opinions suspect. But what this kind of book shows us is that auteurism, with its default cinephilia, still represents the one theoretical stance open to scholars who hope to apply their talents to trade publications. As Betz puts it so neatly, "the predominance of the director as subject of study" has been a crucial force of "continuity" linking little books through the present day.⁶¹

What does this all add up to? Crossover publications reinforce art cinema's most cinephilic values through their persistent stress on art, on form, on canon—and on the auteur in particular. In this way, they help to stabilize the category in the eyes of the public, making its foundational concepts seem impervious to fashion, academic fashion included. That film scholars take part in these publications is crucial to this effect, I think, for their participation can suggest to individuals located outside academia that the more radical or progressive aspects of film studies are symptoms of an academic flakiness that scholars are unwilling to pursue in the most high-profile forums available, where they instead corroborate the cultural distinction that mainstream critics have accorded auteurs, art films, and canon. Thus, despite film studies' deconstructive paradigms, in this field the field itself has lent abundant legitimacy to the conservative values that anchor the festival system.

Only by crafting institutional accounts like those above will we be in a position to deflect Thanouli's suggestion that "art cinema," a term that has facilitated the distribution of a diversity of themes and styles and institutions under a single heading, may in the end be too vacuous to be useful. I hope to have shown here that "art cinema" is *exceptionally* useful—and like "auteurism," it is not going to go away just because we have had enough of its

**Sight &
Sound**

THE INTERNATIONAL FILM MAGAZINE

December 09

Volume 19 Issue 12 £3.95

MICHAEL HANEKE

THE WHITE RIBBON INTERVIEW

PL

Jane Campion on Keats: **Bright Star**   The Coens go back to their roots:
A Serious Man | Henri-Georges Clouzot's lost comeback: **Inferno**
The obscure genius of **Straub/Huillet** | Steven Soderbergh on **The Informant!**
Every new film reviewed

The December 2009 issue of *Sight & Sound*, a crucial art-cinema institution.
This crossover magazine reinforces auteurist premises throughout its pages,
starting with its cover. Used by permission of *Sight & Sound*, published by the
British Film Institute.

dizzying forms and equally dizzying illogics. Instead, we should construct an institutional theory of art cinema that understands the formal heterogeneity implied by this useful heading not through a narrative lens or a formalist sensibility, but through a supple cultural schema that relates the category's diversity to its institutions, including the art house, the festival, and the discipline of film studies. These accredited sites of evaluation have in effect fixed the value of art movies on their first release and have regulated that value over the long-term, often relying on art cinema's flexible ideologies, such as auteurism, to complete the ritual. But to grasp all this, we need *the term*. For whether we are unreformed cinephiles writing reviews or myth-busting scholars in dark sunglasses taking in the festival scene, the term "art cinema" is indispensable to all our projects.

CHAPTER 10

Art Cinema, the Distribution Theory

Though film studies has come a long way since the heyday of the auteur theory in the 1960s and 1970s, the field still circulates many auteur biases. Such biases are plainly evident in what I call the "bad old story" of movie distribution, which amounts to any anecdote that presents distributors as moneygrubbing philistines who interfere with the activities of cinematic artists, especially auteurs. Because this interference is usually imagined as happening *after* production has been finished, distributors often come off even worse in this sort of story than do executive producers, whose overlapping (and frequently identical) financial functions seem to enable the creative process in a more direct way.[1] Hence, the legend in which Joseph Levine let Jean-Luc Godard know that an early cut of *Le mépris* (1963) didn't have "enough ass in it" represents an iconic embodiment of the bad old story, for in it an American distributor crudely directs a French auteur to modify an art film the auteur considered finished so that it would generate more cash.[2] But there are so many other noteworthy cases—here we need only mention Harvey Weinstein to confirm the point—that we needn't limit ourselves to Levine and Godard. In its elements, the bad old story is inscribed, it seems, in our very brains.[3]

What we may be more surprised to discover is that variants of this anecdote often seem today to *grease* movie distribution. Art-cinema industries often promote films and auteurs by defending their authenticity through antidistribution narratives like the bad old story. At times, this means that distributors must voluntarily fill the role of "the heavy" to further their own interests, which are tied to those of the auteurs whose work they distribute. For example, Weinstein has shown a consistent willingness to play the vulgarian villain, and it is tempting to think he understands that doing so has made the art movies of "pure" auteurs like Peter Greenaway more valuable to

A production still showing Helen Mirren as Georgina in Peter Greenaway's film *The Cook, the Thief, His Wife, and Her Lover* (1989). Distributor Harvey Weinstein played "the heavy" in the controversy that this film spurred in its American release. © 1989 Allarts Cook and Elsevira, © 1990 Miramax Films.

his distribution labels; a similar dynamic is visible in the dealings of major-studio distributors like Universal and Warner Bros. with directors like Todd Solondz or Stanley Kubrick.[4] All in all, it seems that the bad old story is today a conventional component of art-cinema distribution, from world cinema and the avant-garde to mainstream cinema. But the idea of art-cinema distribution that this use of the anecdote suggests is so peculiar it cannot be explored through traditional ideas alone. It forces us to find a more nuanced way of imagining movie distribution, one that imagines it as more than a pipeline for movies run by distribution agents.

The pipeline idea, which I refer to as the "transit metaphor," is the most traditional idea of distribution available. Its virtue is clarity, and the cost of such clarity is nuance. If our models are to draw on more complex variables such as cultural status and high-art idealism, we must develop a far more flexible, extended definition of distribution that encompasses more elements and that has broader applications. For me, an extended definition construes movie distribution not as a mere pipeline but as a shifting segment in a wider, more interactive network of cultural exchange. The advantage of this model is that it helps us to re-imagine a movie-distribution industry that interfaces with many different cultural "flows," all of which may ultimately have an impact on art-movie form. In this way, the network model avoids the decontextualization that makes it seem as if films are circulated outside a dense fabric of social relations—an illusion that is particularly vivid in discussions of art cinema, whose primary discourses seem to encourage it. Clearly, the extended definition must be treated with care, for it could lead us into the conceptual ether. But we don't have a choice as to whether to use it, for the realities of movie distribution—and the striking peculiarities of art-cinema distribution—mandate it. And in the end, the extended definition has one other advantage, too: it encourages scholars to re-imagine art cinema as an active, collective category of high art.

From the Transit Metaphor to an Extended Definition

To reconceive art-cinema distribution, we should review how the topic of movie distribution has been dealt with in the past. The bad old story is a popular approach. But a more neutral approach to distribution has long been available in the vast literature of the movie business. Here the routine way of conceptualizing distribution has been to imagine it as a highway, bridge, or pipeline. For example, industry analyst Harold Vogel manages to combine all three metaphors when he observes that "ownership of entertainment distribution capability is like ownership of a toll road or bridge. No matter how good or bad the software product . . . is, it must pass over or cross through a distribution pipeline in order to reach the consumer."[5] This conventional view of distribution—which deems the distributor a "local monopolist," as Vogel puts it—has definite utility, for it explains why certain cinemas have proved viable in certain contexts.

Examples of this idea of distribution may be found in textbooks like Jason Squire's collection *The Movie Business Book* (1983/2004) and in popular studies such as Edward Jay Epstein's *The Big Picture: The New Logic of Money and Power in Hollywood* (2005). For instance, the first book contains a chapter titled "Theatrical Distribution," by Warner Bros. executive Daniel Fellman, and another chapter titled "Independent Distribution," by Newmarket Films executive Bob Berney.[6] In overviews such as these, movie distribution is always a question of acquisition (i.e., distributor–producer relations) or dissemination (i.e., distributor–exhibitor relations). These topics cover issues like pickup deals, financing, licensing, horizontal integration, changes in technology, test screening for playability, and advertising and marketability. Distribution is construed here, then, almost exclusively in terms of issues that affect *distributors* and *distribution agents*—that is, the companies and people who transport movies from artists to exhibitors and on to consumers. Even when looking at the circulation of art-house movies, these pieces remain focused on business activities that grow profit by moving movies from producers to consumers while experiencing minimal friction from *distribution constraints*.

Historians and critics have drawn useful information from these business guides. This utility is reflected in the fine work of scholars like Thomas Guback, Justin Wyatt, and Tino Balio.[7] Unfortunately, the transit metaphor has its limitations. We can use it to imagine distribution as speeding movies toward viewers; we can also use it to imagine distribution speeding dollars back to distributors in a feedback loop. But this metaphor cannot account for the interactive networks of social exchange that movie distribution has actually energized in the world. Nor can it make sense of the cinema's place in wider circuits of human circulation, where biological as well as sociological currents are exchanged. Indeed, if flows of prestige, fame, ambition, sexual desire, cinephilia, and cultural identity could be added to the transit metaphor, it might be easier for scholars to justify its application to a heavily eroticized, status-laden movie genre such as art cinema. Unfortunately, the transit metaphor depends on the ready economic quantification of variables and is much too brittle to support such an approach.

Today, supple and holistic concepts of distribution are emerging in a variety of subfields. These ideas seem especially popular in the scholarship on world cinema and the "transnational," where concepts of cultural exchange and interdependence are taken for granted.[8] They are also popular among media scholars like Sean Cubitt who are versed in ideas of communication. These new concepts of movie distribution often define their topics quite broadly and loosely,[9] making distribution a richer, more culturally relevant topic—but also making it more difficult for media theorists to use such concepts systematically. That said, there is a tradition in the sociology of art that uses an extended definition in a systematic way. This tradition begins with the work of Howard Becker.

In "Distributing Art Works," a chapter in his landmark book *Art Worlds* (1982), Becker lays out principles relevant to both high and low art worlds.[10] Becker's book is organized by his belief that all "artistic work, like all human activity, involves the joint activity of a number, often a large number, of people"—and this idea is nowhere truer than in the area of distribution.[11] Becker perceives the "joint activity" of art as leading naturally to the creation of art worlds. These distribution contexts "provide distribution systems which integrate artists into their society's economy, bringing art works to publics which appreciate them and will pay enough so that the work can proceed."[12] Subject to pressures and laws, these distribution contexts are hardly autonomous. Before people can organize an art world justified by making and distributing "objects or events defined as art, they need sufficient political and economic freedom to do that, and not all societies provide it."[13] Even in cultures where organized art worlds already exist, the capacity to make and distribute art is never divided equally. Almost from the start, then, we see that art—*all* art, whether popular or fine—amounts to an active process of social exchange. We also see that the phenomenon we call "distribution" is a specialized example of that active form of social exchange. And finally, we see that both kinds of social exchange remain contingent on broader cultural factors, including political freedom.

Though Becker makes many fine points, the most crucial may be his belief that "distribution has a crucial effect on [artist] reputations. What is not distributed is not known and thus cannot be well thought of or have historical importance."[14] Hoping to reach an audience and looking out for their own fame, status, and survival, artists respond to the needs of a delivery system (like a studio label or a film festival) by introducing elements of standardization into their artworks that Becker refers to as "marks of the system." This distribution system in turn fits into a larger distribution context and the overall cultural system that shapes it; a distribution system has only as much leeway to accommodate artist and audience preferences as the broader systems allow.[15] Most artists accept the constraints of their distribution system, but some artists attempt to reshape those constraints by overpowering that system through their own marketability or by joining with other artists to inaugurate new distribution systems. Other collective factors, such as art traditions, audience expectations, linguistic backgrounds, political trends, changes in technology, and market segmentations, are all in play here, as are many people, some all but invisible, who shape an artwork and bring it to its public—including the public itself, whose desires mold the works and which are in turn molded by them. In sum, Becker implies that neither artists, nor works, nor audiences are autonomous—for distribution ties them all together.

Where do audiences for new categories of art come from? Today, theorists take it for granted that, as Jane Root once put it, movie distributors "are a vital link in the chain between film production and audiences," for distributors "decide what can be shown where and . . . make crucial decisions about a film's public profile."[16] But what if no audience for a given category of cinema exists? How does one coalesce and start to emerge? Does someone make it? Theorists who rely on the transit metaphor might struggle with this sort of question, since distributors and directors would seem to be their only candidates. But in his book *Hollywood Highbrow: From Entertainment to Art* (2007), Shyon Baumann shows that interlocking social processes are responsible for the formation of movie audiences. To my knowledge, only Baumann has applied Becker's ideas to the art-cinema category. One of the advantages of his research is that it allows us to see that before art movies could have a broad success in the postwar United States, high-art concepts and film-as-art concepts had to be circulating in that context already.

Before focusing on Hollywood, Baumann traces the broad "historical change in the perception of films" that allowed the cinema to be legitimated as art in different times and places.[17] His goal is to explain how one strain of Hollywood production—the New Hollywood—came to be regarded as high art in the 1970s, a curious phenomenon considering Hollywood's vast popularity before 1950 and its efforts to be perceived as a purveyor of entertainment, not art. To explain this curiosity, Baumann begins by describing several factors, like the early appearance of the film-as-high-art idea in France and Italy, as well as Hollywood's use of the auteur theory and other high-art concepts to combat its long commercial decline beginning in the 1950s. Thus he sets up a three-part "legitimation framework" to account for the gradual change in cultural perceptions of Hollywood.[18] His most crucial insight is his idea that the cultural acceptance of *"foreign films as art acted as a pathway for the legitimation of the art world for Hollywood films."*[19] That the film-as-high-art idea originally hailed from Europe added to its legitimacy in

Hollywood and gave it status-conferring power; this legitimacy was in turn reinforced by the success of other ideas of European provenance, especially the auteur theory.

The thing that I most admire about Baumann's account is that it acknowledges that the idea of a Hollywood art cinema was just that: a concept, an idea. The development and circulation of this idea was spurred by global forces of cultural exchange that encouraged the creation of cognitive pathways that allowed the film-as-high-art idea to penetrate the United States. Unlike most commercial movie categories, art cinema has been reliant on its organizing concept; the category is more intellectual than visual, narrative, or aural. It is not unified, then, by objective forms like the frontier backdrop of the western. In a sense, the high-art idea is all that stands between art movies and conceptual chaos. The circulation of the film-as-high-art idea was expanded by postwar phenomena, like the rapid stratification of consumer culture, the huge expansion of the educational system, the emergence of an increasingly expert class of critics, and the precipitous decline in the popularity of film as mass entertainment. In other words, though the circulation of art cinema's high-art concept was impeded by many historical factors before the middle of the century, many of those impediments were removed after the Second World War.

It is easy to see how this kind of account might be expanded. If Baumann were to dispense with the social-constructionist premises that orient not only his study but also many research programs in the social sciences, he could expand his sociology into biocultural areas, perhaps by speculating on how the circulation of New Hollywood films dovetailed with the evolutionary and specifically sexual impulses of human nature. Distribution paradigms might account for our physiological and cognitive constraints as well as for our cultural, subcultural, and industrial constraints.[20] But before we delve into this possibility too deeply, we should come up for oxygen, as it were. We have traveled a very long way in a very short period, moving from the bad old story and a brittle transit metaphor to a diffuse idea of distribution as a variety of "biocultural circulation." Some review is in order.

First, art is a collective human activity that takes place in a social world. Because this world is collective and material, art is never "free." Some of its constraints operate at the level of cultural politics while others are subcultural, operating through various art worlds. An even narrower level of constraint is industrial. Professional artists who want to improve their standing must exhibit their work institutionally, which in the cinema means they must acquire corporate distribution. Such distribution is rarely divided equally, so its acquisition is a competitive process in which artists strive at once to distinguish their work and to standardize the same in accord with the constraints of a delivery system. This process entails that artists must work within artistic concepts that are fairly accessible to audiences targeted by their delivery system; their individual contribution is limited by the flexibility of those concepts, audiences, and systems. Often, the most elastic organizing concepts, like "high art," are simply unavailable within a given art world due to cultural, subcultural, and industrial factors. Such categories and ideas emerge in art worlds only gradually, in concert with a number of other historical developments.

Throughout the arts, distribution agents have a great deal of power, but this power is limited. As "middlemen," distributors must negotiate layers of constraint: some that are put in place by the culture, which usually endorses some degree of censorship; some that are put in place by the art world, whose audiences are limited in what they can accept or tolerate; some that are put in place by the industry, which relies on fixed constraints to optimize the overall profitability of a delivery system; and some that are put in place by the categories of artwork they are working with, categories that can mandate specific and even *peculiar* promotional activities. For instance, in art cinema, one peculiar tactic is distributors' use of the bad old story, whose antidistributor trajectory would seem a counterintuitive tool for a distributor to use were it not for art cinema's high-art biases.

The Bad Old Story and Subcultural Status

Art cinema is built on a high-art concept that first developed and thrived through capitalist forces. As the product of labor innovations that disrupted art markets during the Renaissance, this concept was a defensive response to market constraints. What made this idea odd as a capitalist tool was that it denied the relevance of the market and of all other commercial concerns. Given these factors, it is not too surprising that a high-art sector of the cinema has consistently—and always implausibly—aspired to get beyond commerce. And it is almost predictable that distributors, who more than anyone represent commerce, are the most reviled figures in art cinema. This revulsion against distributors is one way the purity of auteurs is thrown into relief, much as art cinema's purity ostensibly stands out against the corrupt mainstream.[21] But we should recognize that in this equation distributors represent exchange and collaboration, notions that would not automatically be vilified were it not for a high-art framework that idealizes individualism, autonomy, anticommercial purity, and disinterest. That these industrial agents use this negative rhetoric is a function of their place in art cinema—and it is intriguing that they have learned to use it in a way that foments the process this rhetoric nominally rejects (i.e., industrial distribution). Indeed, between Levine's time and ours, distributors like Weinstein have often used such rhetoric to promote their films. Thus the mechanics of the bad old story are worth scrutinizing, especially as they relate to subcultural status.

One striking use of the bad old story occurred in the hoopla surrounding the release of Todd Solondz's *Happiness* (1998), a $3 million art film produced in the indie sector by Good Machine through a distribution agreement with October Films, then a boutique division of Universal. According to this anecdote, when a Universal executive screened this award-winning indie film, he was so upset by its masturbation scene that he "ordered October to dump *Happiness* from its slate."[22] After this information got out, Solondz's status in indie sectors actually rose, partly because his spat with the studio and the MPAA resulted in an unrated, indie release of his film.[23] But as Michael Z. Newman reports, the problem with this parable is that Universal also supplied Good Machine with "under the table" financing so *Happiness* could get proper distribution. When this detail leaked, Solondz's reputation suffered. "Solondz had autonomy precisely because he stood up to Universal," Newman notes.[24] So the "fact that his film was distributed with the help of the studio's dirty money is an inconvenient detail," one that has been left out of conventional accounts that accept the notion of Solondz's autonomy at face value.

If we accept the fact that a professional artist or auteur is at some level a businessperson who must conduct his or her business through many layers of constraint, we might see that the only problem for Solondz was that the story leaked. He could not censor his film for the studio if he wanted to maintain his "cred." But his cred wouldn't do him much good if his film was not seen. As for Universal, its decision to give Good Machine a secret loan was the best way to navigate its own constraints. The studio had to defend its family-friendly image and maintain its status as an upstanding member of the MPAA; at the same time, it wanted to defend its interest in October and *Happiness*, whose publicity would have gone south had it muscled through cuts. By distancing itself from a provocateur, accepting the bad *indie* press that resulted, and financing the release of *Happiness* privately, Universal put itself in a win-win position, for it managed to protect its family-oriented reputation while also defending its financial investment in an artist-oriented indie project.

This story tells us that an auteur's subcultural status hinges on perceptions of his or her autonomy as an author of a film. Though indie auteurs like Solondz must make compromises large and small when producing a movie, they must keep those realities out of the public eye to keep their subcultural status (and their movies) flowing. Indie cred amounts to an indie auteur's symbolic capital. When it is as strong as Solondz's was after the success of *Welcome to the Dollhouse* (1995), it implies a following that can cement the auteur's reputation over the long term. These considerations are of economic import, for they can convince investors to back future projects. It is no wonder, then, that an indie auteur's apparent independence from corporate backers is a crucial illusion. Still, it is not so crucial that an auteur would automatically abandon a film's distribution for it, since distribution is also crucial to an auteur's reputation. Solondz was, in other words, in a sticky position once Universal, a corporate distributor that was itself caught in a web of relations, began to slowly back away from his film.

This story also confirms Becker's belief that the "interests of the intermediaries who operate distribution systems frequently differ from those of the artists whose work they handle."[25] Distributors have a hard time sharing the prestige that is the main benefit of this category for its other participants, including artists and audiences. Indeed, *inside* art cinema,[26] the distributor role is fairly thankless unless distributors manage to brand themselves, à la Daniel Talbot or Cyrus Harvey in past time periods or James Schamus in our own, as indie operators with an "authentic" feel for art—and this careful positioning could backfire if distributors were to reveal any commercial ambitions. Consider that, as I see it, Weinstein has done more for art cinema in the United States than any single auteur, yet he is reviled in indie circles as an anti-art figure and openly mocked as "Harvey Scissorhands." Granted, Weinstein has reportedly done his share of unattractive things.[27] But by itself, the fact that his several distribution labels, Miramax especially, enlarged the circulation of indie films and world cinema in the United States, re-establishing art cinema's mainstream circulation through Hollywood distribution, testifies to his cultural impact—a legacy that might have offset his indiscretions had he been a Godardian auteur rather than a Levinian distributor.

These dynamics have global applications. They explain the scorn that has greeted distributors when they've crossed auteurs like Kubrick, Greenaway, Samuel Peckinpah, and Donald Cammell.[28] And they explain the scorn that has greeted the distributors of French, German, Hungarian, Russian, and Chinese auteurs who have done the same. We also hear echoes of the bad old story in academic debates over the authenticity of world cinemas "compromised" by global money and global distribution. Moreover, the antidistributor logic manifest here is also evident across art cinema's cultural stratifications, encompassing avant-garde and cult regions. For example, while running the New York Film-Makers' Cooperative—the nonprofit system that helped spread the film co-op movement across the globe, stimulating experimental production as never before—Jonas Mekas endured the animosity of artists like Jack Smith, who painted him as a commercially minded empire-builder.[29] In a very different niche, softcore auteurs Alexander Gregory Hippolyte and Tom Lazarus expressed their displeasure at the distributors who limited their creativity.[30] In contexts high and low, then, distributors have found it difficult to seem like anything but profit-seeking "middlemen." No wonder that the dream of indie cinema and art cinema generally is to eliminate distributors entirely.[31] But what makes this dream self-defeating is that distributors are central to the winnowing processes that create status and canon. Even today, when "films" are actually digital software and when many movies, old and new, are streaming directly to consumers, the bad old story is not really obsolete because to become an auteur a director must still watch out for his or her reputation while securing the most prestigious distribution available. As long as there is art and aspiration, this will remain true—regardless of the new channels like YouTube, Netflix, and Facebook.

So why would distributors want to distribute art cinema? Clearly, they must have financial incentives—and, as Roman Lobato has noted, distribution *is* where the money is.[32] Unlike artists and viewers, distributors have direct access to art cinema's economic capital if not to its symbolic capital. Then again, art cinema is hardly the most lucrative kind of cinema to monetize. But there is another commercial incentive to consider here, too. Art cinema is flexible, for distributors can use its myths of value and the free pass they yield to minimize friction from distribution constraints (including rating systems, national borders, and cultural norms) that would block the flow of genres lacking its prestige. This is what has made art cinema's markers so attractive to distributors in genre-branded areas where the circulation of certain vehicles might well be stanched if not for the credentials gleaned from auteur stylization. As Weinstein has shown, for an experienced distributor, it is not at all difficult to enhance the flow of a movie by marketing it as an art film, using a dash of old-fashioned controversy as well as more legitimate promotions that focus on style, festival awards, and parables of indie authenticity.

The Influence of Distribution on Art Cinema Form

The main thing that auteurs complain about within or through the bad old story is having to modify their movies to suit distributors. At the rhetorical level, auteurs resist such demands or at least cast them in a negative light—but it is safe to conclude that distributors have often succeeded in having their demands met, as Levine did in an ironic fashion with *Le mépris*. In other sectors, this type of influence is not cause for alarm. For instance, when studying softcore, I came across a wide variety of distributor effects on movie form. I saw examples in the 1990s softcore industry of executive producers being instructed by their distributors to tone down the violence and sexism of their films to bring them in line with the postfeminist prescriptions of late-night-cable distribution. This influence helped reform the wild, often misogynist genre known during the 1960s and 1970s as "sexploitation" into the tamer, more female-friendly softcore of the 1990s. Because softcore has typically been misperceived as a non-auteurist category, scholars and insiders alike seemed uninhibited by aestheticist bias and were thus fairly open about the influence of distributors on actual movies. But in more traditional art cinema, this influence has been underreported, often because of this category's strict ideals of authorship.

On the other hand, this super-genre is parasitic on multiple genres, so in studying softcore I did observe many examples of distribution's formal influence on *softcore* art movies. This influence was not always a product of outside demands—for as Becker has noted, the main way distribution affects form is through the internalized desires of artists, who standardize their works to win distribution in the most prestigious contexts available. One interesting example of this effect involved Radley Metzger. In the 1960s and 1970s, arty sexploitation directors such as Metzger added highbrow content to their films, hoping to play all the theatrical circuits open to American sex films, including art houses, drive-ins, and grindhouses.[33] The presence of art-house forms and styles within their films won these auteurs a measure of cultural distinction, which insulated them from litigation even as the grindhouse content ensured audience appeal. These processes were even more feasible if the director was, like Metzger, his or her own distributor—and was willing to ape famous European auteurs (whose techniques Metzger understood due to his former employment at Janus Films). Though at times this commercial strategy resulted in highbrow critics condemning these directors as inauthentic, middlebrow interlopers,[34] this result was in some quarters taken as proof of enhanced prestige, for it meant serious critics were reviewing these directors.

Upon finishing my softcore study, I was no longer certain that the European auteurs whom the sexploitation auteurs had aped had been immune to distribution pressures. After all, as Becker puts it, art works "always bear the marks of the system which distributes them,"[35] so I presumed that traditional art films were marked by distribution pressures no less than softcore art movies were, albeit in different ways. Nor was I still certain that there was anything wrong with such pressures and their "marks," since it seemed extremely unlikely that a communal system of film distribution could exist without them. The basic difference between the two areas relative to distribution was not the *fact* of its effect on form, which could rarely be avoided, but that legitimate art cinemas put subcultural pressure on insiders to talk about this effect only in certain ways, as if the cost of this sort of legitimacy was intellectual freedom. One obvious result of this subcultural pressure was the bad old story, which often serves to exculpate auteurs for the inevitable formal impact of commercial distribution on their art movies.

Scholars studying art cinema outside crossover forums have moved beyond the bad old story, though they have rarely done so in a self-conscious way that allows them to dispense with this "common sense" in a direct fashion. Such scholarship tends to interpret form and production in terms of distribution and exhibition. For example, Rosalind Galt and Karl Schoonover's collection *Global Art Cinema: New Theories and Histories* (2010) includes several excellent pieces that utilize distribution-based methods. These include Sharon Hayashi's essay on pink art cinema, which looks at transformations in a culturally debased kind of Japanese sex film through its exchanges with the global festival circuit; Azadeh Farahmand's essay on Iranian cinema, which examines how this national cinema emerged as an acclaimed art cinema through changes in Iranian politics and its creators' use of tactics accessible to festival-goers; Randall Halle's essay on transnational funding, which considers how European financing "exoticized" films made outside Europe for European consumption; and, finally, Betz's article on the persistence of the "parametric" tradition in global art cinema and the festival circuit.[36]

Four generalities may be extracted from these pieces, all of which should sound familiar to students of Becker. First, cinema is a joint activity that reflects a wide array of human interactions over time. Second, movie distribution exerts an influence over the formation of movie categories, movie form, and the subcultural status of movie insiders like auteurs. Third, when films circulate in new milieus, they often seem *very* new—for they are received in very new ways. The last two points are most striking in Hayashi's essay, which shows a movie (Koji Wakamatsu's *Secrets Behind the Wall*, 1965) and an entire strain of cult production circulating out of the illegitimate world of "subcinema" into the more legitimate world of global art cinema through a shift to film-festival distribution—a phenomenon that recalls how Metzger once outfitted his softcore art movies to circulate through art houses and grindhouses. According to Hayashi, the transformation of the pinks into an art cinema reflected a postwar milieu that featured the sexual revolution; the global politics

OCT 23, FRIDAY, 7PM
Film Studies Center
Cobb Hall 307

Introduction by MICHAEL RAINE,
Assistant professor of East Asian Languages and
Civilizations and Cinema & Media Studies

Wakamatsu Koji, 1965, 75min, Japan,
35mm, Japanese with English subtitles

Considered one of Japan's leading directors of the 1960s, Wakamatsu Koji began making
exploitation films in 1960, eventually opening his own production company to produce erotic "pink
films." Independently produced on very low budgets, the "Pink Godfather's" films challenged
Japanese censorship laws with a strange and unique blend of transgressive sexuality, extreme
violence, satire and radical politics

A poster for a university screening of *Secrets Behind the Wall* (1965), a Japanese
pink film by Koji Wakamatsu. Koji's successful transition into global circulation
elevated his cinema. Used by permission of the Film Studies Center at the
University of Chicago.

of the postwar era; the decline of the Japanese studio system; and the zest of
postwar world audiences to interpret Japanese cinema, *any* Japanese cinema,
as art cinema.[37] It also reflected the impact of distribution on form.

But if we look, finally, at Betz's article, we will also see that distribution
pressures can encourage auteurs like Jia Zhangke, Apichatpong Weerasethakul, Lucrecia Martel, Aleksandr Sokurov, Béla Tarr, or Claire Denis to maintain the traditions of even the most overtly difficult formats.[38] The standardization that Becker saw as an inevitable mark of a delivery system need not,
then, be confined to homogenizing systems; it can also be considered in terms
of the idiosyncrasy or common difficulty of movies across a given distribution system or market niche. This point is clearer if we turn away from the
global festival circuit and look instead at the alternative circuit of cooperatives, university cinemas, and microcinemas that have distributed avant-garde
cinemas. As Michael Zryd and Kathryn Ramey have shown, this kind of distribution has not only supported experimental cinema but has encouraged
the common inaccessibility of many categories of avant-garde film made by
filmmakers as different as Stan Brakhage, Joyce Wieland, and Marlon Riggs.[39]

Despite their intriguing methods, these scholars have not produced a materialist theory of distribution whose explanatory potential is rich and portable. One reason is that they have not reflected self-consciously on their use of distribution concepts and, as a result, are not always unfriendly to the bad old story themselves. On the other hand, historicist scholars like Anthony McKenna who *are* unfriendly to the bad old story do not always take a wide enough view, and their contextual parameters prevent them from recognizing that the antidistributor biases of the bad old story are a product of a pervasive high-art ideology that cannot be entirely escaped in art-cinema contexts.[40] In my view, art-cinema insiders cannot really be blamed for circulating such biases, for these biases are a result of a faith that orients their milieus—but scholars working through peer review *can* be so blamed, for such biases hardly reflect academic ideals of honesty, truth, and impartial inquiry. Thus, as I have suggested in a variety of ways in this book, film scholars should maintain clear lines between their work and that of movie critics who are more directly involved in the art-cinema industry.

Video installation in Cobb 310
Conversation in the Arts/Interview by Esther Harriott: Hollis Frampton (59 min, 1978)
Screening Room with Robert Gardner: Hollis Frampton (74 min, 1977)
On Art and Artists: Hollis Frampton: An Interview (42 min, 1978, courtesy of Video Data Bank)

Conference funded by the Andrew W. Mellon Foundation through 2008 Distinguished Achievement Award recipient Tom Gunning

Conference coordinators Tom Gunning, Bruce Jenkins, Matt Hauske

Film Studies Center staff Julia Gibbs, Sabrina Craig, Chloe Connelly

Support staff Michelle Walsh, Paula Horner, Jake Smith

Projection staff Becca Hall, Todd Cooke, Emily Ponder

Photo Marion Faller, 1975

FILM STUDIES CENTER   5811 S. Ellis, Cobb 307
773.702.8596
filmstudiescenter.uchicago.edu
All events are free and open to the public

THE LEGACY OF HOLLIS FRAMPTON

**CONFERENCE FEBRUARY 5-7 2010
UNIVERSITY OF CHICAGO FILM STUDIES CENTER**

5811 S. ELLIS AVENUE, COBB 307-310
CHICAGO IL 60637 773.702.8596
FILMSTUDIESCENTER.UCHICAGO.EDU

A program for a university conference on the work of experimental filmmaker Hollis Frampton. In the United States, the avant-garde legacy is maintained in part by the academy, which has helped encourage idiosyncrasy across avant-garde films. Used by permission of the Film Studies Center at the University of Chicago.

Films by Pat O'Neill and Ernie Gehr

Friday May 29, 7pm

FREE - Univ. of Chicago Film Studies Center

5811 S. Ellis Ave, Cobb Hall 307

http://filmstudiescenter.uchicago.edu

PRESENTED BY THE EXPERIMENTAL FILM CLUB. The EFC is pleased to present films by Ernie Gehr and Pat O'Neill, central figures in American experimental film since the late 1960s. Gehr brought a sense of delicate, lyrical poetry to "structural" film. His films are often based in the apparatus, commenting on the basic techniques and materials of the cinema in a way that creates rapturous and wholly unique viewing experiences, transcendent explorations of light and shadow. Gehr's work provides an interesting counterpart to the films of Pat O'Neill, whose visual mastery reveals similar concerns with the materials of film. This program includes O'Neill's SAUGUS SERIES, seven astonishing short films of virtuosic, hallucinatory images.

Sponsored by the Film Studies Center, Student Fine Arts Fund, CMS Dept.

A university poster for a twin bill of experimental films by Pat O'Neill and Ernie Gehr. Notice the evaluative hallmarks of cinephile discourse in the text of this poster; this kind of rhetoric frequently appears in academic commentary on the relatively little-known figures of the avant-garde. Used by permission of the Film Studies Center at the University of Chicago.

In Place of a Conclusion

I would close with two thoughts. One reason the bad old story bothers me so much is that it is so reductive: it diminishes the ethical context of art movies to questions of auteur integrity. In this story, auteurs and audiences "win" if the auteur refuses to compromise his or her vision to satisfy a distributor. But as filmmakers know, their institutional role involves ethical concerns that stretch well beyond "vision." What if a situation simply demands that the auteur compromise his or her vision, as when a distribution deal—on which the livelihood of an entire cast and crew may rely—hinges on basic modifications to a film? Thought of in the context of community survival, questions of personal cinema might seem precious. Or what if such vision is used to rationalize unethical habits? As Joan Hawkins has argued, low-art movies, often pigeonholed as exploitative, might be thought of as *more* ethical than high-art movies if the latter includes films like Yoko Ono and John Lennon's avant-garde, cinema verité film *Rape* (1969), with its dubious production history.[41] At the highest levels, art cinema's free pass has at times extended to production practices, with auteurs feeling at liberty to violate ordinary ethics in their filmmaking—a phenomenon apparent in Godard's dealings with Levine.

Second, if we can as scholars agree that the bad old story is inadequate both as an ethical measure and as an industrial metaphor, how should we supplant it? Perhaps by substituting in its stead a distribution theory that positions the cinema as a value-neutral phenomenon that comprises interactive flows of movies, ideas, and status, which are in turn linked to noncinematic forms of experience. This sense of inclusivism, of effervescent interconnectedness, makes such a theory especially useful in revisionary analyses of a privileged super-genre such as art cinema, whose exclusivism is part of its historical identification with high-art ideology. High-art ideology has encouraged critics to see art cinema through its culturally valued parts (e.g., its auteurs, masterworks, styles) and its negative anecdotes (i.e., the bad old story) rather than through its modes of cultural and subcultural circulation, which have interlinked its many parts, regardless of individual judgments of aesthetic value or collective judgments of legitimacy. Consequently, when a category like art cinema is subjected to this fresh distribution approach, something new and odd happens: for once, this super-genre emerges as a living, breathing whole. Here, art cinema is an evolving human network of cultural and subcultural flows of movie forms, film concepts, and human capital all unified by the idea of cinema as a high art. In the postwar era, these currents have grown ever-more byzantine, characterized by new-wave movements, categorical diversity, and complicated modes of cultural and subcultural exchange.

Beyond, Before Cinephilia

Cinephilia has played a structuring role in art cinema from the silent era onward. Since that time, the passionate love of serious movies and serious moviegoing has led to what Sigmund Freud might have called *the overestimation of the object*—for there could be no art cinema if people could not mystify their experience of objets d'art through their own love, their own passionate enthusiasm. Cinephilia went mainstream in the postwar era, when it became synonymous not just with a love of film as a medium but also with a passion for specific films, particular auteurs, exact movements, and definite kinds of experience. Since then, cinephiles have often been framed as highbrows who think that other cinephiles should accept their tastes as universally valid. In this way, cinephilia has been crucial to the canonical processes that have "made" art cinema.

Here one might wonder why, if cinephilia is so crucial, I have waited until my epilogue to address it. The reason is that, as a form of love, cinephilia is a very fuzzy, even amorphous emotion, one that scholars like me find difficult to quantify or even verify.[1] But even if cinephilia "cannot," as Jenna Ng believes, "be fully contained in objective theory," we can still acknowledge that this culturally legitimate form of cultural love is at the center of one of art cinema's central institutions, the film festival.[2] Indeed, since the days of André Bazin, the film-festival network has bound moviegoers into communities of likeminded cinephiles, all ostensibly devoted to the pursuit of the art movies that seem worthy of adulation. What is more, ambitious movies of this sort appear to signal the cinephilia of their makers, for today we often equate the desire to make aspirational movies with the cinephile passion of directors like François Truffaut or Jean-Luc Godard. This means that experimental art cinemas are cinephile cinemas, too, for as Kathryn Ramey has noted, "avant-garde filmmakers say that they persist in such economically unviable activity" because of their "professed 'love' of the work. Many film-makers speak about their own production as being somehow inevitable, what they do because they cannot imagine doing anything else."[3] The presumptive purity of cinephilia—as verified by the anticommercial practices of home-grown experimentalists—confirms its cinematic products as forms of high art and hence as forms of art cinema, too.

But, if I have done nothing else in this book, I hope that I have shown that this self-consciously serious passion is not restricted to the legitimate art cinemas alone. If cinephilia has grown steadily more mainstream in the postwar era, its objects have in that interval been found within a widening array of contexts, some of which even qualify as "mainstream." Thus schol-ars are beginning to realize that the classic cinephilia ascribed to Bazin and Truffaut in France or Andrew Sarris and Susan Sontag in the United States cannot account for all the peculiar forms of cinephilia that have emerged during the postwar era—and since the 1980s in particular, when cult cinema took its current form and one technological change after another began to fracture the marketplace.[4] This democratization of cinephilia has not made it useless to scholars, though. If anything, it has made cinephilia *more* useful to us, for we can use it as another tool to identify cult-art cinemas, main-stream art cinemas, and world art cinemas as they emerge—for example, in untraditional national contexts, such as the Philippines or Nollywood. Like many aestheticisms, cinephilia is an adaptable affection whose passions and lamentations can be expressed through variations that often resemble one another across art-cinema subcultures. But even when very personal distinc-tions seem paramount, cinephilia remains at bottom a human affection that culminates in concepts of high-art value that are applied in temporally and subculturally specific ways.

In academia, this equivalence is becoming especially clear to scholars inter-ested in both cinephile values and cult values. Thus, in a recent *Cineaste* essay titled "Cult Film or Cinephilia by Any Other Name" (2008), Elena Gorfinkel expresses her "nagging sense that these seemingly distinct forms of cinematic feeling and connoisseurship are in many ways actually one and the same," leading her to conclude that "the cultist and the cinephile have in the present become indistinguishable from each other."[5] The evidence for this point of view is clarified in books like Jonathan Rosenbaum and Adrian Martin's *Movie Mutations: The Changing Face of World Cinephilia* (2003) and Marijke de Valck and Malte Hagener's *Cinephilia: Movies, Love and Mem-ory* (2005), as well as in the dossiers on cinephilia that Jonathan Buchsbaum and Gorfinkel have edited for *Framework* and that Mark Betz has edited for *Cinema Journal*. These collections have brought together essayists who often identify today's cinephilia as one that explores new areas, that crosses subcultural borders, that builds bridges among many diverse communities, whether legitimate or illegitimate.[6] Ergo, the "contemporary cinephile is," as de Valck and Hagener write, "as much a hunter-gatherer as a merchant-trader, of material goods as well as of personal and collective memories, of reproducible data streams and of unique objects"; this new cinephile "embraces and uses new technology while also nostalgically remembering and caring for outdated media formats."[7]

Clearly, the sense of cinephilia's past glory is present in this updated vision of it. Therefore, the question orienting the *Framework* dossier—"What is being fought for by today's cinephilia(s)?"—takes for granted that the cinephiles of the classic new-wave era were fractious and political, often rushing the barricades over matters of taste and social justice, which they saw as inextricably intertwined. But what I have taken from these volumes on cinephilia is that no activist idealism is now possible, since cinephiles are too busy establishing a new identity, with many hoping to establish a more pluralist cinephile profile. Cinephiles used to be semi-unified under a vaguely European identity that was politically progressive and culturally highbrow, but the foundations of this unity have since been eroded not just by emerging traditions and emergent technologies but by a global array of culturalisms, historicisms, post-structuralisms, and postmodernisms that cinephiles ignore at their own peril. As a result, cinephile intellectuals can no longer present themselves, in Thomas Elsaesser's words, as the "happy few"; they must instead find a way to reconnect with broader publics "for the benefit of the many."[8] Indeed, there is little question, I think, that this global pluralism, which insists not on cinephilia but on cinephilia*s*, is the future. What remains to be seen, though, is whether this odd, aggregate cinephilia—which must be inclusive to be truly pluralist and value-seeking to be truly cinephile—can summon the partial unity necessary to form a common political front.[9]

At the very least, I hope that in academia this new concept of cinephilia foments more respect for art cinema's subcultural diversity, allowing academics to see through the processes that have in the past led them to differentiate cult fans (i.e., "fanboys") and mainstream fans ("mass audiences") from the "devotees" of the traditional art cinemas (i.e., "cinephiles" understood as the elect, as the "happy few") through the status-heavy labels that tend to reinforce the status quo rather than simply explain it. This respect seems most possible in the academy because its tolerance is, at least in theory, a function of its institutional respect for logic and peer review. And make no mistake: when it comes to cinephilia, pluralism has an ironclad logic to its credit.

We can see the force of this logic if we look at examples of the debates now being conducted among cinephiles, traditional and untraditional. These debates were quickened by the 1996 publication of Sontag's essay "The Decay of Cinema," which lamented the passing of a "certain taste"—and a certain kind of cinephile—from the cultural scene.[10] Of course, this polemical essay, in keeping with the style of lamentation long favored by cinephiles, overstates the matter somewhat, for traditional cinephiles such as Jonathan Rosenbaum still have prominent platforms to publicize their tastes. Rosenbaum has often written about cinephilia as a force that in effect dislodged him from academia, sending him back to journalism. Rosenbaum relates that the academy due to "its anti-art biases" "soured" cinephilia for him.[11] Of course, Rosenbaum does not mean anti-*art* so much as anti-*high*-art—and I would quarrel even with this perspective, given my view that the academy has been responsible for circulating and promoting both cinephile discourse and a variety of auteurist biases. But Rosenbaum is surely correct to see that in its ideals the academy *is* anti-high-art—for its respect for logic and peer review *should* blind it to the biases of the "happy few." But if the academy's analytic potential gives cinephiles justifiable pause, this is no excuse for them to collect their marbles and go home—unless, of course, they insist on having their own tastes exclusively prioritized on the cultural stage. For one positive effect of the academy's analytic potential is that it has made room for many tastes, many legitimacies—leading to an impure, "promiscuous" cinephilia that the scholar Lucas Hilderbrand has framed as opening cinephiles to new technologies and new experiences, allowing us "to love more of the cinema."[12]

Another aspect of contemporary cinephilia that Rosenbaum has at times deplored is its Internet orientation.[13] There is an obvious institutional explanation for this dislike of the Internet: print critics are being displaced by Internet critics who find readers through websites, blogs, chat rooms, user reviews, and cyber "top tens." But the deeper reason for Rosenbaum's aversion to these new electronic vistas may be that the Internet, like many modern technologies, has been a great equalizer that has made it more possible for more fans to attain an impressive authority. Thus the expertise that Rosenbaum has spent his life amassing is not necessarily unusual on the Internet, much as his cinephilia brings no necessary distinction within the academy. We can see variations on this gripe portrayed in Gerald Peary's recent documentary *For the Love of Movies: The Story of American Film Criticism* (2009). As this movie shows, print critics have been fighting a rearguard action to retain their rights to the cinephile label as part of their larger battle against the forces of technological and economic change. This is a lost cause, in my view, and one whose terms highlight the arbitrary nature of the cultural authority that print critics have traditionally enjoyed. Consequently, when this documentary surveys traditional critics to determine their qualifications, the best that they can come up with is their *love of movies* and *the knowledge generated by said love*. Yet this documentary also frames their Internet competitors as cinephiles of a certain age, a certain background, a certain knowledge — and it shows the print critics trying to confirm their own greater legitimacy by pointing to their Internet competitors' *lack* of qualifications and *lack* of standards.

I am with Hilderbrand, not Rosenbaum. In fact, I am not even sure that art cinema has *any* proprietary right to cinephilia — not even after we expand our notion of the term to include all the untraditional art cinemas and all the untraditional cinephiles who love them. After all, what is it that we love about art movies? That they excite our bodies. That they fill us with horror, sympathy, outrage. That they drive us to political or intellectual insight. That they offer dazzling experiences full of richness and light. That they tie our brains in knots. That they fill us with an idealism that binds us to others. Something of this multifarious power was suggested recently when the Danish auteur Lars von Trier criticized his own film *Antichrist* (2009) by claiming that it was "too beautiful overall."[14] (This is a "danger" of the category, apparently.) But once we have admitted that even the least traditional art movies may have these powers, too, we should not rest on our laurels, feeling smug about our new, more defensible hold on the cinephile label. For the fact is that from the early cinema on, many categories of movie have triggered this set of human reactions — and not just those in an acclaimed category that has, through the prestigious gestures and the official institutions that structure it, attained the cultural or subcultural status of "art movie." Indeed, because our cinephilias often gain shape through these gestures and institutions, it is easy to forget that our ability to love the cinema can latch onto *any* movie — including the animated extravaganza that takes us unawares during some sleepy matinee with our children. (That is how I first came across the truly miraculous cinema of Hayao Miyazaki, after all.) This ability does not, in other words, need to conform to a cinephilia that is either traditional or untraditional. Our love of cinema can be unnamed, unjustified. It can be that movie love that is beyond, before cinephilia.

Perhaps my message will gain in authenticity if I confess that I am a cinephile, and a lapsed traditionalist at that. I have loved movies since boyhood, but I felt the first stirrings of an articulate cinephilia at Cornell University, where the college theater and the local art houses like Cinemapolis gave me glimpses of what that feeling could mean. Later, I did graduate work at SUNY Stony Brook, which had university theaters, art houses, and access to New York City to recommend it — and whose video collections allowed me to school myself on art-house classics. Later still, I saw Hal Hartley's *Henry Fool* (1997) in New York after a bizarre taxi ride that still seems vivid today even though I left the theater so exuberant that I cannot remember the ride home. Soon after, I placed my first peer-reviewed article in *Film Criticism*—and it was on Hartley, not on the literary auteurs who were the focus of my dissertation. Later still, in Chicago, I had access to even more art houses, university theaters, museums, and DIY spaces—and it was there I viewed David Lynch's *Mulholland Drive* (2001) for the first of two dozen times. Thus my passion generated another article, this one in the *Journal of Film and Video*.

But during that same year, I let my enthusiasm draw me into cult cinema: and lo, a book popped out. And now another. My cinephilia is only expanding. I still feel the joy that I felt at Cornell. It is just that there is, in Hilderbrand's words, *more of it*. In other words, I keep seeing more of the elephant—and, no longer anxious that I might be examining the wrong parts, I am always grateful for the opportunity to see more of the animal. That is why I have never regretted this project, which has familiarized me with so many unfamiliar movies, movements, and auteurs. And it is why I have tried to watch at least one movie per day while performing the happy labors associated with this project. It is even why I persisted in this discipline long after it became clear that my method would allow me to refer to just a handful of the artists and movies that were dazzling my eyes and ears, mind and body, each night from seven to eleven.[15] *Love works in mysterious ways.*

Notes

Introduction

1. As Michael Z. Newman puts it, "mainstream" is a theoretical "category that niche cultures or subcultures construct to have something against which to define themselves and generate their cultural or subcultural capital. I do not believe that there is a mainstream that exists independent of this process of classification." *Indie*, 5. See also Jancovich, "Introduction," 1–2.

2. Baumann, *Hollywood Highbrow*, 177.

3. Ibid., 77. See also Kovács, *Screening Modernism*, 22–25. According to Kovács, the split in art cinema between the avant-garde movie and the art film occurred because the latter needed, in the words of Germaine Dulac, to be somewhat *"commercial, but not enough to pander to nervous ignorants."* Quoted in ibid., 23 (Dulac's italics). This led in turn to a "semicommercial" art cinema that required both specialized audiences and state support. Ibid., 24.

4. I don't mean to use "myth" in a confrontational way. I simply want to underline that art cinema's anticommercialism has typically had commercial outcomes. Most often, art cinema's anticommercialism has allowed promoters to attach an anti-Hollywood identity to their art cinemas, including *Hollywood* art cinemas, thus attracting a particular demographic to those films.

5. For example, Mike Budd has shown that in the United States some of the earliest ideas of art cinema arose through the oppositional value assigned via institutional processes to imports like Robert Wiene's *Das cabinet des Dr. Caligari*. See Budd, "National Board of Review and Early Art Cinema in New York."

6. See, for example, Lev, *Euro-American Cinema*, 7–8.

7. Slingerland, "Two Worlds," 223.

8. See Levine, *Highbrow/Lowbrow*; and Shiner, *Invention of Art*.

9. Sklar, *Movie-Made America*, 18–19.

10. Rees, *History of Experimental Film and Video*, 30; see 30–33. See also Kovács, *Screening Modernism*, 16–32; Andrew, *Film in the Aura of Art*, 3–10; and Abel, "French Silent Cinema."

11. See Balio, *Foreign Film Renaissance on American Screens*, 25.

12. There is disagreement about when these institutions and the ideas of value that they generated first took root. As Kovács notes, the "origins of the concept of the 'art film' as an institutional form of cinema can be traced back to the late 1910s." Kovács, *Screening Modernism*, 22; see 22–27. But scholars have dated the first film festival to 1898 in Monaco. See Society for Cinema and Media Studies, "Film and Media Festivals Scholarly Interest Group." In any event, Baumann is doubtless correct when he argues that cinema began to be legitimated as an art at different times in different places; thus, in the middle of the twentieth century, France and Italy were able to export auteurist ideas and films to the United States because the cinema had become legitimate there earlier than in America. Baumann, *Hollywood Highbrow*, 82.

13. We should remember, though, that this was not the auteur-oriented Hollywood Academy of today. Even directors who won Academy Awards in the Hollywood of the time only rarely thought of themselves as artists. For more, see ibid., 55–56, 60–64.

14. See Schaefer, *"Bold! Daring! Shocking! True!"* 331–337.

15. Three excellent books chronicle these developments: Wilinsky, *Sure Seaters*; Wasson, *Museum Movies*; and Balio, *Foreign Film Renaissance on American Screens*.

16. Sexuality is rarely the focus of studies of this high-status genre. Balio's book, which is clear in articulating the role that sex appeal played in the popularization of art films during the postwar period, is an exceptional addition to the scholarship. See *Foreign Film Renaissance on American Screens*, 8.

17. The term is Baumann's. See *Hollywood Highbrow*, 21–52.

18. Ibid., 127–128.

19. See, for example, Schaefer, *"Bold! Daring! Shocking! True!"* 331; and Lewis, *Hollywood v. Hardcore*, 145.

20. Baumann, *Hollywood Highbrow*, 22.

21. Allen and Gomery, *Film History*, 71; Carroll, *Theorizing the Moving Image*, 1–4.

22. Michael Zryd has written two pieces on this subject. See "The Academy and the Avant-Garde"; and "Experimental Film and the Development of Film Study in America."

23. Sarris, "Why the Foreign Film Has Lost Its Cachet." See also Balio, *Foreign Film Renaissance on American Screens*, 249.

24. See Balio, "A Major Presence in all of the World's Important Markets," 64–67.

25. See Wyatt, "Formation of the 'Major Independent,'" 76–84. See also Newman, *Indie*.

26. Among the peer-reviewed portfolios are Buchsbaum and Gorfinkel, "Cinephilia Dossier"; and Betz, "In Focus." See also Rosenbaum and Martin, *Movie Mutations*; and de Valck and Hagener, *Cinephilia*.

27. *Hollywood Highbrow* does not distinguish between high-art ideas and other ideas of art, which makes it difficult to know what Hollywood's consecration as art meant. Baumann also fails to consider Hollywood's current production of art movies through its indie-style "boutique" divisions, and ignores subcultural manifestations of the art-cinema idea; nor does his book consider biocultural ideas. On the whole, though, these critiques seem almost *ungrateful* when the book's generous insights are taken into account.

28. Baumann, *Hollywood Highbrow*, 14–18.

29. Jancovich et al., *Defining Cult Movies*; Mathijs and Mendik, *Cult Film Reader*.

Chapter 1

1. Thanouli, "'Art Cinema' Narration."
2. Tudor, "Rise and Fall of the Art (House) Movie," 125.
3. Though this history has indeed led us there. For convincing demonstrations that the cinema is an art form, see Carroll, *Theorizing the Moving Image*.
4. Tudor, "Rise and Fall of the Art (House) Movie," 125. Tudor thinks that art cinema's claims to intrinsic value were fundamentally rooted in the elevation of art over commerce that grew out of many post-Renaissance market pressures. Consequently, the art house, which was devoted to the film-as-art approach, created a highbrow preserve where art cinema "could be defended as relatively immune" from market "pollution and utilized as a basis for establishing distinction and symbolic capital." Ibid., 138.
5. "Meanwhile, there has been a proliferation of sectarian audiences," Tudor writes. "What was once primarily the domain of the artistic *avant garde* now hosts cult movies, the 'fans' who cluster around, for example, video distributed horror or semi-pornographic material to which they attribute aesthetic, moral, or social radicalism, as well as the kind of independent cinema familiar in earlier periods." Ibid. (Tudor's italics).
6. Ibid.
7. See, among many possible examples, Betz, "Art, Exploitation, Underground"; and Hawkins, "Culture Wars."
8. Diane Negra calls these complexes "art-house miniplexes" or "art miniplexes." See "Queen of the Indies." See also Newman, *Indie*, 77–79.
9. Bordwell, "Art Cinema as a Mode of Film Practice," 716. This claim is problematic because many movements had already been described as "art cinemas" that produced "art films." It seems preferential to define a concept with a long history in terms of a single set of prestigious movements like Italian neorealism or the French New Wave. See Rees, *History of Experimental Film and Video*, esp. 30–33.
10. Bordwell, "The Art Cinema as a Mode of Film Practice," 717.
11. Ibid. (Bordwell's italics).
12. See Thanouli, "'Art Cinema' Narration."
13. Galt and Schoonover, "Introduction," 3, 6.
14. Bordwell's article was published near the end of the New Hollywood era, when art cinema was most explicitly tied to Hollywood and when it was a decidedly big business. Indeed, Bordwell even notes in his essay that an art cinema was emerging in the New Hollywood—a point he expands in *Narration in the Fiction Film* (1985). Bordwell, "Art Cinema as a Mode of Film Practice," 723; and *Narration in the Fiction Film*, 231–232. But Bordwell still finds it possible to say in his article that "the art cinema is of little economic importance in the United States today." Bordwell, "Art Cinema as a Mode of Film Practice," 717. The reason for this apparent contradiction is that Bordwell does not consider Hollywood art cinema an *authentic* art cinema, a designation that in his view depends on European conventions of narration that are not reducible to cause–effect plotting or to Hollywood genre motifs.
15. Indeed, even scholars who focus on form are careful to avoid reductiveness. For example, Mark Betz has recently argued that art cinema is marked by a "'parametric' tradition," a term he borrows from Bordwell to describe a modernist narrative foregrounding form and style. Betz qualifies this by noting that "parametric" narration is but "one

strand of an 'international style' for contemporary world cinema, indeed contemporary *art* cinema"—one that has "since the late 1980s continued in Western Europe but has also proceeded in parallel in Eastern Central Europe, sub-Saharan Africa, and especially East Asia." See "Beyond Europe," 33 (Betz's italics). Similarly, András Bálint Kovács has mapped out significant strains and styles in art cinema, but he never reduces art cinema to any particular elements. Thus he argues that modernism, which he equates with the commercial art cinema, is "not a particular style in the cinema; it is rather the impact of different modernist movements *in the narrative art cinema*, engendering different (modern) film styles." Kovács, *Screening Modernism*, 52 (Kovács's italics). See also Nowell-Smith, "Art Cinema," 569–570; and Sconce, "Smart Cinema," 429–430. See also Sconce, "Irony, Nihilism, and the New American 'Smart' Film," 350–352.

16. Dominique Russell refers to the definition of "art cinema" as "nebulous" and insists that while it has been associated with "high culture, intelligence, and prestige," it is "by no means a static category, and has meant different things at different times." See Russell, "Introduction," 3.

17. Forbes and Street, *European Cinema*, 40.

18. Gabara, "Abderrahmane Sissako," 320–321.

19. Thanouli, "'Art Cinema' Narration," 9.

20. Ndalianis, "Art Cinema," 87.

21. Weitz, "Role of Theory in Aesthetics," 151–152.

22. See Dickie, *Art Circle*; and Carroll, *Philosophy of Mass Art*.

23. Dickie, *Art and Value*, 33.

24. Quoted in ibid., 34.

25. Davies, *Definitions of Art*, 42.

26. Indeed, this is how R. G. Collingwood, a twentieth-century functionalist, relegates the form to non-art status. See Dickie, *Art and Value*, 33–34. See also Collingwood, *Principles of Art*, 84–85.

27. For persuasive critiques of the neo-Kantian idea of aesthetic disinterest, see Dickie, *Evaluating Art*, 15–79; and "Myth of the Aesthetic Attitude."

28. When Immanuel Kant published his *Critique of Judgement* in 1790, the Prussian philosopher had no idea that his notion of disinterested contemplation, which he sketched in a section titled "Analytic of the Beautiful," would become the catchall it is today. See *Critique of Judgement*, 35–74. Kant's concept, which demands a spectatorship so pure it is indifferent to the existence of its object, considers any action "pure" if that action is performed for its own sake; such an action cannot be impelled by other desires, purposes, or emotions, all of which might qualify as "ulterior." When this concept was codified through neo-Kantian ideas and applied to art, the result was a neo-Kantian aesthetic that detached art from desire, utility, and emotion, without regard for actual cultural and physiological experiences of art—which are, as George Dickie later argued, awash with those seemingly undesirable elements. See Dickie, "Myth of the Aesthetic Attitude." Nevertheless, this neo-Kantian aesthetic—which aestheticians like Monroe Beardsley identified with idealized forms of spectatorship—gained force in the eighteenth and nineteenth centuries and held sway through the middle of the twentieth. Ironically, it gained much of its significance from the fact that it was a useful basis for art evaluation and a useful rationale for modernist codes of "serious" contemplation in museums and concert halls. See Shiner, *Invention of Art*, 144–145, 154, 218. This ideal reached its peak influence in the United States in the middle of the twentieth century, when art houses were spreading rapidly. But the

utility of the concept didn't end there. As Noël Carroll puts it, "somewhere along the line" art critics made the mistake of "transferr[ing] the notion of disinterestedness from the spectator to the art object." *Philosophy of Mass Art*, 96. Thus influential critics such as Clement Greenberg helped transform the ideal of disinterest from a "mere" critical attitude into an influential artistic method (whereby serious modernist artists might be identified by their pure or disinterested creative methods) and a preferred modernist style (often imagined as austere and abstract, not just because abstraction was the twentieth century's most privileged art style but also because it was easy to connect abstraction to the purity and unworldliness implicit to the concept of disinterest). Consequently, as Shyon Baumann puts it, today "artists need to profess a degree of 'disinterestedness' in economic matters to enjoy credibility." This aspect of their art making is a large part of what makes them seem "serious." Baumann, *Hollywood Highbrow*, 168.

29. Carroll, *Philosophy of Art*, 232–239.

30. Carroll, *Philosophy of Mass Art*, 26, 52, 56–57, 295–299.

31. Dickie, *Art and Value*, 45. See also Davies, *Definitions of Art*, 169.

32. For example, Amy Taubin calls *In the Cut* "one of the great art horror films." See "Horrors!" 53.

33. Quoted in Allen and Gomery, *Film History*, 85.

34. Owen, "Genres in Motion," 1393.

35. This does not mean there aren't strong contenders among the forms and the techniques of the art movie, including the art-film motifs, themes, and psychological tactics analyzed by André Bazin, Bordwell, and other crucial critics. For example, the long take and the tracking shot are two candidate techniques that critics have suggested create a distinct sense of art-film form—and these techniques persist to this day on the global festival circuit, where they still animate the award-winning art films of auteurs such as Hou Hsiao-hsien, Wong Kar-wai, Apichatpong Weerasethakul, Lisandro Alonso, and Béla Tarr. But no form or technique is apparent in *every* example of the art film. For instance, does the relative absence of tracking shots in Yasujirô Ozu's movies somehow impugn their status as art films? When we look beyond the art film across art cinema's other formats, questions like these become even more pointed. Indeed, the sense of universality conveyed by the persistence of certain art-film techniques may be an illusion that is generated by global festival distribution, a phenomenon that suggests that the values of a fairly small yet *horizontal* subculture in world cinema are tantamount to universal cultural values.

36. Of course, advocates of the aesthetic attitude might correlate art cinema's techniques with a "properly" disinterested effect/affect, but this notion does not do justice to the range of bodily responses that art movies elicit—and are *meant* to elicit—from viewers.

37. See, for example, Rivette et al., "Six Characters in Search of Auteurs," 65.

38. von Trier and Vinterberg, "Dogme 95," 83.

39. Linda Ruth Williams, *Erotic Thriller in Contemporary Cinema*, 405 (Williams's italics); see also 396–406.

40. Altman, *Film/Genre*, 5.

41. See, for example, Sorrentino, *Something Said*, 325–330.

42. Upon first talking to softcore director Tony Marsiglia, I assumed he would agree that his films were "softcore," given that they were low-budget movies produced and promoted by a softcore label, and given that they included persistent softcore spectacle. But not only did Marsiglia *not* talk of his films as softcore, he often did not speak of them as *art movies*, preferring the more universal category of "Art." Marsiglia, "Re: Some Ques-

tions." It is not too difficult to compare such an attitude to that of an acclaimed director like Stanley Kubrick, who once claimed that a movie "has no responsibility to be anything but a work of art." See Kubrick, *Stanley Kubrick*, 130.

43. See, for example, Waugh, "Canon," 59–61. Waugh's explanation of the canon is valuable for the emphasis it puts on the way politically minded groups, like feminists, have exposed the gendered competitions that direct canonical processes. Feminists are right about this. Still, I would argue that the exclusionary aspect of the canon has not simply limited the canon along the lines of gender, race, and sexual identity but also along the lines of taste, which may be where those processes are most confounding. It is one thing to realize that feminist critics or queer theorists can be as exclusive as anyone else in advocating on behalf of marginalized female auteurs or of queer cinemas. It is quite another thing to hear cult theorists endorse exclusivity in endorsing low-culture films and directors for canonization.

44. One interesting thing about the festival is that it extends the mantle of high art to all its participants, thus providing a comprehensive "artfilmness," without necessarily canonizing further any individual film. Thus, in a sense, the festival field as a whole is canonized; but individual films within that field only find success, individual canonical success, through further jockeying. Indeed, Cindy H. Wong has discussed how the festival works to canonize certain films through "a process of creation that involves both artists and finance, often triangulated through festivals. After a film has found a place in a festival, film critics, festival programmers, and scholars may extend or curtail its reputation, distribution, and the career of its director/auteur beyond the festivals." *Film Festivals*, 101. But again, festival inclusion guarantees a film only "artfilmness"; it doesn't canonize that film, for "most films and directors screened in film festivals do not enter the elusive, ever changing world of competing film canons."

45. See Connolly, *Place of Artists' Cinema*.

46. In considering this, we should focus *not* on the fact that genres are usually deemed identical to a set of conventions but instead on the fact that genres are usually treated inclusively. Genres have conventions, true; but we do not typically deny genre membership to movies that realize those conventions as best they can. The fact that *Planet of the Apes* (1968) is a sci-fi film does not make it more difficult to accept that *Play-Mate of the Apes* (2002), a low-budget softcore spoof heavily reliant on tinfoil and cheap red lights, is also a sci-fi film. What, then, should we say about *Dr. Jekyll and Mistress Hyde* (2003), a low-budget softcore flick that draws on *Mulholland Drive* (2001)? *Mistress Hyde* aspires to be an art movie in the same way that *Play-Mate* aspires to be a sci-fi movie—but whereas we grant the latter aspiration based on some campy props, we don't necessarily grant the former. This is the subcultural dilemma of art cinema.

47. Sconce, "'Trashing' the Academy," 382.

48. Wong, *Film Festivals*, 100–103.

49. Cousins et al., "The Mad, the Bad, and the Dangerous"; see cover.

50. Kermode, "It Is What It's Not," 34–36. This article adopts an anti-genre stance, applauding *Let the Right One In* by distinguishing it from horror movies and other genre motifs to situate it as art cinema. Such articles are crucial to the movie's legitimation because this example of Swedish art horror has also been claimed by cult fans through its success at cult festivals and in illegitimate forums devoted to horror like *Fangoria* and *Rue Morgue*.

51. Quoted in Hawkins, "Culture Wars."

52. Nowell-Smith, "New Concepts of Cinema," 759.

53. See Cohen, "High and Low Art, and High and Low Audiences."

Chapter 2

1. Ciment, "Letter to the Editors," 96.

2. Schatz, *Hollywood Genres*, 7. See also Caughie, "Introduction," 15.

3. See Astruc, "The Birth of a New Avant-Garde." For more on Astruc, see Gerstner, "Practices of Authorship," 6–7. See also Staiger, "Authorship Approaches," 34–35.

4. Edward Buscombe argues that Sarris translated a set of critical *policies* into a full-blown *theory*, creating the sense that la politique des auteurs was meant to explain cinema—something that the *Cahiers* critics did not intend. See Buscombe, "Ideas of Authorship," 22. See also Sarris, "Toward a Theory of Film History"; and "Auteur Theory Revisited."

5. See Caughie, "Introduction"; and Buscombe, "Ideas of Authorship." See also Gerstner, "Practices of Authorship"; and Staiger, "Authorship Approaches." Finally, see Naremore, "Authorship," 18–22. For an exhaustive overview, see Cook, "Authorship and Cinema."

6. The phrasing is Cook's. See "Authorship and Cinema," 479. This observation was obvious to scholars as early as 1983, when Paul Kerr, referring to the anti-auteurist thrust of Caughie's anthology, noted in the pages of *Screen* that "auteurism refuses to go away," for it is "difficult—if not altogether impossible—to entirely dispense with it." Kerr, "My Name Is Joseph H. Lewis," 234.

7. Schatz, *Genius of the System*, 5.

8. Caughie, "Introduction," 13. Caughie contends that "the attention to *mise en scène*, even to the extent of a certain historically necessary formalism, is probably the most important positive contribution of *auteurism* to the development of a precise and detailed film criticism, engaging with the specific mechanisms of visual discourse, freeing it from literary models, and from the liberal commitments which were prepared to validate films on the basis of their themes alone" (Caughie's italics). Grant agrees, arguing that auteurism's "legacy is that it encouraged a more serious examination of the movies beyond mere 'entertainment' and helped move the nascent field of film studies beyond its literary beginnings to a consideration of film's visual qualities." See "Introduction," 5.

9. Gerstner, "Practices of Authorship," 5. The most nuanced sociological treatment of this theme is found in Baumann, *Hollywood Highbrow*. Baumann argues that the distribution of auteur-driven art films across the globe led to new cinephile markets and indirectly created "a pathway for the consecration of Hollywood films as art." See *Hollywood Highbrow*, 10, 61–64, 113, 149, 177.

10. Staiger attributes the notion of the auteur as a "prime mover" to anti-auteurists like Pauline Kael. See Staiger, "Authorship Approaches," 31–32.

11. Sarris, *American Cinema*, 35.

12. Godard, "Face of French Cinema Has Changed."

13. Truffaut was engaged in a form of taste warfare that sought, through an auteur policy that elevated his favorite French directors, to upset the assumptions that privileged the "tradition of quality" with its stress on literature, adaptation, and politics. This is why John Hess launched his famous counterattack on Truffaut in the second installment of

his *Jump Cut* analysis of la politique des auteurs. See Hess, "*La politique des auteurs*, Part Two," 22.

14. Rivette et al., "Six Characters in Search of Auteurs," 69. Schatz gives Bazin credit for the phrase "genius of the system," which Bazin used in reference to Hollywood in 1957. See Schatz, *Genius of the System*, xiii.

15. Rivette et al., "Six Characters in Search of Auteurs," 69.

16. Gerstner, "Practices of Authorship," 8–9; and Staiger, "Authorship Approaches," 37–38. See also Sarris, *American Cinema*, 19–37.

17. For example, as John Hess explained in his 1974 critique of the theory, one thing the auteur critics were rebelling against was the idea that the cinema should be political. Cinema in France after the Liberation was often political, reflecting a range of postwar concerns that privileged the collective over the individual. Hess saw critics like Truffaut reversing that trend in classical French cinema. But time was not on the auteurs' side, as reflected by the increasing radicalism of Godard's output in the 1960s, the growing leftism of American auteur critics like Susan Sontag, and the conflicts evident in period dramas like Bernardo Bertolucci's *The Dreamers* (2003). In retrospect, the auteurs' quest for some apolitical aestheticist autonomy seems like a brief interlude between the political storms of 1945 and 1968. See Hess, "*La politique des auteurs*, Part One."

18. Caldwell, *Production Culture*, 198–201. See also Staiger, "Authorship Approaches," 40–43.

19. Quoted in Cook, "Authorship and Cinema," 410. See also Gerstner, "Practices of Authorship," 9; and Staiger, "Authorship Approaches," 38–40.

20. See Petrie, "Alternatives to Auteurs," 110–112.

21. In *Auteurs and Authorship*, Barry Keith Grant provides variations on this anti-auteurist gambit, including everything from Richard Koszarki's essay on the contributions of Hollywood camera operators ("Men with the Movie Cameras") and Richard Corliss's ("Notes on a Screenwriter's Theory") and Gore Vidal's ("Who Makes the Movies?") essays on the contributions of screenwriters, to Jerome Christensen's ("Studio Authorship, Corporate Art") and Matthew Bernstein's ("The Producer as Auteur") essays on the contributions of studios and producers. Grant also includes Bruce Kawin's brilliant essay "Authorship, Design, and Execution," which in a sense draws the lesson of this pattern by making a case for a collective idea of authorship. Similarly, in a talk at the University of Chicago, Giaime Alonge argued that the anti-auteur critics who elevated screenwriters like Ben Hecht continued the "myth of the author" under a new name. See Alonge, "Hacks and Authors."

22. For example, Corliss ends his essay by promoting the idea of the "multiple auteur," which is one part of a "giant matrix of coordinate talents." See "Notes on a Screenwriter's Theory," 147.

23. Kawin, "Authorship, Design, and Execution," 199.

24. Naremore, "Authorship," 17–18.

25. Here Caughie's *Theories of Authorship* is most helpful, for it contains essays and excerpts from the most relevant contributors to *Cahiers* and *Screen*, including the original auteur critics as well as Wollen, Buscombe, Jean-Louis Comolli, Geoffrey Nowell-Smith, Stephen Heath, and others.

26. Naremore, "Authorship," 19.

27. See Wollen, *Signs and Meaning in the Cinema*, 113.

28. For more on the structuralist and post-structuralist critiques of auteurism, see Gerstner, "Practices of Authorship," 10–17; and Staiger, "Authorship Approaches," 43–49. Barthes's essay "The Death of the Author" (1968) is reprinted in Grant, *Auteurs and Authorship*.

29. See also Grant, "Secret Agents."

30. For two particularly successful overviews of this kind of critique, see Gerstner, "Practices of Authorship," 17–21; and Staiger, "Authorship Approaches," 49–52.

31. See, for example, Heise and Tudor, "Constructing (Film) Art"; Tudor, "Rise and Fall of the Art (House) Movie"; Ramey, "Between Art, Industry, and Academia"; and Baumann, "Intellectualization and Art World Development." See also Baumann, *Hollywood Highbrow*.

32. Baumann, *Hollywood Highbrow*, 61–66. For definitions of "opportunity space," see ibid., 14–15.

33. See, for example, Carroll, *Evolution and Literary Theory*; and Dutton, *Art Instinct*.

34. As Martin Heisenberg has explained in *Nature*, the concept of free will has recently been "under attack as never before" in science and philosophy. See "Is Free Will an Illusion?" 164. For two very different dismantlings of free will, see Ridley, *Genome*, 301–303; and Wegner, *Illusion of Conscious Will*.

35. Neale, "Art Cinema as Institution," 37.

36. Naremore, "Authorship," 21.

37. See Betz, "Little Books."

38. Dutton, *Art Instinct*, 172–176.

39. Ibid., 174.

40. Ibid., 175–176.

41. If, as Caughie avers, it is crucial that scholars who are intent on transcending auteurism understand "the fascination of the figure of the *auteur*, and the way he is used in the cinephile's pleasure," it is also crucial that these scholars consider that such pleasure may be part of the cinephile's biological inheritance—and that it would not *be* that pleasure if the cinephile construed the auteur as a constructed "figure" rather than as a real historical person. See "Introduction," 15.

42. Dutton, *Art Instinct*, 176.

43. Ibid.

44. Ibid., 175. For more on the biocultural mechanisms that connect sexual selection to art and authorship, see Brian Boyd, Joseph Carroll, and Jonathan Gottschall's edition of *Evolution, Literature, and Film: A Reader* (2010), especially the contributions of Geoffrey Miller and David Buss.

45. von Trier and Vinterberg, "Dogme 95," 83.

46. See Gerstner, "Practices of Authorship," 17–21; Staiger, "Authorship Approaches," 49–52; and Cook, "Authorship and Cinema," 468–473. Feminists who have argued against applying a classic idea of auteurism to women directors include Angela Martin, who, in discussing Kathryn Bigelow, has suggested that auteurism can benefit some women while still hurting *all* women, since women tend to be thought of as auteurs in particularly restrictive ways. See Martin, "Refocusing Authorship in Women's Filmmaking," 130–131. See also Grant, "Secret Agents."

47. Naremore, "Authorship," 20.

48. See, for example, Scalia, "Review of *Authorship and Film*."

49. Many essays in this anthology call for new understandings of traditional ideas of auteurism while also calling for reappraisals of a given auteur and noting under-recognized points of genius in said auteur's work.

50. Schatz, *Genius of the System*, 5.

51. Kerr, "My Name Is Joseph H. Lewis," 247. See also Stanfield, *Maximum Movies—Pulp Fictions*, 73–76, 174.

52. Kerr, "My Name Is Joseph H. Lewis," 247.

53. Hayashi, "Fantastic Trajectory of Pink Art Cinema from Stalin to Bush," 48.

54. Ibid.

55. For more on Marsiglia's work, see Andrews, *Soft in the Middle*, 246–249.

56. See Carroll, *Philosophy of Art*, 260–266. See also Davies, *Definitions of Art*, 167–169. This approach is explained in brief in the previous chapter.

57. Such an approach would not be necessary in the case of a low-budget horror flick like Nacho Cerdà's *The Abandoned* (2006). In this film, Cerdà's mimicry of Tarkovsky's technique is clear, making it tempting to formulate an art-historical narrative that culminates in labeling his movie a cult-art movie based on form alone. But even a cursory Internet search turns up evidence that Cerdà's mimicry of Tarkovsky *was* intentional. See, for example, Lamkin, "*The Abandoned*." Such historical evidence should be the primary basis for any narrative tying one auteur to another.

58. For more evidence of this, see Sconce, "'Trashing' the Academy."

Chapter 3

1. This usage is still evident in some fairly mainstream outlets, particularly Netflix, which employs the "foreign movies" designation.

2. Stevenson, "And God Created Europe," 18.

3. See Wilinsky, *Sure Seaters*, 31.

4. Sarris, "Why the Foreign Film Has Lost Its Cachet."

5. See Andrews, *Soft in the Middle*, 35–36.

6. Schaefer, *"Bold! Daring! Shocking! True!"* 332.

7. Ibid., 333.

8. Ibid., 334. See also Stevenson, "And God Created Europe."

9. Balio, *Foreign Film Renaissance on American Screens*, 8. See also Betz, "Art, Exploitation, Underground," 205–210; and Schaefer, *"Bold, Daring, Shocking, True!"* 334–335.

10. Quoted in Schaefer, *"Bold, Daring, Shocking, True!"* 336.

11. Quotation of *Variety* in Wilinsky, *Sure Seaters*, 37.

12. Schaefer, *"Bold, Daring, Shocking, True!"* 335.

13. See Lev, *Euro-American Cinema*, 13.

14. Quoted in Schaefer, *"Bold, Daring, Shocking, True!"* 335. To see how this chain of influence and counter-influence works, we should consider that the "beautiful and disturbing" nudity in Machatý's *Ecstasy* was by Bergman's own admission an influence on Bergman's work. See Bergman, *Bergman on Bergman*, 138.

15. Lev, *Euro-American Cinema*, 13.

16. Becker, *Art Worlds*, 39.

17. Baumann, *Hollywood Highbrow*, 22.

18. Schaefer, *"Bold, Daring, Shocking, True!"* 336.

19. Baumann, *Hollywood Highbrow*, 103. This trend was particularly pronounced in the case of *Et Dieu . . . créa la femme*, which Columbia managed to distribute in the United States by acquiring Kingsley International; a later high-profile case was the acquisition of Lopert Pictures by United Artists. See Balio, *Foreign Film Renaissance on American Screens*, 44, 114–116.

20. Balio, *Foreign Film Renaissance on American Screens*, 95; and Gorfinkel, "Radley Metzger's 'Elegant Arousal,'" 38. See also Wilinsky, *Sure Seaters*, 132–138.

21. See Wilinsky, *Sure Seaters*, 30–31. Today, American "indie" films most often perform "the social functions previously performed by foreign art films." Newman, *Indie*, 2.

22. The American audience was also useful because it provided such a diverse testing ground for the film industry. If a movie could please this audience across its many regional and ethnic differences, it was more likely that that movie could also please viewers across the world. For more, see Thanouli, "Narration in World Cinema," 7.

23. The most common difference is language, with English being the Hollywood default. This has led to the class-conscious practice of subtitling foreign films for art-house consumption and dubbing them into English for mass audiences, if the film has greater commercial potential. For insights on subtitling and dubbing, see Betz, "Name Above the (Sub)Title," 2–5.

24. Chirilov, *Lucian Pintilie*, 5.

25. Becker, *Art Worlds*, 39, 107.

26. Farahmand, "Disentangling the International Festival Circuit," 272–276. See also Wong, *Film Festivals*, 109–112, 117–122.

27. Farahmand, "Disentangling the International Festival Circuit," 275.

28. Ibid., 277. One of the most searing images of the 1979 Iranian Revolution was that of crowds burning down cinemas—so the fact that filmmakers like Mohsen Makhmalbaf and Jafar Panahi were prominent in the Iranian protest movement of 2009–2011 has had tremendous resonance.

29. For more on Jia, see Wong, *Film Festivals*, 153–156.

30. Though unlikely, such a rollback is hardly impossible. After all, directors like Jiang Wen, who was banned from filmmaking for seven years after finishing his festival-decorated war comedy *Devils on the Doorstep* (2000), still routinely face censure.

31. Andrew, "Atlas of World Cinema," 19.

32. Ibid.

33. Ibid.

34. This is the sort of definition at work in Badley and Palmer, "Introduction," 1–3.

35. Dennison and Lim, "Introduction," 6.

36. Andrew, "Atlas of World Cinema," 21.

37. Ibid., 19.

38. Nagib, "Towards a Positive Definition of World Cinema," 33.

39. Ibid., 30.

40. Galt and Schoonover, "Introduction," 11.

41. Nagib calls for "a method in which Hollywood and the West would cease to be the centre of film history, and this would be seen as a process with no single beginning," a demand that is in keeping with her larger view of "world cinema" as "the cinema of the world. It has no centre. It is not the other, but is us. . . . World cinema, as the world itself, is circulation." "Towards a Positive Definition of World Cinema," 34–35.

42. See Thanouli, "Narration in World Cinema," 7, 13–14.

43. Chaudhuri, *Contemporary World Cinema*, 1.

44. One reason that the terminological debate over "world cinema" is so pointed is that it is a function of a more urgent debate over the costs and benefits of global art cinema as a whole. The participants of the latter debate worry that global art cinema (whose Euro-style networks use corporate funding to reach into Africa and South America, looking for new material and new talent) is more costly to the developing world than it is bene-ficial—which is to say that it is more exploitative, more neocolonialist, and so forth. But as Cindy H. Wong points out, there is no final way of mollifying this anxiety, for global art cinema is too complex both in its local virtues and in its moments of exploitation. See Wong, *Film Festivals*, 158.

45. Another way of thinking of this particular usage is through older, more explicitly racist terms such as "ethnic cinema" or "ethnic film." As Barbara Wilinsky has noted, in the postwar era, Mexican films had trouble achieving the status of art films in the United States. Instead, they were often relegated to the lower cultural status of "ethnic films." Mexican films formed a world cinema in the United States that struggled to achieve the status of an art cinema that could take advantage of higher-class screenings, venues, and audiences. Wilinsky, *Sure Seaters*, 32.

46. Baumann, *Hollywood Highbrow*, 113.

Chapter 4

1. Newman seems conflicted in making this point, as if he wants to call indie films "art films" but is not ready to depart from film-history convention. See *Indie*, 76.

2. Tudor, "Rise and Fall of the Art (House) Movie," 127.

3. Wasson, *Museum Movies*, 1–31; and Wilinsky, *Sure Seaters*, 41–79. See also Balio, *Foreign Film Renaissance on American Screens*, 25–26.

4. Baumann, *Hollywood Highbrow*, 1.

5. Ibid., 22, 31, 82, 115.

6. Neale, "Art Cinema as Institution," 16–29.

7. Baumann, *Hollywood Highbrow*, 113, 148–155.

8. As exploitation distributor David Friedman once put it, American viewers weren't excited about Bergman only because of "his creativity or because he was a great film direc-tor"; they were also excited "because he showed some ass and some tits." Morton, "Inter-view with Dave Friedman," 102.

9. Mark Betz has written extensively on this topic. See "Name Above the (Sub)Title," 2–5. This article is reprinted in Betz, *Beyond the Subtitle*, 45–92.

10. Neale, "Art Cinema as Institution," 30–33. See also Stevenson, "And God Created Europe." In *The Foreign Film Renaissance on American Screens*, Balio deals very well with the idea that the distribution of art cinema was expanded in the United States due to the sexuality of the foreign art films.

11. See Baumann, "Intellectualization and Art World Development," 408–409. See also Baumann, *Hollywood Highbrow*, 54–59.

12. See Dubie, "Obscene History in the Heights." On *Les amants*, see Balio, *Foreign Film Renaissance on American Screens*, 145–148.

13. Quoted on the IMDb site. Available at http://www.imdb.com/title/tt0330099 /awards. Accessed April 4, 2009.

14. Quoted on the IMDb site. Available at http://www.imdb.com/title/tt0330099/. Accessed April 4, 2009.

15. Becker, *Art Worlds*, 95.

16. Testa, "Soft-Shaft Opportunism," 41, 52, 43.

17. For example, Patricia Zimmermann notes that "independent exhibitors call American indie films 'art films without subtitles.'" "Digital Deployment(s)," 248. Michael Z. Newman takes a more nuanced position in *Indie: An American Film Culture*, where he admits that indie films have a similar set of sociological functions as art films but are not art films, presumably because they are not foreign art films. See *Indie*, 76.

18. Michael Z. Newman makes this clear in "Indie Culture."

19. The finest discussion of these issues may be found in Newman, *Indie*; see 2–12 in particular.

20. Bennett, "How Indie Is Indie?" 96.

21. This sentiment has been evident in many post-2008 articles on the state of independent film published in mainstream forums like the *New York Times* or *Sight & Sound*. See, for example, Cieply, "As Studios Cut Budgets, Independent Filmmakers Distribute on Their Own." For Newman, a strict construction of indie logic presupposed that the union of a Miramax and a Disney was impossible, because the indies opposed studio ownership. Yet as he notes, these unions were often quite successful, such that the "mainstreaming of indie amplified rather than diminished its salience as a cultural category." See "Indie Culture," 17. These unions worked because the indies and studios were all part of the commodity system. Indeed, the indies, despite their rhetoric, offered "products, objects for sale in the culture market." Ibid., 34. It made sense, then, that if the studios handled their new indie divisions with care, they could market them more effectively than could smaller, less-capitalized indie outfits. As a result, consumers of indie products grew reliant on Hollywood distribution and were naturally quite resentful when much of that distribution was suddenly withdrawn around 2008—even if that withdrawal seemed to uphold their own view of Hollywood as *in it only for the money*.

22. For more on this, see Webb, *Understanding Bourdieu*, 167.

23. See, for example, Farahmand, "Disentangling the International Festival Circuit"; Halle, "Offering Tales They Want to Hear"; and Wong, *Film Festivals*.

24. Peter Lev focuses at length on this subject in *Euro-American Cinema*, xi–xiv. See also Balio, *Foreign Film Renaissance on American Screens*; and Guback, *International Film Industry*.

25. Lev, *Euro-American Cinema*, 25. Lev draws on Guback for this statistic.

26. Betz, "Name Above the (Sub)Title," 15 (Betz's italics).

27. Ibid., 9.

28. See Hawkins, "Culture Wars."

29. Neale, "Art Cinema as Institution," 30–33.

30. Ibid., 33.

31. For the best available discussion of hardcore cinema, see Williams, *Hard Core*.

32. Here I refer to the speculations of another article; see Andrews, "Toward a More Valid Definition of 'Pornography.'" One of my arguments is that evolutionary psychology, the branch of biology devoted to the idea of human nature, may soon have something to teach us about porn. Though noted evolutionists have disputed that evolutionary science can say anything rigorous about the arts, they have admitted that evolutionary psychology's claims about the adaptive roots of human behavior are strongest in areas such as

sexuality. Thus Jerry Coyne agrees with the evolutionary psychologists that "human males are largely promiscuous and females choosy (this despite the socially enforced monogamy that prevails in many societies)." See *Why Evolution Is True*, 228. To me, it seems inevitable that evolutionary theorists will one day draw on this consensus to (1) interpret the pleasure of pornography as rooted in an evolved sex drive that leads heterosexual men to mate with as many women as possible, and to (2) read our traditional bias against porn as a cultural by-product of genetic differences between the sexes, one that is as reliable as society's bias against promiscuity. Ergo, our antiporn biases may be as slow to change as human nature.

33. Lewis, "Real Sex."

34. James Quandt coined this term. See "Flesh and Blood," 126–132. For examples of how critics have used this term, see Hawkins, "Culture Wars."

35. Williams, "Cinema and the Sex Act," 23; Downing, "French Cinema's New 'Sexual Revolution,'" 276.

36. For an example of this sort of distinction, see Downing, who concludes that the films of the New French Extremism "are not porn. Nor are they even art films *about* porn. Rather, they are attempts to disrupt, fragment or destroy the naturalized relationship between the voyeur and the desired spectacle in cinema." "French Cinema's New 'Sexual Revolution,'" 279.

37. McNair, "Not Some Kind of Kinky Porno Flick," 16.

38. Williams, "Cinema and the Sex Act," 22–23.

39. As Chris Lee documents, Soderbergh even admits "to a certain degree of exploitation" of Sasha Grey. "Soderbergh gave Grey the lead role in the film . . . fully intending to milk her X-rated fame for all it is worth. 'I was very much counting on the fact that the interest in her would be greater than the interest in the movie,' Soderbergh said. 'We would be drafting off her notoriety rather than vice versa. I needed her. That's no different than getting Brad Pitt to be in your movie, albeit in a different context.'" Lee, "Porn Star Sasha Grey Gets Mainstream Role." This crossover trend can be seen to some extent among the auteurs, too. For example, *Baise-moi*, a movie whose contributions to this hard-core trend in the traditional art film is beyond dispute, was codirected by Coralie Trinh Thi, who has starred in many hardcore movies—including hardcore *art* movies like Blake's *Paris Chic* (1997). Not incidentally, *Baise-moi* also stars women who have acted in European hardcore projects.

40. Zuromskis, "Prurient Pictures and Popular Film," 9–13.

41. Given the existence of this tradition, it is interesting that Breillat has said that *Romance*—a film whose advertising campaigns relied on the idea that the film goes places other art films haven't—was inspired by Oshima's notorious art movie. See Anton, "Catherine Breillat Opens Up About *Romance*, Sex, and Censorship." See also Williams, "Cinema and the Sex Act," 20.

42. Russell, "Introduction," 6.

43. Several recent sociological studies have investigated similar dynamics. For example, in "'Typically French'? Mediating Screened Rape to British Audiences" (2010), Martin Barker does a study of "Frenchness" to figure out whether this national stereotype serves British viewers as a "cover for potentially dangerous and arousing experiences," such that it is an "art-house excuse, so that middle-class elites can get to see and relish things that aren't 'safe' for ordinary folks." See "'Typically French'?" 146. Barker exposes substantial variation concerning British perceptions of Frenchness, but stereotypes of French "seri-

ousness" clearly exist, which give distributors and cultural guardians alibis that permit the circulation of "typically" French movies.

44. Baumann, *Hollywood Highbrow*, 6, 176.

Chapter 5

1. Juno, "Interview," 17.

2. Mathijs and Mendik, "Editorial Introduction," 11.

3. Jancovich, "Introduction," 1–2.

4. This point of view is evident throughout *Defining Cult Movies* and was to my knowledge first proposed by Jeffrey Sconce. See "'Trashing' the Academy."

5. The Softcore Reviews website demonstrates that the cult world's dominated nature is often made tangible through embarrassment and self-consciousness. The cult reviewers of this site construct their own criteria for evaluation, but then they often mock these, re-inforcing the dominance of traditional criteria and undercutting their own. See Andrews, *Soft in the Middle*, 199–204.

6. See Jancovich, "Cult Fictions," 151.

7. See, for example, Hawkins, *Cutting Edge*; and Betz, "Art, Exploitation, Under-ground," 202–222.

8. On cult cinema's oppositionalism, see Sconce, "'Trashing' the Academy," 381.

9. Mathijs and Mendik, "Concepts of Cult," 20.

10. For one example of this institutional growth, see Bill Landis's account of why he became a grindhouse chronicler and tastemaker. Landis and Clifford, *Sleazoid Express*, xii.

11. See Mike Hale's discussions of the "Cinemania" offerings at Tribeca. Hale, "Under-side of a Film Festival, Where Some Dark Treasures Dwell." See also Hale, "Tribeca's Taste of All Things Grim and Gory." Another reliable festival exhibitor of cult films, one with crossover potential, is South by Southwest in Austin.

12. I recently verified this observation at a Chicago screening of Nobuhiko Obaya-shi's *House* (1977), which took place on March 3, 2010, at 8:00 p.m. at the Gene Siskel Film Center, a venue that is both a first-run art house and a repertory theater. The packed hipster audience had been primed to laugh by months of promo campaigns and by word-of-mouth—and thus it was laughing boisterously at the trailers and advertisements even before the movie began. To get a different glimpse of what cult interactivity and populism can mean in the context of art cinema, see *All the Love You Cannes!* (2002), Lloyd Kauf-man's documentary about Troma's experience at the globally renowned film festival.

13. The cult nexus also fetishizes the substance of film and its modes of projection; and more recently, cult insiders have begun to similarly fetishize video and VHS-viewing.

14. Mathijs and Mendik, "Editorial Introduction," 6.

15. For more on *Donnie Darko*'s cult-indie status, see Newman, *Indie*, 211–213.

16. This "bad" aesthetic is traced in the aforementioned research by Sconce, Jancovich, Mathijs, and Mendik; it is also discussed from a nonacademic point of view by Landis and Clifford.

17. For a discussion of these effects in a particularly subtle example of this phenome-non, see Gorfinkel, "Dated Sexuality," 124–126.

18. For a subtly different take on these questions, see Bozelka, "Exploitation Films and Success."

19. Hawkins, "Culture Wars."

20. On "art horror" in Argento, see de Ville, "Menopausal Monsters and Sexual Transgression in Argento's Art Horror," 62–64.

21. Ohbayashi's *House* and Herk Harvey's *Carnival of Souls* (1962) are a few of the many cult-art movies distributed by the art-house label Criterion Collection on DVD.

22. Cousins et al., "The Mad, the Bad, and the Dangerous." In the United States, early signs of cult eclecticism have been evident at a number of traditional art-cinema institutions, including early film festivals as well as in exhibition contexts like the Museum of Modern Art, which has been famous for seemingly legitimating the most illegitimate forms. For further discussion, see Wasson, *Museum Movies*; and Wilinsky, *Sure Seaters*.

23. Jones, review of *Out of the Past*, 188. On film noir, see Naremore, *More Than Night*.

24. To get an idea of what I mean by "cult mutation," see Johnnie To's *Breaking News* (2004), a film whose first sequence is a marvel of the swooping camera and the long take, all used in the service of relentless action. The critical response to this film and to this "master director" has typically taken breathless account of this combination of art-film technique and generic purpose.

25. Though scholars like Sconce and Nathan Hunt take it for granted that the cultural capital of a given cult sector works only *in* that sector, this is not always the case regarding the high-art canons of that sector. The subcultural capital of cult-art movies has a limited "cultural" dimension, for it is accepted in other cult sectors and sometimes beyond the cult nexus as a whole. See, for example, Hunt, "Importance of Trivia," 198.

26. These opinions are supported vis-à-vis Metzger, Dark (aka Gregory Hippolyte), Lazarus, and Marsiglia, respectively, in Andrews, *Soft in the Middle*, 34–37, 143–146, 218–227, 246–249.

Chapter 6

1. For a description of one set of hipster scenes, see James, "LA's Hipster Cinema." The term "university-made" is Kathryn Ramey's. See "Between Art, Industry, and Academia," 26.

2. This account sees avant-garde cinema as "a specific cinematic practice" that "differs from classical cinema as well as from modernist art cinema precisely by virtue of the difference of its practice. Virtually all verbal proclamations of avant-garde filmmakers show a lesser or greater amount of hostility toward commercial filmmaking. It opposes not just the Hollywood-type film industry but the European art-film industry as well." See Kovács, *Screening Modernism*, 32.

3. On these subjects, see Rees, *History of Experimental Film and Video*, 30–31, 33; and Kovács, *Screening Modernism*, 21–25. Kovács is valuable for how he touches on the origins of the split in art cinema between art films and avant-garde movies. For recent examples of crossover critics who refer to both avant-garde movies and video art as "art cinema," see Young and Duncan, "What is 'Art Cinema'?" in Young and Duncan, *Art Cinema*, 9–11. See also Baumann, *Hollywood Highbrow*, 114–116. Baumann is crucial in that he documents how in the United States the idea of film-as-art existed in the interwar period mainly in avant-garde journals rather than in mainstream discourses; thus, in American contexts, the

idea of an "art cinema" was an avant-garde perception until after the Second World War, when a confluence of events, including the broad distribution of state-subsidized foreign art films from Europe, made the idea more common. See also Connolly, *Place of Artists' Cinema*.

4. See, for example, Arthur, *Line of Sight*, xv, 153.

5. Skoller, *Shadows, Specters, Shards*, 93.

6. See Blaetz, "Introduction," 1. Commentators like Jonas Mekas and Michael Zryd have claimed that in the United States the term "experimental" was more apt than "avant-garde" until 1970, when critics familiar with European traditions began referring to it in that way. Still, if we credit Peter Bürger, whose *Theory of the Avant-Garde* (1974) defines the avant-garde in terms of its resistance to institutions, the un-institutionalized, pre-1970 period was *the* period when American experimental cinema had the most authenticity *as* an avant-garde. See Mekas, "Independence for Independents," 35–36; Zryd, "Experimental Film and the Development of Film Study in America," 182–185.

7. This comes with a significant caveat, though: terms like "underground" have at times referred to popular avant-garde cults, like the New York underground of the 1960s. On the use of the terms "experimental" and "underground," see Kovács, *Screening Modernism*, 27–29.

8. For thorough reviews of this topic, see Neale, "Art Cinema as Institution"; Wilinsky, *Sure Seaters*, 33–40; and Kovács, *Screening Modernism*, 7–32.

9. Rees, *History of Experimental Film and Video*, 8. Kovács uses a distinct terminology that is similar in meaning. See, for example, *Screening Modernism*, 27–32.

10. Rees, *History of Experimental Film and Video*, 31; see also Kovács, *Screening Modernism*, 23–24.

11. Rees, *History of Experimental Film and Video*, 51.

12. Still, even before these necessities emerged, the impetus toward political content had forced much of the narrative avant-garde in more "normative directions," as Rees puts it. Ibid.

13. James, *Most Typical Avant-Garde*, 20–38. In an unpublished work-in-progress that draws on the ideas of Pierre Bourdieu, Chuck Kleinhans refers to the largely forgotten American experimental films made between 1921 and 1947 that the film historian Lewis Jacobs cited in "Experimental Cinema in America: Part One" (1947); these works include some fifteen films that Jacobs claimed were directly influenced by Dziga Vertov. See Kleinhans, "Producing the Field of Experimental Film/Video," 4–5. Kleinhans wishes to acknowledge the contributions of B. Ruby Rich to an earlier formulation of this piece, which was presented as "Avant Garde and Radical Political Film in the U.S." at the Society for Cinema Studies conference in March 1980 and later published in the French journal *Cinémaction*. Kleinhans and Rich, "Le Cinéma d'avant-garde et ses rapports avec le cinéma militant."

14. Mekas, "Independence for Independents," 35.

15. See Kael, "Movies, the Desperate Art," 70.

16. See Arthur, *Line of Sight*, xv.

17. See Wasson, *Museum Movies*; see also the MoMA's informational pages at http://www.moma.org/learn/resources/circulatingfilm.

18. This interconnected history is increasingly covered by institutional histories such as Comer, *Film and Video Art*.

19. See Comer, *Film and Video Art*; and Connolly, *Place of Artists' Cinema*.

20. For more on this subject, see MacDonald, *Canyon Cinema*.

21. James, *Most Typical Avant-Garde*, 205.

22. Ramey, "Between Art, Industry, and Academia," 26–27.

23. See, for example, Bürger, *Theory of the Avant-Garde*. The avant-garde's anti-institutional bearing is central to this book. Bourdieu explains this resistance as a desire "at any price to avoid assimilation to bourgeois art and the effect of social ageing it determines," which leads in turn to the refusal of "the social signs of consecration—decoration, prizes, academies and all kinds of honours." Bourdieu, *Rules of Art*, 123. On the relation of Bürger's theory of the avant-garde to art cinema, see Kovács, *Screening Modernism*, 14–15.

24. Wollen, "Two Avant-Gardes," 171.

25. Ibid., 172.

26. Ibid., 172–173. For a separate account of Wollen's essay, see Kovács, *Screening Modernism*, 29–30.

27. Wollen, "Two Avant-Gardes," 173.

28. Ibid.

29. Ibid., 175.

30. Ibid.

31. See Hanlon, "Traveling Theory, Shots, and Players," 353–355. Hanlon notes that the Third Cinema directors of the New Latin American Cinema tended to agree with Godard that he was "trapped inside the fortress" of Second Cinema (art cinema), despite the fact that he was an aesthetic revolutionary who also happened to be sympathetic to the politically revolutionary principles of Third Cinema. Thus they "understood Godard, Straub, and others as having succeeded in purging their filmic texts of bourgeois ideology," but "also felt that despite this achievement they had merely created a subset of bourgeois art cinema with revolutionary content, which became obvious when the audiences who went to see these films were taken into account." Ibid., 354.

32. Of course, context makes a difference, since Godard films were not always shown in the same venues as Antonioni's films. For example, in France, the films that Godard made between 1968 and 1972 were shown in relatively "funky" art-and-essay theaters, while Antonioni films of the same period were shown in the boulevard movie theaters. My gratitude to Chuck Kleinhans for pointing this out.

33. For evidence of this influence, see the Frameworks archive at http://www.hi-beam .net/fw/index.html. It includes a number of references to *Riddles of the Sphinx*, including threads like this one: http://www.hi-beam.net/fw/fw40/0300.html. Accessed January 3, 2010.

34. Ramey, "Between Art, Industry, and Academia," 22.

35. Ibid.

36. Ibid., 26–27.

37. Ibid., 23.

38. Ibid., 35.

39. See Zryd, "The Academy and the Avant-Garde," 26–27, 28.

40. I don't mean that Zryd is *intentionally* updating Ramey; after all, he cites a different piece by Ramey, and only once. See ibid., 24. Besides that, there is no necessary disjunction between these two essays. Ramey stresses the motivations and status games of *individuals* in experimental cinema while *also* theorizing the larger field. By contrast, Zryd concentrates on that larger field while simultaneously taking a more jaundiced view

of the naïve and uncompromising avant-garde rhetoric articulated at the individual level. By looking at these pieces in tandem, we can see that the *field* of avant-garde cinema as a whole is quite secure, perhaps more secure than ever, even though the lives of its individual members are often marked by insecurity and economic hardship.

41. Ibid., 27–28.

42. Bourdieu, *Rules of Art*, 251.

43. Ibid., 253.

44. Ibid., 123, 254.

45. Ramey, "Re: Experimental Cinema," 2.

46. Bourdieu, *Rules of Art*, 242–243. As Bourdieu notes here, the "reason the field has a directed and cumulative history is because the very intention of *surpassing* which properly defines the avant-garde is itself the result of a whole history, and because it is inevitably situated in relation to what it aims to surpass, that is, in relation to all the activities of surpassing which have occurred in the very structure of the field and in the space of possibles it imposes on new entrants" (Bourdieu's italics).

47. Ibid., 28–29.

48. Ibid., 253–254.

49. Kleinhans, "Producing the Field of Experimental Film/Video," 3. For the way in which Sitney created the "dominant model" for looking at the New American Cinema — one that "is essentially an internal art history approach to the avant-garde" — see ibid., 3–4.

50. Sitney, *Visionary Film*, 209. For more of this mythmaking in action, see the extended Brakhage homage, "Stan Brakhage: Correspondences," which dominates a special double issue of the *Chicago Review*.

51. Colin Still, dir., "Brakhage on Brakhage I" (1996). Brakhage often ties his poverty to his purity and artistic focus in the four documentary segments included in this anthology of his works.

52. Sitney, *Visionary Film*, 155.

53. Ibid., 174, 209.

54. See Mekas and the New York Film-Makers' Cooperative, "First Statement of the New American Cinema Group."

55. James, *Most Typical Avant-Garde*, 203.

56. Ibid.

57. Zryd, "The Academy and the Avant-Garde," 27. See also the "Let's Remain Disorganizedly Organized" section of the first chapter of Paul Arthur's *Line of Sight*, 6–16.

58. See Arthur, *Line of Sight*, 14–16.

59. See MacDonald, "Cinema 16," 28–30. See also Arthur, *Line of Sight*, 6–16; and Ramey, "Between Art, Industry, and Academia," 25.

60. MacDonald, "Cinema 16," 28.

61. Behrens, "Re: Experimental Cinema," 1.

62. Bayma, "Art World Culture and Institutional Choices," 84.

63. Quoted in ibid.

64. Behrens, "Re: Experimental Cinema," 1. See also Ramey, "Between Art, Industry, and Academia," 26–27.

65. I have heard experimentalists express similar sentiments on many occasions, one example of which I have in writing (though its author wishes to remain anonymous). See Anonymous, "Re: Experimental Cinema," 1. Somewhat less often, I have come across evi-

dence of various gatekeepers reacting against the peculiar venom that often greets their decisions in this field. See, for example, the thread on this subject in the Frameworks archive at http://www.hi-beam.net/fw/fw40/0313.html, dated June 11, 2009, and accessed January 3, 2010.

66. Ramey, "Between Art, Industry, and Academia," 25.

67. Quoted in Zryd, "The Academy and the Avant-Garde," 36n13.

68. Bourdieu, *Rules of Art*, 254.

69. For more, see Ramey, "Between Art, Industry, and Academia," 25–26, 30–31; and Bayma, "Art World Culture and Institutional Choices." See also Bourdieu, *Rules of the Game*, 122–123.

70. Denis Dutton speculates that as a population people don't have the built-in capacities for such forms, which deviate far from the normative tastes of human nature. Instead, the taste for avant-garde art varies according to non-heritable factors like education. In this perspective, avant-garde taste has to be relearned with each generation, rather than being inherited via reproduction. See Dutton, *Art Instinct*, 36–38.

71. Quoted in Zryd, "The Academy and the Avant-Garde," 24. For details of *Spiral*'s brief existence in the Los Angeles of the 1980s, see James, *Most Typical Avant-Garde*, 247.

72. See, for example, Fischer, "Experimental Film." See also Arthur, *Line of Sight*, 158–159.

73. See Arthur, *Line of Sight*, 156–160.

74. This anti-institutional posture can have different outcomes, as a brief glance at the websites of Craig Baldwin's Other Cinema (http://www.othercinema.com/) and Andrea Grover's Aurora Picture Show (http://www.aurorapictureshow.org/) demonstrates.

75. For example, in a telephone interview conducted on April 22, 2009, Andrea Grover of the Aurora Picture Show noted that her microcinema is devoted first to the artists, whom it has supported financially and around whom it has built a community, complete with outreach programs. She also indicated her intent to foment an anti-institutional atmosphere. Nevertheless, despite its user- and artist-friendliness, Aurora has been carefully programmed, complete with guest and in-house curation and an awards night that has honored high-profile experimentalists like William Wegman, Isaac Julien, Miranda July, and Steina and Woody Vasulka. For more, see the Aurora website, http://www.aurorapictureshow.org/. See also Ramey, "Between Art, Industry, and Academia," 29.

76. As Grover explains, private foundations have fewer mandates and have "represented Aurora's largest contributors to date"; by contrast, for "government funding, there are incentives to meet audience numbers in terms of diversity, tourists, seniors, and youth served, which means some programming has to have wide appeal." Government funding has also raised censorship concerns for Aurora. See Grover, "Re: Images and Permission," 1.

77. Zryd, "Experimental Film and the Development of Film Study in America," 200.

78. Ramey, "Between Art, Industry, and Academia," 31.

79. Ramey has noted that experimental filmmakers in fine-art positions can be forced by tenure pressures into making their art more conservative so as to win the particular institutional validations (e.g., at festivals "of a certain caliber") required by their tenure committees—a pressure that is only reinforced when their committees refuse to consider a candidate's scholarship, however penetrating it may be. See Ramey, "Re: Experimental Cinema," 2. That said, if the avant-gardist's insider status is based on a critical role (as in the case of Sitney or Arthur) rather than an artistic role (see Ramey), such obstacles might

be easier to circumvent. That said, we should not underestimate the subtle difficulties that critic–scholars face when assimilating academic values.

80. See Birchall, "Avant-Garde Archive Online." Of course, there have always been commercial distributors that have tried to circulate avant-garde films on a broader scale—for example, see Freude Bartlett's Serious Business Company, which expired in 1983 after twelve years of specializing in avant-garde films, feminist films, and animation—but the Internet seems to have opened the avant-garde to a new and more commercial range of viewers in a more permanent way than has ever seemed possible before. For more on Bartlett, see Hess and Kleinhans, "Doing Serious Business."

81. See Arthur, *Line of Sight*, 111–131; and James, *Most Typical Avant-Garde*, 320–336.

82. Arthur, *Line of Sight*, 113.

Chapter 7

1. According to Michael Z. Newman, the "mainstream" is "a category that niche cultures or subcultures construct to have something against which to define themselves and generate their cultural or subcultural capital." Hence, he doesn't believe "there is a mainstream that exists independent of this process of classification." See *Indie*, 5.

2. Kaufman, "IA," xiv.

3. Jancovich, "Introduction," 1. See also Newman, *Indie*, 212.

4. See, for example, Hollows, "Masculinity of Cult"; and Read, "Cult of Masculinity."

5. The latter tendency goes back to the class-driven manifestos of highbrows like Clement Greenberg and Dwight MacDonald. See Greenberg, "Avant-Garde and Kitsch." See also Macdonald, *Against the American Grain*, 54.

6. See, for example, Cindy H. Wong's *Film Festivals: Culture, People, and Power on the Global Screen*, a book that asks a very pertinent question: if we know what a nonmainstream, festival film is, what, "by contrast, is a mainstream film?" At first, Wong pretends to find the difference in the distinction between serious, mid-budget art films and nonserious, big-budget Hollywood films; then she begins to break down the solidity of that distinction through reference to what she calls "crossover films" like *Pulp Fiction* (1994) and *The Wrestler* (2008), which had major Hollywood success though they "shared the laurels of the 'A'-level festivals." Ibid., 69, 71.

7. Kaufman, "IA," xiv.

8. Didion, *Slouching Towards Bethlehem*, 150.

9. As Jancovich puts it, "Rather than investigate the contradictory and problematic nature of this [mainstream] concept, [Sconce] conflates it with an equally problematic term, 'Hollywood,' which he defines as 'an economic and artistic institution that represents not just a body of films, but a particular mode of film production and its accompanying signifying practices.'" See Jancovich, "Cult Fictions," 152.

10. See, for example, Neale and Smith, "Introduction," xiv–xv.

11. See Balio, "Major Presence in All of the World's Important Markets," 61–62.

12. See Caldwell, *Production Culture*.

13. Balio, "Major Presence in All of the World's Important Markets," 59–64.

14. Ibid., 58–59; Maltby, "Nobody Knows Everything," 37; Wyatt, *High Concept*.

15. Balio, "Major Presence in All of the World's Important Markets," 58.

16. Two examples: during the early 1990s, Paramount was the major distributor of cult studio Full Moon Pictures, which at that time featured a softcore label (Torchlight); and in 1989, Warner Brothers even held the American video rights for Troma's sequel to *The Toxic Avenger*.

17. Consider, for example, that Harvey Weinstein's films have over the past decades secured almost three hundred Oscar nominations and over sixty wins all by themselves; many of these movies were produced through labels with Hollywood affiliations.

18. Farber, "Underground Films," 163.

19. Ibid., 165, 166. Farber's incipient auteurism clearly represents a midpoint in the transition from cultural perceptions of Hollywood as a site of entertainment and craft to perceptions of it as a potential site of genius and high art. See Baumann, *Hollywood Highbrow*, 60–63.

20. That these Eastwood films form a kind of "middle" art cinema is suggested by the details of their exhibition. For example, just after their initial runs, I saw *Unforgiven* and *Gran Torino* in repertory art houses—and it is worth noting that their Hollywood status was emphasized there, as when *Gran Torino* was segregated into an "Oscar Worthy" category by the University of Chicago's Doc Films on its Spring 2009 film schedule.

21. Baumann, *Hollywood Highbrow*, 168.

22. See Dargis, "Seduction by Machine Gun."

23. These business numbers are from IMDb. Available at http://www.imdb.com/title /tt0468569/business. Accessed May 9, 2009.

24. Schatz, *Hollywood Genres*, 6–7.

25. Ibid., 7.

26. As the Australian director Fred Schepisi put it, the most freedom that a foreign-born director could expect inside Hollywood was the freedom to do something original *within* Hollywood genre constraints. See O'Regan, "Cultural Exchange," 265.

27. Anonymous, "Cinema."

28. See Cagle, "Two Modes of Prestige Film."

29. Baumann, *Hollywood Highbrow*, 92–97. As Baumann puts it, although these expensive prestige "productions did *not* redefine film as art, they *were* a precursor to such a redefinition." Ibid., 96 (Baumann's italics).

30. See Schatz, *Genius of the System*, 491. The directors of the postclassical era have often "put forth a fantasy image of [Hollywood] filmmaking as a field of restricted production, an image that film reviewers and the press participated in constructing"—and an image that in the 1960s and 1970s "matched emerging values and preferences." See Baumann, *Hollywood Highbrow*, 88.

31. On the authenticity of indie-style films, see Newman, "Indie Culture."

32. Quoted in Janisse, "Cult of Suffering," 19.

33. See Hess, "*La politique des auteurs*, Part Two," 20.

34. To get a sense of how auteurist and art-oriented even the French directors opposed by the auteur critics really were, look at the interview segment with Clément included on Criterion's *Jeux interdits* DVD (2005), in which he comes off as the ultimate cinephile.

35. Yabroff, "Straight Outta Denmark." See also Bier, "Searching for a Place 'In a Better World.'"

36. Wood, "Cultural Space as Political Metaphor."

37. For an overview of recent events in Iranian cinema, see Farahmand, "Disentangling the International Festival Circuit," 268–276.

38. Rajadhyaksha, "Hindi Cinema," 218. See also Nowell-Smith, "Art Cinema," 574–575; and http://www.culturalindia.net/indian-cinema/art-cinema.html.

39. Andrews, *Soft in the Middle*, 205–229.

40. Ibid., 218–220.

41. In an example of this subcultural acclaim, Softcore Reviews, at one time a prominent softcore website, once referred to *Word of Mouth* as "the *Citizen Kane* of softcore." Ibid., 201.

42. This last point holds true even if we construe a mainstream movie as one that hews to the "contingent universals" favored by human nature, especially its preference for "clarity" in speech, story, and action. See Carroll, *Theorizing the Moving Image*, 80. If we adopted this point of view, we might think it "unnatural" to favor a fairly opaque art cinema over a cinema that maximizes its accessibility. But we needn't look at the issue this way, for our tendency to demean the mainstream may depend on equally natural urges: for instance, our need for social status, which is often responsible for our participation in discourses that favor oppositional cinemas. Whether a movie technique or technology is relatively "unnatural" in that it seems unsuited to human physiology—an argument that Roger Ebert has recently made vis-à-vis 3-D technology—does not then suggest that it "deserves" a lower sociological status. See Ebert, "Why I Hate 3-D." After all, what would happen to the avant-garde, which so often elevates films that are difficult or headache-inducing, if this were the case? In the end, appeals to "nature" offer no final, bulletproof justification for elevating or degrading a cinema at the social level.

Chapter 8

1. Becker, *Art Worlds*, 360.

2. Doll, "Werner Herzog Dreams in 3-D." For related comments, see Wigley, "Out of the Darkness."

3. Rohter, "Prehistoric Cave with a Hornet on the Wall."

4. For the *New York Times* critic A. O. Scott in his review of *Pina*, "One of the interesting and unexpected film stories of 2011 is about 3-D, which simultaneously lost commercial potency and gained artistic credibility. Those who dismiss the format as the industrial gimmick (and excuse for price gouging) that it frequently is may need to reconsider now that a handful of certified auteurs have given it a try."

5. For coverage of this topic in the context of contemporary Hollywood, see Neale and Smith, *Contemporary Hollywood Cinema*.

6. Nowell-Smith, "Art Cinema," 567.

7. Galt and Schoonover, "Introduction," 7.

8. Forbes and Street, *European Cinema*, 47. See ibid., xii, 45–48, for the presence of star systems in European cinemas that were opposed, at least rhetorically, to Hollywood norms, including the use of celebrities.

9. Dyer, *Stars*, 63 (Dyer's italics).

10. Ibid., 10–12.

11. Lev, *Euro-American Cinema*, 13.

12. Betz, *Beyond the Subtitle*, 121–131. See also Balio, "Brigitte Bardot and Hollywood's Takeover of the U.S. Art Film Market in the 1960s"; and Dyer, *Stars*, 70–73.

13. Vincendeau, "Brigitte Bardot," 492 (Vincendeau's italics). See also Stevenson, "And God Created Europe," 35; and Russell, "Introduction," 5.

14. Czach, "Cinephilia, Stars, and Film Festivals," 145. One way that art cinema's difference from mainstream cinema is maintained in many (though not all) traditional art films is through its use of facial expressions. For example, one recognizable tradition that helps viewers identify an art film as "nonmainstream" involves the use of exaggerated detachment, especially in faces of its female characters. Indeed, though art cinema has promised us an investigation of female ecstasy since 1933, when Gustav Machatý tightened on Hedy Lamarr in *Ecstasy*, the Czech art film, it has more often given us signs of "serious" female detachment instead. Hence, this movie category has often been identified through the "inexpressive expressivity" of signature actresses, like Bardot, Deneuve, and Béart as well as Jeanne Moreau, Vanessa Redgrave, Monica Vitti, Liv Ullmann, Charlotte Rampling, Faye Dunaway, Delphine Seyrig, Tilda Swinton, Isabelle Huppert, Juliette Binoche, and Gong Li.

15. Negra, "Queen of the Indies," 71.

16. Ibid.

17. Neale, "Art Cinema as Institution," 36.

18. For an authoritative account of this "almost" movie, see Lewis, "Real Sex."

19. Neale, "Art Cinema as Institution," 24.

20. See Andrews, *Soft in the Middle*, 194, 240–243.

21. Lee, "Porn Star Sasha Grey Gets Mainstream Role."

Chapter 9

1. Thanouli, "'Art Cinema' Narration."

2. Ibid. On the connection of "smart cinema" to "art cinema," see Sconce, "Irony, Nihilism, and the New American 'Smart' Film'"; and "Smart Cinema."

3. Thanouli, "'Art Cinema' Narration."

4. Several extended critiques of Bordwell's account have appeared lately. Besides Thanouli, see Betz, "Beyond Europe"; and Kovács, *Screening Modernism*. While these critiques show respect for Bordwell's work, they also manifest some disenchantment with it. I share in both feelings. I respect Bordwell immensely, but I see how his achievements have constrained alternative perspectives on art cinema. What I find most problematic is that Bordwell realizes that what he calls "art-cinema narration" is one strand of a larger phenomenon he calls "international art cinema." See *Narration in the Fiction Film*, 205. Even a conservative view of this broader phenomenon could position it as potentially encompassing everything from prewar films d'arts, to the interwar avant-gardes, to particular examples of classical Hollywood narration, to the art movies of the New Hollywood, and to the many art movies that *Narration in the Fiction Film* in effect distinguishes from art cinema by categorizing them under alternate headings ("historical–materialist narration," "parametric narration," and Godardian narration). Bordwell gives one of these categories, art-cinema narration, preferential status as the "true" art cinema, not just through the label itself but also through the fact that he bluntly refers to its vehicle as the "art film." Even if Bordwell's narrative categories held water, which there is growing reason to doubt, this taxonomy would be misleading and incomplete—for it would not explain how so many

other types of art movie have managed to *function* as art cinema within the rubric of the "international art cinema" without actually being art cinema.

5. Thanouli, "'Art Cinema' Narration." Bordwell has appended an "Afterword" to a reprint of his essay in *Poetics of Cinema*. In this addendum, he makes many good points and apologizes at the start for being too general, with "no fine gradations allowed," when writing "The Art Cinema as a Mode of Film Practice" back in the 1970s. See "Afterword," 158. Bordwell also acknowledges here the growth of many art-cinema institutions, especially the festival circuit, which he considers "the world's alternative to Hollywood's theatrical distribution system." Ibid., 160. However, from this addendum, it is clear that he has retained the germ of his form- and narrative-based idea of art cinema, for he still sees this category as fundamentally rooted in "European art-cinema principles." Ibid., 163. He has not, then, moved toward the institution-, subculture-, and value-based idea of art cinema that I propose here.

6. See, for example, Bordwell, "Art Cinema as a Mode of Film Practice," 723, where he refers to the New Hollywood as "an art cinema" but claims that American art films cannot be art films in the European sense, since they "warp art-cinema conventions in new directions (as the work of Altman and Coppola shows)." He makes a similar point in his book, which builds on this essay, as well as his recent addendum to this essay. See Bordwell, *Narration in the Fiction Film*, 232; and Bordwell, "Afterword," 163.

7. Galt and Schoonover, "Introduction," 3–9.

8. Thanouli, "'Art Cinema' Narration."

9. Ibid.

10. Ibid.

11. This is the most traditional understanding of the rise of the postwar European art cinemas, but some innovative ideas have recently emerged. For example, Betz has argued that the postwar European art cinemas were generated not through opposition to Hollywood but through "the nostalgia produced by the loss of imperial power and unified national identity that the nation states of France and Italy encountered in their similar yet distinct relations to decolonization and modernization." Betz, *Beyond the Subtitle*, 99. *Beyond the Subtitle* is also applicable to this chapter in that it compares the Bordwell and Neale pieces discussed here. See ibid., 10–14.

12. Neale, "Art Cinema as Institution," 11.

13. The institutional approach profits Neale, then, by enabling him to see the obvious: that art cinema developed into a category that did not "belong" to one industry or region but was instead a niche in which different Hollywood art cinemas (including Euro-Hollywood coproductions, the New Hollywood, and the indie-style labels) might compete. Indeed, Hollywood could dominate certain art-movie markets, as it did in the United States after Miramax merged with Disney. This isn't to claim that the opposition between Hollywood and European art cinema ever went away as a structuring mythology. It is instead to claim that there was nothing to prevent Hollywood from exploiting this myth on its own.

14. Ibid., 15–16.

15. Kovács, *Screening Modernism*, 24.

16. Neale, "Art Cinema as Institution," 16–20.

17. Ibid., 24; see also 21–25.

18. Ibid., 27–28.

19. Ibid., 20.

20. Ibid., 35–37.

21. Ibid., 35.

22. Wasson, *Museum Movies*, 1–31.

23. Wilinsky, *Sure Seaters*, 41–79.

24. Tudor, "Rise and Fall of the Art (House) Movie," 136.

25. As Cindy H. Wong asks, artistic "integrity may be the criteria for selection, but what is it?" When auteurs can be seen adapting their styles to the needs of festivals and other funding mechanisms, the reality of their illusory "autonomy" becomes apparent. See *Film Festivals*, 157.

26. Baumann, *Hollywood Highbrow*, 67.

27. See Galt and Schoonover, "Introduction," 3–8.

28. Elsaesser, "Film Festival Networks," 84. See also Kovács, *Screening Modernism*, 25–26.

29. James, "Whose Cinephilia?" 5. The same figures are cited in Roddick, "Window Shopping," 13. Bordwell counts "about 250" major film festivals, "with hundreds more serving local, regional, and specialist audiences." See "Afterword," 160. For an excellent online compendium of film-festival research, see Film Festival Research Network, "Film Festival Research."

30. See Baumann, "Intellectualization and Art World Development," 408–409. See also Baumann, *Hollywood Highbrow*, 54–59; on U.S. festivals, see 56–57.

31. For an excellent book-length analysis of the festival world—one that is not governed by cinephilia—see Wong, *Film Festivals*. Though this book does not have much to say about the global system's intersections with cult cinema and "fantastic" festivals, it does have a great deal to say about festivals that are specialized in other ways (e.g., by their focus on gay-and-lesbian issues).

32. Bordwell, "Afterword," 160.

33. Elsaesser, "Film Festival Networks," 87.

34. Ibid., 86.

35. Ibid.

36. Baumann, "Intellectualization and Art World Development," 409.

37. Elsaesser, "Film Festival Networks," 99; Farahmand, "Disentangling the International Festival Circuit," 266.

38. de Valck, *Film Festivals*, 186–187.

39. Elsaesser, "Film Festival Networks," 107n28. For more on the business details of the festival circuit, see Peter Biskind's book *Down and Dirty Pictures: Miramax, Sundance, and the Rise of Independent Film* (2004), Steve Montal's article "Film Festivals and Markets" (2005), and Richard Porton's collection *dekalog³: On Film Festivals* (2009), which contains a number of essays like Mark Peranson's contribution, which describes the centrality of the sales agent in the commercial hierarchies of the film festival. See Peranson, "First You Get the Power, Then You Get the Money."

40. Elsaesser, "Film Festival Networks," 92–93.

41. Ibid., 91. It is for this reason that theorists like Neale and Kovács identify the festival with the global character of art cinema. See, for example, Kovács, *Screening Modernism*, 25.

42. Elsaesser, "Film Festival Networks," 93.

43. Thanouli, "'Art Cinema' Narration," 9.

44. As Farahmand has put it, festivals "exert a direct or indirect influence on film production because of the role they play in helping a film transition from local economies to the global market." See "Disentangling the International Festival Circuit," 267. Later, she explains how this process has worked in the context of recent Iranian art films. Ibid., 272–276. See also Wong, *Film Festivals*, 129–158, who offers insight into the logistics of funding art films through festival constraints and festival funding mechanisms. Betz also touches on this process. See "Beyond Europe," 31–32.

45. Thanouli, "'Art Cinema' Narration," 7–8.

46. Wong, *Film Festivals*, 99.

47. Farahmand, "Disentangling the International Festival Circuit," 265.

48. Elsaesser, "Film Festival Networks," 100. See also Wong, *Film Festivals*, 159–179. The April 2012 Side by Side LGBT International Film Festival in Moscow, a city in which the rights of gays and lesbians have been severely suppressed, highlights the activist potential of such festivals.

49. On gay-and-lesbian festivals, see Wong, *Film Festivals*, 179–188.

50. Mike Hale has written often on this phenomenon. See "Underside of a Film Festival, Where Some Dark Treasures Dwell."

51. Hawkins, "Culture Wars."

52. This is the pattern of *dekalog*³: *On Film Festivals*, which not only reprints the Bazin essay but follows it with essay after essay lamenting the corruption of the international festival circuit, whose overweening commercialism it depicts as an affront to cinephilia and to the larger idea of film as high art. As Robert Koehler puts it in this volume, the "central problem with film festivals . . . is not so much a willingness to show bad films. . . . It is their general and unexamined aversion to cinephilia, and an unwillingness to place cinephilia at the centre of festivals' activities." Koehler, "Cinephilia and Film Festivals," 81. This attitude of continual lamentation over the commercialization of a festival circuit that was once pure has been ritually restated in crossover forums and cinephile forums alike; for another recent example, see Roddick, "Window Shopping," 13.

53. Baumann, "Intellectualization and Art World Development," 409–410.

54. Neale, "Art Cinema as Institution," 37.

55. See Baumann, *Hollywood Highbrow*, 66–69, 111–160.

56. Grieveson and Wasson, "Introduction," xxiv. See also Polan, "Beginnings of American Film Study."

57. Grieveson and Wasson, "Introduction," xxiv.

58. Near the start of his essay, Neale pithily indicates the importance that a crossover publication like *Sight & Sound* has played in maintaining the institutions of art cinema: "During the 1960s and early 1970s, at a time when the polemics surrounding 'popular culture' and Hollywood were at their height, Art Cinema was often defined as the 'enemy': as a bastion of 'high art' ideologies, as the kind of cinema supported by *Sight and Sound* and the critical establishment, therefore, as the kind of cinema to be fought." See "Art Cinema as Institution," 12.

59. Betz, "Little Books," 323.

60. Ibid., 340.

61. Ibid.

Chapter 10

1. This chapter does not make a strict distinction between distributors who are only distributors and the many distributors who, like Joseph Levine or Harvey Weinstein, have also acted as executive producers as well.

2. A. T. McKenna takes issue with Peter Lev's retelling of this legend. See McKenna, "Guilty by Association." See also Lev, *Euro-American Cinema*, 83–89.

3. Indeed, there may be a sense in which the bad old story *is* inscribed in our brains — for it could be that forces of natural and cultural selection have favored the bad old story's high-art prejudices, including its anticommercial and auteurist thrusts, in complex ways. Though this possibility would help explain the persistence of such stories, I don't have space for such speculation here.

4. Weinstein never seemed to take particular care to cover up the industrial pressures he placed on directors to modify their films to conform with his commercial aims. In the case of *The Cook, the Thief, His Wife, and Her Lover* (1989), Weinstein gleefully played both sides, pressuring Peter Greenaway to change his movie to suit the ratings board but then surrendering the X assigned the film when the director held firm, opting to distribute the movie unrated instead. It is as if Weinstein understood that acting this way would attract many audiences, including cinephiles aghast at the distributor interference.

5. Quoted in Balio, "'Major Presence in All of the World's Important Markets,'" 61–62.

6. See Fellman "Theatrical Distribution"; and Berney, "Independent Distribution." See also Schamus, "To the Rear of the Back End."

7. One recent example is Tino Balio's extraordinary book *The Foreign Film Renaissance on American Screens, 1946–1973*, which contains a wealth of data on art-film distributors in the United States during the postwar period.

8. See, for example, O'Regan, "Cultural Exchange"; and Thanouli, "Narration in World Cinema."

9. See, for example, Cubitt, "Distribution and Media Flows"; and Lobato, "Subcinema."

10. Becker, *Art Worlds*, 93–130.

11. Ibid., 1.

12. Ibid., 93.

13. Ibid., 39.

14. Ibid., 94, 95.

15. Ibid., 39.

16. Root, "Distributing 'A Question of Silence,'" 58.

17. Baumann, *Hollywood Highbrow*, 1. See also Baumann, "Intellectualization and Art World Development."

18. Baumann, *Hollywood Highbrow*, 3; see also 14, 161.

19. Ibid., 113 (Baumann's italics).

20. That is why I have tried to formulate my distribution theory, nascent though it is, according to Brian Boyd's belief that an "evolutionary analysis of art [must] consider the costs and benefits of art as a behavior in general." See "Art and Evolution," 438. In other words, a holistic distribution theory would measure art behavior in terms of biocultural incentives and biocultural constraints.

21. What I find intriguing about *Heaven's Gate* (1980) is that time has inexorably trans-

formed its legend from a cautionary tale emphasizing the destructive effects of auteur *excess* into a tale of auteur *integrity*, one in which a director's heedless spending proved his artistic rather than mercenary intent. In this variant of the bad old story, it doesn't matter that Michael Cimino's film was a box-office flop that took down United Artists—and may have taken the New Hollywood down with it.

22. Newman, "Indie Culture," 24. See also Biskind, *Down and Dirty Pictures*, 334.

23. Newman, "Indie Culture," 25–26.

24. Ibid., 27.

25. Becker, *Art Worlds*, 93.

26. I am stipulating "inside" because I don't mean to simplify the function of non-economic forms of capital in society. As long as Weinstein is acting outside traditional art-cinema institutions, where art cinema's high-art ethics may be less clearly understood, he can presumably draw on the category's prestige. A good example of this dynamic is his continual use of the Academy Awards to draw positive exposure for himself and his movies in mainstream quarters outside the most traditional art-cinema institutions.

27. See Biskind, *Down and Dirty Pictures*.

28. On Cammell, see Williams, *Erotic Thriller in Contemporary Cinema*, 404–406.

29. See Arthur, *Line of Sight*, 14–16.

30. On Hippolyte, see Andrews, *Soft in the Middle*, 143. For similar statements about Playboy auteur Tom Lazarus, see ibid., 218–220. Low-budget auteurs like Hippolyte and Lazarus flouted the postfeminist values that dominated their softcore contexts, making films that would have had very little hope of distribution were it not for their stylization and the auteurist rhetoric that surrounded them.

31. In American indie art cinemas, these sentiments were repeated even more forcefully in reaction to the 2008 downturn, which caused more traditional distributors to cut back. See, for example, Cieply, "As Studios Cut Budgets, Independent Filmmakers Distribute on Their Own."

32. Lobato, "Subcinema," 115.

33. See Gorfinkel, "Radley Metzger's 'Elegant Arousal.'"

34. This happened to Metzger repeatedly. For one expression of such a critique, see Testa, "Soft-Shaft Opportunism."

35. Becker, *Art Worlds*, 94.

36. Hayashi, "Fantastic Trajectory of Pink Art Cinema from Stalin to Bush"; Farahmand, "Disentangling the International Festival Circuit"; Halle, "Offering Tales They Want to Hear"; Betz, "Beyond Europe."

37. See Hayashi, "Fantastic Trajectory of Pink Art Cinema from Stalin to Bush," 49, 59–60.

38. Betz, "Beyond Europe," 31–33. See also Wong, *Film Festivals*, 98, 157. The picture Wong draws is of festival directors acting as distributors; thus, in cinephile discourse, they often come off badly, like a Levine or a Weinstein, for they force "autonomous" auteurs to adapt to festival mandates to secure festival circulation. But the difference between a festival director and a more commercial distributor is that the festival director often enforces a common seriousness or difficulty across a field of festival films.

39. See Zryd, "The Academy and the Avant-Garde"; and Ramey, "Between Art, Industry, and Academia."

40. See McKenna, "Guilty by Association."

41. Hawkins, *Cutting Edge*, 139. From Erich von Stroheim, Leni Riefenstahl, and

Henri-Georges Clouzot to Stan Brakhage, Béla Tarr, and Vincent Gallo, the history of art cinema is replete with auteurs who have blurred moral distinctions during the production of their films, using "art" as a rationale. Some of these rationales seem paper-thin in retrospect. For example, Werner Herzog in an Anchor Bay DVD extra that accompanies *Aguirre, the Wrath of God* (1972/2000), defended his decision to take a 35mm camera from the Munich Film School by saying, "I knew it was not theft . . . I had a natural right to take it"—presumably because he later made films like *Aguirre* using said camera.

Epilogue

1. To cite just two examples, see Ng, "Love in a Time of Transcultural Fusion," 75; and Ramey, "Between Art, Industry, and Academia," 35n1.

2. Ng, "Love in a Time of Transcultural Fusion," 75. Ng makes a similar point in "Myth of Total Cinephilia," 151. The importance of festivals to the experience of cinephilia is often cited by participants in the recent cinephilia debates; see, for example, Czach, "Cinephilia, Stars, and Film Festivals."

3. Ramey, "Between Art, Industry, and Academia," 35n1.

4. See, for example, de Valck and Hagener, "Introduction," 12. See also Elsaesser, "Cinephilia or the Uses of Disenchantment," 41.

5. Gorfinkel, "Cult Film or Cinephilia by Any Other Name," 33, 38.

6. Buchsbaum and Gorfinkel, "Cinephilia Dossier." In this dossier, the clearest expressions of a new cinephilia are found in the essays by Zachary Campbell, Lucas Hilderbrand, Girish Shambu, and Laurent Jullier, though other essayists speak of it and to it. See also Betz, "In Focus"; and Rosenbaum and Martin, *Movie Mutations*.

7. de Valck and Hagener, "Introduction," 22.

8. Elsaesser, "Cinephilia or the Uses of Disenchantment," 41.

9. Who—or what—might be the common enemy of this new cinephilia? One answer this dossier gives is global capital, with its stress on copyright and property. According to Zachary Campbell, "today's cinephilia" fights "for its autonomy, its right and capacity to use technologies—such as email, the Internet, digital piracy—unhindered by commercial or corporate statutes that exist not for culture and daily life and pleasure, but for the milked profits of regulated leisure." See "On the Political Challenges of the Cinephile Today," 212.

10. Sontag, "Decay of Cinema." This piece is cited by many contributors to de Valck and Hagener's collection as well as by many writers in Mark Betz's recent "In Focus" section of *Cinema Journal* devoted to cinephilia. Sontag seems to have crystallized the thoughts of many, fomenting a lively debate that has continued since her death in 2004. Another central resource of the recent cinephilia debates is the work of Antoine de Baecque, especially *La cinéphilie*.

11. Rosenbaum, "Reply to Cinephilia Survey," 182. For a different expression of the same view, see Rosenbaum, *Essential Cinema*, xii–xiii. Rosenbaum has also recently expressed a happier view of the new cinephilias. See *Goodbye Cinema, Hello Cinephilia*, xii–xiii, 3–7.

12. Hilderbrand, "Cinematic Promiscuity," 217.

13. Rosenbaum, "Reply to Cinephilia Survey," 182.

14. Björkman, "Making the Waves," 19.

15. In this, I may reflect a passage from Christian Metz's *Imaginary Signifier* that I saw quoted in George Toles's essay for Betz's cinephilia portfolio. See Toles, "Rescuing Fragments," 159. In this passage, Metz discusses how he learned to distance himself from his cinephile self while still recalling that self clearly; in this way, he integrated his cinephilia into film theory without damaging the latter. Thus Metz doesn't lose sight of the old cinephile but instead chooses to keep "an eye on him." See *Imaginary Signifier*, 15. If there is coldness to Metz's double approach, experience tells me that there needn't be any in actual life. For me, the coldness of theoretical reflection has allowed me to re-open myself to a variety of cinemas, thus expanding the scope of "hot" cinephile consumption through "chilly" anti-cinephile analysis.

Filmography

This list offers standard details (titles, alternative titles, dates of release, and director names) on all the movies mentioned above, including those that are in no sense "art" movies. Generally, I have placed original titles first, except in the many places where those titles seem unlikely to be familiar to English speakers.

8 ½ (1963), Federico Fellini
8 ½ Women (1999), Peter Greenaway
9 Songs (2004), Michael Winterbottom
12:08 East of Bucharest | A fost sau n-a fost? (2005), Corneliu Porumboiu
The Abandoned (2006), Nacho Cerdà
À bout de souffle | Breathless (1960), Jean-Luc Godard
The Act of Seeing with One's Own Eyes (1971), Stan Brakhage
Adaptation (2002), Spike Jonze
"Aftermath" (1994), Nacho Cerdà
Aguirre, der Zorn Gottes | Aguirre, the Wrath of God (1972), Werner Herzog
Ai no corrida | In the Realm of the Senses (1976), Nagisa Oshima
Ali: Feat Eats the Soul | Angst essen Seele auf (1974), Rainer Werner Fassbinder
À l'interieur | Inside (2007), Alexandre Bustillo and Julien Maury
All the Love You Cannes! (2002), Lloyd Kaufman, Gabriel Friedman, and Sean McGrath
Les amants | The Lovers (1958), Louis Malle
À ma soeur | Fat Girl (2001), Catherine Breillat
Amateur (1994), Hal Hartley
Anatomie de l'enfer | Anatomy of Hell (2004), Catherine Breillat
"Anémic cinema" (1926), Marcel Duchamp
Angels and Insects (1995), Philip Hass
L'année dernière à Marienbad | Last Year at Marienbad (1961), Alain Resnais
À nos amours | To Our Loves (1983), Maurice Pialat
Anthony's Desire (1993), Tom Boka
Antichrist (2009), Lars von Trier
L'argent (1983), Robert Bresson

Arraya (1959), Margot Benacerraf

Art School Confidential (2006), Terry Zwigoff

Ashes and Diamonds / Popiół i diament (1958), Andrzej Wajda

L'assassinat du duc de Guise / The Assassination of the Duke de Guise (1908), André Calmettes and Charles Le Bargy

"The Astrum Argentium" (2006), Jon Behrens

Audition / Ôdishon (1999), Takashi Miike

Au hasard Balthazar (1966), Robert Bresson

The Auteur (2008), James Westby

Avatar (2009), James Cameron

L'avventura / The Adventure (1960), Michelangelo Antonioni

Badlands (1973), Terrence Malick

Bad Lieutenant: Port of Call—New Orleans (2009), Werner Herzog

Baise-moi / Rape Me (2000), Virginie Despentes and Coralie Trinh Thi

The Ballad of Cable Hogue (1970), Samuel Peckinpah

"Ballet mécanique" (1924), Fernand Léger and Dudley Murphy

Basket Case (1982), Frank Henenlotter

Basquiat (1996), Julian Schnabel

Batalla en el cielo / Battle in Heaven (2005), Carlos Reygadas

Battleship Potemkin / Bronenosets Potyomkin (1925), Sergei Eisenstein

The Beat That My Heart Skipped / De battre mon coeur s'est arête (2005), Jacques Audiard

Behind the Green Door (1972), the Mitchell brothers

Being John Malkovich (1999), Spike Jonze

Belle de jour (1967), Luis Buñuel

La belle noiseuse (1991), Jacques Rivette

Betty Blue / 37°2 le matin (1986), Jean-Jacques Beineix

The Bicycle Thief / Ladri di biciclette (1948), Vittorio de Sica

The Big Combo (1955), Joseph Lewis

The Big Lebowski (1998), the Coen brothers

Bijou (1972), Wakefield Pool

The Birth of a Nation (1915), D. W. Griffith

Black Sabbath / I tre volti della paura (1963), Mario Bava

Blood and Black Lace / Sei donne per l'assassino (1964), Mario Bava

Blood Feast (1963), Herschell Gordon Lewis

Blow Job (1963), Andy Warhol

Blow-Up (1966), Michelangelo Antonioni

Bonnie and Clyde (1967), Arthur Penn

Book of Life (1998), Hal Hartley

"Brakhage on Brakhage I" (1996), Colin Still

Breaking News / Dai si gin (2004), Johnnie To

A Brighter Summer Day / Gu ling jie shao nian sha ren shie jian (1991), Edward Yang

Bright Star (2009), Jane Campion

Bring Me the Head of Alfredo Garcia (1974), Samuel Peckinpah

Broken Embraces / Los abrazos rotos (2009), Pedro Almodóvar

Broken Flowers (2005), Jim Jarmusch

The Brown Bunny (2003), Vincent Gallo

Buffalo '66 (1998), Vincent Gallo

Das cabinet des Dr. Caligari / *The Cabinet of Dr. Caligari* (1919), Robert Wiene
Caché (2005), Michael Haneke
Camille 2000 (1969), Radley Metzger
Caravaggio (1986), Derek Jarman
Carlos (2010), Olivier Assayas
Carmen, Baby (1967), Radley Metzger
Carnival of Souls (1962), Herk Harvey
Cave of Forgotten Dreams (2010), Werner Herzog
Chantal (2007), Tony Marsiglia
Che (2008), Steven Soderbergh
La chiave / *The Key* (1983), Tinto Brass
"*Un chien andalou*" (1929), Luis Buñuel
Children of Men (2006), Alfonso Cuarón
La ciénaga / *The Swamp* (2001), Lucretia Martel
Citizen Kane (1941), Orson Welles
A City of Sadness / *Bei qing cheng shi* (1989), Hou Hsiao-hsien
Cléo de 5 à 7 / *Cleo from 5 to 7* (1962), Agnès Varda
A Clockwork Orange (1971), Stanley Kubrick
The Connection (1962), Shirley Clarke
The Cook, the Thief, His Wife, and Her Lover (1989), Peter Greenaway
The Cow / *Gaav* (1969), Daryoush Mehrjui
Crash (1996), David Cronenberg
Cremaster cycle (1994–2002), Matthew Barney
Cries and Whispers / *Viskningar och rop* (1972), Ingmar Bergman
The Curious Case of Benjamin Button (2008), David Fincher
Daisies / *Sedmikrásky* (1966), Vera Chytilová
La dame aux camélias / *Camille* (1911), André Calmettes and Henri Pouctal
Dans ma peau / *In My Skin* (2002), Marina de Van
The Dark Knight (2008), Christopher Nolan
Days of Heaven (1978), Terrence Malick
Dead Ringers (1988), David Cronenberg
The Death of Mr. Lăzărescu / *Moartea domnului Lăzărescu* (2005), Cristi Puiu
Deep Throat (1972), Gerard Damiano
Demain on déménage / *Tomorrow We Move* (2004), Chantal Akerman
Detour (1947), Edgar G. Ulmer
The Devil in Miss Jones (1973), Gerard Damiano
The Devils (1971), Ken Russell
Devils on the Doorstep / *Guizi lai le* (2000), Jiang Wen
Les diaboliques (1954), Henri-Georges Clouzot
Et Dieu . . . créa la femme / *. . . And God Created Woman* (1956), Roger Vadim
Dogtooth / *Kynodontas* (2009), Giorgos Lanthimos
La dolce vita (1960), Federico Fellini
Donnie Darko (2001), Richard Kelly
Do You Like Hitchcock? (2005), Dario Argento
The Dreamers (2003), Bernardo Bertolucci
Dr. Jekyll and Mistress Hyde (2003), Tony Marsiglia
L'eclisse / *Eclipse* (1962), Michelangelo Antonioni

Ecstasy | Ekstase (1933), Gustav Machatý
Edward Scissorhands (1990), Tim Burton
Election | Hak se wui (2005), Johnnie To
Emmanuelle (1974), Just Jaeckin
Empire (1964), Andy Warhol
L'Enfant (2005), the Dardenne brothers
Enter the Void (2009), Gaspar Noé
Eraserhead (1976), David Lynch
D'Est | From the East (1993), Chantal Akerman
Eternal Sunshine of the Spotless Mind (2004), Michel Gondry
The Evil Dead (1981), Sam Raimi
Evil Dead 2 (1987), Sam Raimi
The Evil Eye | La ragazza che sapeva troppo (1963), Mario Bava
Exit Through the Gift Shop (2010), Banksy
Eyes Wide Shut (1999), Stanley Kubrick
Fahrenheit 9/11 (2004), Michael Moore
Fallen Angels | Duo luo tian shi (1995), Wong Kar-wai
Faster, Pussycat! Kill! Kill! (1965), Russ Meyer
Fight Club (1999), David Fincher
Five Easy Pieces (1970), Bob Rafelson
Flandres | Flanders (2006), Bruno Dumont
Floating Weeds | Ukigusa (1959), Yasujirô Ozu
Following (1996), Christopher Nolan
For the Love of Movies: The Story of American Film Criticism (2009), Gerald Peary
Freaks (1932), Tod Browning
From Dusk till Dawn (1996), Robert Rodriguez
Frontière(s) | Frontier(s) (2007), Xavier Gens
Fulltime Killer | Chuen jik sat sau (2001), Johnnie To and Wai Ka-fai
Funny Ha Ha (2002), Andrew Bujalski
Le gai savoir | Joy of Learning (1968), Jean-Luc Godard
The Game of Love | Le blé en herbe (1954), Claude Atant-Lara
The Getaway (1972), Samuel Peckinpah
The Girlfriend Experience (2009), Steven Soderbergh
The Girl from Monday (2005), Hal Hartley
The Glamorous Life of Sachiko Hanai | Hatsujô kateikyôshi: Sensei no aijiru (2004), Mitsuru Meike
Glen or Glenda (1953), Ed Wood
The Goalie's Anxiety at the Penalty Kick | Die Angst des Tormanns beim Elfmeter (1972), Wim Wenders
The Godfather (1972), Francis Ford Coppola
The Good, the Bad, the Weird | Joheunnom nabbeunnom isanghannom (2008), Kim Jee-woon
Gran Torino (2008), Clint Eastwood
Greed (1924), Erich von Stroheim
Guess Who's Coming to Dinner (1967), Stanley Kramer
Gummo (1997), Harmony Korine
Gun Crazy (1949), Joseph Lewis
"Hapax Legomena II: Poetic Justice" (1972), Hollis Frampton

Happiness (1998), Todd Solondz
Hard Boiled / *Lat sau san taam* (1992), John Woo
Hardcore (1984–1993), Richard Kern
Hard Edge (2003), Andrew Blake
Haute tension / *High Tension* (2003), Alexandre Aja
The Headless Woman / *La mujer sin cabeza* (2008), Lucretia Martel
Heat (1995), Michael Mann
Heaven Can Wait (1943), Ernst Lubitsch
Heaven's Gate (1980), Michael Cimino
Henry Fool (1997), Hal Hartley
Henry and June (1990), Philip Kaufman
High Art (1996), Lisa Cholodenko
Hiroshima mon amour (1959), Alain Resnais
Histoire d'O / *The Story of O* (1975), Just Jaeckin
The Host / *Gwoemul* (2006), Bong Joon-ho
Hostel (2005), Eli Roth
House / *Hausu* (1977), Nobuhiko Obayashi
House of Love (2000), Tom Lazarus
I Am Curious (Yellow) / *Jag är nyfiken—en film i gult* (1969), Vilgot Sjöman
I, a Woman / *Jeg—en kvinde* (1965), Mac Ahlberg
Idioterne / *The Idiots* (1998), Lars von Trier
I Heart Huckabees (2004), David O. Russell
In a Better World / *Hævnen* (2010), Susanne Bier
Inception (2010), Christopher Nolan
Inga (1968), Joseph Sarno
Inglourious Basterds (2009), Quentin Tarantino
Inland Empire (2006), David Lynch
In the Company of Men (1997), Neil Labute
In the Cut (2003), Jane Campion
In the Mood for Love / *Fa yeung nin wa* (2000), Wong Kar-wai
Intimacy (2001), Patrice Chéreau
Intolerance (1916), D. W. Griffith
L'intrus / *The Intruder* (2004), Claire Denis
Invictus (2009), Clint Eastwood
Irma Vep (1996), Olivier Assayas
Irréversible / *Irreversible* (2002), Gaspar Noé
The Isle / *Seom* (2000), Kim Ki-duk
Jackie Brown (1997), Quentin Tarantino
Jeanne Dielman, 23 Quai du Commerce, 1080 Bruxelles (1975), Chantal Akerman
La jetée / *The Pier* (1962), Chris Marker
Jeux interdits / *Forbidden Games* (1952), René Clément
Jules et Jim / *Jules and Jim* (1962), François Truffaut
Junior Bonner (1972), Samuel Peckinpah
Ken Park (2002), Larry Clark
Kids (1995), Larry Clark
The Killer / *Dip huet seung hung* (1989), John Woo
The Last House on the Left (1972), Wes Craven

The Last Seduction (1994), John Dahl
Latex (1995), Michael Ninn
The Legend of Sleepy Hollow (1999), Tim Burton
Let the Right One In | Låt den rätte komma in (2008), Tomas Alfredson
Lies | Gojitmal (1999), Jang Sun-woo
Lie with Me (2005), Clément Virgo
Lolita (1962), Stanley Kubrick
Lord of the G-Strings (2003), Terry West
Lord of the Rings trilogy (2001–2003), Peter Jackson
Lorna's Silence | La silence de Lorna (2009), the Dardenne brothers
Lost Highway (1996), David Lynch
Lucía y el sexo | Sex and Lucia (2001), Julio Medem
Lust for Dracula (2004), Tony Marsiglia
La maman et la putain | The Mother and the Whore (1973), Jean Eustache
Man Bites Dog (1992), Rémy Belvaux, André Bonzel, and Benoît Poelvoorde
"Manhatta" (1921), Paul Strand and Charles Sheeler
Man with a Movie Camera | Chelovek s kino-apparatom (1929), Dziga Vertov
Marat/Sade (1967), Peter Brook
Martha Marcy May Marlene (2011), Sean Durkin
Martyrs (2008), Pascal Laugier
The Masque of the Red Death (1964), Roger Corman
Memento (2000), Christopher Nolan
Memories of Murder | Salinui chueok (2003), Bong Joon-ho
Memories of Underdevelopment | Memorias del subdesarrollo (1968), Tomás Gutiérrez Alea
Le mépris | Contempt (1963), Jean-Luc Godard
"Meshes of the Afternoon" (1943), Maya Deren and Alexander Hammid
Miami Vice (2006), Michael Mann
The Miracle | Il miracolo (1948), Roberto Rossellini
The Mirror | Zerkalo (1975), Andrei Tarkovsky
Mom and Dad (1945), William Beaudine
Mona: The Virgin Nymph (1970), Howard Ziehm
Morte a venezia | Death in Venice (1971), Luchino Visconti
Mouchette (1967), Robert Bresson
Mudhoney (1965), Russ Meyer
Los muertos (2004), Lisandro Alonso
Mulholland Drive (2001), David Lynch
Mysterious Object at Noon | Dokfa nai meuman (2000), Apichatpong Weerasethakul
Mystic River (2003), Clint Eastwood
Naked (1993), Mike Leigh
The Naked Kiss (1964), Samuel Fuller
The Naked Venus (1959), Edgar G. Ulmer
New Wave Hookers (1985), Greg Dark
The New World (2005), Terrence Malick
Night and Day | Bam guan nat (2008), Hong Sang-soo
Night of the Living Dead (1968), George Romero
The Night Porter | Il portiere di notte (1974), Liliana Cavani
La notte | The Night (1961), Michelangelo Antonioni

Oasis (2002), Lee Chang-dong
Oldboy (2003), Park Chan-wook
Olympia (1938), Leni Riefenstahl
One Summer of Happiness | Hon dandsade en sommar (1951), Arne Mattsson
The Opening of Misty Beethoven (1975), Radley Metzger ("Henry Paris")
Out of the Past (1947), Jacques Tourneur
Paris Chic (1997), Andrew Blake
Paris, Texas (1984), Wim Wenders
The Passenger | Professione: Reporter (1975), Michelangelo Antonioni
Pather Panchali (1955), Satyajit Ray
Persona (1966), Ingmar Bergman
Le petit soldat (1960), Jean-Luc Godard
Phantom of the Paradise (1974), Brian De Palma
La pianiste | The Piano Teacher (2001), Michael Haneke
The Piano (1993), Jane Campion
Picnic at Hanging Rock (1975), Peter Weir
The Pillow Book (1996), Peter Greenaway
Pink Flamingos (1972), John Waters
Plan 9 from Outer Space (1959), Ed Wood
Planet of the Apes (1968), Franklin J. Schaffner
Planet Terror (2007), Robert Rodriguez
Plastic City | Dangkou (2008), Nelson Yu Lik-wai
Platform | Zhangtai (2000), Jia Zhangke
The Player (1992), Robert Altman
Play-Mate of the Apes (2002), John Bacchus
Pola X (1999), Leos Carax
The Pornographer | Le pornograph (2001), Bertrand Bonello
The Prestige (2006), Christopher Nolan
Pretty Woman (1990), Garry Marshall
Private Vices, Public Pleasures | Vizi privati, pubbliche virtù (1976), Miklós Jancsó
"The Production and Decay of Strange Particles" (2008), Jon Behrens
Un prophète | A Prophet (2009), Jacques Audiard
Prospero's Books (1991), Peter Greenaway
Public Enemies (2009), Michael Mann
Pulp Fiction (1994), Quentin Tarantino
Quai des orfèvres (1947), Henri-Georges Clouzot
Les quatre cents coups | The 400 Blows (1959), François Truffaut
Raise the Red Lantern | Da hong deng long gao gao gua (1991), Zhang Yimou
Ran (1985), Akira Kurosawa
Rape (1969), Yoko Ono and John Lennon
Rashômon (1950), Akira Kurosawa
Ratatouille (2007), Brad Bird and Jan Pinkava
Red Psalm | Még kér a nép (1972), Miklós Jancsó
Reefer Madness (1936), Louis Gasnier
Reenactment | Reconstituirea (1969), Lucian Pintilie
Reservoir Dogs (1992), Quentin Tarantino
Resurrection of Eve (1973), the Mitchell brothers

"Le retour à la raison" / "Return to Reason" (1923), Man Ray
Ride the High Country (1962), Samuel Peckinpah
Riddles of the Sphinx (1977), Peter Wollen and Laura Mulvey
robZtv: Robert Zverina Epic Video Memoir (2010), Robert Zverina
The Rocky Horror Picture Show (1975), Jim Sharman
Romance (1999), Catherine Breillat
Roma, città aperta / Open City (1945), Roberto Rossellini
Roommates (1981), Chuck Vincent
Russian Ark / Russkiy kovcheg (2002), Aleksandr Sokurov
Salò o le 120 giornate di Sodoma / Salo, or the 120 Days of Sodom (1975), Pier Paolo Pasolini
Le sang d'un poète / Blood of a Poet (1932), Jean Cocteau
Sátántangó / Satan's Tango (1994), Béla Tarr
The Searchers (1956), John Ford
Sébastiane (1976), Derek Jarman
Secrets Behind the Wall / Kabe no naka no himegoto (1965), Koji Wakamatsu
Serbis / Service (2008), Brillante Mendoza
A Serious Man (2009), the Coen brothers
Seul contre tous / I Stand Alone (1998), Gaspar Noé
sex, lies, and videotape (1989), Steven Soderbergh
Sex: The Annabel Chong Story (1999), Gough Lewis
Shame (2011), Steve McQueen
Shock Corridor (1963), Samuel Fuller
Shortbus (2006), John Cameron Mitchell
The Silence / Tystnaden (1963), Ingmar Bergman
Sin City (2005), Robert Rodriguez
Sinful (2006), Tony Marsiglia
Sleep (1963), Andy Warhol
Sleeping Beauty (2011), Julia Leigh
Solaris (2002), Steven Soderbergh
Sommaren med Monika / Summer with Monika (1953), Ingmar Bergman
Sonic Outlaws (1995), Craig Baldwin
Spring, Summer, Fall, Winter . . . and Spring / Bom yeoreum gaeul geurigo bom (2003), Kim Ki-duk
Story of Qiu Ju / Qiu Jud a guan si (1992), Zhang Yimou
Stranger Than Paradise (1984), Jim Jarmusch
Straw Dogs (1971), Samuel Peckinpah
Stroszek (1977), Werner Herzog
The Sun / Solntse (2005), Aleksandr Sokurov
Suspiria (1977), Dario Argento
Sympathy for Mr. Vengeance / Boksuneun naui geot (2002), Park Chan-wook
"Symphonie diagonale" (1924), Viking Eggeling
Syndromes and a Century / Sang sattawat (2006), Apichatpong Weerasethakul
Synecdoche, New York (2008), Charlie Kaufman
Taste of Cherry / T'am e guilass (1997), Abbas Kiarostami
A Taste of Honey (1961), Tony Richardson
Teenage Catgirls in Heat (1994), Scott Perry
Tenebre / Unsane (1982), Dario Argento

The Texas Chainsaw Massacre (1974), Tobe Hooper
Therese and Isabelle (1968), Radley Metzger
They Live (1988), John Carpenter
The Thin Red Line (1998), Terrence Malick
Thirst (2009), Park Chan-wook
This Girl's Life (2003), Ash Baron-Cohen
This Sporting Life (1963), Lindsay Anderson
Three Kings (1999), David O. Russell
Tie Me Up! Tie Me Down! | ¡Átame! (1990), Pedro Almodóvar
Titanic (1997), James Cameron
Tokyo Story | Tôkyô monogatari (1953), Yasujirô Ozu
El Topo (1970), Alejandro Jodorowsky
Touch of Evil (1958), Orson Welles
The Toxic Avenger (1984), Lloyd Kaufman
Traffic (2000), Steven Soderbergh
Trees Lounge (1996), Steve Buscemi
Tribulation 99 (1991), Craig Baldwin
Triumph of the Will | Triumph des willens (1935), Leni Riefenstahl
Tromeo and Juliet (1996), Lloyd Kaufman
Trouble Every Day (2001), Claire Denis
Twentynine Palms (2003), Bruno Dumont
Two in the Wave (2010), Emanuel Laurent
Under the Skin of the Night | Zir-e poost-e shab (1974), Fereydun Gole
Unforgiven (1992), Clint Eastwood
Until the Light Takes Us (2009), Aaron Aites and Audrey Ewell
(Untitled) (2009), Jonathan Parker
Vampyros Lesbos (1971), Jess Franco
Videodrome (1983), David Cronenberg
Virgin Stripped Bare by Her Bachelors | Oh! Soo-jung (2000), Hong Sang-soo
Viva (2007), Anna Biller
"A Visit from the Incubus" (2001), Anna Biller
Voyeur Confessions (2002), Tom Lazarus
Walkabout (1971), Nicolas Roeg
Wavelength (1967), Michael Snow
The Wayward Cloud | Tian bian yi duo yun (2005), Tsai Ming-liang
Le week-end | Week End (1967), Jean-Luc Godard
Welcome to the Dollhouse (1995), Todd Solondz
Werckmeister Harmonies | Werckmeister harmóniák (2000), Béla Tarr and Ágnes Hranitzky
When a Woman Ascends the Stairs | Onna ga kaidan wo agaru toki (1960), Mikio Naruse
White Dog (1982), Samuel Fuller
White Material (2009), Claire Denis
The White Ribbon | Das weisse Band—Eine deutsche Kindergeschichte (2009), Michael Haneke
Who's Afraid of Virginia Woolf? (1966), Mike Nichols
The Wild Bunch (1969), Samuel Peckinpah
Woman in the Dunes | Suna no onna (1964), Hiroshi Teshigahara
Word of Mouth (1999), Tom Lazarus

The World | Shijie (2004), Jia Zhangke
The Wrestler (2008), Darren Aronofsky
Yearning | Midareru (1964), Mikio Naruse
Yeelen (1987), Souleymane Cissé
Zabriskie Point (1969), Michelangelo Antonioni
Zodiac (2007), David Fincher
Zombie Strippers (2008), Jay Lee
Zoo (2007), Robinson Devor
Zorns Lemma (1970), Hollis Frampton

Bibliography

Abel, Richard. "French Silent Cinema." *The Oxford History of World Cinema*. Ed. Geoffrey Nowell-Smith. Oxford: Oxford University Press, 1996. 112–116.

Allen, Robert, and Douglas Gomery. *Film History: Theory and Practice*. New York: Knopf, 1985.

Alonge, Giaime. "Hacks and Authors: Ben Hecht, the *Politique des Auteurs*, and Scriptwriting in Classical Hollywood." Unpublished lecture. University of Chicago. March 16, 2010.

Altman, Rick. *Film/Genre*. London: British Film Institute, 1999.

Andrew, Dudley. "An Atlas of World Cinema." In Dennison and Lim, eds. 19–29.

———. *Film in the Aura of Art*. Princeton: Princeton University Press, 1984.

———. "Foreword." In Galt and Schoonover, eds. v–xi.

Andrews, David. "Art Cinema as Institution, Redux: Art Houses, Film Festivals, and Film Studies." *Scope*, vol. 18 (October 2010). Available at http://www.scope.nottingham.ac.uk/article.php?issue=18&id=1245. Accessed December 29, 2010.

———. "Convention and Ideology in the Contemporary Softcore Feature: The Sexual Architecture of *House of Love*." *Journal of Popular Culture*, vol. 38, no. 1 (2004): 5–33.

———. "One Filmmaker's 'Personal Journey' into the World of Soft-Focus: A Conversation with Playboy's Tom Lazarus." *Bridge*, vol. 12 (October/November 2004): 26–32.

———. "Revisiting 'The Two Avant-Gardes.'" *Jump Cut*, no. 52 (Summer 2010). Available at http://www.ejumpcut.org/currentissue/index.html. Accessed September 12, 2010.

———. *Soft in the Middle: The Contemporary Softcore Feature in Its Contexts*. Columbus: Ohio State University Press, 2006.

———. "Toward a More Valid Definition of 'Pornography.'" *Journal of Popular Culture*, vol. 45, no. 3 (2012): 457–477.

———. "Toward an Inclusive, Exclusive Approach to Art Cinema." In Galt and Schoonover, eds. 62–74.

———. "What Soft-core Can Do for Porn Studies." *Velvet Light Trap*, vol. 59, no. 1 (2007): 51–61.

Anonymous. "Cinema: Prestige Picture." *Time*, August 16, 1937. Available at http://www.time.com/time/magazine/article/0,9171,770806,00.html. Accessed May 6, 2009.

Anonymous. Internet posting. *The Insider*, May 4, 2007. Available at http://www.theinsider.com/. Accessed March 12, 2009.

Anonymous. "Re: Experimental Cinema." Personal e-mail to the author. April 25, 2009. 1.

Ansen, David. "Shock and Yawn." *Newsweek*, October 26, 2009: 48–50.

Anton, Saul. "Catherine Breillat Opens Up About *Romance*, Sex, and Censorship." On-line interview. *Indiewire*, September 23, 1999. Available at http://www.indiewire.com /article/interview_catherine_breillat_opens_up_about_romance_sex_and_censor ship/. Accessed May 23, 2009.

Arthur, Paul. *A Line of Sight: American Avant-Garde Film Since 1965*. Minneapolis: University of Minnesota Press, 2005.

Astruc, Alexandre. "The Birth of a New Avant-Garde: La Camera-Stylo." 1948. *The New Wave: Critical Landmarks*. Ed. Peter Graham. Garden City, NY: Doubleday, 1968. 17–23.

Badley, Linda, and R. Barton Palmer. "Introduction." *Traditions in World Cinema*. Ed. Linda Badley, R. Barton Palmer, and Steven Jay Schneider. New Brunswick: Rutgers University Press, 2006. 1–12.

Baker, Jayson. "Guess Who's Off the Hook: Inventing Interracial Coupling in Global Art Cinema." *Wide Screen*, vol. 1, no. 1 (2009): 1–14.

Balázs, Béla. "Theory of the Film." 1953. In Talbot, ed. 201–215.

Balio, Tino. "The Art Film in the New Hollywood." *Hollywood and Europe: Economics, Culture, and National Identity*. Ed. Geoffrey Nowell-Smith and Stephen Ricci. London: British Film Institute, 1998. 63–73.

———. "Brigitte Bardot and Hollywood's Takeover of the U.S. Art Film Market in the 1960s." *Trading Culture: Global Traffic and Local Cultures in Film and Television*. Ed. Sylvia Harvey. Eastleigh, UK: John Libbey, 2006. 191–201.

———. *The Foreign Film Renaissance on American Screens, 1946–1973*. Madison: University of Wisconsin Press, 2010.

———. "'A Major Presence in All of the World's Important Markets': The Globalization of Hollywood in the 1990s." In Neale and Smith, eds. 58–73.

Barker, Martin. "'Typically French'?: Mediating Screened Rape to British Audiences." In Russell, ed. 149–158.

Barkow, Jerome, Leda Cosmides, and John Tooby, eds. *The Adapted Mind: Evolutionary Psychology and the Generation of Culture*. Oxford: Oxford University Press, 1995.

Barthes, Roland. "The Death of the Author." 1968. In Grant, ed. 97–100.

Baumann, Shyon. *Hollywood Highbrow: From Entertainment to Art*. Princeton: Princeton University Press, 2007.

———. "Intellectualization and Art World Development: Film in the United States." *American Sociological Review*, vol. 66 (June 2001): 404–426.

Bayma, Todd. "Art World Culture and Institutional Choices: The Case of Experimental Film." *Sociological Quarterly*, vol. 36, no. 1 (1995): 79–95.

Bazin, André. "An Aesthetic of Reality." 1948. In Fowler, ed. 56–63.

———. "The Festival Viewed as a Religious Order." 1955. In Porton, ed. 13–19.

———. *What Is Cinema?* Vol. 1. Trans. Hugh Gray. Berkeley: University of California Press, 1967.

———. *What Is Cinema?* Vol. 2. Trans. Hugh Gray. Berkeley: University of California Press, 1971.

Becker, Howard. *Art Worlds*. 1982. Berkeley: University of California Press, 2008.

Behrens, Jon. "Re: Experimental Cinema." Personal e-mail to the author. December 14, 2009. 1–2.

Bennett, Charlie. "How Indie Is Indie?" E-mail to the editors. *Sight & Sound*, vol. 19, no. 3 (2009): 96.

Berger, John. *Ways of Seeing*. London: BBC/Penguin, 1972.

Bergman, Ingmar. *Bergman on Bergman: Interviews with Ingmar Bergman by Stig Björkman, Torsten Manns, and Jonas Sima*. 1970. New York: Simon and Schuster, 1973.

Berney, Bob. "Independent Distribution." In Squire, ed. 375–383.

Bernstein, Matthew. "The Producer as Auteur." 2006. In Grant, ed. 180–189.

Betz, Mark. "Art, Exploitation, Underground." In Jancovich et al., eds. 202–222.

———. "Beyond Europe: On Parametric Transcendence." In Galt and Schoonover, eds. 31–47.

———. *Beyond the Subtitle: Remapping European Art Cinema*. Minneapolis: University of Minnesota Press, 2009.

———, ed. "In Focus: Cinephilia." *Cinema Journal*, vol. 49, no. 2 (2010): 130–178.

———. "Little Books." In Grieveson and Wasson, eds. 319–349.

———. "The Name Above the (Sub)Title: Internationalism, Coproduction, and Polyglot European Art Cinema." *Camera Obscura*, vol. 16, no. 1 (2001): 1–45.

Bier, Susanne. "Searching for a Place 'In a Better World.'" Interview with Larry Rohter. *New York Times*, February 22, 2011. Available at http://carpetbagger.blogs.nytimes .com/2011/02/22/searching-for-a-place-in-a-better-world/. Accessed February 22, 2011.

Biller, Anna. "Re: Hi David." Personal e-mails to the author. November 2009. 1–6.

Birchall, Danny. "The Avant-Garde Archive Online." *Film Quarterly*, vol. 63, no. 1 (2009): 12–14.

Biskind, Peter. *Down and Dirty Pictures: Miramax, Sundance, and the Rise of Independent Film*. New York: Simon & Schuster, 2004.

Björkman, Stig. "Making the Waves." Lars von Trier interview. *Sight & Sound*, vol. 19, no. 8 (2009): 16–19.

Blaetz, Robin. "Introduction: Women's Experimental Cinema, Critical Frameworks." In Blaetz, ed. 1–19.

———, ed. *Women's Experimental Cinema*. Durham: Duke University Press, 2007.

Bordwell, David. "Afterword." *Poetics of Cinema*. New York: Routledge, 2008. 158–169.

———. "The Art Cinema as a Mode of Film Practice." 1979. *Film Theory and Criticism: Introductory Readings*. Ed. Marshall Cohen and Leo Baudry. New York: Oxford University Press, 1999. 716–724.

———. *Narration in the Fiction Film*. Madison: University of Wisconsin Press, 1985.

Bordwell, David, and Noël Carroll, eds. *Post-Theory: Reconstructing Film Studies*. Madison: University of Wisconsin Press, 1995.

Borger, Lenny. "Production Notes: The 'Quai' of Inspector Clouzot." Rialto Pictures pressbook, 2002. Available http://www.webcitation.org/5vRTYoJEy.

Bourdieu, Pierre. *Distinction: A Social Critique of the Judgement of Taste*. 1979. Trans. Richard Nice. Cambridge: Harvard University Press, 1984.

———. *The Rules of Art: Genesis and Structure of the Literary Field*. 1992. Trans. Susan Emanuel. Stanford: Stanford University Press, 1996.

Boyd, Brian. "Art and Evolution: The Avant-Garde as Test Case: Spiegelman in *The Narrative Corpse*." 2008. In Boyd, Carroll, and Gottschall, eds. 433–454.

Boyd, Brian, Joseph Carroll, and Jonathan Gottschall, eds. *Evolution, Literature, and Film: A Reader*. New York: Columbia University Press, 2010.

Bozelka, Kevin John. "Exploitation Films and Success: The Half-Told Melodramas of Andy Milligan." In Weiner and Cline, eds. 171–190.

Brakhage, Stan. "Stan Brakhage: Correspondences." Ed. Eirik Steinhoff. *Chicago Review*, vol. 47, no. 4, and vol. 48, no. 1 (2001/2002): 5–199.

Brand, Peggy Zeglin. "Disinterestedness and Political Art." *Aesthetics: The Big Questions.* Ed. Carolyn Korsmeyer. Malden, MA: Blackwell, 1998. 155–171.

Buchsbaum, Jonathan, and Elena Gorfinkel, eds. "Cinephilia Dossier: What Is Being Fought for by Today's Cinephilia(s)?" *Framework*, vol. 50, nos. 1–2 (2009): 176–228.

Budd, Michael. "Authorship as a Commodity: The Art Cinema and *The Cabinet of Dr. Caligari.*" 1984. In Grant, ed. 249–254.

———. "The National Board of Review and Early Art Cinema in New York: *The Cabinet of Dr. Caligari* as Affirmative Culture." *Cinema Journal*, vol. 26, no. 1 (1986): 3–18.

Bürger, Peter. *Theory of the Avant-Garde.* 1974. Minneapolis: University of Minnesota Press, 1984.

Buscombe, Edward. "Ideas of Authorship." In Caughie, ed. 22–34.

Buss, David. "Evolutionary Psychology: The New Science of Mind." 2008. In Boyd, Carroll, and Gottschall, eds. 21–37.

Cagle, Chris. "Two Modes of Prestige Film." *Screen*, vol. 48, no. 3 (2007): 291–311.

Caldwell, John Thornton. *Production Culture: Industrial Reflexivity and Critical Practice in Film and Television.* Durham: Duke University Press, 2008.

Campbell, Zachary. "On the Political Challenges of the Cinephile Today." In Buchsbaum and Gorfinkel, eds. 210–213.

Carr, Kevin. "Exclusive: Jenna Jameson to Produce Horror Movies." *Film School Rejects*, April 28, 2008. Available at http://www.filmschoolrejects.com/news/exclusive-jenna -jameson-to-produce-horror-movies.php. Accessed May 31, 2009.

Carroll, Joseph. *Evolution and Literary Theory.* Columbia: University of Missouri Press, 1995.

Carroll, Noël. *Philosophy of Art: A Contemporary Introduction.* London: Routledge, 1999.

———. *The Philosophy of Horror: Or, Paradoxes of the Heart.* New York: Routledge, 1990.

———. *A Philosophy of Mass Art.* Oxford: Oxford University Press, 1998.

———. "Prospects for Film Theory: A Personal Assessment." In Bordwell and Carroll, eds. 37–68.

———. *Theorizing the Moving Image.* Cambridge: Cambridge University Press, 1996.

Caughie, John. "Introduction." In Caughie, ed. 9–16.

———, ed. *Theories of Authorship: A Reader.* 1981. London: Routledge, 1988.

Chaudhuri, Shohini. *Contemporary World Cinema: Europe, the Middle East, East Asia, and South Asia.* Edinburgh: Edinburgh University Press, 2005.

Chirilov, Mihai, ed. *Lucian Pintilie.* Promotional pamphlet. New York and Chicago: Romanian Cultural Institute in New York, 2012.

Christensen, Jerome. "Studio Authorship, Corporate Art." 2006. In Grant, ed. 167–179.

Cieply, Michael. "A Rebuilding Phase for Independent Film." *New York Times*, April 25, 2010. Available at http://www.nytimes.com/2010/04/26/business/media/26indie.html?hpw. Accessed April 27, 2010.

———. "As Studios Cut Budgets, Independent Filmmakers Distribute on Their Own." *New York Times*, August 12, 2009. Available at http://www.nytimes.com/2009/08/13 /business/media/13independent.html?hp. Accessed August 13, 2009.

Ciment, Michel. "Letter to the Editors." *Sight & Sound*, vol. 19, no. 6 (2009): 96.

Clair, René. "How Films Are Made." 1953. In Talbot, ed. 225–233.

Cline, John, and Robert Weiner, eds. *From the Arthouse to the Grindhouse: Highbrow and Lowbrow Transgression in Cinema's First Century.* Lanham, MD: Scarecrow, 2010.

Clover, Carol. *Men, Women, and Chain Saws: Gender in the Modern Horror Film.* Princeton: Princeton University Press, 1992.

Cohen, Ted. "High and Low Art, and High and Low Audiences." *Journal of Aesthetics and Art Criticism*, vol. 57, no. 2 (1999): 137–143.

Collingwood, R. G. *The Principles of Art.* 1938. New York: Galaxy, 1960.

Comer, Stuart, ed. *Film and Video Art.* London: Tate, 2009.

Connolly, Maeve. *The Place of Artists' Cinema: Space, Site, and Screen.* Bristol, UK: Intellect, 2009.

Cook, Pam. "Authorship and Cinema." In Cook, ed. 387–483.

———, ed. *The Cinema Book.* 1985. London: British Film Institute, 2007.

Corliss, Richard. "Notes on a Screenwriter's Theory, 1973." 1974. In Grant, ed. 140–147.

Cousins, Mark, et al. "The Mad, the Bad, and the Dangerous." *Sight & Sound*, vol. 19, no. 9 (2009): 22–36.

Coyne, Jerry. *Why Evolution Is True.* New York: Viking, 2009.

Cubitt, Sean. "Distribution and Media Flows." *Cultural Politics*, vol. 1, no. 2 (2005): 193–214.

Czach, Liz. "Cinephilia, Stars, and Film Festivals." In Betz, ed. 139–145.

Danto, Arthur. "The Artworld." *Journal of Philosophy*, vol. 61, no. 19 (1964): 571–584.

———. *Transfiguration of the Commonplace: A Philosophy of Art.* Cambridge: Harvard University Press, 1981.

Dargis, Manohla. "Seduction by Machine Gun." *New York Times*, July 1, 2009. Available at http://movies.nytimes.com/2009/07/01/movies/01enemies.html?8dpc. Accessed July 1, 2009.

———. "Talking About a Revolution (for a Digital Age)." *New York Times*, January 31, 2010. Available at http://www.nytimes.com/2010/01/31/movies/31dargis.html?hpw. Accessed January 31, 2010.

Davies, Stephen. *Definitions of Art.* Ithaca: Cornell University Press, 1991.

Dawkins, Richard. *The Selfish Gene.* New York: Oxford University Press, 1976.

de Baecque, Antoine. *La cinéphilie: Invention d'un regard, histoire d'une culture, 1944–1968.* Paris: Fayard, 2003.

Dennison, Stephanie, and Song Hwee Lim. "Introduction: Situating World Cinema as a Theoretical Problem." In Dennison and Lim, eds. 1–15.

———, eds. *Remapping World Cinema: Identity, Culture, and Politics in Film.* London: Wallflower, 2006.

Derrida, Jacques. *The Truth in Painting.* 1978. Trans. Geoff Bennington and Ian McLeod. Chicago: University of Chicago Press, 1987.

de Valck, Marijke. *Film Festivals: From European Geopolitics to Global Cinephilia.* Amsterdam: Amsterdam University Press, 2005.

de Valck, Marijke, and Malte Hagener, eds. *Cinephilia: Movies, Love, and Memory.* Amsterdam: Amsterdam University Press, 2005.

———. "Introduction: Down with Cinephilia? Long Live Cinephilia? And Other Videosyncratic Pleasures." In de Valck and Hagener, eds. 11–24.

de Ville, Donna. "Menopausal Monsters and Sexual Transgression in Argento's Art Horror." In Weiner and Cline, eds. 53–75.

Dickie, George. *The Art Circle.* 1984. Evanston: Chicago Spectrum Press, 1997.

———. *Art and Value.* Malden, MA: Blackwell, 2001.

———. *Evaluating Art.* Philadelphia: Temple University Press, 1988.

———. "The Myth of the Aesthetic Attitude." *American Philosophical Quarterly*, vol. 1 (January 1964): 56–65.

Didion, Joan. *Slouching Towards Bethlehem.* New York: Farrar, Straus and Giroux, 1968.

Dimaggio, Paul. "Cultural Entrepreneurship in Nineteenth-Century Boston: The Creation of an Organizational Base for High Culture in America." *Media, Culture, and Society*, vol. 4 (January 1982): 33–50.

Dissanayake, Wimal. "Issues in World Cinema." *World Cinema: Critical Approaches.* Ed. John Hill and Pamela Church Gibson. Oxford: Oxford University Press. 527–534.

Doll, Susan. "Werner Herzog Dreams in 3-D." *Facets Features* blog entry. April 20, 2011. Available at http://facetsfeatures.blogspot.com/2011/04/werner-herzog-dreams-in-3-d.html. Accessed April 24, 2011.

Downing, Lisa. "French Cinema's New 'Sexual Revolution': Postmodern Porn and Troubled Genre." *French Cultural Studies*, vol. 15, no. 3 (2004): 265–280.

Dubie, Sven. "Obscene History in the Heights: The Case of Nico Jacobellis and *Les Amants.*" Cleveland Historical Society website. Available at http://chhistory.org/FeatureStories.php?Story=Obscene History. Accessed October 11, 2009.

Dutton, Denis. *The Art Instinct: Beauty, Pleasure, and Human Evolution.* New York: Bloomsbury Press, 2009.

Dwyer, Susan, ed. *The Problem of Pornography.* Belmont: Wadsworth, 1995.

Dyer, Richard. *Stars.* 1979. London: British Film Institute, 1998.

Eamon, Christopher. "An Art of Temporality." In Comer, ed. 66–85.

Ebert, Roger. Review of *The Brown Bunny.* Online review. *Chicago Sun-Times*, September 3, 2004. Available at http://rogerebert.suntimes.com/apps/pbcs.dll/article?AID=/20040903/REVIEWS/409020301/1023. Accessed April 5, 2009.

———. "Why I Hate 3-D (and You Should Too)." *Newsweek*, March 10, 2010. Available at http://www.newsweek.com/2010/04/30/why-i-hate-3-d-and-you-should-too.html. Accessed March 5, 2011.

Elsaesser, Thomas. "Cinephilia or the Uses of Disenchantment." In de Valck and Hagener, eds. 27–43.

———. *European Cinema: Face to Face with Hollywood.* Amsterdam: Amsterdam University Press, 2005.

———. "Film Festival Networks: The New Topographies of Cinema in Europe." In Elsaesser, *European Cinema.* 82–107.

Epstein, Edward Jay. *The Big Picture: The New Logic of Money and Power in Hollywood.* New York: Random House, 2005.

Farahmand, Azadeh. "Disentangling the International Festival Circuit: Genre and Iranian Cinema." In Galt and Schoonover, eds. 263–281.

Farber, Manny. "Underground Films." 1957. In Talbot, ed. 163–174.

Fellman, Daniel. "Theatrical Distribution." In Squire, ed. 362–374.

Festival Research Network. "Film Festival Research." Online scholarly resource. Available at http://www.filmfestivalresearch.org/. Accessed March 3, 2011.

Fischer, Craig. "Experimental Film: The Contemporary Scene." Online reference guide. Available at http://www.filmreference.com/encyclopedia/Criticism-Ideology/Experimental-Film-THE-CONTEMPORARY-SCENE.html. Accessed April 13, 2009.

Forbes, Jill, and Sarah Street. *European Cinema: An Introduction*. New York: Palgrave, 2000.

Fowler, Catherine, ed. *The European Cinema Reader*. London: Routledge, 2002.

Gabara, Rachel. "Abderrahmane Sissako: Second and Third Cinema in the First Person." In Galt and Schoonover, eds. 320–333.

Galt, Rosalind, and Karl Schoonover, eds. *Global Art Cinema: New Theories and Histories*. Oxford: Oxford University Press, 2010.

———. "Introduction: The Impurity of Art Cinema." In Galt and Schoonover, eds. 3–27.

Gerstner, David. "The Practices of Authorship." In Gerstner and Staiger, eds. 3–26.

Gerstner, David, and Janet Staiger, eds. *Authorship and Film*. New York: Routledge, 2003.

Gibson, Pamela Church, ed. *More Dirty Looks: Gender, Pornography and Power*. London: British Film Institute, 2004.

Gledhill, Christine. "Rethinking Genre." *Reinventing Film Studies*. Ed. Christine Gledhill and Linda Williams. London: Arnold, 2000. 221–243.

Godard, Jean-Luc. "The Face of the French Cinema Has Changed." 1959. *Godard on Godard*. New York: Da Capo Press, 1986. 146–147.

Goldman, Michael. "Digitally Independent Cinema." *Filmmaker Magazine: The Magazine of Independent Film* (Winter 2008). Available at http://www.filmmakermagazine.com /winter2008/projection.php. Accessed April 13, 2009.

Gomery, Douglas. "Hollywood Corporate Business Practice and Periodizing Contemporary Film History." In Neale and Smith, eds. 47–57.

Gorfinkel, Elena. "Cult Film or Cinephilia by Any Other Name." *Cineaste*, vol. 34, no. 1 (2008): 33–38.

———. "Dated Sexuality: Anna Biller's *Viva* and the Retrospective Life of Sexploitation Cinema." *Camera Obscura*, vol. 26, no. 3 (2011): 95–137.

———. "Radley Metzger's 'Elegant Arousal': Taste, Aesthetic Distinction, and Sexploitation." In Mendik and Schneider, ed. 26–39.

Gracyk, Theodore. "Pornography as Representation: Aesthetic Considerations." *Journal of Aesthetic Education*, vol. 21, no. 4 (1987): 103–121.

Grant, Barry Keith, ed. *Auteurs and Authorship: A Film Reader*. Malden, MA: Blackwell, 2008.

———. "Introduction." In Grant, ed. 1–6.

Grant, Catherine. "Secret Agents: Feminist Theories of Women's Film Authorship." *Feminist Theory*, vol. 2, no. 1 (2001): 113–130.

Greenberg, Clement. "Avant-Garde and Kitsch." 1939. *Mass Culture: The Popular Arts in America*. 1957. Ed. Bernard Rosenberg and David Manning White. New York: Free-Macmillan, 1964. 98–107.

Grieveson, Lee, and Haidee Wasson. "Introduction." In Grieveson and Wasson, eds. xi–xxxii.

———, eds. *Inventing Film Studies*. Durham: Duke University Press, 2008.

Grodal, Torben. *Embodied Visions: Evolution, Emotion, Culture, and Film*. New York: Oxford University Press, 2009.

Grover, Andrea. "Re: Images and Permission." Personal e-mail to the author. January 1, 2010. 1–3.

Guback, Thomas. *The International Film Industry*. Bloomington: Indiana University Press, 1969.

Guest, Haden. "Experimentation and Innovation in Three American Film Journals of the 1950s." *Inventing Film Studies*. In Grieveson and Wasson, eds. 235–263.

Hale, Mike. "Tribeca's Taste of All Things Grim and Gory." *New York Times*, April 21, 2011. Available at http://www.nytimes.com/2011/04/22/movies/tribeca-film-festivals-crime -and-horror-section.html?ref=movies. Accessed April 23, 2011.

———. "The Underside of a Film Festival, Where Some Dark Treasures Dwell." *New York Times*, April 22, 2010. Available at http://www.nytimes.com/2010/04/23/mov ies/23cinemania.html?8dpc. Accessed April 22, 2010.

Halle, Randall. "Offering Tales They Want to Hear: Transnational European Film Fund-ing as Neo-Orientalism." In Galt and Schoonover, eds. 303–319.

Hanlon, Dennis. "Traveling Theory, Shots, and Players: Jorge Sanjinés, New Latin Ameri-can Cinema, and the European Art Film." In Galt and Schoonover, eds. 351–366.

Hansen, Miriam Bratu. "The Mass Production of the Senses: Classical Cinema as Ver-nacular Modernism." *Reinventing Film Studies*. Ed. Christine Gledhill and Linda Wil-liams. London: Arnold, 2000. 332–350.

Hawkins, Joan, "Culture Wars: Some New Trends in Art Horror." *Jump Cut*, vol. 51 (Spring 2009). Available at http://www.ejumpcut.org/archive/jc51.2009/artHorror/index .html. Accessed June 21, 2009.

———. *Cutting Edge: Art-Horror and the Horrific Avant-Garde*. Minneapolis: University of Minnesota Press, 2000.

Hayashi, Sharon. "The Fantastic Trajectory of Pink Art Cinema from Stalin to Bush." In Galt and Schoonover, eds. 48–61.

Heise, Tatiana, and Andrew Tudor. "Constructing (Film) Art: Bourdieu's Field Model in a Comparative Context." *Cultural Sociology*, vol. 1, no. 2 (2007): 165–187.

Heisenberg, Martin. "Is Free Will an Illusion?" *Nature*, vol. 459, no. 14 (2009): 164–165.

Hess, John. "*La politique des auteurs*, Part One: World View as Aesthetics." *Jump Cut*, vol. 1 (May/June 1974): 19–20.

———. "*La politique des auteurs*, Part Two: Truffaut's Manifesto." *Jump Cut*, vol. 2 (July/August 1974): 20–22.

Hess, John, and Chuck Kleinhans. "Doing Serious Business." Freud Bartlett interview. *Jump Cut*, vol. 31 (March 1986): 30–34.

Hilderbrand, Lucas. "Cinematic Promiscuity: Cinephilia After Videophilia." In Buchs-baum and Gorfinkel, eds. 214–217.

Hollows, Joanne. "The Masculinity of Cult." In Jancovich et al., eds. 35–53.

Holmlund, Chris, and Justin Wyatt, eds. *Contemporary American Independent Film*. Lon-don: Routledge, 2005.

Hunt, Nathan. "The Importance of Trivia: Ownership, Exclusion, and Authority in Sci-ence Fiction Fandom." In Jancovich et al., eds. 185–201.

Hutchings, Peter. "The Argento Effect." In Jancovich et al., eds. 127–141.

Iordanova, Dina. "The Film Festival Circuit." *Film Festival Yearbook 1: The Festival Cir-cuit*. Ed. Dina Iordanova and Ragan Rhyne. St. Andrews: St. Andrews Film Studies, 2009. 23–39.

Itzkoff, Dave. "The Man Behind the Dreamscape." *New York Times*, June 30, 2010. Avail-able at http://www.nytimes.com/2010/07/04/movies/04inception.html?_r=1&hpw. Accessed July 3, 2010.

Jacobs, Lewis. "Experimental Cinema in America: Part One, 1921–1941." *Hollywood Quar-terly*, vol. 3, no. 2 (1947–1948): 111–124.

―――. "Experimental Cinema in America: Part Two, the Postwar Revival." *Hollywood Quarterly*, vol. 3, no. 3 (1948): 278–292.

Jacobsen, Thomas. "Beauty and the Brain: Culture, History, and Individual Differences in Aesthetic Appreciation." *Journal of Anatomy*, vol. 216 (February 2010): 184–191.

James, David. "LA's Hipster Cinema." *Film Quarterly*, vol. 63, no. 1 (2009): 56–67.

―――. *The Most Typical Avant-Garde: History and Geography of Minor Cinemas in Los Angeles*. Berkeley: University of California Press, 2005.

James, Nick. "The *Gummo* Factor." *Sight & Sound*, vol. 20, no. 1 (2010): 5.

―――. "Whose Cinephilia?" *Sight & Sound*, vol. 19, no. 11 (2009): 5.

Jancovich, Mark. "Cult Fictions: Cult Movies, Subcultural Capital, and the Production of Cultural Distinctions." 2002. In Mathijs and Mendik, eds. 149–162.

―――. "Introduction." In Jancovich et al., eds. 1–13.

Jancovich, Mark, et al., eds. *Defining Cult Movies*. Manchester: Manchester University Press, 2003.

Janisse, Kier-La. "The Cult of Suffering." An interview with Pascal Laugier. *Rue Morgue*, vol. 87 (March 2009): 16–19, 22.

Jones, Kent. Review of *Out of the Past*. 1997. *The Village Voice Film Guide: 50 Years of Movies from Classics to Cult Hits*. Ed. Dennis Lim. New York: Wiley, 2007. 188.

Juno, Andrea. "Interview: Frank Henenlotter." In Vale and Juno, eds. 8–17.

Kael, Pauline. *The "Citizen Kane" Book: Raising Kane*. Boston: Little, Brown, 1971.

―――. "Movies, the Desperate Art." 1956. In Talbot, ed. 51–71.

Kahler, Erich. "What Is Art?" 1959. In Weitz, ed. 157–171.

Kant, Immanuel. *Critique of Judgement*. 1790. Trans. James Creed Meredith. 1952. Oxford: Clarendon Press, 2007.

Kaufman, Anthony. "Is Foreign Film the New Endangered Species?" *New York Times*, January 22, 2006. Available at http://www.nytimes.com/2006/01/22/movies/22kauf.html. Accessed April 17, 2006.

Kaufman, Lloyd. "IA: I-Won't-Suck-the-Mainstream Art." In Mendik and Schneider, eds. xiii–xvii.

Kawin, Bruce. "Authorship, Design, and Execution." 1992. In Grant, ed. 190–199.

Keller, Alexandra, and Frazer Ward. "Matthew Barney and the Paradox of the Neo-Avant-Garde Blockbuster." *Cinema Journal*, vol. 45, no. 2 (2006): 3–16.

Kendrick, Walter. *The Secret Museum: Pornography in Modern Culture*. 1987. Berkeley: University of California Press, 1996.

Kermode, Mark. "It Is What It's Not." *Sight & Sound*, vol. 19, no. 5 (2009): 34–36.

Kerr, Paul. "My Name Is Joseph H. Lewis." 1983. In Grant, ed. 234–248.

Kleinhans, Chuck. "Producing the Field of Experimental Film/Video, 2.7." Unpublished work-in-progress. 1–16.

Kleinhans, Chuck, and B. Ruby Rich. "Le Cinéma d'avant-garde et ses rapports avec le cinéma militant." Trans. Katerina Thomadeki. *Cinémaction*, vols. 10–11 (Spring/Summer 1980): 55–68.

Koehler, Robert. "Cinephilia and Film Festivals." In Porton, ed. 81–97.

Koszarki, Richard. "The Men with the Movie Cameras." 1972. In Grant, ed. 135–139.

Kovács, András Bálint. *Screening Modernism: European Art Cinema, 1950–1980*. Chicago: University of Chicago Press, 2007.

Kubrick, Stanley. *Stanley Kubrick: Interviews*. Ed. Gene Phillips. Jackson: University Press of Mississippi, 2001.

Lamkin, Elaine. "*The Abandoned*: Director Nacho Cerdà." Interview with *Bloody Disgusting*. Available at http://www.bloody-disgusting.com/interview/339. Accessed June 2, 2010.

Landis, Bill, and Michelle Clifford. *Sleazoid Express: A Mind-Twisting Tour Through the Grindhouse Cinema of Times Square*. New York: Fireside, 2002.

Lee, Chris. "Porn Star Sasha Grey Gets Mainstream Role." *Los Angeles Times*, May 21, 2009. Available at http://www.latimes.com/entertainment/news/la-et-sasha-grey21 -2009may21,0,7751766.story. Accessed May 31, 2009.

Lehman, Peter. "Introduction: 'A Dirty Little Secret'—Why Teach and Study Pornography?" *Pornography: Film and Culture*. Ed. Peter Lehman. New Brunswick: Rutgers University Press, 2006. 1–21.

———. "Revelations About Pornography." *Pornography: Film and Culture*. Ed. Peter Lehman. New Brunswick: Rutgers University Press, 2006. 87–98.

Lev, Peter. *The Euro-American Cinema*. Austin: University of Texas Press, 1993.

Levine, Lawrence. *Highbrow/Lowbrow: The Emergence of Cultural Hierarchy in America*. 1988. Cambridge: Harvard University Press, 1990.

Lewis, Jon. *Hollywood v. Hard Core: How the Struggle over Censorship Saved the Modern Film Industry*. New York: New York University Press, 2000.

———. "Real Sex: Aesthetics and Economics of Art-House Porn." *Jump Cut*, vol. 51 (Spring 2009). Available at http://www.ejumpcut.org/archive/jc51.2009/artHorror /index.html. Accessed September 11, 2012.

Lobato, Roman. "Subcinema: Theorizing Marginal Film Distribution." *Limina: A Journal of Historical and Cultural Studies*, vol. 13 (2007): 113–120.

Loist, Skadi, and Marijke de Valck. "Film Festival/Film Festival Research: Thematic, Annotated Bibliography." 2nd ed. Film Festival Research Network, 2010. Available http://www1.uni-hamburg.de/Medien/berichte/arbeiten/0091_08.html. Accessed September 11, 2012.

Longino, Helen. "Pornography, Oppression, and Freedom: A Closer Look." *The Problem of Pornography*. Ed. Susan Dwyer. Belmont: Wadsworth, 1995. 34–47.

Macdonald, Dwight. *Against the American Grain*. New York: Random House, 1962.

MacDonald, Scott. *Canyon Cinema: The Life and Times of an Independent Film Distributor*. Berkeley: University of California Press, 2008.

———. "Cinema 16: Documents Toward a History of the Film Society," *Wide Angle*, vol. 19, no. 1 (1997): 3–48.

Maltby, Richard. "'Nobody Knows Everything': Post-Classical Historiographies and Consolidated Entertainment." In Neale and Smith, eds. 21–44.

Marcus, Steven. *The Other Victorians*. New York: Basic, 1964.

Marsiglia, Tony. "Re: Some Questions." Personal e-mails to the author. September 2004. 1–5.

Martin, Angela. "Refocusing Authorship in Women's Filmmaking." 2003. In Grant, ed. 127–134.

Mathijs, Ernest, and Xavier Mendik, eds. *Alternative Europe: Eurotrash and Exploitation Cinema*. London: Wallflower, 2004.

———. "Concepts of Cult." *The Cult Film Reader*. Ed. Ernest Mathijs and Xavier Mendik. New York: Open University Press, 2008. 15–24.

———, eds. *The Cult Film Reader*. New York: Open University Press, 2008.

———. "Editorial Introduction: What Is Cult Film?" In Mathijs and Mendik, eds. 1–11.

McKenna, A. T. "Guilty by Association: Joe Levine, European Cinema, and the Culture

Clash of Le Mépris." *Scope*, vol. 14 (June 2009). Available at http://www.scope.notting
ham.ac.uk/article.php?issue=14&idea=1135. Accessed June 17, 2009.

McNair, Brian. "'Not Some Kind of Kinky Porno Flick': The Return of Porno-Fear?"
Bridge, vol. 11 (August/September 2004): 16–19.

Mekas, Jonas. "Independence for Independents." In Holmlund and Wyatt, eds. 35–40.

Mekas, Jonas, and the New York Film-Makers' Cooperative. "The First Statement of the
New American Cinema Group." 1962. Online posting. Available at http://www.film
-makerscoop.com/about/history. Accessed April 4, 2009.

Mendik, Xavier, and Graham Harper, eds. *Unruly Pleasures: The Cult Film and Its Critics*.
New York: FAB Press, 2000.

Mendik, Xavier, and Steven Jay Schneider, eds. *Underground USA: Filmmaking Beyond the
Hollywood Canon*. London: Wallflower, 2002.

Metz, Christian. *The Imaginary Signifier: Psychoanalysis and Cinema*. 1977. Trans. Celia
Britton, Annwyl Williams, Ben Brewster, and Alfred Guzzetti. Bloomington: Indiana
University Press, 1982.

Miller, Geoffrey. "Arts of Seduction." 2000. In Boyd, Carroll, and Gottschall, eds. 156–173.

Montal, Steve. "Film Festivals and Markets." In Squire, ed. 315–330.

Morawski, Stefan. "Art and Obscenity." *Journal of Aesthetics and Art Criticism*, vol. 26,
no. 2 (1967): 193–207.

Morton, Jim. "Interview with Dave Friedman." In Vale and Juno, eds. 102–107.

Mulvey, Laura. "Visual Pleasure and Narrative Cinema." *Screen*, vol. 16, no. 3 (1975): 6–18.

Nagib, Lúcia. "Towards a Positive Definition of World Cinema." In Dennison and Lim,
eds. 30–37.

Naremore, James. "Authorship." *A Companion to Film Theory*. Ed. Toby Miller and Robert
Stam. Malden, MA: Blackwell, 2004. 9–24.

———. *More Than Night: Film Noir in Its Contexts*. 1998. Berkeley: University of California Press, 2008.

Ndalianis, Angela. "Art Cinema." In Cook, ed. 83–87.

Nead, Lynda. "'Above the Pulp-Line': The Cultural Significance of Erotic Art." In Gibson,
ed. 216–223.

Neale, Steve. "Art Cinema as Institution." *Screen*, vol. 22, no. 1 (1981): 11–39.

———. *Genre*. London: British Film Institute, 1980.

Neale, Steve, and Murray Smith, eds. *Contemporary Hollywood Cinema*. London: Routledge, 1998.

———. "Introduction." In Neale and Smith, eds. xiv–xxii.

Negra, Diane. "'Queen of the Indies': Parker Posey's Niche Stardom and the Taste Cultures of Independent Film." In Holmlund and Wyatt, eds. 71–88.

Newman, Michael. *Indie: An American Film Culture*. New York: Columbia University
Press, 2011.

———. "Indie Culture: In Pursuit of the Authentic Autonomous Alternative." *Cinema
Journal*, vol. 48, no. 3 (2009): 16–34.

Ng, Jenna. "Love in a Time of Transcultural Fusion: Cinephilia, Homage, and *Kill Bill*."
In de Valck and Hagener, eds. 65–79.

———. "The Myth of Total Cinephilia." In Betz, ed. 146–151.

Nowell-Smith, Geoffrey. "Art Cinema." *The Oxford History of World Cinema*. Ed. Geoffrey
Nowell-Smith. Oxford: Oxford University Press, 1996. 567–575.

———. *Making Waves: New Cinemas of the 1960s*. New York: Continuum, 2008.

―――. "New Concepts of Cinema." *The Oxford History of World Cinema*. Ed. Geoffrey Nowell-Smith. Oxford: Oxford University Press, 1996. 750–759.

"The Oberhausen Manifesto." 1962. Twenty-six German signers. In Fowler, ed. 73.

O'Regan, Tom. "Cultural Exchange." *A Companion to Film Theory*. 1999. Ed. Toby Miller and Robert Stam. Malden, MA: Blackwell, 2004. 262–294.

Osterweil, Ara. "Andy Warhol's *Blow Job*: Toward the Recognition of a Pornographic Avant-Garde." *Porn Studies*. Ed. Linda Williams. Durham: Duke University Press, 2004. 449–451.

Ostrowska, Dorota. *Reading the French New Wave: Critics, Writers, and Art Cinema in France*. London: Wallflower, 2008.

Owen, Stephen. "Genres in Motion." *PMLA*, vol. 122, no. 5 (2007): 1389–1393.

Passmore, John. "The Dreariness of Aesthetics." *Mind*, vol. 60, no. 239 (1951): 318–335.

Peckham, Morse. *Art and Pornography: An Experiment in Explanation*. New York: Basic, 1969.

Peranson, Mark. "First You Get the Power, Then You Get the Money: Two Models of Film Festivals." In Porton, ed. 23–37.

Perkins, V. F. *Film as Film: Understanding and Judging Movies*. New York: Penguin, 1972.

Petrie, Graham. "Alternatives to Auteurs." 1973. In Grant, ed. 110–118.

Petrolle, Jean, and Virginia Wright Wexman. *Women and Experimental Filmmaking*. Urbana: University of Illinois Press, 2005.

Pinker, Steven. *The Blank Slate: The Modern Denial of Human Nature*. New York: Penguin, 2002.

―――. *How the Mind Works*. 1997. New York: Norton, 2009.

Polan, Dana. "The Beginnings of American Film Study." *Looking Past the Screen: Case Studies in American Film History and Method*. Ed. Jon Lewis and Eric Smoodin. Durham: Duke University Press, 2007. 37–60.

Porton, Richard, ed. *dekalog³: On Film Festivals*. London: Wallflower, 2009.

Prime, Samuel. "A Generation of Filmmakers Influenced by Whom? Tracing the Origin of Mumblecore, the New American Independent Film Movement." Unpublished conference paper. Popular Culture Association Conference, St. Louis. April 1, 2010.

Projansky, Sarah, and Kent Ono. "Making Films Asian American: *Shopping for Fangs* and the Discursive Auteur." In Gerstner and Staiger, eds. 263–280.

Quandt, James. "Flesh and Blood: Sex and Violence in Recent French Cinema." *Artforum*, February 2004: 126–132.

Rajadhyaksha, Ashish. "Hindi Cinema." In Cook, ed. 217–221.

Ramey, Kathryn. "Between Art, Industry, and Academia: The Fragile Balancing Act of the Avant-Garde Film Community." *Visual Anthropology Review*, vol. 18, nos. 1–2 (2002): 22–36.

―――. "Re: Experimental Cinema." Personal e-mail to the author. December 21, 2009. 1–3.

Read, Jacinda. "The Cult of Masculinity: From Fan-Boys to Academic Bad-Boys." In Jancovich et al., eds. 54–70.

Rees, A. L. *A History of Experimental Film and Video: From the Canonical Avant-Garde to Contemporary British Practice*. London: British Film Institute, 1999.

―――. "Movements in Art, 1941–79." In Comer, ed. 46–65.

Richerson, Peter, and Robert Boyd. *Not By Genes Alone: How Culture Transformed Human Evolution*. Chicago: University of Chicago Press, 2005.

Ridley, Matt. *Genome: The Autobiography of a Species in 23 Chapters.* New York: Perennial, 2000.

Rivette, Jacques, Erich Rohmer, André Bazin, Jacques Doniol-Valcroze, Pierre Kast, and Roger Leenhardt. "Six Characters in Search of Auteurs: A Discussion About the French Cinema." 1957. In Fowler, ed. 64–72.

Roddick, Nick. "Window Shopping." *Sight & Sound*, vol. 19, no. 12 (2009): 13.

Rohter, Larry. "Prehistoric Cave with a Hornet on the Wall." *New York Times.* April 22, 2011. Available at http://www.nytimes.com/2011/04/24/movies/werner-herzogs-cave -of-forgotten-dreams-filmed-in-chauvet-cave.html?pagewanted=1&hpw. Accessed April 24, 2011.

Root, Jane. "Distributing 'A Question of Silence': A Cautionary Tale." *Screen*, vol. 26, no. 6 (1985): 58–64.

Rosen, Philip. "Notes on Art Cinema and the Emergence of Sub-Saharan Film." In Galt and Schoonover, eds. 252–262.

Rosenbaum, Jonathan. *Essential Cinema: On the Necessity of Film Canons.* Baltimore: Johns Hopkins University Press, 2004.

———. *Goodbye Cinema, Hello Cinephilia: Film Culture in Transition.* Chicago: University of Chicago Press, 2010.

———. "Reply to Cinephilia Survey." In Buchsbaum and Gorfinkel, eds. 181–182.

Rosenbaum, Jonathan, and J. Hoberman. *Midnight Movies.* New York: Harper & Row, 1983.

Rosenbaum, Jonathan, and Adrian Martin, eds. *Movie Mutations: The Changing Face of World Cinephilia.* London: British Film Institute, 2003.

Russell, Dominique. "Introduction: Why Rape?" In Russell, ed. 1–12.

———, ed. *Rape in Art Cinema.* New York: Continuum, 2010.

San Filippo, Maria. "A Cinema of Recession: Micro-budgeting, Micro-drama, and the 'Mumblecore' Movement." *CineAction*, vol. 85 (October/November 2011). Available at http://cineaction.ca/issue85sample.htm. Accessed April 25, 2012.

———. "Unthinking Heterocentrism: Bisexual Representability in Art Cinema." In Galt and Schoonover, eds. 75–91.

Sarris, Andrew. *The American Cinema: Directors and Directions, 1929–1968.* 1968. Chicago: University of Chicago Press, 1985.

———. "The Auteur Theory Revisited." In Sarris, *American Cinema.* 269–278.

———. "Notes on the Auteur Theory in 1962." In Grant, ed. 35–45.

———. "Toward a Theory of Film History." In Sarris, *American Cinema.* 19–37.

———. "Why the Foreign Film Has Lost Its Cachet." *New York Times*, May 2, 1999. Available at http://www.nytimes.com/1999/05/02/movies/summer-films-international -why-the-foreign-film-has-lost-its-cachet.html. Accessed January 6, 2011.

Scalia, Bill. "Review of *Authorship and Film.*" *Journal of Film and Video*, vol. 56, no. 1 (2004): 51–53.

Schaefer, Eric. *"Bold! Daring! Shocking! True!" A History of Exploitation Films, 1919–1959.* Durham: Duke University Press, 1999.

Schamus, James. "To the Rear of the Back End: The Economics of Independent Cinema." In Neale and Smith, eds. 97–105.

Schatz, Thomas. *The Genius of the System.* New York: Pantheon, 1988.

———. *Hollywood Genres: Formulas, Filmmaking, and the Studio System.* Philadelphia: Temple University Press, 1981.

Schoonover, Karl. "Neorealism at a Distance." *European Film Theory*. Ed. Temenuga Trifonova. New York: Routledge, 2008. 301–318.

Sconce, Jeffrey. "Indecipherable Films: Teaching *Gummo*." *Cinema Journal*, vol. 47, no. 1 (2007): 112–115.

———. "Irony, Nihilism, and the New American 'Smart' Film." *Screen*, vol. 43, no. 4 (2002): 349–369.

———, ed. *Sleaze Artists: Cinema at the Margins of Taste, Style, and Politics*. Durham: Duke University Press, 2007.

———. "Smart Cinema." *Contemporary American Cinema*. Ed. Linda Ruth Williams and Michael Hammond. London: McGraw-Hill, 2006. 429–430.

———. "'Trashing' the Academy: Taste, Excess, and an Emerging Politics of Cinematic Style." *Screen*, vol. 36, no. 4 (1995): 371–393.

Scott, A. O. Review of *Pina*. *New York Times*, December 22, 2011. Available at http://movies.nytimes.com/2011/12/23/movies/pina-a-documentary-by-wim-wenders-review.html. Accessed December 22, 2011.

———. "Wallowing in Misery for Art's Sake." *New York Times*, October 7, 2009. Available at http://www.nytimes.com/2009/10/07/movies/07festival.html. Accessed November 2, 2009.

Shiner, Larry. *The Invention of Art: A Cultural History*. Chicago: University of Chicago Press, 2001.

Sitney, P. Adams. *Visionary Film: The American Avant-Garde, 1943–2000*. 1974. Oxford: Oxford University Press, 2002.

Sklar, Robert. *Movie-Made America: A Cultural History of American Movies*. New York: Vintage, 1975.

Skoller, Jeffrey. *Shadows, Specters, Shards: Making History in Avant-Garde Film*. Minneapolis: University of Minnesota Press, 2005.

Slingerland, Edward. "Two Worlds: The Ghost and the Machine." 2008. In Boyd, Carroll, and Gottschall, eds. 219–223.

———. *What Science Offers the Humanities: Integrating Body and Culture*. New York: Cambridge University Press, 2008.

Smith, Murray. "Darwin and the Directors: Film, Emotion, and the Face in the Age of Evolution." 2003. In Boyd, Carroll, and Gottschall, eds. 258–269.

———. "Theses on the Philosophy of Hollywood History." In Neale and Smith, eds. 3–20.

Soble, Alan. *Pornography: Marxism, Feminism, and the Future of Sexuality*. New Haven: Yale University Press, 1986.

Society for Cinema and Media Studies. "Film and Media Festivals Scholarly Interest Group." Available at http://www.cmstudies.org/?page=groups_filmfestivals. Accessed April 23, 2011.

Sontag, Susan. *Against Interpretation*. 1966. New York: Anchor, 1990.

———. "The Decay of Cinema." *New York Times*, February 25, 1996. Available at http://www.nytimes.com/books/00/03/12/specials/sontag-cinema.html. Accessed September 11, 2012.

Sorrentino, Gilbert. *Something Said: Essays*. 1984. Normal, IL: Dalkey Archive Press, 2001.

Squire, Jason, ed. *The Movie Business Book*. 1983. New York: Fireside, 2004.

Staiger, Janet. "Authorship Approaches." In Gerstner and Staiger, eds. 27–58.

Stallybrass, Peter, and Allon White. *The Politics and Poetics of Transgression*. London: Methuen, 1986.

Stanfeld, Peter. *Maximum Movies—Pulp Fictions: Film Culture and the Worlds of Samuel Fuller, Mickey Spillane, and Jim Thompson*. New Brunswick: Rutgers University Press, 2011.

Stevenson, Jack. "And God Created Europe: How the European Sexual Myth Was Created and Sold to Post-War American Movie Audiences." *Fleshpot: Cinema's Sexual Myth Makers and Taboo Breakers*. Ed. Jack Stevenson. Manchester: Critical Vision, 2002. 17–48.

Talbot, Daniel, ed. *Film: An Anthology*. 1959. Berkeley: University of California Press, 1972.

Taubin, Amy. "Horrors! On the Riviera This Year, If It Bled, It Led." *Film Comment*, vol. 45, no. 4 (2009): 50–53.

Testa, Bart. "Soft-Shaft Opportunism: Radley Metzger's Erotic Kitsch." *Spectator*, vol., 19, no. 2 (1999): 41–55.

Thanouli, Eleftheria. "'Art Cinema' Narration: Breaking Down a Wayward Paradigm." *Scope*, no. 14 (June 2009). Available at http://www.scope.nottingham.ac.uk/issue.php ?issue=14. Accessed June 17, 2009.

———. "Narration in World Cinema: Mapping the Flows of Formal Exchange in the Era of Globalisation." *New Cinemas: Journal of Contemporary Film*, vol. 6, no. 1 (2008): 5–15.

Toles, George. "Rescuing Fragments: A New Task for Cinephilia." In Betz, ed. 159–166.

Tooby, John, and Leda Cosmides. "Does Beauty Build Adapted Minds? Toward an Evolutionary Theory of Aesthetics, Fiction, and the Arts." *SubStance*, vol. 30, nos. 94–95 (2001): 6–27.

Tran, Dylan. "The Book, the Theater, the Film, and Peter Greenaway." 1991. *Peter Greenaway: Interviews*. Ed. Vernon Gras and Marguerite Gras. Jackson: University Press of Mississippi, 2000. 129–134.

Trope, Alison. "Footstool Film School: Home Entertainment as Home Education." In Grieveson and Wasson, eds. 353–373.

Truffaut, François, "Une certain tendance du cinéma français." *Cahiers du cinéma*, no. 31 (January 1954): 15–29.

———. "A Certain Tendency of the French Cinema." 1954. In Grant, ed. 9–18.

Tudor, Andrew. "The Rise and Fall of the Art (House) Movie." *The Sociology of Art: Ways of Seeing*. Ed. David Inglis and John Hughson. London: Basingstoke, 2005. 125–138.

Turman, Suzanna. "Peter Greenaway." 1992. *Peter Greenaway: Interviews*. Ed. Vernon Gras and Marguerite Gras. Jackson: University Press of Mississippi, 2000. 147–153.

Vale, V., and Andrea Juno, eds. *Incredibly Strange Films*. 1986. San Francisco: RE/Search Publications, 1988.

Vidal, Gore. "Who Makes the Movies?" 1976. In Grant, ed. 148–157.

Vincendeau, Ginette. "Brigitte Bardot." *The Oxford History of World Cinema*. Ed. Geoffrey Nowell-Smith. Oxford: Oxford University Press, 1996. 492.

Vogel, Amos. *Film as a Subversive Art*. New York: Random House, 1976.

von Trier, Lars, and Thomas Vinterberg. "Dogme 95—the Vow of Chastity." 1995. In Fowler, ed. 83.

Wasson, Haidee. *Museum Movies: The Museum of Modern Art and the Birth of Art Cinema*. Berkeley: University of California Press, 2005.

Waugh, Patricia. "Canon." 1992. *A Companion to Aesthetics*. Ed. David Cooper. Cambridge, MA: Blackwell, 1996. 59–61.

Webb, Jen, et al. *Understanding Bourdieu*. Sage: London, 2002.

Wegner, Daniel. *The Illusion of Conscious Will*. Cambridge: MIT Press, 2002.

Weiner, Robert, and John Cline, eds. *Cinema Inferno: Celluloid Explosions from the Cultural Margins*. Lanham, MD: Scarecrow, 2010.

Weitz, Morris, ed. *Problems in Aesthetics*. New York: Macmillan, 1963.

———. "The Role of Theory in Aesthetics." 1956. In Weitz, ed. 145–156.

Wigley, Samuel. "Out of the Darkness: Werner Herzog's *Cave of Forgotten Dreams*." Interview with Werner Herzog. *Sight & Sound*, vol. 240 (April 2011). Available at http://old.bfi.org.uk/sightandsound/feature/49713. Accessed May 4, 2011.

Wilinsky, Barbara. *Sure Seaters: The Emergence of Art House Cinema*. Minneapolis: University of Minnesota Press, 2001.

Williams, Linda. "Cinema and the Sex Act." *Cineaste*, vol. 27, no. 1 (2001): 20–25.

———. *Hard Core: Power, Pleasure, and the "Frenzy of the Visible."* 1989. Berkeley: University of California Press, 1999.

Williams, Linda Ruth. *The Erotic Thriller in Contemporary Fiction*. Edinburgh: Edinburgh University Press, 2005.

Winston, Brian. *Technologies of Seeing: Photography, Cinematography, and Television*. London: British Film Institute, 1996.

Wollen, Peter. "The Auteur Theory: Michael Curtiz and *Casablanca*." In Gerstner and Staiger, eds. 61–76.

———. *Signs and Meaning in the Cinema*. 1969. Bloomington: Indiana University Press, 1973.

———. "The Two Avant-Gardes." *Studio International*, vol. 190, no. 978 (1975): 171–175.

Wong, Cindy H. *Film Festivals: Culture, People, and Power on the Global Screen*. New Brunswick: Rutgers University Press, 2011.

Wood, Mary. "Cultural Space as Political Metaphor: The Case of the European 'Quality' Film." Unpublished conference paper, 2000. Available at http://www.mediasalles.it/crl_wood.htm. Accessed January 20, 2011.

Woods, Alan. *Being Naked Playing Dead: The Art of Peter Greenaway*. Manchester: Manchester University Press, 1996.

Wyatt, Justin. "The Formation of the 'Major Independent': Miramax, New Line, and the New Hollywood." In Neale and Smith, eds. 74–90.

———. *High Concept: Movies and Marketing in Hollywood*. Austin: University of Texas Press, 1994.

Yabroff, Jennie. "Straight Outta Denmark." *Newsweek*, February 28, 2011: 54.

Young, Ed. *Seven Blind Mice*. New York: Philomel, 1992.

Young, Paul, and Paul Duncan, ed. *Art Cinema*. Cologne: Taschen, 2009.

Zangwill, Nick. "UnKantian Notions of Disinterest." *British Journal of Aesthetics*, vol. 32, no. 2 (1992): 149–152.

Zimmermann, Patricia. "Digital Deployment(s)." In Holmlund and Wyatt, eds. 245–264.

Zryd, Michael. "The Academy and the Avant-Garde: A Relationship of Dependence and Resistance." *Cinema Journal*, vol. 45, no. 2 (2006): 17–42.

———. "Experimental Film and the Development of Film Study in America." In Grieveson and Wasson, eds. 182–216.

Zuromskis, Catherine. "Prurient Pictures and Popular Film: The Crisis of Pornographic Representation." *Velvet Light Trap*, vol. 59 (Spring 2007): 4–14.

Index